B. Whistler Dabney

# SIMONE WEIL

## A FELLOWSHIP IN LOVE

by Jacques Cabaud

'I was made for
fellowship in love
not fellowship in hate.'
Sophocles, ANTIGONE

Channel Press
NEW YORK

*Printed in Great Britain*
*by Collins Clear-Type Press*
*London and Glasgow*
*Published in the United States*
*by Channel Press, an affiliate of*
*MEREDITH PRESS*
*Des Moines and New York*

*Simone Deitz has generously agreed to collaboration on aspects of Simone Weil's life in which she was directly involved and which form a portion of the last two chapters*

# Contents

# Contents

# Illustrations

# Illustrations

# Acknowledgement

The collaboration of Simone Deitz in certain sections of the last two chapters has been invaluable: I am thankful to her for allowing me to highlight my own text with her recollections which offer much insight into the character of Simone Weil. I am equally indebted to her for comments and corrections relating to other sections of this biography.

From *L'Expérience vécue de Simone Weil* (Plon, 1957) came the nucleus from which *Simone Weil: A Fellowship in Love* was developed. For invaluable assistance in this development I am indebted to Amalia Elguera and David Lutyens for their editorial and translating skill. It was not possible, however, to merely adapt the French book for an English speaking audience. Progress in research warranted many additions, shifts in perspective, rewriting—in short, a new book. At this stage, the editorial and corrective measures of Janet Egleson of New York University helped me incalculably, and I watched with admiration the surety of her touch, the finesse of her insight, the alacrity with which she wrought order out of disorder, gave style to what was formless. In matters of philosophy or political science, I relied heavily upon Paul Peeters whose vast knowledge runs second only to his kindness.

I benefited from the benevolent help of Carol Wagner and Margaret Barker. Cade Ware and Jay Taylor assisted in the arduous work of proof-reading. I am deeply grateful to all those mentioned above, as to all the named or unnamed witnesses of Simone Weil's life who supplied the material from which this biography is drawn.

I must also express my debt to Messrs. Routledge and Kegan Paul, the English publishers of Simone Weil's works, who have allowed me to make free use of their translations, or alternatively, to supply my own version.

May I hopefully acknowledge in advance with my thanks any communication from readers possessing information on Simone Weil which is missing from this book. I have merely stated what I knew. Much remains to be found for which I am still searching.

# Introduction

In March 1934, Simone Weil wrote these words about a biography of Karl Marx, which she disliked: 'If one writes the biography of a great man in such a way as to separate his life from his work, one necessarily emphasizes his shortcomings, since it is in his work that he puts the best of himself . . .

'. . . Is it not better to study the life of a great man so as to uncover in it signs of a greatness which only his works fully reveal? One would not gloss over his shortcomings, but they would appear as limitations rather than as essential elements of his genius. Modern biographies as a general rule do just the opposite; they don't present the life of a great man but rather the life of a very little man who by some miracle did great things.'

As Alain has said, one has duties towards the dead.[1] The first of these is truth. Yet there frequently is, for those who die before their prime, a compensatory process of mythification which does not consult truth. Posterity takes unto itself the half-finished business of a broken life, and ends it in its own way. Biography, however, based as it is on careful research, on the questioning of hundreds of witnesses, runs counter to the myth-making trend of the times. But it also recognizes the inevitable law of gravity: the logic of what Simone Weil has said postulates that which, still unsaid, cut off in the mid-sentence of her thoughts, may yet be traced back to her, as an offshoot of her interrupted writings. And her life, as it is traced herein, is but the outline of the inner life embodied in her thoughts.

Truth, then, is in the hands of the reader, who sees it in the facts which are placed before him. For truth is life.

Only God is worth concern;
nothing else is.

Simone Weil, *La Connaissance
surnaturelle*

# PART ONE

# CHILDHOOD AND UNIVERSITY

1909-1931

# I

# Childhood and Adolescence

## 1909-1925

*Water! Water! I want to wash. A child's cry*

SIMONE WEIL was born in Paris, 19 Boulevard de Strasbourg, on
the third of February, 1909.[2] From infancy, chronic illness
imperilled her life, a pattern of ill-health from which she never
completely escaped. In 1912, the family moved to an apartment
on the third floor of 37 Boulevard St Michel, where they remained
for two years. Simone Weil's earliest impressions, therefore, were
of the city. Perhaps that was the macrocosm from which she drew
the pulsing energy, the nervous enthusiasm that was to be hers
throughout life. Nevertheless, by the time she was three and a
half, she had already revealed a quick wit and verbal precocity
that would have been remarkable in even a healthy child. While
she was in hospital having her appendix removed, for example, she
astonished the doctors and nurses with her vocabulary and
expression. One day in a tramway on the Montrouge-Gare de l'Est
route, she chattered so busily with her brother, André, that a
woman got up from her seat sputtering: 'I'm getting out of here!
I can't listen to all that! Fancy bringing children up to be
parrots!'

Early tastes and preferences and other aspects of her behaviour
already showed glimpses of the personality she was to become.
She loved Grimm's fairy tales. Later, she said that the story of the
Mary of gold and the Mary of pitch influenced the whole bent of
her character. Like all children, she and her brother André, three
years her elder, fought and pulled one another's hair. But no
matter how the fight ended, she never cried, for Simone Weil was
a born stoic. Before she was five years old, she was washing in

cold water, shivering all over, and repeating the famous words of Turenne, general to Louis XIV (uttered on the battlefield, when he was in danger): 'You tremble, carcass . . .' Soon after, there were intellectual contests with André. They learned Racine by heart, and in the evening they would challenge each other to recitations of whole scenes. The one who 'dried up' got a smack from the other. (As can be expected, Simone was the one who most often got smacked.)

Doctor Bernard Weil, Simone's father, was called up almost immediately when war broke out in 1914. The family moved with him, renting houses in Neufchâteau (Vosges), in Menton, in Mayennes for two years; then Chartres and Laval. Finally came the return to the apartment in Paris, 37 Boulevard St Michel—home. As a result of all this moving about, the education of the children was continually interrupted. They were aware of the conflict, and played their part in the war by denying themselves sugar and chocolate which they sent to soldiers at the front whom they had adopted.[3] André did his lessons by correspondence, and worked out equations for fun. Simone wrote later that it was 'a childhood and youth like Pascal's'.[4] When she was in London she said to Mme Closon: 'Oh yes! I spent my time reciting mathematical formulas to my brother.' He had taught himself to read, and one day he decided to teach Simone, who was then six, as a birthday present for Doctor Weil. They worked as many as eight hours a day, under the table-cloth if need be so as not to be seen. On New Year's Day, 1915, André said in front of his father: 'Go on, Simone, read the newspaper to Papa!' 'Papa' was astonished. Simone was actually able to read, although slowly.

When she was about six, Simone tried her hand at 'bouts-rimés' with equal diligence and no small success:

> *Unhappy me, the wretched shepherd cried:*
> *My stepmother has wrecked my life. Inside,*
> *She fills my heart with such bitter gall,*
> *She makes me wish, my God, you'd end it all.*

In 1916, Simone's family arranged private lessons for her in Chartres. The following year, she was regarded as a very keen pupil in the Laval Lycée where her education was continued. Extremely pretty when she was eight years old, her delicate

18

features never again had the charm they then took from the radiance of her expression. Her fine, black, almond-shaped eyes suggested those of the Byzantine frescoes. She had black, curly hair dressed in the Salomé style of Henri Regnault's painting. A playful child, she nevertheless did not take part in strenuous games. André was also not given to sports. He spent hours reading, and at this time of their life, André seemed more gifted than Simone: he was even credited with genius. Like everyone else, Simone admired him. Brother and sister were happy, studious, and precocious, and they filled the hearts of their family with pardonable pride.

Simone was, however, not a demonstrably affectionate child. Gustave Thibon, among a host of others, has noted that Simone knew nothing of 'the sensible and carnal side of tenderness ... embraces repelled her'. Without indulging too much in parlour psychology, it may be worth while speculating on the influence of Elie Metchnikoff, a celebrated bacteriologist and an old friend of her family, in the light of certain kinds of behaviour. For example, the following incident took place in the house of a medical friend of Simone's parents. Charmed by her childish grace, the friend bent down unexpectedly and kissed her hand. Simone burst into tears and ran away crying: 'Water! Water! I want to wash!' Could some overheard conversation of Metchnikoff's have been the cause of Simone's early aversion to being kissed? Later, she got over this fear of catching germs through physical contact and declared: 'I like being kissed by men with moustaches. It stings!' Another time, Simone 'sat down in the snow and refused to go on because her parents had given her brother the heaviest luggage to carry'.[5]

Hers was a Roman soul and all her life she remained as inflexible as she was as a child.

The Weil family spent the holidays of 1919 and 1920 in Brittany, at the seaside resort of Penthièvre. On the beach Simone read English children's books and translations from Greek. Sometimes she spent whole hours watching the sunset. Often she was asked; 'Why don't you go and play?' 'This is so beautiful,' she would reply, 'I'd much rather watch the sunset than play!' Sometimes, however, she did play with her young companions—but in her own way, and at games with a distinctly moral tone. There was the time, for instance, when she and her friends swore the celebrated oath of the Horatii and the Curiati never to walk from the village to the beach with their shoes on—an oath which was kept poorly except by Simone herself.

At the age of ten or eleven, Simone Weil wrote a fairy-tale, 'The Fire Sylphs', which has recently been published in the *Figaro Littéraire* (Dec. 1, 1962). At first reading, it appears to be merely the work of a child endowed with a vivid and poetic imagination: a short story with puzzling undertones. The mysterious element could well be explained by the author's extreme youth: at such an early age a fairy-tale is pure fantasy. But the use of Greek vocables and certain sentences which have an odd philosophical ring might lead to an assumption of a well-defined allegorical meaning.

The sylphs robed in 'red, yellow or golden orange' hues, are called the *phlogos* (flames): they are the souls of children 'not yet born' who await their turn to become men. They dance, following their leader, the *Megistos* (the mighty one), 'stopping now and then to kiss his burning feet'. A 'pale blue' flame which represents the 'phantom of *Phaidros*' (the gay one) goes through several dramatic phases, during which he almost dies, because *Emera* (daylight, Time) has stolen his robe and his talisman; but he survives, succeeds in killing his aggressor, and ends up marrying his 'beautiful betrothed' in the golden dress. The tale ends with a frenzied *orchesis* (dance) which whips faster than the wind, throwing sparks in a 'dust of gold'.

In this small prose poem, with its cycle similar to that of the days (or to that of the souls in Plato's myth), Simone Weil already reveals her astonishing gift for composition on several levels which is the mark of the true artist.

At the end of 1919, Simone entered the Lycée Fénelon, a public high school and junior college for girls, on the Left Bank close to the Latin Quarter in Paris. From that time her studies took on an unaccustomed regularity, even though they were continually disrupted by her poor health. Perhaps she really had little need for instruction. Her teacher in literature complained that she upset the class and made the other students learn the whole of *Athalie* by heart.

She was gifted in mathematics, but bad at drawing. Her circulation was poor and her hands were swollen. When one of her drawing teachers gave her a low mark, a sympathetic friend tried to persuade him that Simone's clumsiness wasn't her own fault. It was not manual skill Simone lacked, the teacher said, and touching her head: 'It's there that something's missing!'

No end of dramas occurred over geography. Simone wore herself out in her efforts to draw maps, until at last she was offered a consolation prize if she came last in the subject (as indeed she did, in map-drawing), but was first in answering the questions.

Simone followed the Cours Sévigné for several weeks, but she begged her parents to let her withdraw. Invariably she was first, and she disliked receiving so many compliments. Moreover, all these studies were too narrow for her; her field of interests was wider. She was attracted by politics and had already taken a definite stand on current issues. Years later, in her *Letter to Georges Bernanos*, she refers to the disgust aroused in her by the Treaty of Versailles:

'Up to then, I had been patriotically thrilled as children are in war-time. But the will to humiliate the defeated enemy which revealed itself so loathsomely everywhere at that time (and in the following years) was enough to cure me once and for all of that naïve sort of patriotism. I suffer more from the humiliations inflicted by my country than from those inflicted upon her.'[6]

This declaration is significant. All evidence indicates that Simone Weil's revolutionary tendencies date from the years of her childhood.[7] Whether they took the form of sympathy for conquered and humiliated Germany or, (as she wrote to Bernanos) of an attraction towards 'those organizations which spring from the lowest and least regarded social strata' does not matter. The seed was in the furrow and it bore its fruit in time.

Simone Weil's parents brought her up in complete agnosticism. They left her in ignorance of the fact that there were Jews and Gentiles. But one relative let her know that she would rather see her dead than married to a 'Goy'. Because the agnosticism of her environment did not tend towards proselytism or orthodoxy, she was able to accept 'the Christian attitude as the only possible attitude' for herself.

Nevertheless she forbade herself ever to think about a future life, although she believed that the 'moment of death is the norm and purpose of life'. Later, she could not remember having been without a sense of detachment from material things. And she had, from earliest childhood, 'the Christian notion of love for one's neighbour', to which she gave (as did the Neo-Platonists in the Middle Ages) the name of justice which becomes it so well.

When she was about twelve, Simone began to suffer from the headaches which plagued her all her life. It was this physical problem, along with emotional and intellectual ones, which brought about a serious crisis during her adolescence. A boundless despair engulfed her. Her teens were a decisive time in her life: perhaps without knowing it, she then found a definite direction for her whole subsequent development. In a letter to Father Perrin she writes as follows: 'At fourteen . . . I seriously thought of dying because of the mediocrity of my natural faculties. The exceptional gifts of my brother . . . brought my own inferiority home to me. I did not mind the lack of visible successes, but what did grieve me was the idea of being excluded from that transcendent kingdom which is only accessible to the truly great and wherein truth abides. I preferred to die rather than to live without that truth. After months of inward darkness, as in a flash, there was born in me the everlasting conviction that no matter what human being, even though practically devoid of natural faculties, can penetrate to the kingdom of truth reserved for genius, if only he longs for truth and always concentrates all his attention upon its attainment.'[8]

This confession not only places the moment of her moral and spiritual adolescence, it also conveys the true measure of her agnosticism. She says in the same letter: 'From childhood, I considered the question of God's existence as a problem for which data could not be obtained here below.' The only way not to reach a wrong solution to it—that is, the worst solution—is not to pose it at all. Being in this world, isn't it our business to take the best possible attitude towards the problems which belong to this world? Moral problems, like all those which confront man, contained an answer which was intrinsic, and not transcendental, to the terms in which they were stated; or they offered a solution based on analogy on a perceptible scale of comparison. The beauty of a mountain landscape ushered into Simone Weil's mind the notion of 'purity'. It came to her at sixteen, after she had passed through several months of 'the emotional unrest natural to adolescence'; it conveyed to her 'all that this word can imply for a Christian' and became in turn a term of reference for values both ethical and aesthetic, as shown by the constant use of the word in her writings.

Since God had not spoken, how could she have listened to him in her youth? Simone Weil pondered this, much later, in her *American Journals*: 'To obey God, one must receive his commands. How can it be that I received them in adolescence whilst I professed atheism?'[9]

While struggling with the undercurrents of her inner life, the stream of outer life continued to carry her along. On 22nd June 1924, Simone Weil was admitted to the *baccalauréat* in the classical section. On 1st October, she registered as a non-resident at the Lycée Victor Duruy, a girls' public high school and junior college near the Invalides.

Simone had difficulty in making up her mind whether to specialize in mathematics or in philosophy: the first was the more challenging, since it was her brother's subject; the second ought to have been the obvious choice, considering her natural gifts. Some say she solved the dilemma by tossing a coin.

On the advice of several friends, Simone chose the Lycée Victor Duruy for her year of philosophy. It is said she went there to study under Le Senne.[10] But Le Senne himself explains: 'This was the first time that a man ever taught in a girls' lycée.' In any case, there is no evidence that Le Senne's teaching was important in Simone Weil's mental development. He acknowledged that she was his best pupil, but nothing more: 'The real Simone Weil did not appear until later.'

Le Senne's judgment was not altogether true. For Simone Weil showed a strong personality even then, and its principal characteristics were already formed. She was, among other things, absent-minded and rather careless. One day, when she was

23

wearing a fairly new beige dress, she unthinkingly put an ink-pot into one of her pockets, covering it with large stains. Her generosity and need for affection were not always evident; other, more average, pupils of the Lycée sometimes felt hurt by her. A former fellow-student credits the utter lack of comradeship between herself and Simone to her 'making such a show of her unconventional attire, and of a political extremism that seemed rather an affectation in one so young'. She intimidated others, says Sister Françoise Copeau, who knew her at the Lycée Duruy, by the depth of her interests—and all the more so because she was herself embarrassed by the strained feelings she sometimes caused. She wasn't inclined to talk a great deal, even to friends; when she did, her speech was slow and diffident. Later, when 'Édi' Copeau entered a convent, Simone supported her decision with an 'ardent, almost tender approval' and continued to write to her and see her.

On the 27th of June, 1925, Simone Weil took her *baccalauréat* in philosophy. It was understood that after the holidays she was to enter the Lycée Henri IV—the equivalent of junior and senior years in an English school or an American college—to prepare for the entrance examination at the university.

## 2

# University

1925-1931

'Geometry, like all thought, perhaps, is the daughter of labour's fortitude.' Simone Weil, *Perception, or the Adventure of Proteus*

SIMONE WEIL became a first-year student at Henri IV in October 1925. The term reports of the three years that she spent there enable us to follow her intellectual development: 'She has cogency, lucidity, and often distinction in her powers of analysis. The general perspectives are less clear: she has to learn how to construct a coherent argument. She already shows an original mind and much may be expected of her.' Very soon the tone of these reports rose to a higher key. 'An excellent pupil, who learns and develops with remarkable rapidity and confidence. Her style is not quite equal to her thinking, but one can anticipate brilliant results which may well prove astonishing.' Finally, at the end of the first year: 'An excellent pupil, who is capable of far-ranging ideas, and whose appreciation of the best authors is of the utmost originality. The results are almost always of the highest order, although they are marred by a certain obscurity, from which she will no doubt free herself.'[1]

This obscurity is continually mentioned in the reports of 1926-1927. 'A very good pupil; really gifted, who should, above all, be on her guard against over-abstruse reflections, expressed in almost impenetrable language. She knows perfectly well, however, how to compose her essays, elucidate her argument, and arrange her thoughts in writing. Her success depends upon herself.'

There is nothing academic about these reports. They present a graphic picture of the young Simone and suggest a quite

25

personal relationship between master and pupil. Again, for the years 1927-1928, we read that 'she shows considerable power and consistency, although she sometimes goes too fast and without sufficient preparation. Her examination thesis cannot but prove outstanding.' And finally: 'Hers is an already extensive culture; she has a mind of unusual power. Her thoughts at times outdistance her class exercises. Thence arises an understandable difficulty, which sometimes paralyses her capacity for giving form and structure to her thoughts. Nevertheless one can foresee for her a brilliant success.'

These reports reveal the hand of Émile Chartier, otherwise known as Alain. His preponderant influence on the spirit of Simone Weil is unquestionable. She among others was never to succeed in freeing herself wholly from his influence. His written work alone would scarcely explain the importance he had for successive pupils and, in fact, for a whole generation. To this day, Alain is no doubt the real target of the polemics of Sartre and Merleau-Ponty, for example, since they were exposed to his influence, directly or indirectly, at the outset of their careers. Yet he had no wish to be an innovator, and the idea of starting a new philosophical system would surely have amused him. His only wish was to carry on the great French philosophical tradition, to re-evaluate Descartes in the light of Kant, whose major ideas had been transmitted to him by his teacher, Jules Lagneau. Alain's teaching consisted of a free commentary on the major philosophers: Plato, Descartes, Kant, Hegel. Yet, far from trying to accentuate the discrepancies in their doctrines, his principal concern was to emphasize what was most valuable in each of them. 'Let us say boldly: to philosophize is to explain, in the popular sense of the word, the obvious by the obscure.'[2]

Alain was a splendid figure of a man; he had the swagger of a musketeer. Although temperamental by nature, he was on guard against violence. All forms of metaphysical *angst* or religious anxiety were foreign to him; he was anti-clerical and radical in the spirit of 1900. He remained a bachelor well into his sixties and was fiercely hostile to all the mundanities of life. He combined politics with philosophy, and in his youth had been militantly political and a Dreyfusard. As for socialism, he deplored what he regarded as its blind faith in an economic transformation of society. His antithesis between the bourgeois who lives by illusion and the proletarian whom work has immunized against fallacious values was familiar to all his students: he continually referred to the son of Aesop who is neither crass nor asleep, but only abandoned. His political theory was experimental and independent and opposed to all systematic formulations. In 1914, although exempted by age from conscription, Alain joined the French forces as a private, because he was convinced that he would remain freer at the front than behind the lines.

Such was the man who came to have an extraordinary influence on Simone Weil's life. René Château, a colleague of Simone's, tells us that she had a slack and badly formed handwriting. When she was in 'Khâgne', the class of 'Première Supérieure' (the year of preparation for admission to the École Normale), Alain told her that she ought to take pains to write more legibly. Human beings can become what they want to be, he said, and to write well implies a control of one's passions. Simone therefore applied herself to improving her handwriting, because she was convinced that she would thereby learn to think. She took pains also to avoid erasures—those repentances of thought—for in his spiritual autobiography Alain had explained how and why he had decided never to correct his text: either you leave what has been written or you begin all over again. He believed that everyone whether he were a genius or not ought to spend at least two hours a day at his writing-desk.

Another colleague of Simone Weil, Étienne Borne, tells how she applied herself to imitating Alain in all things. Here and there in his works can be found the ideas that she adapted and made her own. One of these was the concept of what is 'social': society resists the spirit; the spirit, in turn, resists society. 'All use of power is an abuse.' An organized religion, however, belongs to a social order; therefore, a free spirit should oppose religion too. And yet, apart from its ecclesiastical organization, Christianity is precisely the cult of the crucified spirit, a cult which was already fore-shadowed in the *Republic* of Plato.

What Alain lacked was not so much the Christian interpretation of the Greek tradition but the torment and anguish of the

Absolute. This metaphysical affliction was well known to Jules Lagneau, as it came to be to Simone Weil. Alain's significant contribution was to bring Weil into contact with Lagneau. 'God,' wrote Lagneau, 'confronts us in the act wherein we confront him. That is to say that, in the act of reflection upon God, we attain that absolute sphere of the creative power; we enter into the creative act.' In order to accomplish this act of reflection, we must have recourse simultaneously to affirmation and to negation. Atheism is this negation. It is, therefore, more than merely a form of intellectual asceticism; it is a phase of faith itself. It seals off all the ways towards idolatry. And in this void, God creates. 'Certitude is', therefore, 'an absolute creation of the spirit; it is the spirit itself, it is the absolute, it is God who creates it in us'. These words awakened profound echoes in the soul of Simone Weil.[3]

And yet—did her absorption in philosophy endanger her chances of success in other areas? This is a question that may be answered with the help of her teachers' reports. At the end of her first term, Gautier, who instructed his class in French and Greek texts, found in his pupil 'some literary taste, but also some bad taste'. Fedel, professor of Latin, writes that she 'knows a little Latin, but her translation is clumsy and her style crude and cumbersome'. Salomon, professor of history, tersely describes her as 'an intelligent amateur'.

The reports of the second term corroborated those of the first in their assessment of Simone's character and aptitudes. 'Inclined to let her fancy run away with her; she is apt to talk rather too much in class.' According to Fedel, 'she explains the text well enough. Her translation from Latin is of middling ability. Her translation into Latin is weak, and marred by gross lapses.' But Salomon writes: 'An intelligent young girl who evidently feels that she is above history.'

In the last term's report, we learn that Simone did no history for this term; and Gautier writes: 'She has not kept up the success she had in French at the beginning of the year. She tries too hard to achieve originality and becomes eccentric.'

The scholastic year 1926-27 apparently did not result in any real progress in French. Simone Weil continued to show great

originality, her teachers agreed. She was 'very individualistic'—
in fact *too* individualistic. 'She gives free rein to her imagination'
and her 'behaviour leaves much to be desired', they declared.
A final complaint: she stayed away from all lectures during most
of the third term.

Only Fedel noted some progress. But he also wrote that she
stayed away from class too often during the last term.

Salomon's reports predicted a catastrophe: he reports of her
first term of the year 1926-1927: 'She is still eccentric: she seems,
however, to have less confidence in herself and a little more in the
value of exercises that are moderate enough for her.' His second
term's report is categorically unfavourable: 'She has done no
history at all this term. History may well be her downfall if she
wants to get into the École Normale.' During the third term,
Simone Weil did not work at history, either.

She took her test, with catastrophic results. Questioned on
the Eastern situation, she made twenty statements about the
Sublime Porte in her examination paper: it was all she knew about
the subject. She received seven points out of twenty—a score
which did not in itself eliminate her, but for which she could
not compensate. Thus failure was inevitable.

Doubtless this failure could be attributed to Alain, for he
inculcated in his pupils a scorn for psychology and, some said,
a disdain for history.

Whatever the case, Simone Weil loyally blamed no one but
herself. She had wasted her time, smoking cigarettes in cafés.
The set-back humiliated her, but it had an enlightening, strength-
ening and sobering effect. Her progress was immediate. Alba,
her professor of history in 1927-28, writes that 'she ought to aim
at more simplicity in presentation and at fewer philosophical
speculations about the subject. However, one must pay tribute
to her reflection; her thought is often profound.' Chevaillier, her
professor of French, writes in the report of the first term that
'her theses are original essays rather than set themes for class work.
They are very brilliant and very vigorous.' Only Travers, her
English professor, had grounds for complaint against her during
this year. In his first term report, he declares, 'I regret to say that
it is impossible at times to have her in the class unless she is

isolated from the others.' His complaint becomes even more bitter during the second term: 'Simone Weil is determined to profit from this class as little as possible, and she succeeds.'

But on the whole, as Chevaillier records, 1927-1928 was 'a very good year'. And what struck her teachers most was not so much the calibre of the school work as the personality of their prize pupil. For her character was striking. Alba described later 'her need to seek the truth, and once she had found it to express it with an indomitable courage; her absolute rejection of all compromise, in little things as in big'. Her talents were recognized and given the opportunity to develop.

On the 30th January 1926, the star pupils of the Lycée gathered for the traditional feast of St Charlemagne. Simone Weil was commissioned to compose a poem for the event. Her last verses contain an invocation to St Geneviève:

> *Rather than Charlemagne, invoke this saint*
> *Whose greatness of heart made her*
> *More strong than death; it is she whom*
> *The Frenchman invoked in his fear,*
> *When he saw her, without threat and without complaint,*
> *Keep watch over the sleeping town.*

On hearing these lines, Alain observed, smiling: 'Everyone begins by writing bad verse.'

It was also at this epoch in her student life that Simone composed the vigorous verses: 'To a rich young girl', a satire on society and morals. Another poem, 'Sonnet to Mme Bessarabo', a jest on the theme of a celebrated murder, dates from the years at the Lycée Fénelon.

Simone's activities extended outside the school, too. Shortly after her admission to the Lycée Henri IV, Thévenon writes: 'She was attracted by revolutionary syndicalism [trade unionism]. She was already giving courses of instruction to young syndicalist railwaymen.'[4] (These courses had been organized by Simone's railwayman friend, Cancouet.)

Meanwhile, her home environment continued to be warm and pleasant. In 1928, Simone Weil's parents settled in an apartment on the seventh and eighth floors of a new building, 3 rue Auguste Comte, facing the Jardin du Luxembourg. From their windows a vast and beautiful panorama stretched over most of the western half of Paris, from the Sacré Cœur in Montmartre to the Eiffel Tower. There they remained until 1940. In 1924 or 1925 they had also acquired a small country house at Chevreuse, to the south-west of Paris, where they spent week-ends with their children during the warmer months.

In March 1928 Simone fell ill and forgot to enter her name for the coming examination. On 17th April 1928, her father had to write to the Minister of Education to request that she be put down for it *extra-tempora*. This request was supported by the head-master of the Lycée Henri IV, who wrote a letter on her behalf to the Rector of the Academy, who in turn forwarded it to the Minister.

For it is the Minister of Education who controls the whole state-supported educational system in France, from the lowest École Primaire (ages 6 to 12-13), through the Lycées (ages 6 to 16-17) and the Lycées Supérieurs (ages 18 to 19 or 20), to the universities such as the Sorbonne. The École Normale Supérieure was the school where the boys who had received a state scholarship were entitled to live and study. In exchange they signed a ten-year contract for teaching in the French state-run Lycées. (They automatically received army commissions after completing their exams. It was possible to buy their way out of the teaching contractual requirement, but few took advantage of this.) In Simone Weil's day, the École Normale's classes had only very recently been opened to girls. Before then, girls attended the École de Sèvres, in the suburbs of Paris, where standards were not so high.

Simone Weil was permitted to sit for the examination. The 'indomitable courage' of which her teacher Alba had spoken enabled her to surmount the obstacle of registering late, and she made a favourable impression on her examiners. Presented at the same time as Simone de Beauvoir, she came in first; Simone de Beauvoir was the runner-up. These two remarkable young women were at the top of a list of thirty men.

At the end of 1928, Simone entered the École Normale Supérieure, where she rejoined the three women who had been enrolled the year before and who were nicknamed 'the three

31

gleaners' a reference to Millet's picture. Simone was often counted as one of them.

The image of Simone, student of the École Normale, is still fresh in the memory of all those who knew her during this period of her life. She was considered an 'astute girl', but very much a tomboy. She went to cafés with other students, took part in discussions, and perfected the art of debunking, an indispensable aspect of student life. A chain-smoker, she rolled her own cigarettes, but since she was not skilful at it she often had shreds of tobacco in her mouth.

Her features were still delicate and beautiful, but large horn-rimmed spectacles, for myopia, detracted from her appearance. She had retained her girlish bearing, but she walked awkwardly, leaning forward, with long, jerky steps. Her usual costume was a loose tailored dress, of masculine cut, with large side-pockets that were always full of tobacco, worn with the low-heeled shoes of a little girl.

It was said that Simone Weil was anti-clerical. If true, this attitude seems to have been a pose and partly the result of her left-wing views. According to Professor Puesch, now at the Collège de France, everyone took her for a communist. He was astonished when, in response to his suggestion that she take the 'idea of progress' as a theme to prepare for her examination, 'she left in a violent temper, saying that the idea had no meaning'.

Simone had a sharp, restless glance. In contrast with a certain vivacity of facial expression, her speech emerged with a controlled and purposeful slowness, and her delivery was staccato and monotone. She dealt out the words one by one, dwelling upon them to the end; as if she were speaking in a foreign accent. She had a way of aspirating almost all her *h's*. The tone of her voice was of middle register, rather dull and on the nasal side. She always spoke in the same tone of voice, sniffing after each phrase. Her friends said she sounded like a woman preaching for the Salvation Army.

What was most striking about her despite this description was her desire to be like everyone else, and the impossibility of ever achieving this. Nevertheless, she made constant and pathetic efforts to conquer herself. Hoping to remedy her extreme

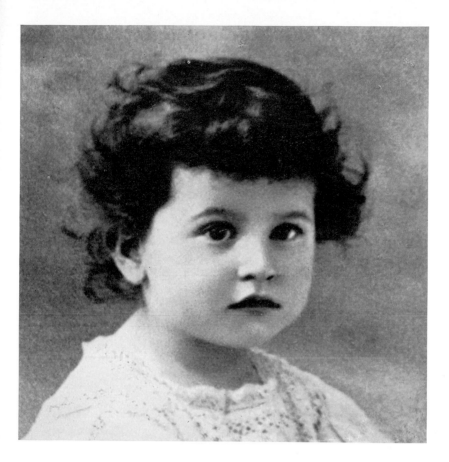

Simone aged two, Paris, 1911

With her father at Mayenne, 1915

Simone at Knokke (Belgium), summer of 1922

clumsiness, she joined the first women's rugby team in the 'Femina' athletic club. People remember seeing her return from the playing field, covered with mud and bruises, and a prey to a sort of inner despair that these excesses did little to conceal. Her health continued to be poor, but for that she had a sovereign disregard. The determined efforts she made to overcome her physical disabilities were instrumental in the development of a physical condition that adversely affected her future. On her return from a game of rugby one cold day in 1930, she was prostrated by an agonizing headache, worse than those she had grown accustomed to suffering. It was the first attack of sinusitis, not properly diagnosed until 1939, which was to torment her to the end of her life.

At the École Normale Simone continued to attend Alain's courses in philosophy. She was not alone in this: a good many of the students of the École Normale spent more time at the Henri IV than in their own lecture-rooms. Alain was a quasi-spiritual source of inspiration to Simone. Like him, she banished from her intellectual horizon all easily demonstrable truths. She submitted her writings to him; he published them in his periodical, *Libres Propos*. It was in this periodical, on the 20th May 1929, that she published her first essay, a paper written for the university on the nature of perception, in which she applied the Homeric myth of Proteus : ' *De la perception ou l'Aventure de Protée* '. The style is somewhat stiff, and her analysis owes as much to poetry as it does to metaphysics. Her principal thesis amounts to the assertion that the problem of perception is closely bound up with the problem of work. 'What, then, truly understood, is work? Work, in contrast to reflection, to persuasion or to magic, is a sequence of actions that have no direct connection either with the initial emotion, or with the end aimed at . . .'

The attributes of things, the forms they assume, the distances between one thing and another are, in this essay, ambiguous aspects of Proteus. They govern all work.

The core of the essay may be found in this passage: '. . . Colours, sounds, dimensions can change, while the law of work, which is to be unceasingly indifferent to what has preceded and to what will follow, never changes. Proteus can take this or that form at will, but the mind is not thereby freed from observing the same law in its activity and therefore from encountering the same matter. Qualities, forms and distances change, but the law of work remains the constant factor to which qualities, forms and distances serve only as signs. It is the very same law of exterior relations that defines space. For to see space is to grasp work's raw material, always passive, always outside one's self—as soon as space is formed, Proteus is conquered.'

The concluding phrase of this essay delighted École Normale circles: 'Geometry, like all thought, perhaps, is the daughter of labour's fortitude.'

It is significant that this first printed essay by Simone Weil expressed such concern about the nature of labour, for it became one of her life's obsessions. And although the ideas owe much to Alain, the statement is original.

On 20th August 1929, *Libres Propos* published '*Du temps*', an essay which Simone Weil had written on the nature of time. After asserting that man endures suffering, feels desire, entertains doubt, and is prone to ignorance, Simone went on: 'These are so many ways of saying that what I am does not satisfy me and has become me without my consent; what I am, I endure.'

The future is defined for man by the fact that he is not immediately in his own power. 'Tomorrow is an I that now I cannot change. It is this relation between the present and the future that constitutes time.'

Time, then, being that separation between what one is and what one would like to be, work is the only road from self to self. 'I cannot, therefore, free myself from time, save by conforming my actions to this, the condition which time imposes upon me. Insofar as time expresses the complete impotence of my will to legislate without doing, time is beyond time, time is eternal, time is, in some fashion, present by the very presence of this alien existence which imposes it upon me. Thus I do not have to go outside myself to discover what is foreign to me. In any impression whatever, there is only one thing that is not mine, and that is the law by which I cannot pass on to another impression without passing through intermediate steps alien both to that which I am feeling and that which I want to feel—impressions foreign to one

34

another except that each of them comes after another, and that each one is foreign to any other impression. And this is the very law of time as perceived by the genius of Kant. It is by this law of time as a form of work that, in every sense-impression, I am aware of the existence of the world.'

All the ideas whereby sense-data constitute themselves into an object are, as Kant saw it, 'the daughters of time'. 'Let us then wake up anew to the world; that is, let us return to work and to perception, and not fail in courage to observe that rule by which alone what we are doing can truly be work, and what we feel, perception: let us humble our own bodies to the status of tools, and our emotions to the rank of signs.'

These vigorous ideas are not overly lucid. They resist any summary analysis. Alain believed that Simone was capable of writing a conclusive commentary on Kant and Spinoza. He had read pages she had written on Spinoza 'which were positively outstanding'.[5] He advised her, among other things, to cut out pages from the works of Kant, or Spinoza, and paste them on large white sheets of paper on which she could then write her comments. He expressly directed that these sheets be large, for he maintained that blank white space is in itself a discipline to thought.

There was, then, a sort of natural kinship of ideas between Simone Weil and Chartier; a common attitude of mind. Both sought to reduce every question to its essentials, often at the cost of a symbolic interpretation of texts; both felt the same devotion and respect for the wisdom of the Greeks; both had the same skilful way of resolving an intellectual difficulty with a dazzling statement. And yet, paradoxically, the remarkable affinity of spirit which attached Simone Weil so closely to the instruction of Alain rendered her far freer from his influence than the majority of his disciples.

Most of Alain's pupils copied him slavishly. There was a coterie around him, a cult of Alain, of which Michel Alexandre was the moving spirit. Marcou, Le Tellier, Ganuchaud, and Château were generally regarded as his pre-eminent followers. In discussions among his students, these men used to remain silent for some time; then they would deliver a terse and solemn judgment, from which there could be no subsequent appeal. The master had spoken. No scepticism was tolerated: irony on the subject of Alain was ruled out of court.

But Simone, who had made all Alain's ideas her own, broke the spell by taking his notions to their logical conclusion. This was nothing short of heterodoxy. Alain's orthodox followers felt that Simone's excesses were injurious to Alain's teaching. Both friends and foes joined in regarding her as eccentric. Her eccentricity was her wish to get to the depths of the matters that concerned her—an illustration of a dichotomy between her own ideas, the ideas she expressed, and the ideas she was seeking.

In truth, Simone Weil could not have had anything in common with Alain's eclecticism. The professor's attitudes seemed to be almost a form of intellectual philandering beside her impassioned standpoint. Simone committed herself to her ideas at once and entirely and felt bound to put them into immediate action; she could tolerate no compromise whatever. This characteristic was widely recognized among her fellow students at the École Normale, who called her 'the Categorical Imperative in skirts'.

Simone Weil was, in this and in other respects, in conflict with her milieu. True, the conflict was latent in the beginning, but it went deep and arose from her natural force of spirit. She was even more alone than she realized. Besides her intellectual isolation, she was wholly shut off from the free-and-easy, boy-girl relationships of student life. Young men considered her unfeminine, and her lack of femininity was ridiculed, sometimes grossly. Some thought that she deliberately tried to look ugly; others simply thought her so in fact. Her hair, of which another girl would have been proud, her excellent complexion, went unnoticed under her general untidiness. From the moment that she was permitted to choose her own clothes, she had preferred to wear what was least becoming. As though in self-justification, she pretended that she had no desire to be regarded as a girl by her fellow-students. The result was that very few realized that she had any need for the affection and attention that a woman usually desires. But there were times when the young woman in her showed through, and then she would blush enchantingly. One summer day, when she was picking plums in the country, she climbed a

wall and couldn't get down again. A young man stretched out his
hands to her. At the implication behind this gesture, either from
modesty or because she felt bound to refuse assistance, she
trembled all over. Beneath her spectacular assertions of independence, there seems to have been an intensity of affective life which
no one understood.

In a sense, Simone Weil denied herself the emotional security
offered her by her own family; she wanted to cut herself off completely from all that makes life easy and to dispense absolutely
with comfort. She believed that this was essential to escape from
the middle-class spirit she hated.

At the École Normale, Simone followed the fashion of being
insolent towards the professors of the Sorbonne. Fate had in store
for her two chosen victims: first, there was Bouglé, the actual
director of the school studies. One day he lectured on the meaning
and feeling of Patriotism—a thorny subject. At the end of the
hour, he asked if there were any questions. Simone took the floor
and read, without comment, a speech from the *Official Gazette* of
1912, in which Poincaré seemed to recommend an invasion of
Belgium. When she had finished, there was a moment's pause.
Bouglé took out his watch and said: 'It's twelve o'clock; it's time
for lunch.' This reply quickly became a catch-word, repeated,
with the appropriate gesture, whenever a student couldn't find
an answer to a disconcerting question.

Then, as now, it was fashionable for students to draft petitions.
At that time, however, student petitions attracted the attention of
the general public far more than today and were a thorn in the
flesh of the Directors of the École. Simone subscribed to them
all, naturally. An anti-militarist petition drawn up by Château
which fired Simone with enthusiasm was the most unwelcome of
them all, although the issue turned out to be unimportant. Eighty-
three Normaliens had requested that recruitment for the ROTC
should be voluntary rather than compulsory; the conservative
press commented unfavourably. The spirit of the movement
was one of intellectual individualism, of pacifism, and also of the
personality of Alain, 'whose many-faceted essays', said *L'École
Émancipée* on 30th December 1928, 'often conceal nothing more
than a paltry philosophical radicalism'. Bouglé summoned the

ring-leaders of the group, lectured them, and said: 'If you repeat what I say to you here, I shall simply say that it is not true.' Nothing could have been more absurd or more odious to Simone Weil. She never forgave him, and she took every chance of making him aware of it. He called her 'the Red Virgin' and is rumoured to have remarked disparagingly of her in public: 'As for Simone Weil, we will leave to her the organization of *le Grand Soir* (i.e., the Revolution).' He followed her activities unsympathetically. Once, however, when she came begging for funds, he gave her twenty francs with a warning that the donor must remain anonymous. Some days later, he saw a sign on the bulletin-board: 'Follow the example of your Director. Be an anonymous donor to the unemployment benefit fund.'

Simone Weil's other victim was Léon Brunschvicg. There was abundant cause for friction between them. At times he indulged in irony. For instance, he called Alain, 'M. Chartier the tapestry-weaver'. Such a remark was considered a challenge. In addition, Brunschvicg couldn't abide Rousseau. After reading a student paper on Rousseau, he declared that Rousseau 'shammed sincerity'. This was sacrilege to anyone sympathetic with Alain's views on Rousseau, and the remark provoked a clamour of protest. Alain's devotees also disliked Brunschvicg's coolness toward Kant, for whom, he said, 'duty is Duty, with a capital D'. Brunschvicg gave Simone ten points out of twenty for her diploma-monograph: *Science and Perception in Descartes* (1930). Apparently, he found it intolerable that she could have so personal a point of view and such faith in Alain—and, at the same time, so little respect for his own views and teaching on philosophical subjects. There is a story that Alain, on meeting Brunschvicg, teased him by saying, 'Ten out of twenty! Simone deserves zero out of twenty or eighteen out of twenty, but that, never! Would you like to know why you gave her ten out of twenty? Because she is Jewish.' (Brunschvicg himself was a Jew.)

In Simone's monograph there are the same illustrative enumerations and unqualified categorical assertions characteristic of Alain's style, along with his entire teaching on Descartes. And yet there are also Simone's extensive and thorough knowledge of the subject, a somewhat excessive boldness to contradict the great philosopher's conclusions, and even a will to reduce them to absurdity. The exact, serious, and solid critical apparatus which Simone deploys in her scholarly analysis on the one hand, and her ingenuousness, subtlety, and independence of mind on the other, give her thesis a very peculiar character. It astonishes, shocks, irritates and disturbs. Simone Weil is visibly feeling her way but she has already won through to a startling freedom of thought. No doubt she disappointed Léon Brunschvicg. Had Léon Brunschvicg disappointed her? The question would not have occurred to her, for she never expected anything of him.

To sum up, during the years at Normale, all that Simone Weil really learned beyond the prescribed limits of her studies was to properly evaluate Alain and to free herself from him, and that only to a limited extent. But her time at the École was decisive in introducing her into the trade-union movement. We know that her attraction to Marxism began at an early date. She also took part, although rather reservedly, in the activities of the 'Union for Truth' meetings of students and intellectuals inspired by Gide, Martin du Gard, and other writers of the *Nouvelle Revue Française*. Another activity also won her dedicated interest. Château and Ganuchaud had founded, at 3 rue Falguière, a kind of working men's college. The aim of this college was to enable railway employees to graduate from manual labour to white-collar work. They also hoped to provide for the proletariat a grounding in cultural subjects. Simone gave herself heart and soul to this benevolent teaching, working hand-in-hand with Guindey, Marcou, and the three founders.

It is hardly possible to exaggerate the importance of the contacts Simone made at the rue Falguière. One day a workman asked if he could talk about matters outside the syllabus. He made an appointment with his teachers in the Luxembourg Gardens, and when they met it became clear that he had been reading Plato and Descartes and had acquired a very sound grasp of their meaning. This incident might have been unimportant to others, but to Simone Weil it was a revelation confirming both Alain's views on the proletariat and the worth of the vocation, the special type of sainthood, which she now regarded as the whole orientation of her life. Simone had confidence *a priori* in the good sense of the working class; it was the postulate she needed in order to give coherence to her inmost aims and ideals.

Simone also was connected with the Fourteenth Chapter of the League for the Rights of Man, of which Cancouet was then President. She was to say later to a Parisian journalist: 'The League for the Rights of Man is, from my point of view, the trade-union movement itself.' From her connection with the anti-militarist manifesto of the Normaliens and from other activities, Simone Weil acquired a reputation as a pacifist during her years at the École Normale. Her pacifism was undeviating and wholehearted, and well established at the time of the dispute (see page 37) which led to the resignation of 83 Normaliens from the officers' reserve corps. Students of the École Normale had protested against compulsory enlistment as a violation of individual liberty, but they were badly organized. The majority of students who had resigned their commissions had every intention of serving, but only as privates. Sixty-two of the eighty-three signatories of the petition declared in *L'Oeuvre*, on the 3rd December 1928, that they had no wish whatever to attack the army. Thus the cause was undermined through lack of unity and resolution, and the undertaking proved abortive.

But *Libres Propos* of July 1931 registered a new protest against the 'militarization of intellectuals' in a document signed by Bénichou, Romain Rolland, Sartre and other former students of the École Normale, and by Simone Pètrement, Lucien Roubaud, Jean Weil, and Simone Weil, all current students. Simone also was affiliated although indirectly, with Madeleine Vernet's 'The Will to Peace' movement.

From these years at college Simone Weil also dated her first experiences with the actual, day-to-day life of the working classes. During the holidays, which she spent at the home of an aunt, she worked ten hours a day digging potatoes. Two summers in succession she visited the mother of her friend Pierre Le Tellier at St Malo de Lalande, near Coutances in Normandy. There she exhibited a frantic kind of energy during the five or six weeks of harvest time. In the fields the thistles harvested by the reapers were separated from the wheat and piled into heaps. Simone would gather them up in her bare arms. 'Leave them,' she was told, 'there are men coming with prongs to pick those up.' She stopped momentarily, embarrassed, fearing that she may have done something not according to the accepted routine. But she recovered herself quickly, and picking up her thorny bundle once more said: 'Why them, and not me?' In the evening, she made the same reply when the farm-hands tried to stop her from helping unload 'her' cart; she lifted sheaves bigger than herself over her head, working at the same rate as the men. One day a farm-hand who had worked with her observed: 'You know, when I think of her, why, I think Joan of Arc was like that!'

In 1928, word spread at Normale that a certain Cérésole had created what he called 'le Service Civil'. He meant by this a union of pacifists throughout the world. Pacifists should prove at last, he said, that they are in earnest. He proposed that they should hold themselves in readiness against any public catastrophe as proof of their real spirit of international co-operation. In 1928, members of 'le Service Civil' decided to go to the Principality of Lichtenstein, which had been devastated by floods. Simone was bent on being among them, although the women of the movement, dubbed 'Sœurs', had no jobs allotted them except cooking. Sister Weil, who had no talent for cooking whatever, begged to be taken as a navvy, but the others would not allow it.

Such extravagant notions concealed a heart as yet unaware of itself. Georges Hourdin tells of the time Simone was walking with her student-friends in the Luxembourg Gardens. She took one of them by the lapel and said: 'How can you laugh, when children are suffering in China?'[6] One fine spring day, according to Raymond Aron, she appeared sad and downcast: 'There's been a strike in Shanghai, and they've been shooting at the strikers!' She possessed a faculty common to poets—that of isolating a single event in space and time and converting it into a drama of cosmic importance. 'Everyone knows,' she was to write later, 'that the scale of human problems, the importance of men, the gravity of injustice, the intensity of suffering, diminish with distance. . . . Here is a phenomenon for which one might try to establish the mathematical formula. No doubt, as with the law of gravity, the ratio varies in inverse proportion to the square of the distance. Distance makes injustice and oppression weigh less in themselves and on our spirits, in the same way as it influences the weight of matter.'[7]

Simone's heart, 'capable of missing a beat for what took place at the other end of the universe', evoked the admiration of Simone de Beauvoir, who relates, in her *Mémoires*, the only discussion she ever had with Simone Weil: 'She asserted in a strident voice that only one thing matters today on earth and that is the Revolution which is to feed the whole world. I retorted, in a no less peremptory fashion, that the problem was less how to increase human well-being than how to discover the meaning and value of human existence. She looked me up and down: "It is easy to see you have never been hungry." '[8]

On July 1931, Simone Weil received her *agrégation*. In France *agrégation* is a final examination taken by those being graduated from the École Normale and from the Universities; only a fraction pass the examination and are thenceforward called *agrégés*. They enjoy thereafter special promotional privileges. And as a general rule, candidates to a doctorate are recruited amongst the *agrégés*. Her Ministry of Education dossier states that Simone Weil was admitted 7th *ex aequo* along with 11 others out of 107 candidates. It includes the following estimate: 'A brilliant candidate, who appears to be well informed not only about philosophy, but also about literature and contemporary art. She tends to run ahead of herself, however, ignoring difficulties and objections.' It was rumoured that she owed her placement to Brunschvicg. In reality, she owed it especially to Lalande, president of the jury, who questioned her on the *Chanson de Roland* and gave her nineteen points out of twenty. During the year Simone had been following the course which Bédier gave on this subject, so her answers were brilliant. The witnesses say that as the questioning proceeded, the face of the examiner lit up.

When the problem of finding a teaching post for Simone Weil arose, the Director of the École Normale is supposed to have said: 'We'll give her a job as far away as possible. Then at last we'll hear no more of her!' But for this, Simone had to approach him first, to ask him to find her a post. On Saturday, August 1st, Roustan of the Ministry of Education received the *agrégés*, and Simone

Weil was not able to tell him that day that she was requesting a post for the year 1931-32. On 10th August, however, she wrote to the Minister in the hope that she might obtain a post 'preferably in a port (Le Havre, if possible) or in an industrial town in the North or the Centre'. To support her request for Le Havre, she had got the recommendation of M. E. Pascaud, a deputy of the Charente; on 22nd August he wrote that Simone Weil's nomination as a teacher at the girls' Lycée of Le Puy was not at all what he had asked for. Evidently the Ministry of Education had sent her as far away as possible. But Bouglé was mistaken if he thought that 'the Red Virgin' would not be heard of again.

The nomination to Le Puy could hardly have been pleasing to the young graduate. Proof of her dissatisfaction exists in her file in the Ministry of National Education: 'Having learned that the post of teacher of philosophy at the Lycée of Valenciennes is not at present occupied by a university graduate,' the candidate has the honour to beg the academic authorities to put forward her name for this post instead of that to which she has been appointed. The Minister's answer was the equivalent of a flat refusal: 'If an *agrégée* has the right to a post in a lycée, that does not signify that she has the right to choose her post, or to annul any appointment whatever in order to possess herself of the post that she desires.' The nomination stood, without change.

Before taking up her job, Simone Weil spent the holidays with her family at Réville, near Saint-Vaast, in the department of La Manche. No sooner did she arrive on the coast of Normandy than she wanted to find out about the living conditions of the fisher-folk. But her reputation as a communist had preceded her; she had the air of the lone wolf and the introvert; and her large hood and heavy spectacles were regarded with suspicion and something akin to fear among those to whom she offered her help.

Marcel Lecarpentier was the only sailor who made her welcome aboard his boat, a thirty-foot eight-tonner which he sailed with the help of his brother and *un homme d'équipage*. She accompanied the three men in their work. They began, in water up to the waist, by fishing for bait by the shore. 'She jumped into the water just like a fish' when they threw out the large net which had to be withdrawn as soon as it closed. Then came the baiting, a three-hour process. And then the equipping of the boat before they could put out to sea.

Marcel and his crew fished by hooks along a line two and a half miles long which each man filled out of his own basket. Simone did not have one, but helped the others with a good will which did not always make up for her inexperience. At night, she studied the stars, as navigators did long ago. Once they ran into a real tempest, but tough weather didn't alarm her in the least. She returned soaked to the skin and sat down dripping wet at her hosts' table as naturally as the house dog comes in from the rain and stretches out by the fire-place.

# PART TWO

# SIMONE WEIL :
# TEACHER, ANARCHIST,
# REVOLUTIONARY

1931-1936

# I

# The Lycée of Le Puy

## 1931-1932

'I have always regarded dismissal as the normal culmination of my career.' Simone Weil

WHILE AT THE ÉCOLE NORMALE, Simone Weil had come into contact with a group which was then the life and soul of a movement called *La Révolution Prolétarienne*. This group, then under the influence of Monatte and Louzon, its guiding spirits, no doubt corresponded more nearly than any other to what Simone Weil was seeking, morally and intellectually, at that time. On principle, she had no sympathy whatever with Stalinist Communism, which, far from liberating the workers, had given rise to a totalitarian state. The alliance between politics and brute force was repugnant to her. But all that was humanitarian, anarchist, syndicalist or revolutionary had an irresistible appeal to her. And the *Révolution Prolétarienne* seemed to symbolize all these qualities.

During this period, the trade unions followed the political directives of two central organizations: on the one hand, there was the Confédération Générale du Travail (CGT), the majority of whose members were not communist; on the other, the United CGT, or CGTU, which was dominated by the Communist Party.

In the CGTU orthodox communists were in a minority, but they were politically dominant in the Confédération. The Trotskyites, for their part, were a majority, but they were too divided among themselves to exercise any influence proportionate to their numbers. There was also a second minority group, the revolutionary syndicalists, who were not ideological communists.

47

They were opposed to the very notion of a political party, and their exclusive concern was specifically with syndicalist trade-union action.

When Simone Weil arrived at Le Puy, she knew little of the realities of syndicalist life. She had, on the other hand, a clear idea of what trade unionism ought to be. She had exactly the same idea about it as Claudius Vidal, a striking personality in the syndicalist movement among the school-teachers of the Haute-Loire region: Unionism 'is a practice in search of a theory.' Fate favoured her in putting her in touch with the group organized around *La Révolution Prolétarienne*.

'What was of most interest to her . . . was the fundamental movement. Could the *syndicats* [trade unions] really form the basis of a society where the workers would not be exploited? Were they really now working to provide the workers with the means of achieving their own emancipation?'[1] It was in her eagerness to get answers to these questions that Simone visited Thévenon during the autumn of 1931. He was then the assistant secretary of the Loire Branch of the Federated Syndicalist [trade union] Movement. Holding in her hand a sock that she was darning, Albertine Thévenon opened the door. Without introducing herself, Simone Weil brushed past her and strode down the long corridor which led into the apartment.[2] Through Thévenon, Simone Weil plunged immediately into the thick of working-class life. It was with joy that she made the journey at least once a week from Le Puy to Saint-Étienne.

Thévenon's chief concern was to restore syndicalist unity. He was trying, he wrote, 'to reconsolidate the syndicalist minority and to bring back to the fold of the CGT the regional Federation of Miners, which was then a minority in the CGTU and whose secretary, P. Arnaud, had just been expelled from the Communist Party.'[1]

*L'Effort* of the 21st November 1931 printed Simone Weil's article on 'an intersyndicalist meeting' at Le Puy. It reveals the extent to which she was then fighting, with complete conviction, for syndicalist unity. She makes the following distinctions: 'Existing syndicalist organizations, which are the most precious achievement of the whole working-class movement, must be respected, but unity must be achieved, if necessary without the support of these organizations—even in some cases despite them.' We are, in fact, impaled on the horns of a dilemma: 'The working class will either have to solve this problem, which seems insoluble, or it will have to condemn itself to atrophy as a revolutionary force.' In other words: without true unity among trade unions we shall have no true trade unions. There will never be a revolution, in the proper sense of the word, so long as syndicalism remains merely political.

Syndicalist collaboration is necessary *because* collaboration between the classes is a deception. This is the tenor of Simone Weil's argument in the *Libres Propos* of 10th October 1931: 'The advantages that the syndicalist leaders boast of having obtained through their collaboration with governmental organizations do not seem to be a gain as much as a bone thrown to the people in a period of prosperity.'

Thus the collaboration between the classes disguises the exploitation of the proletariat and is no remedy for it. In November, Simone Weil reverts to this theme in an article entitled 'Reflections on the Economic Crisis'—in effect, an attempt at reformulating Marxist doctrine. In this article, she attacks the principle of production bonuses. In a period of economic expansion, she shows that 'to encourage the output of the workers, the master class establishes . . . an artificial system of bonuses'. The illusory social collaboration which results from this is a pure fabrication, according to Simone; what sort of collaboration, she asks, can exist between exploiters and exploited? What is strange, she says, is that the dangerous myth of collaboration is not necessarily exposed by a slump. On the contrary: according to classical economic theory, in a slump managers and workers may seem to have the same interests to a greater extent than ever. This illusion is the core and kernel of the problem. Such crises are said to be a 'natural' scourge. But, Simone Weil insists: 'Nothing could be less natural than that the abundance of useful products should bring about poverty.' The vice is inherent in the system itself, true. If the system can't be remedied, then crises and periods of prosperity will continue to succeed one another as inevitably as the night follows the day. But can the workers really be said to have 'the same interest as capitalists in discovering some means whereby they can be exploited afresh as rapidly as possible'? For this is what the collaboration between the classes entails in a slump period. Is there no alternative but to believe that the present system will endlessly perpetuate itself? She rebels against this idea, concluding that 'there is nothing to be gained in trying to lessen a crisis; that cannot be done except with the assent and under the domination of the ruling class .... One has got to reckon with the fact that there can be no interest in common between the exploiters and the exploited.'[3]

Her reasoning is shaped by enthusiasm for her subject. There is far less of Simone's more profound thinking here than in the article which she wrote on 30th January 1932, in *L'Effort*: 'It is not enough to revolt against a social order founded on oppression: one has to change it, and one can't change it without understanding it.'

This was, for Simone Weil, a true observation of lasting relevance. It was also a warning and an avowal of some uneasiness in her mind created by the postulate that revolution was the only possible solution to the evils of society. Simone Weil expresses her uneasiness in *L'Effort* on 12th March 1932, where she discloses that her purpose is to assist in leading the syndicalist movement towards genuine reforms. A desire for real reform, she maintains, is the only safeguard of the revolutionary spirit: 'To re-establish the worker's control over the processes of work, without destroying the collective form that capitalism has imposed upon production. The resolution of this problem is the beginning and the end of revolution.'

In April 1932, she published in *La Révolution Prolétarienne* a letter whose frankness must have astonished some readers. Louzon had written an article in July 1931 on the origins of the slump. He attributed the crisis to a lack of man-power. This theory threw Simone Weil into 'perplexities without end'. She wrote that Louzon's article had fascinated her 'by its characteristic clarity and mathematical precision'. 'What he failed to do was to evaluate fully in the light of this theory all the facts on hand after a careful examination of the whole history of the slump. A precise and exhaustive history of the crisis up to the present moment seems to me to be of cardinal importance now. In this period of turmoil and confusion, the *Révolution Prolétarienne* should remain, on the theoretical level at least, equal to the situation.'

Meanwhile another prominent interest occupied Simone Weil. Thévenon was a member of the Advisory Council of the Labour Exchange of Saint-Étienne; he was co-founder, with Claveyrolas, of a circle of working-class studies there. Simone, who had acquired an aptitude for this sort of work in Paris, took part in the scheme as fully as possible. She helped to make it a going concern by buying books with her *prime d'agrégation* (a fixed sum added to the salaries of the *agrégés*), which she regarded, in any case, as an intolerable privilege. She supported the circle of working-class studies with all her enthusiasm and never ceased to attack the suspicion shown by certain trade-union leaders towards centres of education for workers. Simone Weil distinguished between two approaches to working-class culture: the political, against which she warned those who would listen, whose only aim, she said, 'is to reinforce the power of the intellectual over the working class'; and the contrary approach, which strives to free the working class from such domination. The latter, rightly understood, was, she believed, the real goal of working-class education.

From the bottom of her heart—and here at least she was able to quote Karl Marx without the slightest reserve—Simone Weil desired to work for the abolition of the degrading division between intellectual work and manual labour. In an eloquent plea she urged the working class to prepare itself to take possession of 'the whole heritage of preceding generations', in which she included above all 'the heritage of human culture . . . for the whole essence of the Revolution consists in entering into this heritage'. This central idea of Simone Weil's reveals both the extent of her idealism and the weakness of her revolutionary orthodoxy.

To hasten the coming of the great day, Simone devoted herself to teaching. *L'Effort* of 12th December 1931 refers to the Committee for working-class studies: meetings took place on Saturday night and Sunday morning at the office of the Labour Exchange.

'Comrades Thévenon (a teacher at Saint-Étienne) and Simone Weil (an instructor at the Lycée of Le Puy) will supervise the work of this study-group. A lending library will be available for the participants.' Simone Weil brought her own books to the meetings. Whenever she quoted a passage from any of these, she showed her audience the underlined text. Pierre Arnaud observed: 'One could see that she felt an intimate pleasure at being in the company of workers who earned their living with their hands.'[2] That is why she was so deeply attached to the work of the study-group. How could anyone, inspired by the same ideal, have resisted the charm of such a life, with all its astonishing encounters? Simone Weil wanted to get to know all the workers of the circle personally, including the 'bad boys' and the toughs. In her room at Le Puy where the sparse furnishings consisted of a sofa, a large table, planks thrown across a trestle, and packing-cases which served for chairs, she put up on the wall the photograph of a 'big tough' and said: 'There, that's my kind of man!'

Big toughs or not, the miners of Saint-Étienne spoke of Simone Weil with affection. Of course, they never took her for one of themselves, but tended to regard her as a kind of big-hearted mascot. After much begging, she succeeded one day in inducing a small mine-owner near Rive-de-Gier to let her go down the pit, where she had an opportunity to wield the miners' pneumatic drill. It jolted her thoroughly, especially her head, already so sensitive through her previous violent headaches. To go down the shaft of a mine is 'to penetrate to the heart of the proletariat', she said. Everything is stark. Each movement is painful. Even the light seems to be in thrall: light itself 'is merely a tool of toil'. As for the drill, she felt she was shackled to it, and all the miners of the whole world with her. Again she draws the moral: 'It will not be enough for the miners to expropriate the mine-owners, to become themselves the masters of the mines. Political revolution, economic revolution, will only become realities on condition that they lead on to a revolution in the whole technical process, whereby the worker will re-establish, even within the mine and the factory, that control over the terms of work which it is the workers' function to exercise.'[4]

Although up to her ears in work at Saint-Étienne, Simone

Weil was nevertheless also a teacher of philosophy in the girls' lycée of Le Puy.*

Her reputation for being 'a young and brilliant graduate' had gone before her into the little town, and she got the benefit of this inclination in her favour. On the first day of the term, she was wearing a hat which was afterwards replaced by a beret. A little frightened, she went up to her desk with the step of an automaton and, without looking at a soul, drew out sheets of paper covered with her regular writing, put her head in her hands, and began to address the class in a monotone: 'Philosophy is a science; but a science that is quite different from the ordinary sciences. It is a reflection, a thought about thought itself. To begin with, men were interested in things for their own sake; they could not help it. The first free activity of men was to build temples. Their beauty caused them to reflect. But reflection upon such beautiful works was not yet philosophy, but rather religion. In this primitive sort of society human activity was of two kinds: work and religion. Religion has united in itself all the free thoughts of men. Philosophy comes after everything else. The scope of philosophy is the whole of human thought and nothing else.'[5]

Simone Weil would start a sentence, then interrupt herself, and remarking that words are incapable of expressing all the subtle shades and gradations of thought, would ask the help of her audience. In this way, she kept her class on tenterhooks. She used none of the usual artifices of pedagogy and was far more concerned with forming than with informing her pupils. They were always astonished that she had managed to hold them spellbound without having recourse to any device outside the actual subject of consideration. The clumsy way in which she took up a piece of chalk had at first amused them, but this type of distraction soon wore off. The impression of painful awkwardness that she had made on the first day disappeared, too. Her teaching was far too absorbing for her students to dwell upon

*Situated 70 miles to the south-west of Lyons, Le Puy is a picturesque town of 15,000 inhabitants. It is famous for its beautiful Romanesque cathedral, which rises on a steep hill above the city, and for its traditional lace manufacture.

minor details of instruction that she herself overlooked. She was no ordinary teacher.

Her pupils' notebooks (later to be searched for scandalous matter) trace the dominant themes of her teaching: 'Man's life does not begin with labour. The life of man begins with culture. It is not for the human mind to pass from the order of success to the order of values. There is an abyss between these two orders, an abyss that cannot possibly be bridged. It is from the higher of these two orders that man begins.'

And, on the subject of the past: 'Piety towards men exists among all men. All our thoughts are nourished by piety towards our human past.'

Evidence can be found, in countless pages, of her interest in myths, proverbs, legends, and epics. She is reported to have said, on the subject of Claude Farrère and marriage versus free love, that she was not in the habit of speaking about what she did not know; several rash commentators have pounced upon this phrase. She did not give the course on God, no doubt for the same reason; she spoke of him in her lectures, however. One can also find, in the notes of her pupils, some quotations from Lagneau and some concepts which are as rigorously defined as anything that she was to write in the future. Several notebooks, for instance, contain the following sentence: 'God is, in a sense, the only way of eliminating God.' And: 'Mystics who pass beyond the limits of space and time remain immobile. The condition of the state of ecstasy is immobility. There is one other way of entering into eternity: that is to take possession of space and time.'

'God,' writes Lagneau, 'cannot be said to exist, for he cannot be apprehended in the context of experience.'

'It can be said . . . that religion serves no purpose whatever. It is one of those things that lead to no results . . . . One can say that a man practises religion with an eye to enjoying happiness in the other world. But this would be a grossly superficial way of considering religion.'

'The only way to express religion is through works of art. Religion is a sort of pity towards nature which does not prevent us from being ourselves.'

'To be aware of the horror that the wretched inspire one must attain the spirit of Charity.'

It is this very outlook that we find in quotations from Claudel's *l'Ôtage*:

> *And I recall what the Indian monks say, that all*
> *    this evil life*
> *Is vain appearance, and only persists among us*
> *    because we are moving with it,*
> *And all we need to do for it to leave us*
> *Is to sit down and desist from movement.* (I, 1)

These were the ideas closest to the heart of Simone Weil, often illustrated by such simple images as flies in a bottle or a blind man's staff.

It is possible to extract from these notebooks interesting passages on attention, imagination, time and necessity; for example: 'Time alone creates the distinction between abstract necessity and actual necessity. The element of unreality in our dreams is ascribable to the fact that time plays no part in their unfolding. Time is the solid part of reality. Necessity is the antithesis of fatality. Sensations incessantly modify our being. The flow of time prevents us from belonging to ourselves; it is represented in an abstract way in poetry and music by rhythm. Time flows as fast for the unhappy as for the happy. There is no idea of necessity in our enslavement to time.'

From this quotation, it is possible to form a fairly exact estimate of the teaching methods of Simone Weil. She kept the main theme on a leash, as it were, otherwise allowing everything else complete freedom of movement. By touching upon all ideas related to it, she progressively clarified the principal idea without attenuating it. We owe to her pupils these interesting observations on power: 'As a general rule, man's starting point is to avail himself of forms of action, which are conducive to power. For man, the question of ends does not arise until later. There are people in power who allege that their objective is the public good; in reality, their aim in achieving power has been to possess power.'

Napoleon and Molière's miser are singled out as prototypes: 'A peasant tries to enlarge his holding. He has no other reason for doing so except to possess still more land. . . . The merchant sells so as to make his shop still larger and the owner of a factory works to enlarge his factory. . . . Thus, there can be lives that are lived altogether without reflection. Ordinarily, it is in adolescence that one is most reflective. Often, afterwards, life is spent with no other end in view but success. It is possible to live and die in this way, so long as you do not encounter a situation which compels you to ask the question why and not the question how.'

Simone Weil was prone to epigrams with a sting in their tail; one can find them still vibrant, amidst the dead matter which often fills the notebooks of pupils:

'Instinct is a worker without a conscience. But a worker without a conscience is not a worker at all,' says Hegel.

'Labour is the only thing that makes us grasp the idea of necessity.'

'Algebra conjures away all difficulties. . . . To be doing algebra is to be losing one's time.'

'Moments of attention and insights of genius are not different in kind.'

'Labour is human because it presupposes thought.'

'Labour corresponds with the heroic moment, the moment when man separates himself from matter and his own body; he considers himself as something apart from himself with which he must do what he wants . . .'

'Labour is the only way whereby we can pass from dream to reality.'

'The world is a web of necessity.'

'Slaves cannot liberate themselves by revolt, but through the progress of humanity.'

'Greek culture was the abstract form of the perfect society modelled upon human nature.'

'Great thoughts surge up under the pen, they do not come by reflection before writing.'

Simone did not follow the fixed curriculum, nor did she use text-books. But if her pupils did not learn what they were supposed to learn, did they at least learn what she taught? In April, there was a school-wide inspection of teachers. The inspector who sat in on one of her classes spent his whole time taking notes. When a pupil confided this to Simone after class, she replied: 'He did that in order to understand after reflection.' A wise and distinguished literary man, the inspector, Gendarme de Bévotte took care not to commit himself on the subject of Simone's lecture, but took her to task on a point on which he knew he was stronger: 'That's all very learned what you are saying . . . but your pupils do not look as though they understand it.' Thereupon, Simone Weil handed him her class-register and asked him to question the pupils himself. He was astonished by their answers. Acknowledging his surprise, he revealed what was at the back of his mind: 'What you are doing is very good indeed; but not more than two of your pupils will get their *baccalauréat*.'

'Monsieur l'Inspecteur,' Simone replied, 'that's all the same to me.'

And in fact, of the fourteen pupils whom she taught that year, seven went up for the examination, three proved admissible and only two passed.

In spite of this shocking failure, the pupils did not turn against her. The young women liked her; they called her 'la Simone', or sometimes 'Mother Weil'. The inspector of schools, M. Chardon, says that she was 'interested in the progress of their minds'. On the surface, she seemed a little lacking in human warmth; often she was severe, and she always applied Alain's pedagogic principle that a higher performance should be demanded of a pupil than he is capable of accomplishing. Her ideal was to enable her students to make a fair showing with every kind of philosophical problem. To do this, she tried to instil good sense, judgment, and style. Simone never tired of repeating, after Descartes, that common sense is the most widely shared thing in the world, and she made her students do their written exercises over and over again. But she also devoted much precious time to correcting their essays. Again and again, she said: 'Write something on any subject you like. Hand it to me, I shall correct it.' These exercises were comparable to the famous little papers dear to Alain in which his pupils exercised their powers of analysis.

In addition, Simone Weil gave an optional Thursday lecture on the history of science. All her students attended, for they understood how much importance she attached to it. They did so without being slavish; in fact, completely on their own. Simone was trying, as she explains in a letter of this period, to show that mathematics consists in the reduction of 'the continuous to the discontinuous'; in other words, that 'modern physics was born with the introduction of the incommensurables'. Later on, in the *Cahiers*, she wrote something about this ambitious project. The most lucid passages are well above an average student's comprehension. It is not likely that the students at Le Puy Lycée were all exceptional.

And so it was Simone's personality, her intellectual honesty, her halo of purity, asceticism, and poverty which captivated her pupils. Was it possible for any student to be insensitive, or even to remain neutral, while this unusual teacher exhibited contempt for conventions and rules, in head-on conflict with an interfering administration? Especially during the scandal which was soon to follow?

Simone Weil fully returned the affection her pupils felt for her. On school holidays she would go down into the court-yard near the dormitories to chat with the boarding pupils. One of her students was unable to pass the *baccalauréat*, for she was poor in Latin. Simone spent many hours tutoring her, and her patience was untiring.

After leaving Le Puy, Simone Weil continued to correspond with some of her students, writing at great length on the German question and the Russian problem. At first sight, perhaps, hers may seem rather dry letters, until the personal element comes through: 'I don't believe there's much point in your following the course on ethics and psychology; you will do yourself much more good by reading.' She then lists her favourite authors: Plato, Descartes, Rousseau, Kant, Marcus Aurelius, Balzac, Stendhal, Comte, Proudhon, Marx, Machiavelli, and Retz. We also find, in one letter, the following very human touch:

'It's hard, the enforced rest at a sanatorium. Or rather it's not so much hard as demoralizing. I hope that you will come out physically and morally undamaged, that all trace of illness will have disappeared, and that this will have been "a retreat", as they used to say in the seventeenth century. Just let yourself go. Don't try too much to fight against it.

'You don't say anything about your way of life, and, in view of what you tell me about your health, I'm very much afraid that you might do something stupid (not sleep, or stop eating, etc.).'

These moments of tenderness are, in their way, pathetic. They are surprising because they are rare, like a smile flitting momentarily across a face marked by profound and sorrowful preoccupation. Simone Weil is usually too serious to relax and smile in her letters. Her correspondence gives us hardly a trace of the sort of humour which those who knew her very well have said they enjoyed in her company, but have rarely attempted to describe.

Scarcely had Simone Weil arrived at the lycée in Le Puy when her extra-professional activities began to get her into trouble. She was disturbed by the lot of the unemployed of Le Puy, who were victims of the slump. On their behalf, the municipal authorities had decided to open a quarry for stone-breaking, as they had done every winter since 1925, and to start work on an embankment. Steps were also taken to organize a communal soup-kitchen. On the 16th December 1931, Doctor Durand, then mayor of Le Puy, received a deputation of the unemployed in his office at the town hall. To his surprise, he spotted a young girl in the group. On being questioned—he asked where she worked—she answered simply that she taught at the girls' lycée. In the course of this interview, the mayor is said to have promised a wage of twenty-four francs per day to the unemployed at the municipal works.[6]

The authenticity of this promise was contested by Mayor Durand at the meeting of the town council on the 18th February 1932. But even before that there was trouble: *La Haute-Loire* reports (19th December 1931) that a meeting of the town council was held on the evening of the 17th of December. Matters on the agenda were already under discussion when a group of eighty workers entered and ranged themselves quietly at the back of the hall. They were led, according to the newspaper, by 'a feminine personality who enjoys a job which shelters her from the economic crisis'.

'This suffragette, still rather a young girl, draws up her followers with smiling authority . . . A bespectacled intellectual with her legs sheathed in sheer silk stockings . . . This young person, paid, we have no doubt, according to her worth, has an agreeably heavy pocket-book at the end of each month, and has no fear of unemployment for herself.' (*Mémorial*, 20th December 1931.)

The presence of such a large audience was unusual, and the council was perplexed. But the mayor was able to deal with the situation by ruling that the council go into secret committee. This having been announced, the leaders of the group stepped forward and asked what the council intended to do to help the unemployed and to ensure that relief was being arranged for them. A quite legitimate question, it was formulated with dignity. The mayor made a purely administrative reply: the question was not on the day's agenda, hence the council could not pronounce upon it. When this statement produced some disturbance, he ordered that the hall be cleared. There was no further incident. The unemployed went to the Labour Exchange; Simone Weil went to a café.

It is hard to imagine what a stir Simone's intervention provoked. The mayor gave the order that she was to be watched. A police report was immediately placed in the hands of the school inspector in Le Puy, in whose office Simone was summoned to appear on the 19th of December. Was it true, she was asked, that she had been the leader of the deputation of the unemployed? Had she, in fact, gone to a café on leaving the town hall with a group of workers and paid for their drinks? Was it true that the following day, she could have been seen to cross the Place Michelet with a copy of the communist newspaper, *L'Humanité*, in her hands? Had she indeed, on the same day, shaken hands with one of the quarry workers?

It was no hanging matter if she had, and Simone knew it. In fact, at the request of the Committee for Working-Class Unity, she agreed to go again to the mayor with two of the unemployed and to hand him an agenda for the next council meeting.

This new action proved to the town council that Simone Weil could not be intimidated. They had no alternative except to take extreme measures—to demand her dismissal. Simone was sent for by M. Jorre, the rector of Clermont; he was struck by her sincerity. Having read the local press, he also instinctively looked down to see if she was wearing the sheer silk stockings mentioned in the *Mémorial*. But her stockings as always were of coarse wool. As a matter of duty, Rector Jorre had to inform Simone Weil officially of the displeasure she had given the civil authorities, and to tell her that her dismissal had been requested.

On the 30th December 1931, a deputation of the unemployed again attended the meeting of the town council, and again intervened at the end of the public session. The mayor advised them that the questions they brought could not be discussed in public session. However, he also said that it was his desire and that of the town council to aid the unemployed, especially by giving them work.

On 11th January 1932, the unemployed who had been put on relief jobs at the municipal works called a strike for the following day. Although she had been present at the meeting, Simone Weil carefully refrained from expressing any opinion.

On the 12th of January at about four o'clock in the afternoon, a group of the unemployed entered the Place Michelet to picket the stone-breakers still on the job. At the same moment, Simone Weil was leaving the lycée, carrying her teacher's portfolio under her arm. She was going to the Board of Inspectors, who had again summoned her. Recognizing some of her comrades, she shook them by the hand, then went on her way. During her absence the police broke through the ranks of the strikers and dispersed them. They met again at the Labour Exchange, where, as soon as she had left the Board of Inspectors, Simone rejoined them. At about five o'clock, as she left the Labour Exchange, she was arrested and taken to the police-station. A policeman who held her by the arm said to her: 'You are beginning to be a nuisance with all these scrapes you get yourself into.' She was released immediately, but not before she had been threatened with detention. Simone's only reaction was to be excited and delighted at having been involved in such an adventure.

Meanwhile, the unemployed formed ranks again and marched past the windows of the mayor in the boulevard Saint-Louis singing the *Internationale*. Simone Weil met them, but did not take part in the march. She limited herself to watching from the pavement.

The people of Le Puy were alarmed by these events. 'The

presence, in the midst of the unemployed, of a teacher at the lycée for young girls, her portfolio under her arm, has provoked extremely severe comments from the public,' wrote the *Haute-Loire* of the 13th January. So great was the public scandal that the mayor of Le Puy requested the prefect to send a full report to Paris and again demanded Simone's dismissal. It is certain that the worthy town of Le Puy had never before seen and probably would never again see a public demonstration to compare with that of the 12th January 1932.

On the 14th of January, Simone was summoned a second time to the rector of Clermont and asked to sign, on the spot, a request for a change of post. She refused. The rector informed her that she might well be officially transferred elsewhere, despite her refusal.

Back at Le Puy, Simone Weil told her friends all about the threat. They were greatly concerned. Fearing prompt sanctions and the removal of Simone from Le Puy, Vidal, the secretary of the teachers' section of the national trade union, sent a telegram of protest to the Minister of Education.

The League for the Rights of Man took up the problem, for the freedom of opinion of state employees was at stake. At a later date, the French League for the Rights of Women also put in their word on the matter. Soon others sprang to the defence of freedom of thought, which was being threatened. But before coming to Simone Weil's aid, these groups had to get to the facts of the case.

The Catholic press took a keen interest in the affair, while the anti-clericals worried about the reputation of the Lycée. On the 14th January, *La Croix* published a story that 'at Le Puy . . . a young lady named Weill [*sic*], on Tuesday at 6 p.m., roused to revolt thirty of the unemployed who tried to induce the stone-breakers to strike. The police intervened . . . The young lady took to flight. The unemployed then made a boisterous demonstration in the town.'

The *Tribune de Saint-Étienne* carried an anonymous account of the events of the 12th, anonymous but clearly from Simone's hand: 'The *Internationale* is not a political song; it is the song of the workers who refuse to be the slaves of the profiteers. Has this refusal a political character? The ruling class wants to think so. This is a class movement of a significance quite distinct from political controversy.'

Following these incidents, the mayor promised, in a vague sort of way, to grant the rate of twenty-five francs per day demanded by the unemployed. On the 22nd of January, a new outburst from Simone Weil appeared in the *Tribune de Saint-Étienne*: 'Ten days later, seeing that nothing had happened, the unemployed sent a new delegation to the mayor.' But as they had neither gone on strike nor demonstrated again, said the article, they were not given what they had asked for. Patently, 'the only relations between them and the dominant class are those of force. Sometimes the public authorities conceal their reliance on force under fine words; at other times, they manifest it openly and then they contribute better than anyone else to the education of the working class.'

This was the signal for fresh incidents, printed propaganda, posters, petitions, and increased violence. On the 3rd of February, a mass demonstration was staged and a procession marched (to the tune of the *Internationale* and the *Carmagnole*) through the centre of town to the residence of the mayor and the prefecture. The demonstration was followed by an edict by the mayor banning all further demonstrations or processions. The next day the unemployed followed instructions to leave their working sites in small groups or separately. They went to the Labour Exchange. When they came out, the police were there to detain, search, and question them, after which they let them go. (All this took place under the amused and ironical eye of the middle-class townspeople of Le Puy.) The workers then formed ranks and left, still demonstrating, headed by a woman carrying a red flag.

The Weil affair had now reached its climax. The *Mémorial* of 3rd February gave an account of a 'communist demonstration . . . ordered from Moscow via Paris for 4th February. . . . Moscow has its correspondent at Le Puy. . . . Moscow has its agent'. They knew all about Simone. She was mentioned by name next day in a report of the demonstration of 4th February: 'Mlle Weill [*sic*], a red virgin of the tribe of Levi, evangelist of the gospel of Moscow, incited the unfortunate people she had led

63

astray. Then, after having formed them into a procession, she declared their destination to be the residence of the Mayor, whom they serenaded.'

Just at that moment when the scandal seemed to have grown almost intolerable, it was suddenly dissipated. It must be understood that Simone's spectacular activities were also rather alarming to the unemployed and to the workers' leaders. They did not really understand her attitude and they thought her eccentric. They had had to pay numerous fines, when they would have preferred to win over the populace to their cause. But the intervention of this young woman—this lecturer—produced just the opposite effect; it alienated the sympathies of the town. They tended to make jokes at her expense; they did not always listen to what she was saying; and now they came to the conclusion that she could have better served the cause of the unemployed in some other way.

The excitement was calming down. The unemployed were to be given unemployment benefit at last, disguised as a rate of sixteen francs per day simply for signing on. The campaign shifted to another front.

Now Simone Weil had to defend herself. Parents of lycée pupils—not her own, it is true—kept an attentive eye on her movements from the porter's lodge of the lycée. The mayor, the prefect, and the police inquired about her. They laid a trap for her: plans were made to arrest her on the pretext that she had jeopardized the freedom to work by having incited the unemployed to strike. But she did not turn up where they had expected to surprise her.

Were they toying with the idea of putting Simone in prison? That seems unlikely. In any case, she wasn't bothered about the possibility. One of her pupils had warned her: 'Be careful; they'll put you in jail.' She replied: 'I don't mind so long as I have enough paper and ink to write with.'

Slowly the situation returned to normal. No reply from the minister had come in answer to the official reports which M. Jorre had sent. What he had said, moreover, had been extremely mild in tone. On the 26th February 1932, for instance, he wrote: 'The value of her professional teaching makes one regret that her

extra-professional activity attracts attention to her.' He refused
to go to Le Puy for an immediate, personal investigation, despite
pressure. Instead, he went in June and sat in for an hour on
Simone Weil's class. After the class, as was customary, she
requested an interview and asked if he had any advice to offer
about her way of teaching. He got the impression that she wished
to embarrass him and to exculpate herself. She asked also if she
would have to deal with the colonial question, as stated in the
curriculum. The only works she had read on the question were
Gide's *Le Retour du Tchad* and another work of an anti-colonial
nature, she confessed, so she wasn't up on the subject. Since the
colonial question was in the curriculum, the rector told Simone
she would have to deal with it. 'You have personal opinions on the
subject: you are bound to show them. For even if you hid them
they would be obvious. But you ought also to give an objective
explanation of the other theories and do them equal justice.'
He advised her to read more widely on the question, so as to be
better informed about it.

If the charges against Simone Weil lacked substance, what
put them even more in question was the fact that the prestige of
Alain was involved. People said: 'She's Alain's pupil? Don't
worry. You can't touch a pupil of Alain.' In addition, the
accused knew how to defend herself: 'The university administration lags several thousand years behind human civilization. It
is still at the stage of the caste system.

'. . . There are people whom a teacher at a lycée can associate
with, if necessary, secretly and behind closed doors, but with
whom she must on no account be seen shaking hands by the
parents of her pupils in the Place Michelet.'

Who were those people? 'Shady bankers, crooked politicians,
old statesmen guilty of having carelessly sacrificed human lives?'
asked Simone Weil. Not at all! 'They were workers whom the
industrial crisis deprived of the work they were trained for and who
were reduced to breaking stones, at the expense of the municipal-
ity, for a ludicrous wage.' In conclusion: 'We demand from the
administration a definite ruling, indicating exactly under what
conditions each category of the teaching body has the right to
fraternize with such and such a social stratum.'[7]

The teachers' union, to which she had affiliated herself instead of to the professors' union, supported Simone, repaying her for her gesture. Her activities in the teachers' union were a source of frustration to those of her colleagues who wanted to help; they could not intervene personally in Simone's affairs, and they had no organizational authority, belonging as they did to a different union. A fellow teacher named Villard, however, who was devoted to her, circulated petitions in her support. The rest simply abandoned her to her fate. There were even some who spoke openly in her favour and intrigued against her in private.

However, Pierre Arnaud and Simone's other friends at Saint-Étienne did not remain inactive. Mme Ranchet, another colleague, says that when Simone Weil left for Paris delegations of workers waited for her in the small stations all along the line from Saint-Étienne. The reaction of the vocal trade-unionists in favour of their champion was strong and well led. The miners' unions, the syndicalist organizations of Saint-Étienne, and the Building Workers' Union of Lyon launched an energetic campaign against her dismissal, and the Committee for Trade-Union Independence vehemently protested against the sanctions threatened by the administration against Comrade Weil, now nicknamed *la Ponote.**

The parents of Simone's own pupils signed a petition which was sent to the Minister of Education on 3rd January 1932. They expressed their hope that she would not be transferred: 'By her interesting courses and her professional integrity, Mlle Weil has won the sympathy and the respect of her pupils. She has taken pains to make her teaching strictly impartial. The class notebooks bear ample witness to this. She has been a most valuable influence upon all the girls she has had in her charge.'

Certain parents, however, had only yielded to the entreaties of their daughters, members of Simone's class in philosophy, and some must have signed the petition with private reservations. Disturbing rumours had come to their ears of the disquieting views which the young teacher had expressed in class: she attacked the idea of saving, alleging that to buy state bonds was to make oneself part of the capitalist régime. It was said that she even repeated the sacrilegious suggestion that the Unknown Soldier might have been

*Ponot, Ponote*, inhabitant of Le Puy.

a deserter shot down by his own officer. As for the colonial question, she referred her pupils to *Le Retour du Tchad* by André Gide, which we have already mentioned.

In the end, the municipal administration achieved its aim and obtained the replacement of Simone Weil. She confided to one of her pupils; 'I don't care if I do get sacked!' That was not the issue, however; she was simply transferred—which ironically was what Simone herself desired with all her heart. Le Puy was much too provincial for her. She needed a more stimulating social climate, an industrial town, an environment animated by an awakened class-consciousness.

She signed her application to be transferred in the presence of the rector of Clermont-Ferrand. It was all in the nature of an amicable arrangement. It is not known to whom she addressed her famous quip: 'Monsieur l'Inspecteur—Monsieur le Recteur—I have always regarded dismissal as the natural culmination of my career.'

It should be noted that the activities of the unemployed described here had taken place quite outside union discipline. Simone herself had let loose, unintentionally and almost without knowing it, the storm that had raged over Le Puy. She had let herself be carried away by the human side of the problem. Wanting to get to know workers, she had spent hours with window-cleaners, for example, and had taken a lively interest in the technical side of all kinds of work. She was heard to say, in conversation with a teacher: 'Why, you wouldn't even know how to unbolt a rail!' Apparently she did, for she not only asked questions but she strove to get the feel of the work so that it 'entered into her body'. Often she would work in the fields helping to dig potatoes; and after her agricultural endeavours, she would give her lectures wearing heavy troopers' shoes covered with mud.

Simone Weil was drawn to the proletariat by their poverty. Her dedication to the poor was heroic. She shared so much of her salary with the unemployed that for a whole winter she went without heat. Her charwoman was paid five francs an hour instead of the usual two. The apartment that she shared with Mlle Antériou, a fellow-teacher, in the Maison Fabre, on the road

67

to Sauges, was open at all hours so that workers could go in and get something to eat. One day the two young women themselves had to go for a meal to the house of a friend, Mme Bardin, because their own larder had been emptied by workmen.

There was nothing spectacular in the workers' coming to Simone Weil, as was supposed, for her right hand knew nothing of her left hand's giving. It was not to the poor that she gave, but to their poverty, with infinite discretion. Indeed there was little for her to give, and thus only few who could benefit from her charity.

One day, one of the unemployed brought Simone a large spray of lilacs. Her joy must have been profound, for the simplicity of that gesture was exactly appropriate to the greatness of soul that inspired her devotion to the unemployed of Le Puy.

## 2

# The Auxerre Lycée

## 1932-1933

'For bureaucracy *always* betrays.' Simone Weil, letter to Thévenon

THE SCHOOL YEAR ENDED, Simone spent the greater part of her holidays in Germany. While still at the École Normale, she had made brief visits to Berlin. There were now early warnings of the drama which was to unfold the following year, and Simone wished to see the situation at first-hand. Staunchly pacifist, she set out for Germany in the summer of 1932. Until then she had always condemned the foreign policy of France, which she called 'the most brutal, the most arrogant, the most oppressive known to the modern world' (*Libres Propos*, March 1932). Her horror of the Treaty of Versailles had not abated over the years, and her keen sympathy for Germany was heightened by the reputation it then enjoyed as the potential home for the revolution.

She found at least part of what she was looking for. On her return, she wrote to Thévenon: 'You could imagine nothing more fraternal, more courageous or more lucid than the young Berlin workers in the midst of an overpowering situation. The cultural level of the German working class is also unbelievable. If I were my own master, I would be off on the wing to Germany forthwith. By comparison one has the feeling that all the French are asleep.'[1]

Simone was also eager to see the German Communist Party at close quarters. Her ideas on the subject of the USSR were already formed, but there was still great confusion in her mind on the subject of communism and the future of the revolution in general. In *L'Effort* of 20th February 1932, she had severely criticized not only the French memorandum at the disarmament conference, but also Litvinov's speech. To her he had seemed to

advocate limited collaboration—although not clearly defined—
with the capitalist countries. He appeared to argue, in effect, that
there could be no lasting peace without universal socialism;
however, until socialism should prevail everywhere, the only way
to international security was by disarmament and mutual pacts of
non-aggression. It was on account of this speech that Simone
Weil declared that the USSR had ceased to be a proletarian state.
'Let the hopes of all proletarians still be turned towards the
USSR. But let the sincere defenders of the working class in the
capitalist countries beware of putting the revolutionary movement
into the hands of the Russian bureaucracy.'

She was, however, continually on the alert for any fresh turn
that Russian policy might take. In *L'Effort* of 2nd July 1932, she
reported an interview which Stalin had given to the German
historian, Emil Ludwig. Stalin had expressed admiration for
American efficiency. 'But America is . . . . the country which, more
than any other, produces for the sake of producing,' Simone
protested. Ergo, Stalin had betrayed the principal tenet of
Marxism. 'This only goes to show that the USSR is still a long
way from possessing the basis of a working-class culture.' She
was disappointed by Stalinist policy, but not yet scandalized by it.

Thus, although Simone came back from Germany full of
enthusiasm for 'their magnificent working-class youth with their
sports, camping, singing, reading and their organizations for
children's recreation,'[2] she had lost all the respect she had
previously felt for the Communist Party. It came to her not as a
discovery but as a kind of alleviation. She wrote to Thévenon:
'I am now of the opinion that all compromise with the party, all
mitigation of censure, is criminal. Trotsky himself seems to have
shown a loss of nerve in this respect, which makes him partly
responsible for the crimes of the Third International in Germany.
However, it is true that any other attitude would have been
difficult for him.'

On 25th August 1932 *La Révolution Prolétarienne* printed the
first instalment of her comments. In it, she noted with astonishment the lack of political agitation, the absence of alarm, the
contrast between the party's revolutionary aspirations and its
complete passivity. Her article was criticized: it was said to

70

consist of mere impressions. But the vociferousness of the reaction showed that she had touched a sensitive point.

It has been said that Simone Weil lacked political instincts. The acuteness of her observations in her articles on Germany tend to prove the opposite. True, she slipped into a number of predictions which events proved wrong, but who can blame her? The situation in Germany was to be affected by unpredictable events; the foreign observer could only make premature judgments.

Simone followed the day-to-day events with passionate interest. In the *Libres Propos* of 25th February 1933, she maintains that Hitler had succeeded only by blackmail. 'Clearly he does not have the power.' In November on the other hand, she evaluates the dazzling electoral victory of the communists and, with great perspicacity, minimizes its importance. 'The power of the Communist Party, when it is reduced to its own strength and when it comes into real action, is precisely nil.'[3]

Simone Weil frequently returns to what she regards as the shocking inertia and passivity of the communists. In *L'École Émancipée* of the 12th February 1933, for instance, she writes that the Communist Party had called for a general strike 'which has come to nothing'. Their reason for calling the strike, she states, was to have an alibi to cover their inaction.

It is not difficult to give credence to Simone Weil's explanation for the passivity of proletarian organizations in Germany. For a long time 'the working-class movement in Germany . . . has had something it wants to preserve at the core of the régime.'[1] She writes: 'Nothing is more reformist, more inherently reformist than the German trade unions.' They are *above all*, societies for mutual aid. They can be dragged along by the masses like dead weights, but that is all.'[4]

According to Simone Weil, the only possible way for the workers to make headway against the menace of Hitler and to prevail against it before it was too late, was: 'On the one hand, to make the masses realize that a nationalist movement, founded upon the union of the classes, would not bring about any new system; and, on the other hand, to make them feel the existence, in opposition to Hitler's forces, of another force, that of the organized proletariat.'

In the headlong rush of events she could do no more than confess the failure of international trade unionism and underline, vigorously, the real character of political communism. At every opportunity she emphasized the points of resemblance between Hitler's national socialism and orthodox communism. When national socialism sought to assume the guise of a working-class movement, she noted, its propaganda had exactly the same sound as communist propaganda. For example, arguments between Nazi workers and communists gave the impression of two factions searching in vain for some point of real disagreement. As for communist activities, Simone Weil wrote: 'By the organization of mass rallies, by ritual slogans and ritual gestures, Communist propaganda is becoming more and more like a religious propaganda; it is as though the revolution were becoming a myth, which, like other myths, merely makes tolerable an intolerable situation.'

That, she declares, is the essence of Stalinism, a corrupted form of communism that 'adorns itself with the glamour of the October Revolution'. The rulers of Russia were, to Simone Weil, behaving exactly like priests 'who deprive their devotees of their critical faculties and conceal direct absurdities under the authority of the Church . . . But whatever revolution is, it is not a religion . . . it is a practical task.' Clearly then, the Russian State is a State like any other, she concludes. And although she concedes that no doubt it is the result of revolution, its origin cannot excuse its betrayal of the German workers for the sake of its own bureaucracy.

Just as Simone Weil's article went to press, the German catastrophe reached its climax: the Reichstag was burnt, and Hitler ordered the arrest of four thousand people, among them the most influential communists. New elections gave Hitler a parliamentary majority, and he called into session at Potsdam the new Reichstag, which was to grant him dictatorial powers on 24th March 1933. As soon as the votes were counted, he turned to the socialists and announced: 'Gentlemen, I have no further need of you.'

Simone Weil felt that her reasons for condemning the Communist International had been confirmed. The Comintern had brought tragedy to the German working class by abandoning the leadership of the German industrial proletariat. 'One would like to know in *what* country the Comintern *has* fulfilled this function,' wrote Simone. Words such as these, and the subsequent develop- ment of the German situation, foreshadowed the desperate struggle into which Simone Weil was about to hurl herself head- long.

Shortly before the end of the school holidays, Mme Weil went to Auxerre with Simone to be with her when she introduced herself to the headmistress of the girls' lycée. Mme Weil helped her daughter move into rooms over a café on the Vaux highway where it joins the road to Preuilly, on the outskirts of the town near a site called 'l'Arbre-Sec'. She saw to it that Simone's rooms were furnished comfortably, but as soon as she left for Paris, Simone rolled up the carpets, took away everything not to her liking, and arranged things according to her own Spartan tastes.[5]

The windows of the apartment looked out on the country side. To the left Simone could see Auxerre, dominated by the silhouette of the massive Gothic cathedral. No less conspicuous from other vantage-points were the church of St Germain with its long nave and flying buttresses, and the white tower of St Pierre, richly ornamented in late *gothique flamboyant*. Set on a semi-circle around a bend in the river Yonne, with bridges thrusting out like the spokes of a wheel, it was a charming little Burgundian town, bordering on Île de France. It also had barracks and a factory, the latter operating part-time because of the depression. Nothing was lacking for Simone except a mine—but there were wine- growers, who were anti-clerical and anti-militarist. It did not take long for her to strike up an acquaintance with one of them; as a result she was able to fulfil her desire of working on the wine harvest.

Simone had chosen Auxerre because it was near Paris. There were no more weekly visits to Saint-Étienne, but this was the only one of her habits that she gave up. She was as careless of her appearance as ever. One witness recalls often seeing her dis- mounting her bicycle as she arrived home. A four-pound loaf of bread which must have lasted her almost a week was tucked under one arm. She wore a pullover which had been put on backward. Her fingers were yellow with tobacco.

At the lycée, relations with the administration began badly and gradually grew worse. When the headmistress, Mme Lesnes, spoke to her, Simone would turn her back. When Mme Lesnes visited the class-room, the students got up deferentially. Simone, however, would remain seated, looking the other way, 'two black eyes flashing fire'. At teachers' meetings, she would hide her face behind a Russian newspaper, smoke, say nothing, keeping herself only to the letter of her obligations. One day, spotting another teacher, Mlle Marchand, hurrying to her class, Simone snapped at her, 'conscience—that's an occupational disease!' It seemed to her colleagues that Simone Weil was courting disfavour—spoiling for an unfavourable reaction. They looked for hidden meanings in everything she said and did.

Apart from caustic barbs, Simone Weil avoided her colleagues: many of them never exchanged a word with her. She remained aloof, estranged, absorbed in her own thoughts. She never went to the staff room. After her classes she would disappear. Her lack of sociability was altogether discouraging to any who might have attempted friendship.

Soon, discouragement turned to scandal: the notebooks of some pupils were found to contain such aphorisms as: 'The family is legalized prostitution.' According to others, she had said: 'The family is organized prostitution,' adding: 'A wife is a mistress reduced to slavery.'[6] Priests and parents protested. The headmistress inspected the notebooks and confiscated them as exhibits for the prosecution.*

Among Simone Weil's class were the daughters of army officers. 'There is going to be fun when we talk about patriotism,' she wrote to Thévenon. Stories began to circulate about Simone's influence over her pupils. After the assassination of President

*I personally have not seen such statements in any of the students' notebooks which I have looked through. The incriminating remarks had perhaps been made in jest—paradoxical sallies. Nevertheless, the reported statements must have had some foundation in fact. An echo of them will be found in the recollections of the students of Bourges (1935-36), to whom, however, Simone Weil will be far less close.

Doumer, she demanded the canonization of 'Saint' Gorgulof who 'had destroyed a capitalist'. It was reported that one of her pupils, the only child of a widow of the First World War, wrote to her mother at Easter: 'I shall not come back home for the holidays. I don't know where I shall go, but I shan't come home.'

For Simone's critics, such reports were confirmed by the very enthusiasm which her pupils showed for her. They even typed out the tracts that she composed for the railway workers.

The voice of public protest finally reached the ears of the school inspector. Had Mme Lesnes complained of the singular liberties that her subordinate was taking with the school? One day a poor man came in from the street, fork and spoon in hand. Asked what he was doing there, he said: 'It's Mlle Weil who told me to come and eat here. She said that if there was enough for 350, there would be enough for 351.' On another occasion, a group of workers installed themselves in the courtyard of the lycée. They were asked their business and replied: 'Waiting for Simone.' No need to inquire further about the identity of 'Simone'! The workers were peremptorily dismissed: 'You can't wait here: you'll have to wait for her outside.' They were ushered out through a postern gate which was carefully locked behind them.

Meanwhile, Simone's philosophy class should have been spectacularly successful: it was made up of the best students the lycée had had in years. Simone began the course with these few words: 'All you can hope for in a year is to be able at the end of it to write something that makes sense. But to become philosophers requires more time than you have at your disposal.' The only texts used were *The Discourse on Method* and the *Philosophical Meditations* of Descartes, the *Prolegomena* of Kant, and the *Republic* of Plato. Simone instilled in her pupils a contempt for standard text-books, for compositions that were well-polished but empty of substance, and for indexing and classifying. Rumpling her hair all the time, she talked on spontaneously, in the clearest manner, repeating formulations that her pupils could easily write down: 'Emotions, associations and language operate through the mediation of the imagination. Doubt is the only remedy.' 'The great-

75

ness of every religion, at the moment when it was created, has been to diminish credulity.' 'We love the truth, so long as the truth does not trouble us.' 'It has to be done: that's the workers' password.' 'Justice—total expression of virtue.'

There were never-ending discussions between teacher and pupils. They spoke of war, of patriotism ('a moribund notion'), of social reform ('However little suffering remains, it will remain of first importance to relieve it'). Simone used mathematical illustrations, which her students were able to understand because she presented them so clearly. She loved to quote Balzac, Tolstoy and Valéry. To emphasize the aesthetic nature of memory, she quoted from Valéry's *La Jeune Parque*:

> *Viens mon sang, viens rougir la pâle circonstance*
> *Qu'ennoblissait l'azur de la sainte distance,*
> *Et l'insensible iris du temps que j'adorai.*

In the course that Simone gave at Auxerre no allusion may be found to the teaching of Alain. It is of Spinoza, Descartes and Kant that she speaks most frequently, but at every turn she reveals the breadth of her learning; here is, for instance, a quotation from Marcus Aurelius: 'Anyone who desires anything that does not exist cuts himself off from the world. He ceases to be a citizen of the world; he becomes a sore in the flesh of the world.'

The following line of Corneille also appears in her students' notes: 'Look into your heart, Octavius, and no longer complain....' And a saying of Goethe, which a later day was to give a more intense meaning, appealed to her: 'I have never heard mention of any crime which I did not feel capable of committing.'

Significant among the pieces she chose to quote is the following passage from the *Nachlass* of Immanuel Kant: 'My thirst for knowledge is boundless; I am harassed by a desire to extend illimitably the frontiers of the known and still more am I desirous of having the satisfaction of knowing that I have done my duty. There was a time when I was convinced that herein consisted all that was honourable in mankind. I had contempt for people who seemed ignorant of this. It was Rousseau who opened my eyes to the error of this way of thinking. Illusory superiority vanished, and I have become aware that I would be of even less value than the common worker if I did not believe that all such studies were profitless unless their outcome was to make others understand that the only thing of value is to make evident the rights of man.'

On every possible occasion, Simone alluded to the problem of God, as she saw it at this phase of her life. She had a certain familiarity with the Gospels of which she speaks with respect, but which she interprets rather freely and symbolically. For example, she refers to the Beatitude of the poor in spirit and compares it with Hegel's idea that 'the subjection of bodily nature is the condition for the freedom of the soul'. No one, Simone Weil maintained, is more dependent on the body than the pure ascetic.

It is clear that at this point Simone was strongly inclined to accept the ontological proof of God's existence. This is a significant detail, for such proof plays its part in the *metaphorical pantheism* to which she was one day to be attracted. Her lecture notes contain also an apology for false gods. She maintains that the idolatry which consists in the adoration of the true God through effigies of wood and stone liberates the worshipper from superstition. This same virtue she attributed to religious rites: 'In the Catholic Church, ceremonies and rites are all the more distinctive in that they are conducted in Latin and are but little understood by the people. The prayers, the Latin words, have to do with man rather than God, and it is precisely because they refer to man that they are of such cardinal importance. It may well be that without religious rites man would never have risen above superstition.'

Her lecture notes also include many interesting passages about the nature of attention and necessity: the affirmation, for example, that the miraculous is by no means an exception to the rule of necessity. Most important, perhaps, the respect which Simone Weil professes for all factual aspects of religion indicates something of the sources of her spiritual inspiration: 'The purely human Greek religion is unique of its kind. The Christian religion is a sort of synthesis between the Greek spirit and the spirit of the Bible. Greek gods are men, somewhat more beautiful, sometimes less strong. And there are only myths, no dogmas of any kind. There is also freedom; three or four versions of each myth among which the imagination is at liberty to roam . . . . The Greek temple is a house. All this is expressive of man's being at home

77

in nature. Everything is human, and is habitable by humans.
They [the Greeks] believed in gods as intelligent children believe
in fairy-tales.'

It is no doubt tempting to find more illumination in these
quotations than really exists; they are far from being without
value, however, for they show how superficial Simone Weil's
agnosticism really was and prove that she must have already
experienced a certain religious disquietude.

As the principal aim of the philosophy course was to learn 'to
write something that makes sense', both teacher and pupils spent
considerable time on 'short papers': essays on such subjects as
labour, a charwoman with her broom, a working-class type. When
an essay was good, Simone had it typed so that the student could
read her own work as objectively as if it had been written by
someone else. In this she followed the example of Freinet, a
teacher at Saint-Paul-de-Vence, an outstanding man who was
summarily dismissed after an intrigue very much like the one
which Simone had been the butt of in Le Puy.

In defence of Freinet, Simone wrote in *Libres Propos* of 25th
June 1933: 'Most readers . . . must surely know already who
Freinet is. He is the initiator of the admirable teaching method
which consists of having school children print their best writings.
In this way the written language at once acquires for small
children at school its true signification—that of being read in
the form of printed prose. Children do not write only with an
eye to being marked and corrected by their teacher, but also with
the intention of being read by all sorts of little friends scattered
over the length and breadth of France.'

At times, Simone's headaches became so excruciating that it
was almost impossible for her to teach. She came to class just the
same and had her students read aloud. Holding her head in her
hands, she gave her pupils all the attention she could divert from
her physical condition. These headaches were the only interrup-
tion of the normal course of study in the philosophy class. Her
students worked enthusiastically throughout the year, encouraged
by the delight of discovering philosophical theories for themselves.
It was slow, uphill work, demanding much patience from both
teacher and pupils, and there was no way of measuring what was

learnt. Only in the third term of the academic year could the pupils themselves begin to be aware, from within, that they had absorbed a great deal.

At that point, the only cloud on the horizon for Simone's pupils was the examination. They had reason to worry about it, for Simone did not cover the ordinary subject-matter of the course. She tried to calm them by saying: 'After all, the *baccalauréat* is only a convention. The first thing is to learn how to write, and the way to do that is to copy out seven or eight lines each day from Pascal's *Pensées* or from Voltaire. And when it comes to the exam there is this golden rule: put down the first point; then a short connecting passage; then, by way of a second point, state the opposite of the first; then another little connecting passage; finally, a third point leading to a conclusion with something new and surprising about it.'

These suggestions, of course, were not enough by themselves, and Simone made a few concessions to scholastic requirements. She made her pupils memorize quotations or principles which characterized a good number of philosophers and which epitomized their attitude towards the most essential problems: 'Perceptions are no more than perfectly consistent dreams' (*Leibnitz*). 'In every man there is a Pyrrhonism that is proof against all dogmatism, and a dogmatism invincible to any Pyrrhonism' (*Pascal*). They also memorized brilliant paradoxes: 'He who loves God cannot wish God to love him in return.' 'The more we understand about particular things, the more we love God.' Last of all, the students wrote some conventional papers—not, Simone felt, that their minds were yet prepared for that kind of exercise, but because they had to. (In Simone's eyes, it was absurd that pupils should write such papers before their minds had passed through a long apprenticeship in reflective thought.)

Several students decided to take private tutoring with other professors to prepare for the examination, but to no avail. The examination was a massive defeat: Mlles Fouilloux, Simaure and Grossot, Simone's best students, were casualties, and only four of her twelve students passed. Simone took full responsibility for the failure. She personally interceded with the authorities at Dijon, trying to excuse her pupils. But the administration of the lycée at Auxerre saw this as their opportunity to get rid of Simone. They abolished the chair of philosophy at the girls' lycée, and Simone was released.

The story of Simone Weil's career at Auxerre emerges in academic reports: the comments of Mme Lesnes, dated 15th December 1932, describe good and bad aspects of her teaching: 'She takes no account of the time she devotes to her pupils . . . She separates herself systematically from the staff . . . her bad health is a hindrance to her work.' The Academy's Inspector sat in on her class on 22nd November 1932; he emphasized her lack of preparatory work in his reports. On 13th March 1933, the rector complained that she had no sense of pedagogy: 'There is a constant diffusion of thought . . . her pupils . . . do all they can to take notes of which they understand nothing.' A detailed description of the philosophy class was written by the rector a month later:

'The subject of the lecture is not very clear: it is about sociology and its methodology. Taking as her starting point the law of the Three States of Comte, the teacher claims to know what positive sociology is by contrast with social philosophy and takes Marx's historical materialism as an example, which is highly paradoxical, since the doctrine of Marx, stemming from Hegelianism, is usually considered a general philosophy of history. Mlle Weil's exposition of this is fairly wide in scope and copious in detail, but lacking in firmness and clarity. She does state, but does not illustrate by well-chosen examples, that for Marx economic phenomena themselves explain social structures or the changes they undergo. She is better at demonstrating how the conditions of the struggle of man against nature are modified by the effects of that struggle itself. But she is all too apt to treat all that can be ascribed to social causes, no matter what kind, as proof of the Marxist thesis. Her exposition is, on the whole, diffuse, even rather confused, and does not sufficiently emphasize key ideas. Moreover, she makes the mistake of speaking without looking at her pupils, she bends over her papers, and she does not pronounce her words clearly. Nevertheless, the teaching she gives seems to me substantial enough; and one is made aware of an effort to inform and of a personal reflection even when the pains she has taken do not produce a very clear or well-constructed lesson.

'Unfortunately, her teaching is also extremely tendentious. It is a respectable point of view, no doubt—even *sympathique* in her sincerity and her conviction. But she often takes a violent or oversimplified position, and her lectures are so full of allusions to events or personalities of the present or recent past that her teaching all too often has the tone of a pamphlet or political broadside. There can be no question that this tendency jeopardizes the best interests of the school where she teaches. Evidently Mlle Weil has wholly failed to understand the reserve that her position requires or the respect she owes to the opinions of her pupils and their families. . . .'

The café where Simone lived was near a factory. Workers came to drink there, and she often came downstairs to join in their conversations. She made friends with a worker who lived near the café. He was a plumber, whom she nicknamed 'Robinet' (tap), and she often worked in his shop. He was a communist, and she used to spend whole hours arguing communism with him, overwhelming him with her arguments. Poor Robinet was upset, it seems, to the point of insomnia. It wasn't he, however, who taught her how to solder a joint, but the workmen who did the repairs at the boys' school. She was very proud of her achievement and used to ask people if they could solder a joint. Since the answer was almost invariably 'no', she used to add in a peremptory voice: 'That's a gap in your education.'

During the year, Simone Weil bought a small printing-press for the use of her students, but it was not popular with them. They didn't want to dirty their hands. After two fruitless attempts to engage their interest, Simone gave up. Her activities as a 'labourer' outside school included digging potatoes on the workers' allotments surrounding the café. She also spent some time in the Auxerre ochre-paint works. What wages she earned, she quietly gave away.

There was a certain superficiality, in these sporadic contacts with the realities of the workers' life, and Simone was aware of it. They seemed to her absolutely essential, however, to her role as a trade unionist of conviction. She was moved both by curiosity and by pity: dispassionate intellectual curiosity, true, but also unrestrained. The ease with which she came and went among the workers disconcerted them; she could not help but realize this. But her character drove her to lead a life of austerity, even privation. It helped her to experience the poverty of the people for whom she felt a genuine compassion.

Simone Weil had now formed her own idea of 'revolution'—the need for objective understanding and the need for empathy—synthesizing two elements which were in themselves disparate. To pursue the revolution intelligently, it was necessary to understand the nature of the problems. To understand the problems of the workers, one must be a worker oneself. But the synthesis that gave cohesion to the strange life of Simone Weil was precarious. It was soon to fall apart.

When she arrived in Auxerre, Simone had resumed her syndicalist activity. At first she wavered between the local branches of the united CGTU and the federated CGT.

Finally, she decided for the CGTU, proving by this act her independence even of her Saint-Étienne friends. She entered the arena flying the flag of opposition to the communist bloc. 'I am trying to demolish it,' she wrote to Thévenon, 'but they resist. . . . All the same, it is a good atmosphere. They are fine people here. There has never been any exclusion on grounds of opinion in this region.'

Simone Weil's attitude towards events in Germany, particularly what she considered the Soviet Union's scandalous conduct with regard to the German working-class parties, precipitated her into a quarrel of extraordinary violence. The quarrel involved many aspects of trade-union politics, but for her the dispute could be reduced to a few simple questions which she felt bound to ask herself and compelled to answer regardless of the consequences.

She wrote to Thévenon: 'Things are bad in Germany. The IC [Comintern] has virtually ceased to exist, it seems to me.

'This is no time to attack honest revolutionaries nor to confine oneself to uncompromising syndicalism.

'This is rather the moment for an all-round understanding among syndicalists, communists, both deviationists and even the orthodox who are basically sincere ... This is the moment, above all—and above all for young people—to get to work seriously to *revise* all our ideas. Seeing that all the workers' organizations have *failed completely*, we can no longer accept at face value any of the pre-war platforms.

'You can see that insofar as revolutionary syndicalism is dogma for you (as the Party is for communists either orthodox or deviationist) I am decidedly no longer with you.

'This does not mean to say that I am drawn towards the communist movement—quite the contrary! But I will no longer recognize any of those notions that before the war were considered articles of faith, were *never* seriously examined, and are now discredited by the whole of post-war history. I want people to discard all these groupings and learn at last to confront the problems honestly—which the politically militant all too rarely do.

'I am stifled in this blindfold revolutionary movement . . . .'

From Simone Weil's point of view, the great lesson to be learnt from the events in Germany was this: the German Communist Party had collapsed without a struggle, although it held all the necessary cards to make a success of the revolution. It is a duty to pass judgment on an event of such importance. But some refuse to do so. Trotsky himself is guilty of that cowardice. He followed 'the German situation as it unfolded from day to day with a probing, incisive analysis that it is impossible not to admire'.[7] Why, then, asked Simone, do the Trotskyite organizations want to avoid, even now, taking a definite stand against the Comintern? 'The situation is far too grave for militant socialists—above all, for a militant like Trotsky—to have the right to an ambiguous viewpoint.'[7] The truth, apparently, was too disagreeable to mention. Thus Simone wrote in an article published in *L'École Émancipée*, 7th May 1933: 'At present, on all important issues, the working-class movement is wholly given over to illusion and lies. We are lost now if we do not remember the great principle that Lenin constantly held up to us: namely, that the truth, whatever it may be, is always salutary for the workers' movement; error, illusion and lies are always fatal.'

Finally, after only two years' contact with the trade-union world a masterly but disquieting article appeared on 25th August

1933 in *La Révolution Prolétarienne*. The definitive version of this article (she did several successive drafts) was written at one sitting, without erasures, between morning and a late hour of the night. It was written with such passion that she refused to stop for food.

Simone Weil had published a previous article about the Russian situation in *L'Effort* of 22nd July, in which she wrote that the USSR was defending its own national interest as a state and not the interests of the world proletariat, and had even allied itself quite unscrupulously with the bourgeoisie against the workers. Now the Russian state, she claimed, was the master of the Comintern—but this the workers did not know. The USSR had closed its frontiers to German communist refugees, while bourgeois Jews in the West did not. Without doubt, she said, the collaboration between Nazi Germany and Soviet Russia was destined to end in a pact of non-aggression. It was a theme which she had treated many times. Indeed, it was one of the leit-motifs of her new article: 'Are we Heading For the Proletarian Revolution?'

Simone began by arguing that capitalism seemed to be arriving at a point beyond which all development is brought to a halt by insuperable barriers. (This, no doubt, was reminiscent of Alain's thesis that the capitalist system abounds in arrant absurdities.) But what goal are we moving towards, she asked? Before answering the question, she defined her own point of view: 'If we wish to survive this calamitous epoch with honour, we must abstain, like the Ajax of Sophocles, from the comfort of hollow hopes.'

After discussing briefly the mechanism whereby, in history, a new form of oppression succeeds an older one, Simone analysed the Stalinist state mercilessly: Trotsky does not go far enough in his condemnation of Stalin's system, she re-asserted, and she quoted Descartes's celebrated aphorism: 'A clock that is out of order is not an exception to the laws of horology but a different mechanism subject to its own laws.' The inherent vice of the Stalinist system, according to Simone Weil, is that of oppression in the name of function. This was, for her, a new idea.

Marx, she said, had seen two things in the capitalist system: first, the oppression inherent in the money-exchange between buyers and sellers; second, the conflict between 'those who control the machines and those whom the machines control'. The Russian experiment shows that one can eliminate the first form of oppression without doing away with the second.

'One can see clearly enough how a revolution can "expropriate the expropriators", but not how a mode of production based on the subordination of working operatives to those who co-ordinate operations can fail to produce, automatically, a social structure defined by the dictatorship of a bureaucratic class.'

There can be no true socialist system, she maintained, until 'productive labour itself becomes the dominating function'. This, for Simone Weil, was the essence of Marxist theory. But she could not see its coming to pass under 'a system of production in which labour itself is subordinated, by means of the machine, to the function which consists in the co-ordination of tasks'. There follows this forceful analysis: 'This bureaucratic machinery . . . thus imperils the very existence of the one element of the bourgeois system that is of real value. In place of the opposition of contradictory opinions, an official opinion admitting no contradiction would be imposed on all subjects. In place of that cynicism characteristic of capitalism, which dissolves all that links man to man and replaces it with relationships based solely on interest, there would be a sedulously cultivated fanaticism designed to make the masses think of their poverty, not as a burden passively borne, but as a sacrifice freely accepted—a blend of mystic devotion and unbridled brutality, a "cult of the State" which would stamp out all individual values, that is to say, all true values.'

Here, Simone began to establish her mature opinions with that matchless force and clarity she was to achieve at her finest moments: 'We wish to uphold not the collectivity but the individual as the supreme value. . . . We wish to give to manual work the dignity which is its due, by giving the worker full knowledge of technique instead of a mere elementary training, by giving his intelligence its proper object, and by bringing him into contact with the world by means of labour.' For, she continued, as is too often forgotten: 'Society itself is a force of nature, as blind as all other natural forces, and no less perilous to man unless he can achieve mastery over it. In actual fact, this force weighs down upon us more cruelly than water, earth, air or fire. . . . True democracy is, by definition, nothing but the subordination of society to the individual; and this is also the true definition of socialism.'

Simone Weil crowns these striking passages with a conclusion as significant as it is contradictory. The spontaneous struggle of the workers has proved unavailing. The proletariat has itself been overtaken by the economic crisis. What hope remains? 'To preserve intact and in action the same hope which critical examination has shown to be almost without foundation—that is the very essence of courage.'

No doubt one should also try to salvage what is still healthy in the workers' movement, yet 'the only hope for socialism resides in those who already have achieved in themselves (so far as it is possible in present-day society) this union of manual labour and intellectual work' which should be the basis of all social organization.

'But the extreme feebleness of the weapons at our disposal compels us to take on another task as well. If, as seems all too likely, we are to perish, let us acquit ourselves so that we shall not perish without having truly existed.'

There is nothing to prevent 'our striving to conceive clearly the object of our efforts; so that, even if we cannot achieve what we want, we should at least have made an effort of will, and not just wished blindly.' Maybe we are too weak to win, 'but not too weak to understand the force that is crushing us'.

'In any event the worst thing that could happen to us would be to die without either succeeding or understanding.'

To perish after having existed: that was a very meagre consolation. The problem was this: how to form a workers' organization without creating a bureaucracy? 'For bureaucracy *always* betrays.'[1] Unorganized action is, of course, pure; but it is also futile. Certainly the revolutionary trade unionists—those nearest to Simone's heart—were for democracy. But, as she saw it, 'syndicalism itself is bureaucratic. And even revolutionary syndicalists have in the end become discouraged and have compromised with bureaucracy.' Could not some principles, at least, survive the compromise? None, excepting perhaps those which are so remote from reality as not even to be 'belied by it'. 'Conclusion: to be on the side of the working class? Yes. To strive, to think and to build with the workers? Yes. But the last aim is impossible for the moment. The first is possible only to a slight extent.

'The revolution is *hard work*; it is a methodical task which those who are blind or blind-folded cannot accomplish. And that is what we all are at this moment.'[1]

An article of such scope and quality could not fail to provoke a powerful reaction. As early as 25th September 1933, Roger Hagnauer, an active contributor to the movement, published a trenchant reply in *La Révolution Prolétarienne*, in which he attacked both the thesis and the personality of the young teacher. 'Simone Weil is surveying the world from on high,' he wrote, suggesting that the public might well wonder what her intellectual resignation had in common with the syndicalist movement. Calling for a more hopeful outlook, he attacked what Monatte had characterized as an 'intoxication with abstractions'. In conclusion, Hagnauer said: 'Simone Weil has enough revolutionary conviction to accept this lesson in optimism.'

From that moment on, articles by Simone Weil were not to pass unnoticed. The first master-stroke reached even Trotsky himself. His reaction was mildly contemptuous. (Later, he was to meet Simone and to complain of her fierce onslaught of questions.) But he wrote a reply entitled 'The Fourth International and the USSR' which appeared in *La Vérité* of October 1933. 'Bemoaning "the regrettable experiences" of "dictatorships of the proletariat", Simone Weil has found consolation in a new cause—the defence of her personality against society. This is a formula of the old liberalism, modernized by a cheap anarchist enthusiasm . . . It will take many years for her and her kind to free themselves from the most reactionary of the petit-bourgeois prejudices.'

He turned the full force of his disdain against *La Révolution Prolétarienne*: 'It is impossible to imagine a publication more flattering to melancholy revolutionaries, to political stockholders living on the interest of a capital of memories, and to those pretentious reasoners who may perhaps rally to the Revolution . . . after it has become a fact.'

## Another Rosa Luxemburg

Simone Weil received lively admiration, however, in the circles about *La Révolution Prolétarienne,* where she was highly praised by Monatte. Marcel Martinet told Thévenon that her article was a work of genius, and that nothing like it had been written since the days of Rosa Luxemburg, one of the leaders of the Communist inspired abortive Berlin revolution which took place after the First World War. The publicity disguised the true state of affairs: intellectually, Simone had already severed her connection with revolutionary syndicalism; henceforth she was attached to it only by ties of affection.

# 3

# Roanne and Saint-Étienne

## 1933-1934

'There is but little hope for the individual, and yet the individual is the only hope.' (p.100.)

SIMONE SPENT THE MONTH OF AUGUST 1933 with her parents at Chambon-sur-Lignon, in the picturesque setting of the Haute-Loire. She invited some of her former Le Puy pupils to visit her there. They arrived in the morning and, later in the day, went for a hike in the mountains.

Simone Weil's own shyness infected her guests, and at first conversation was difficult. But in the relaxed atmosphere of the excursion, tongues loosened: the girls reacted spontaneously to the beauty of the landscape, or complained of limbs unaccustomed to climbing. When the way led down-hill, the girls rejoiced. But from Simone who had wrangled from them the group's complete load of supplies to carry in her own pack, there came a typical 'Weilianism': 'Personally, I don't like going down. I much prefer going up.'

Simone had intended to spend the summer in Spain. But the most important event of the season, undoubtedly, was the Trade Union Congress at Rheims. It came as a climax to the long controversy on the German question which had seriously split the French syndicalists and in which Simone had played an important role. On 30th April *L'École Émancipée* had spoken of Simone's 'truly outstanding' analysis of the German question, while, according to the February issue of *Le Travailleur de l'Enseignement*, she had 'odiously' defamed both the attitude and the activity of the German Communist Party. For many syndicalists her observations appeared as 'monstrous calumnies' which

89

not only grossly misrepresented the course of events in Germany but struck at the tenets of their socialist creed. The subsidiary issues she had also brought into focus were a source of embarrassment to true party followers. How could they explain or ignore the Soviet government's attitude towards the German refugees? They were being asked to justify the internal administration of Russia. It seemed that the whole revolutionary movement was at stake, and French syndicalism was a house divided. But the communists manoeuvred nimbly to kill off any opposition which might threaten their supremacy in the trade unions, in particular in the CGTU.

Simone Weil countered by launching an appeal in *La Révolution Prolétarienne,* 'For trade-union democracy (in the CGTU)'. Its purpose was to bring the political trend of the CGTU to the attention of its members. 'After many half-concealed manoeuvres and perversions, proletarian democracy, without which there can only be a parody of union organization, has been openly and cynically trampled underfoot. In its place, the "apparatus" is slowly installing a system of administrative dictatorship.' Thus David defied Goliath, but the battle had already been lost according to the leading article in *L'Effort* (15th July 1933), and it was too late to save anything. In the editor's view, 'union democracy is now dead in the heart of the CGTU. The party apparatus has to all intents and purposes killed the organization.'

The Congress was held on the 5th, 6th and 7th of August. Simone Weil asked to be allowed to speak, in order to describe the plight of the German communists. Her request was refused. She spoke nevertheless, through uproar and disorder. During the eighth session, she renewed her request to be given the floor and was at last allowed to speak.

Simone recalled an article published in the *Neue Weltbühne* which expressed alarm at Hitler's terrorism and the attitude of the USSR. She read aloud the reply to this article, published by *Gegenangriff,* the organ of the German refugees; it confirmed the reports that the Soviet Union had closed its frontiers to communist refugees. At 4.30 in the morning the president cut her short; consulting with Congress, he declared the debate closed.[1]

Simone's speeches took courage: she was dealing with the unmentionable, the collusion between Hitler and Stalin. On two occasions she was threatened with physical assault, but her comrades, the miners, were watching over their 'human-hearted mascot'. They surrounded her and kept the assailants at bay.

Of those outbreaks of violence she wrote in *L'Effort* of 28th October that they 'would have been impossible in a genuine trade-union organization. But the CGTU, long since degenerated, has no longer anything in common with a trade-union organiza-tion. It is nothing but an appendage of the power of the Soviet State.'

Despite the bullying and insults, the small opposition group in the CGTU did not lose courage. It had 'hardly been able to participate in the Congress except through the insults it suffered'. But the last session of the CGTU had 'to some extent, given cohesiveness to the movement'.

After the Congress, Simone took her new teaching post at the girls' lycée in Roanne, a manufacturing city of 60,000 on the river Loire, 65 miles to the west of Lyons. She rented a room that looked out over red-tiled roofs on the fourth floor of a pleasant building, in the avenue Gambetta. At the first opportunity, she travelled to Saint-Étienne and its neighbour-town, Firminy, to take part in public meetings at the Labour Exchange. One of her ambitions was to raise funds for the construction of a new centre for these meetings, at which she lectured. The militants of the Communist Party were invited to her lectures, but never appeared.[2]

The events in Germany were now of greater concern than ever to Simone Weil. Former members of the *Sozialistische Arbeiter Partei* were her special interest: she did her utmost to find persons who were free to go to their rescue in the concentra-tion camps. Among her acquaintances was a man who tried to do this, and who later spent more than two years in prison. Had Simone influenced him? She spoke of the tortures inflicted on the opponents of the Nazis and used to ask point-blank: 'Would *you* be able to resist torture if you were arrested?' To anyone who answered that he had no fear of torture, she would tell the story (an authentic one) of the trade unionist who himself led the

Gestapo to the places where his friends were hiding and pointed them out one by one after having been tortured for several days.[3]

When the study-groups re-opened in the autumn, Simone described to her trade-union comrades the lamentable fate of the German refugees—driven back at the Soviet frontier posts, forced to knock at the less inhospitable doors of the millionaires in imperialist France and fascist Poland. She distributed leaflets put out by one of the numerous communist minority-groups then operating in Paris, the Democratic Communist Circle led by her friend Boris Souvarine. One such pamphlet described treachery in the port of Hamburg, where militant communists who had taken refuge aboard Soviet ships were put off and handed over to the Nazi authorities. At the same time, Simone also attended meetings of a group of German refugees and French trade unionists which had been formed in Paris. One day, someone remarked that the German parties were the best because they had had their martyrs. She replied tartly that martyrs were no justification for a political party—even the most sinister party might manufacture its martyrs for propaganda purposes (and often has).

Simone Weil distributed petitions among her friends, sometimes asking for signatures herself. On one occasion, she gave Pierre Arnaud, leader of the miners' union, a document which condemned the attitude of the Communist Party. Arnaud lost his temper; his eyes flashing angrily, he shouted: 'Simone, take your filth away! I'm not a counter-revolutionary yet!' Simone's indignation matched his own, but she did not show it. Instead, she handed him another petition, to raise funds for the anti-fascist German refugees. Arnaud took the pamphlet, read it, and said: 'Yes, that's all right, I'll sign that!' His hands were trembling. Simone protested: 'But, Pierre, it means the same thing!' 'No, Simone,' he replied, and both stood speechless. With pursed lips, Simone handed him a fountain-pen; he spread the paper out on the table and signed it.

The better part of her time was now spent on the 65-mile railway trip between Roanne and Saint-Étienne. When her actual business was over and the last train had left, she worked late at the houses of comrades or in a café. Sometimes she would spend the night in a bar facing the Labour Exchange where the proprietor let her stay after closing-hours. When she was worn out, she dozed on the leather-covered banquette and then would catch the first train back in the morning. She found this necessary in order to avoid her friends' hospitality and have more time for work.

Simone's trips to Saint-Étienne were for the purpose of teaching the study-groups which she had created. Past difficulties in getting her ideas across to miners and construction workers had made her cautious: now she built each talk around one idea only and also distributed an outline to her audience for absolute clarity. The outline she used for her talk on Marxism is still extant.

It shows that the lecture was divided into three parts: first, she discussed the definition of Marxism as the application of scientific method to social emancipation; second, she outlined the development of science before Marx; third, attempts at social emancipation before Marx. In conclusion, she investigated the proper definition of a science of society. Thus Simone attempted 'a genuine method of popularization'.[4]

The lecture seemed successful: the hall was crowded; the audience was visibly flattered at being able to follow the speaker; the workers returned in full force for the next lecture. The theme: if there is a science of society, it has to be put into practice.

Her general conclusions of these talks may be summed up as follows: social movements are determined by economic relations; men and their thoughts are determined by their social situation, and what is determined cannot pretend to change that which determines it. Only those who escape from social determinism can make use of a science of society, either by putting it at the service of the masses, or, on the contrary, by using it to enslave the masses and suppress democracy altogether. From this evolves a discussion of the part played by the individual in society: the individual, who alone is able to grasp the nature of the forces which control him, is the only true lever of revolution. Moreover, if we want technicians to rise from the ranks of the proletariat in the future, we must enable the proletariat to free themselves from the network of relations which hold them prisoner. We must re-establish the autonomy of individual enterprises; that is, recreate them in more human dimensions, and at the same time give the worker, both in life and in work, the opportunity 'to divide his time freely between reflection and action'.

Was this not what Simone herself practised? She even included moments of relaxation. Claudius Vidal recalls the films they saw together one day: René Clair's *A nous la liberté*; and, on their last outing together, Eisenstein's *Battleship Potemkin*. Simone had collected the songs of workers, sailors, chain-gang convicts. She was interested in their content of folklore, however slight this might sometimes be. When the occasion or the spirit moved her, she would break out into song. Since she could not really sing, however, she spoke the words rather than sang them, rather in the style of contemporary dramatic leads in musical comedy.

On the eve of 'Sainte-Barbe', the feast of the patron saint of miners, Simone was scheduled to talk about fascism at the end of a party for miners given by the United Syndicate in the hall of the Labour Exchange. Pierre Arnaud sent an escort in a taxi to pick her up at the Saint-Étienne station. Arriving at the hall, Simone mounted the podium and, in a shrill voice, shouted out slogans; the enthusiastic applause disconcerted her. 'We must arm ourselves against fascism. We must arm, not metaphorically, but in fact . . .' She spoke with the pathetic intensity of a Joan of Arc surprised by the enemy without her sword or horse. As the party proceeded, she put on a red paper forage cap to get into the spirit of things. But she was the only one to do so, and her head-gear caused more embarrassment than amusement.

This contrived attempt at humour was the clue to Simone's real inner mood. She was on the outside of the group, a spectator, like the cold-sober man who arrives at a party long after it has begun. Her very lucidity defeated her friendly efforts to be one of the crowd. But, with one or two friends, she could relax and reminisce in her semi-confidential way about her university years or the Quatorze Juillet nights when she wandered quietly from one public ball to another. She did not dance, since she did not know how, and she never explained the reason for her solitary tour. Although Péra, an admirer, could write the following 'beatitude' in *Les Études matérialistes*: 'Blessed are they who loved Simone

94

Weil,' could anyone know whether Simone returned their love? The story goes that, once, when one of her friends sang:

> *And I shall always remember*
> *Simone* (instead of 'Thérèse' as in the song)
> *My little Française* . . .

she took offence at the familiarity, stood up at once, looked around her friends one by one, and left. Such was her fear of any strong personal attachment.

In her letters, however, the full wealth of her sensitivity and her intuitive feeling for people came through clearly. To a friend who confided how hard it was for her to bear the thought of the future, and who asked if that was what Simone meant by the expression 'living just as though you had never existed', she answered: 'No, I love you as you are, living in the present as I do . . . It is through those who live in the present that the present exists, and through them that the chain of time stretching into the future is not just a succession of days without human content.' To another friend who complained of his sense of futility and said he did not know what to do with his life, she replied with words which she could not, ironically, apply to herself: 'There are some of us who can be content to exist for the sake of others who love them.'

To her colleagues at the Roanne lycée, she was always distant. They remember her as a fleeting, mysterious figure immersed in some great German book such as *Das Kapital*. If spoken to, she would reply briefly. She never warmed to a discussion. It amused her occasionally to put someone on the wrong track. One day while they were crossing the square, Mlle Deschamps, a fellow-teacher, said to her: 'I am an atheist.' Though Simone, who might have been termed an agnostic, would certainly not have used such an expression to describe herself, she reacted with a spontaneity which was perhaps misleading: she shook her colleague's hand with warmth and observed that she was personally disturbed by the headway the Young Christian Student Movement was making at the lycée. 'If this continues,' she added, 'I am going to form a materialist study-group.' The two teachers decided to confer with the headmistress about this question, but it is not certain whether they actually did.

Thus Simone acquired the reputation of being both a communist and a confirmed atheist. Any doubt there might have been about her social and political philosophy was dispelled by an event that took place at the end of October. A memorial to the war victims of Saint-Étienne was to be unveiled by President Lebrun. In a city whose workers took pride in their record of wartime strikes in 1917, this was considered a provocation. The CGTU called a meeting of 500 militants at the Labour Exchange on the eve of the ceremony. On their way out, they were intercepted by the municipal police, who had been reinforced for the occasion. A few demonstrators were beaten up, some were arrested. The next day, Sunday the 22nd October, a second meeting was called, but it had to take place on the pavement outside. Protests were made against the closing of the Labour Exchange, the arrests of the previous day, and the brutality of the police. Simone put down the red flag she had been carrying at the head of the miners' procession, had herself hoisted up on to a window-ledge, and gave an account of the functions of the President of the Republic. Plainclothes men tried to move towards her through the gathering crowd of curious bystanders and through the demonstrators under the window; singing the *Internationale*, the latter formed a human chain to block the way of the advancing civil guard. The police, spruced up for the occasion, were unable to disperse the crowd; they were forced to listen to the speech Simone delivered on the prerogative of mercy, that exorbitant right which gave the head of a republic the power of life and death.[5]

This demonstration had less effect than Simone Weil's courage and eloquence deserved. The 'gutter press' of Saint-Étienne did not even refer to it, but restricted itself to noting that the President of the Republic had received a warm welcome. This was not at all surprising, wrote Simone in *L'Effort* on 28th October 1933: 'The State does not distribute secret funds for nothing. It pays, but it imposes conditions. That's why *La Tribune*, like *La Loire* and *Le Mémorial*, has seen nothing but the ovation accorded Lebrun and has refused to mention the workers' demonstrations, thereby approving, by its guilty silence, the lynching of militant workers. Worse still, pacifists, socialists of all kinds, even trade unionists, had turned up all too sparsely at the meeting called by their

96

Place Michelet at Le Puy, as seen from the *Lycée de Jeunes Filles*

Saint-Etienne, a focal point of Simone Weil's activities, 1931-2 and 1933-4

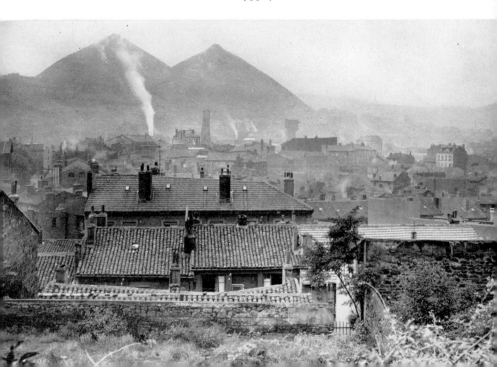

Simone Weil, Madame la Directrice, and four students of philosophy, *Lycée de Jeunes Filles*, Roanne, 1933-4

leaders. Perhaps they had thought nothing would take place because the Labour Exchange was closed. But 'when the Exchange is closed, there is the street, and I've never yet seen a pacifist, a trade unionist or a socialist to be held back by fear of the cops'. Instead of going to see the head of the State, was it not the duty of the masses to come and listen to Simone Weil? (In fact, her lecture had not been planned in advance; though she was the life and soul of the assembly, no one had foreseen that she would become the rallying-point as well.)

Simone worried about the impression made by her awkwardness when she was hoisted up to the window. Thévenon asked if she were afraid of ridicule. She was indeed, she said, but 'only so far as the bourgeoisie can exploit it to minimize the importance of our demonstration'. She had reason to be concerned about the political consequences of the affair, as things turned out, for the communist leaders took the fullest advantage of it. There was a brisk exchange of words between the affiliated (CGTU) and the confederated (CGT) unions. The demonstration misfired and was a humiliation for the confederalists, and they weren't allowed to speak at the trade-union meeting which took place the following Thursday.

Simone was disturbed very little by the possible consequences of her behaviour with the educational authorities. By this time the university administration seemed to be aware of the intrinsic qualities, as well as the dangers, of her teaching. 'She has a keen and open mind,' states her principal in a report sent to the Ministry of Education on 25th January, 1934. 'In philosophy, she develops the personality of her pupils, rather than the knowledge required for the *baccalauréat*.'

On 25th November 1933, there was a general inspection. The inspector, Gastinel, sent the following report to the Ministry: 'Mlle Weil, graduate in philosophy, gives seven hours of instruction in literature to the 5th form [12-year-old pupils]. In carrying out this part of her duties, she shows some distinguished intellectual qualities, a personal feeling for teaching—and also inexperience. At first sight, one has the impression that she cannot have much influence over her pupils: her near-sightedness, her low voice, and her indistinct delivery are liabilities. She speaks without emphasis (the only gesture she makes is a slow extension of one arm), and her hands remain still. But her active, tense intelligence grips her audience. The children feel that they are dealing with a decisive authority . . . they have, above all, the feeling that Mlle Weil takes them out of school exercises and puts them in touch with real life—and, as is natural, they enjoy this feeling very much. Perhaps Mlle Weil does not attach sufficient importance to positive, precise, practical advice: her ideas about the best way to approach a subject are correct, clear, discriminating, and wholly devoid of formal rhetoric. This is as it should be, but while she is quick to point out faults, she all too rarely suggests how these can be corrected. The handling of the subject is too summary, and there is almost no correction of the work of the class as a whole. As an alternative to the set theme (a dead leaf floats on the current of the stream: whence does it come? Where is it going?), Mlle Weil allowed her pupils to deal with any narrative subject of their choice. Half of the class availed themselves of this permission, and the results in general were not happy.

'It is still too soon to know whether Mlle Weil has understood that she must show more circumspection and reserve in her social activities.' One can hardly fail to notice the warning that brings the report to a close.

The meetings on 21st and 22nd October had been organized to demonstrate against the 'arms-manufacturer' Lebrun. The idea was to stage a protest against war-mongers and to curb their 'criminal' machinations. The issue of pacifism, then, was in the air.

In November 1933, Simone Weil published a lengthy article on the subject in *La Critique sociale*. She begins these 'Reflections on War' by drawing up what she calls a 'balance-sheet of traditions'. The workers' movement could scarcely be more confused over the whole issue of war, she points out, for the socialist traditions upon this question are quite contradictory. Up to the First World War, it was true to say that socialist minds were dominated by the memory of the revolutionary war, a war that had been defensive as much as offensive and was regarded not only as legitimate but as one of the most glorious eras in the struggle of the masses against their oppressors. The post-war period evolved 'not indeed another conception (for neither the workers nor the so-called workers' organizations of our epoch can be accused of having conceptions on this or any other subject) but a new moral atmosphere'. Post-war pacifism, evidently, gave way before the triumph of Hitler; old notions, she says, are now floating up to the surface again. 'Such uncertainty and obscurity might well surprise and ought to shame us. . . . It would be even more surprising to have arrived at anything better, however, having started from so utterly mythical and illusory a tradition as that of 1793 and using the most defective of all methods, that of evaluating a war in terms of the aims it pursues rather than the means it employs.'

Before passing any judgments whatever upon a war, Simone continues, it is necessary to study the mechanism of the conflict, that is, to analyse the 'social relationships implied under the given technical, economic, and sociological conditions'. The materialist method is 'first and foremost to examine every human fact, putting less weight on the ends pursued than on the consequences that result from the means employed'.

Now, modern war subordinates the combatants to the instruments of combat. In effect, then, war is a matter of internal politics: it is the war of the State apparatus against its own army. A study of the history of the French and of the Russian revolutions shows this clearly. 'Revolutionary war is the death-knell of revolution.' It is true that a war may provoke a violent reaction against capitalism, but this 'hostility, stifled by the war-time truce in the class struggle, turns to the advantage of the State system, not that of the workers'. The absurdity of fighting fascism by warlike means is therefore, to Simone, obvious.

Any attempt at revolutionary war she sees as an act of despair, doomed to certain defeat 'until we can see the possibility, in the very act of producing or fighting, of freeing the masses from the hold of this mechanical apparatus'. In conclusion, Simone returns to the fundamental theme of the article: that war is an instrument of oppression in the hands of whoever wields it, never a factor for liberation.

'Present-day society resembles a vast machine in which men

99

are continually being caught up and which nobody knows how to control; those who sacrifice themselves for the sake of social progress are like people who try to grasp the wheels and clutch at the transmission-belts in a vain effort to stop the machine. They are crushed in their turn. But the helplessness which one feels at a given moment—a helplessness which one should never consider total—neither excuses one from remaining true to oneself nor justifies surrender to the enemy, whatever disguise the enemy assumes. And whether it calls itself fascism, democracy, or the dictatorship of the proletariat, the supreme enemy remains the administrative apparatus, be it civil or military. The true enemy is not the one in front of us, who is our enemy only insofar as he is the enemy of our brothers: the true enemy is the one who calls himself our defender and makes us his slaves. In no matter what circumstances, the worst betrayal is to consent to subordinate oneself to this administrative apparatus and, in its service, to destroy, in oneself and in others, all true human values.'

Simone's whole argument is drawn from an analogy between capitalist machinery and the mechanism of modern war. The synthesizing genius of Simone Weil took a short-cut that heightened the tragedy of modern oppression: there was but little hope for the individual, and yet the individual was the only hope.

In her article, Simone alluded to the 'dictatorship of the proletariat'. She discussed it again in an article in *L'Effort* of 2nd December 1933. This notion, she wrote, is not only shrouded in fuliginous mists: it has led the workers' movement into serious error. 'The principle known as "reasons of state"—or, to quote the biblical formula, the principle that "it is expedient that one man should die for the people"—can be applied to each of the individuals who compose the people, excepting the masters themselves, and in the end it amounts to the sacrifice of the whole people to the interests of the privileged few.' The example set by Russia indicates that it is normal for the individual to be sacrificed to the good of the revolution. 'The entire Russian people can be legitimately sacrificed in the person of each of its individual members, for an alleged collective interest which is represented by the State bureaucracy.' For Russia has engaged itself fully, and of its own accord, in the game of capitalist competition. Why suppose that it will not have to act like every capitalist, continuing to invest ceaselessly in order to keep abreast of its competitors, a practice which invariably requires the sacrifice of the present for a future that can never be overtaken? Simone concludes that there is little difference between the Soviet State and any other managerial class, 'except that the Russian State, besides controlling production and exchange, also possesses an army and a police force'.

It was to the question of human values that Simone always returned, and it was this that divided her from the hard-core union militants. Another example of it may be found in the review of Otto Rühle's *Life of Karl Marx*, which she wrote for *La Critique sociale* in March 1933. Taking care not to exalt Marx, as so many others did, as the deity of a new cult, Simone criticized the 'dismal games . . . redolent of the most dubious psychology' in which Rühle indulged, in his attempt to explain away the work of Marx as the product of his digestive troubles and an inferiority complex arising from his Jewish origin. What deserves attention here is Simone Weil's assertion that materialism is an absurdity 'when one conceives it not as a method of investigation but as a doctrine capable of explaining all problems'. Such an approach would inevitably lead to the destruction of all humanism.

'The result is to eliminate all values, including those of materialism itself. One can explain everything through materialism except the mind itself which apprehends and comprehends the part played by matter. If one tries to do that, materialism degenerates into a low sort of pragmatism . . . To restore any significance at all to either action or thought, we are bound to invent a mythical goddess called History.'

On 3rd December 1933, Simone took part in the famous 'march of the miners', perhaps one of the most exciting experiences of her life. The demonstration had been planned by the National CGT Miners' Federation of the below-ground workers. In all the collieries, the miners, in protest against unemployment and a wage cut of more than 40 per cent, were to make a symbolic assault on their prefecture, after having marched in procession a distance of over three miles. Pierre Arnaud assembled more than

three thousand miners of the *département* carrying red flags. The
rallying point was to be the statue of Michel Rondet, the pioneer
of trade unionism in the Loire. Simone Weil waited with some
late-comers at a cross-roads which the procession was to pass.
She wore a cap and a drab cloak. Her face and hands (for once
she kept her hands out of her pockets) were blue with cold. She
joined the first rank immediately, slipped in among the militants,
and claimed what had been promised her—the large red flag
of the Labour Exchange of Saint-Étienne. She marched well in
step, with all the gravity her role required. When there was a
lull in the bugle-playing, she was heard to cry out: 'Come on!
Can't the miners sing any more? '

The bourgeois press of Roanne launched a violent attack
against her for having taken part in this demonstration. She is
said to have replied with an article citing the personal rights of
State employees.[6]

While Simone Weil travelled at weekends to Saint-Étienne
for such activities, she carried on her normal teaching schedule
in Roanne. In both cities, the plight of the German political
refugees continued to concern her. One of her colleagues tells us
that she went to a mayor in the region of Roanne one day to enlist
his help in finding work for those who had fled from the Nazis.
Her success can be deduced from the remark she made after her
meeting: 'That's the first time that I haven't addressed a fellow
socialist as "comrade ".' A colleague, Mlle Deschamps, informs
us that Simone tried to go to Russia; but while she herself obtained
the necessary papers without difficulty, Simone's efforts came to
nothing.

Simone's students can still remember waiting in vain for her
to take her class on the first of May. Upon leaving the lycée at
twelve o'clock, they spied her in the front rank of the traditional
*défilé*, holding up her clenched fist, so they said, and chanting
the *Internationale* with the others.

On 12th June 1934, there was again a general strike at Saint-
Étienne. The miners swarmed into the streets and overturned the
tram-cars. National Guards charged the demonstrators on horse-
back. Friends of Simone Weil among the miners had taken good
care not to let her know of the plans, however. When she heard

what had happened, she telephoned to tell them that they were 'swine' for keeping the news from her. Their excuse was that she couldn't run: she was bound to have been arrested. What they did not say was that they would probably have been arrested, too, or beaten up, had she been with them, trying to protect her from the mounted police.

Simone's social preoccupations, which she felt so acutely that they were often translated into immediate action, bore fruit in a literary project which she jokingly called the 'Testament' or the 'Magnum Opus'. Begun in 1933, it was still in progress in 1934; but for various reasons she never finished it. She was never really satisfied with the conclusions of her study, and it is probable that her physical exhaustion and her experiences working in factories in 1934 contributed to her decision to set it aside. It was this study, no doubt, which she described in her letter of 20th June 1934 to the Minister of Education: 'I would very much like to prepare a philosophical treatise dealing with the relationship between modern technology, the basis of large-scale industry, and the essential aspects of our civilization, by which I mean, on the one hand, our social organization, and on the other, our culture.'[6]

She asked for a year's leave starting on 1st October 1934, for 'personal studies'. In a subsequent letter, she informed the Minister that she did 'not wish to receive any salary' during her leave of absence. Her request was formally granted on 12th July.

Simone was excited at the time over a plan which she had been entertaining ever since the year she took her degree, and she was eager to leave Roanne. She asked her mother to pack up her things and to sort out the stack of German newspapers (mainly the two dailies, *Die Rote Fahne* and *Der Völkischer Beobachter*) which she had collected in her room. Her attitude during a syndicalist controversy that broke out just as she was to leave her friends in Saint-Étienne shows, beyond doubt, that she meant this to be more than a temporary absence.

The anarchist-revolutionaries in the unions belonged to the *Révolution Prolétarienne* group. They had written a manifesto entitled: *Power to the Union*. In a letter to the editor published on 25th July, Simone condemned it without qualification as 'a monstrous joke'. The anarchist-revolutionaries of CGTSR belonged to the rival group of the trade-unionist *Combat*; they had drawn up another document entitled: 'The Economy to the Unions—the Social Structure to the Communes.' These two documents were under discussion one day in a café in the presence of Simone Weil. She laughed at the CGTSR manifesto: 'The announcement is somewhat premature.' But as far as their title went, she conceded, they had the better of the *Révolution Prolétarienne*. This title indicated that the eventual control of the economy by the unions had nothing whatever to do with a seizure of power by political parties to install a State-controlled economy. 'Seizing power for the ideal union,' Simone Weil said, 'is like seizing power for the ideal party. Our unions are actual unions. They are not capable of seizing power . . . fortunately.'

# 4

# A Year's Factory Work

## 1934-1935

'Christianity, in its essence, is the religion of the slaves.' Simone Weil, *Waiting on God*

AT THE END OF 1934, Simone Weil was twenty-five years old, almost twenty-six. She had cleared all the easy things out of her life, and she was alone. She envisaged her whole future stretched before her; and firmly and resolutely, made up her mind to make something of it, to steer it from that point to the finish in a pre-determined course. There was, however, a double risk: first, that her energy, her will-power, her capacity for work, might break under the pressure of harsh necessity; second, that her health, never good, might be undermined, and that physical suffering would then drain away her purpose, leaving her only the crushing burden of struggling through life, day by day. Simone was to come face to face with both.

On Tuesday, 4th December 1934, she began work as a factory-hand at Alsthom. The factory was at 364, rue Lecourbe, Paris XVième. She got the job through a friend who knew Auguste Detœuf, the managing director of the company. The friend had been frank about why Simone wanted the job. 'The fact that he understood—that showed a broad-mindedness that was certainly exceptional in a person of his position,' she wrote to one of her students. Later, she spoke of Detœuf even more warmly.[1]

Simone stayed at Alsthom for four months. At the top of the notebook in which she planned to record her impressions, she wrote in Greek: 'Much in spite of thyself, under the pressure of hard necessity.' She also wrote in her 'Factory Journal': 'Not only should man know what he is making but, if possible, *he should see it in use*, so that he may see the modification he works on nature. Each object that a man makes should be for him *an object of contemplation*.' Could this have been the idea she was seeking in the hours she had passed with her plumber friend, 'Robinet'? Now, she believed, she was going to live it.

On that first Tuesday, Simone Weil worked less than three hours: an hour's drilling, an hour's work at the power-press with a new friend, Jacquot, and, at the end of the afternoon, forty-five minutes turning a crank-handle to help Dubois, another new acquaintance, who was making cartons. No one knew her background; no one knew that she was, in fact, a teacher of philosophy. But right from the beginning her eyes smarted, her head ached, fatigue crept through her body, she was bullied and reprimanded. During her first weeks on the job, she noted her experiences and reactions with a scientific detachment, as if the work were a kind of game. She had not been able to escape the feeling that she was a graduate teacher 'on the loose among the working class'; she was not yet able to commit herself to her strange new way of life as if it were her destiny, as if it would go on forever, as if it had been imposed upon her by ineluctable necessity, and not by her own free will.

After a week she wrote to Mme Thévenon that her only fear was that she might lose her job through being unable to keep up the required production rate: 'I am not disappointed. I am very happy to have done what I've dreamt of doing for so long. More and more I'm persuaded that the (relative) liberation of the workers must begin in the workshop itself, and it seems to me that I shall come to see a little what that depends upon. I have the impression that it would not require very considerable changes to turn a factory into a very cheerful place.

'As for the atmosphere here, I am taking to it like a fish to water, as you can imagine.'[2]

Such ties with the past, however, were soon to be forgotten in the fatigue, the monotony, and the ugliness Simone Weil was to find in the work. Before long, every contact with the world from which she had come was to make her present way of life more distasteful. To have dinner at home with her parents, for example, was to increase her suffering. At times, she took a kind of joy in the muscular efforts her work demanded; at other times, she wept over her machine. Only on Saturday afternoons and Sundays was she able to regain her sense of herself and recover sufficient vigour to think creatively.

More and more Simone became aware of the gulf between her expectations and reality. The fourth week she was let off for the Christmas and New Year holidays. She caught cold, ran a fever, and was plagued by maddening headaches. When it was time to return to work, she still felt worn out and still had a cold.

On Wednesday, 2nd January, she was put on the furnace. The work proved far beyond her strength. Headaches, burns, and the drain on her energies exhausted her. The moment arrived when she could not lower the furnace door. The work inside was on the point of ruin when a smith leapt to her rescue. 'How grateful you feel at such moments,' she wrote in her 'Journal'.

In one respect, her part of the factory was extraordinary: the bosses never went there. The workers carried on as one team 'without a trace of servility or meanness'. There was an atmosphere of liberty, of true brotherhood. The boy who lit the furnace for her showed her how to lower the door with a hook, to save her strength. 'Whenever I burn myself,' she wrote, 'the welder smiles at me sympathetically.'

On 9th January, Simone saw an accident: a woman's hair was caught in a machine. A great patch of her scalp was left bald. The accident occurred at the end of the morning; in the afternoon, the woman was back at work.

An 'administrative incident' took place the next day. Ten washers were missing. Since twelve harassed people of progressively higher rank were required to intervene to put the situation right, work was held up; so pressure was relieved for a little while, but not for very long. Simone felt her back breaking under the strain of factory work. She dreamt of digging potatoes. By Monday, 14th January, she was completely exhausted when she stopped her machine at the end of the day, but the quick smile of a young workman and a joke heard in the locker-room restored her morale.

Slowly, gradually, Simone Weil felt her energies drain away until the temptation to just stop thinking obsessed her. It seemed the one and only way to escape the unendurable suffering. To work in an upset condition was impossible; that would lower the output. And, of course, neither could there be a question of complaining about the bosses. Simone wrote to Mme Thévenon: 'One is tempted purely and simply to lose consciousness of everything except what is part of the common daily grind.' Could it be, she asked, 'that the salvation of the worker's soul depends primarily upon his physical constitution'? She could not see how anyone but a healthy brute could avoid falling into some form of despair, turning to crime or vagabondage, or stupefying himself with drink or debauchery. True revolt, she felt, was out of the question. 'You aren't even conscious of the situation any longer; you just put up with it. Any re-awakening of thought is painful.' However, the sense of working-class solidarity, the indignation at the injustices endured, remain intact. But how far can this last thread of spiritual independence be stretched without snapping ?

In spite of Simone's headaches, and even though she ate little and slept less, both the noise of the factory and her physical suffering filled her with a kind of moral exultation, which she notes as a 'very singular sensation'. Suffering and joy became the two poles of her social thinking.

On the 6th of March, Simone Weil felt crushed by fatigue. There was no doubt the work was harder for her than for the ordinary worker: she was, after all, unaccustomed to it, she was naturally awkward, her health was poor, and her movements were rather slow. In addition, her mind was always active: she had not rid herself of her passion for thinking. But Simone had come to grips with a real life experience, and the contradictory impressions that overwhelmed her proved that she had emerged from the world of abstractions. Now she was surrounded with 'real men—good and bad, but really good and really bad'. There was no time, however, for worrying about logical consistency. At the university she had been paid to think, 'or at least to make a show of it'. Here she was in a way paid not to think. Each day she felt the urge to work faster. She couldn't let herself think. This was the *sine qua non* of a good output. And without satisfactory output, there was no job.

## Mystery of the machine

Simone relished hard work and work that was going badly. One day, when she was sifting parts through the strainer, she saw that a good many of them were defective. 'I threw away as many as I could.' Nevertheless, she was alarmed, for she had passed ten thousand which were entered on the chit and the number actually turned in was much lower.

She made a note of this incident in her journal on the day she was laid off. The day before, she had cut her hand badly on her machine, but a bad cut did not prevent her saying once again that work which is going badly 'is much less boring'. In the evening she did not feel tired; in fact she went to Puteaux 'in fine sunshine, and a fresh breeze was blowing'. She had a delightful time there, and went to bed late.

Simone took advantage of her enforced leisure to jot down some reflections on the mystery of factory work: 'Guihéneuf: because the worker has never learnt mathematics, his machine is a mystery to him. He doesn't see a balance of forces in it. Hence, he also lacks confidence in it . . .

'Jacquot and the machine which didn't work: clearly, his machine-press was a mystery to him; and so too was the reason it didn't work. Not just as an unknown factor, but, somehow, in itself. The machine wouldn't work . . . As if it had refused.'

*A fortiori*, to the worker, the process of manufacture as a whole is a mystery. He doesn't know what each thing he makes is for or how it will be combined with other things later on. 'Nothing is *less* informative than a machine.' What is necessary is a reorganization of the whole factory-process so that the worker is able to form a clear impression of the manufacturing process as a whole. The problems of management are wholly outside the worker's ken, Simone observes; but evidently they were somewhat outside her own ken too. She writes that the renewal of obsolete equipment is a 'capitalists' trap', for if one employer renews the equipment he has written off, the other employers have to do likewise whether their own is obsolete or not. 'Next round, the first employer suffers in his turn.' But the main conclusion that Simone could draw from her work at Alsthom was 'how boundless was the unawareness of a man who has never suffered'.

Her diary describes her search for employment. She met two

metal fitters, and one of them told her of his war experiences. Fear apparently had not humiliated him. As far as she could tell he did not understand what was meant by 'the wretched fate of slaves'.

On Easter Sunday, coming out of a church where she had 'hoped (foolishly) to hear Gregorian chants', Simone went to an exhibition to see a Jacquart loom in action. She, who 'had so eagerly, so vainly, studied this process at the Institute of Arts and Crafts', listened to an explanation of the process from a workman who was very proud of his knowledge. It pleased her 'to understand at last—more or less—the relation between the cards, the needles, and the yarn'.

Her search for employment continued. Finally, on 11th April, she got a job with Carnaud at the Forges de Basse-Indre in Boulogne-Billancourt. According to her employment card, she worked there from 11th April to 7th May as a packer—very exacting work in a stifling and malodorous atmosphere. 'This supposedly pleasant little plant proves on closer examination to be anything but small, and above all it's dirty—you have no idea how filthy it is!' In this foul place, there was one particularly loathsome workshop: 'That's mine!' she wrote to Boris Souvarine.[3] By pushing herself to the extreme, she found she could pack 400 pieces in an hour. Towards four o'clock of the first day the foreman, 'a handsome fellow', came to her and said quite politely: 'If you don't do 800 I won't keep you. If you do 800 an hour for the next two hours, *I may perhaps agree* to keep you on. Some of them do as many as 1,200.' Inwardly boiling, Simone worked at full pressure, and managed to do 600. The foreman returned, counted them, and said it was not enough. At 6 o'clock in a cold fury she went in search of the works manager and asked him whether she was to return the next day. 'Come back anyway, we'll see,' he said. But it was clear she would have to work faster. She saw that the factory was a 'sweat-shop (frantic speed, fingers cut over and over again, dismissals without scruple)'. A lovely young girl, strong, healthy, with a fresh complexion, said to Simone one day in the cloakroom: 'We're sick of the day's work. Just wait till the fourteenth of July! Then we'll dance!' Simone Weil asked her if she could dance after ten hours at the job. The girl answered, laughing: 'Of course I can! I could dance all night long.' Then she added sadly: 'It's five whole years since I danced. You long to dance, and then you have to dance in front of the wash-tub.'

Simone was dismissed from the Carnaud factory on 7th May, after a month's work. For the next month she was out of work. It was a trying time, following, as it did, the excessive labour to which she had applied herself, and the 'frightful prostration induced by her headaches'. But she had foreseen that her period as a factory-worker must come to an end.

On 31st May 1935, Simone Weil applied to the Minister of Education for a post as teacher of philosophy for the year 1935-1936. She said that she preferred a town near Paris 'such as Rheims, Lille, Rouen, Le Havre, Valenciennes, Roubaix or Douai'. Meanwhile she continued her experiment of living as a worker. During her last week of unemployment, she decided to spend only three francs fifty a day, 'transport included'. Hunger became a permanent sensation, to which was added the anxiety, the disappointments, the humiliations she endured in queues in front of the personnel offices.

Simone eventually found a job at the Renault works. She began on Thursday, 6th June, 'as a specialized worker, at the cut price of 1.25 francs per hour'. She dreaded 'a workshop of machine-presses, work ten hours a day, brutal shop-stewards, fingers cut off, heat, headaches'. Happily, she was not put to work at the presses. But there was still the rhythm, the speed of the work. She reflects on her experiences at Renault: 'The drawback of a slave's situation is that one is tempted to take as real human beings who are only pale shadows in a cave: e.g. that young skunk, the mechanic.'

When she went to work, each step Simone took was a moral effort; when she left, each step was a physical strain. So she went on, day after day, working from 2.30 in the afternoon until 10 at night. To get a seat in the train home became an obsession.

One day, the packing-case into which she had to drop her completed work was stolen. She lost time looking for another. She hurt herself and had to go to the First Aid Post; when she came out, her case had again disappeared. It was difficult for her to suppress her disgust at incidents of this kind; in time, she came to regard as a special favour those moments when she had nothing to bear 'on account of human brutality'. To be able to get on a bus became a cause for astonishment. How could she, a slave, receive so signal a favour? 'Slavery has made me lose entirely the feeling of having rights.' A few stray bonds of human kinship are established: 'A very nice fellow. . . . He looks at me one day as he passes, while I am painfully transferring heavy bolts with my bare hands into an empty crate. I will always remember this man.' One evening, at a meeting of the *Révolution Prolétarienne* group in Paris, Louzon pretended not to recognize her: he said her face was different and that she looked 'tougher'. She got a letter from Alain, about whom she noted: 'Chartier has only a superficial and elementary notion of mechanization.'

But the state of servitude was not without fleeting moments of joy. One Sunday she visited an exhibition of Italian art. On pay-day, she practised no self-denial: 'A packet of cigarettes, and stewed fruit . . .' Above all, she enjoyed the feeling that in spite of everything she had preserved her human dignity. Later, in her 'letters to the manager of a factory',[4] she explained what she meant by this: 'One day I realized that a few weeks of this existence had almost sufficed to transform me into a docile beast of burden. . . . I swore to myself that I would not leave this working-class condition until I had learnt how to put up with it in such a way as to preserve my human dignity intact. I kept my word. But up to the last day I felt that this feeling of human dignity had always to be achieved afresh, because the conditions of existence continually crushed it and tended to degrade me once more into a beast of burden.'

In what way could she sum up her experiences? A direct and stark encounter with reality; the feeling of possessing no right 'whatever it might be, to anything whatever'; the ability to be morally self-sufficient, to live, without feeling inwardly humiliated in her own eyes, in a state of latent and perpetual humiliation; the capacity to 'taste each moment of freedom or of comradeship to the full, as though it were to last for ever'.

It was not that this or that idea of hers had changed; on the contrary, many of her ideas had been confirmed. There was

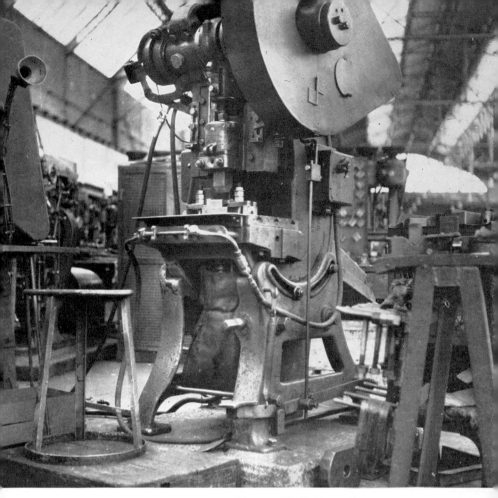

Type of machinery operated by Simone Weil, December 1934-
March 1935, Alsthom's rue Lecourbe plant, Paris

View from Simone Weil's window,
Place Gordaine, Bourges, 1935-6

Simone Weil, Barcelona, August 1936, in uniform of *Confederación Nacional del Trabajo*

infinitely more to it than that; her whole outlook on life and on things had been affected. Doubtless, she would feel joy again, but there had been a certain lightness of heart that she would experience no more. The sense of her own personal dignity, in so far as it derived from her position in society, no longer existed. She had, then, to recreate it differently: and now all her striving was towards preserving this new sense of human dignity at all costs.

Simone's most urgent conviction was that the established social order was not based upon the suffering of the workers, but on their humiliation. Hitler was aware of this when he promised his workers, not the alleviation of toil or suffering, but the joy of the pride that engenders force. Marxist materialism had not understood this; that was what made it 'stupid'; that was the blind spot in Marxism. Humiliation, rather than suffering, was the condition of the class that 'counted for nothing in the eyes of everyone'— and which never would count, no matter what happened, in spite of the well-known verse of the *Internationale*: 'We are nothing, let us become something.'

The full significance of another 'Weilian' observation was later to be revealed: that no matter how inexorable, oppression does not provoke revolt, but submission. 'Acceptance must be substituted for submission' because acceptance entails the free consent of the worker, and submission, the shameful trembling of the slave who bows his head. Such is the problem.

Thus formulated, the situation did not necessarily seem irremediable; for Simone Weil had invariably found: 'Among these simple and unlettered beings, a generosity of heart and an aptitude for general ideas in direct proportion to one another . . . When I think that the Bolshevik leaders claimed to create a *free* working class—when in all probability, *not one of them* . . . had so much as set foot in a factory and, in consequence, could not have had the vaguest idea of the real conditions which determine freedom or servitude for the workers—politics seem to me a sinister sort of buffoonery.'

Even though her experiences had not enabled her to acquaint herself with the problems of management, even though she said that she was overwhelmed by the rhythm imposed upon production, Simone Weil did not close her eyes to the imperatives of modern industrial production. However hard on the workers, these were imperatives which no change of régime could render less essential. Nor did Simone Weil attempt to deny the inevitable irksome character of labour. But, she noted, 'such difficulty can either be seen as that of a victorious struggle over matter and over self . . . or of degrading servitude'. Therefore, as she wrote in a letter to a factory manager, it goes without saying that the workers must both know and understand 'the necessary demands to which the life of a factory is subjected'.[4] When they are understood, they become tolerable, even desirable, although the demands may take the form of a hierarchy of tasks and functions.

Simone Weil did not hesitate to declare that the managerial classes were under a delusion about the revolutionary capacities of the French working class. She knew the working-class movement well—and from the inside—and she now knew the workers of the Paris area. And so she had acquired the conviction (for her, very sad) that not only the capacity for revolution, but even for action pure and simple, of the working class was reduced to almost nothing. Only the bourgeois, she said, could believe in its existence.

For this reason, Simone, more than ever, could not advocate revolution; and that less in the interests of order than of the oppressed themselves. She knew perfectly well that, when one is chained to a cruel necessity, a premature revolt can only be followed by an immediate and crushing defeat; and that one's new condition would be worse than the old.

Simone Weil was convinced that factory owners had excessive power. They enjoyed 'the power of God rather than of man'. The execution of an order 'requires only a passive submission in which neither mind nor heart has any part to play; the subordinate becomes almost a tool manipulated by the intelligence of others'. It is a mistake, declared Simone, to think that the exercise of this power does not cause a profound transformation of soul. As Saint-Just said: 'Only those who are powerful profit by it.'[5]

This, then, was Simone Weil's experience as a worker. Its validity may be contested on grounds of its brief duration, her personality, her past. An accurate evaluation will have to consider the fruits it was to bear.

## The religion of slaves

At the end of Simone Weil's factory days, her soul and body were in tatters. Her parents took her to Portugal. She left them and went to a small fishing village.

Until her last year at the factory, Simone had had no experience of misfortune except her own, to which she had attached little importance. In any case, she regarded her sufferings as far less, being 'biological and not social'.[6] But when she found herself among the workers, as one of them, the meaning of misfortune was illuminated in her mind, as the impact of suffering had left its mark upon her flesh. She had forgotten her past, had come to expect no longer anything of the future, 'being hardly able to imagine the possibility of surviving her fatigue', and she could say, quite truthfully, that nothing separated her from these unfortunates. She had received the brand of slavery upon her soul, 'that mark of the red-hot iron with which the Romans branded the foreheads of their most abject slaves'.

This was her physical and mental state, when she went into the little Portuguese village with its poor hovels ranged along the shore. It was the evening of the parish feast of the local saint. The full moon shone upon a procession of women walking round the fishing boats, singing songs 'certainly very ancient and of a heart-rending mournfulness'. Never, perhaps, had Simone Weil heard anything so poignant.

It was in this setting, before believers whose faith she did not share, that she became convinced that 'Christianity, in its essence, is the religion of the slaves, that slaves can do nothing but adhere to it'—and she among so many others.

# 5

## The Lycée of Bourges and
## Holidays in Spain

### 1935-1936

'I was made for fellowship in love, not fellowship in hate.' Sophocles, *Antigone* (trans. George Young)

SIMONE WEIL arrived at Bourges, exhausted, her mind full of vivid memories of human suffering. During the first months she stayed with Mlle Alice Angrand, a teacher of English at one of the schools in the town. They spent many evenings in conversation: Mlle Angrand begged her guest to speak of her past, and Simone, in her quiet but impassioned manner, recaptured what her experiences as a farm-hand and factory-worker had taught her. She also spoke of Shakespeare, and of the classics. Taking the great Greek tragedies and translating them page by page, she opened the heart of her hostess to the beauties of Greek literature.[1]

Mostly, however, they discussed social issues. One evening Mlle Angrand mentioned someone who owned and managed a factory in Vierzon that produced woodworking machinery. Simone Weil asked for an introduction, she was eager to see the factory. Her hostess agreed, so Simone was welcomed by one of the factory engineers, and was able to spend a whole afternoon talking with the workers.

At the end of her first term in Bourges, Simone moved from Mlle Angrand's house to that of a milliner, in the Place Gordaine. There she rented an attic, sparsely furnished with an iron bedstead, a deal table, and a few chairs. Her room, which opened on to another one, had for view only a narrow shaft; it was neither pleasant nor private nor comfortable. Simone herself did nothing to contribute to its appearance. Though she often railed against herself for her inability to make a bed or to do housework, she always left her lodgings in complete disorder. Her money lay about on the furniture, and one day it disappeared. Simone was not in the least upset. Speaking about the theft to a colleague, she said: 'Whoever took it no doubt needed it, so I'm glad he took it.'

The milliner had a brother who sometimes borrowed Simone's books. One day he took away Kierkegaard's *Diary of a Seducer*, but brought it back without having read much of it. 'The teacher at the girls' lycée,' he told his friends, 'has an odd sort of taste in reading.'

The truth of the matter was that Simone Weil could not read Kierkegaard without feeling moved. Although her rationalist upbringing still shut her off from Kierkegaard's teaching, she was close to him in spirit—so close, in fact, that she did not need to refer to him in her writings.

The year passed without any major conflict with the lycée administration. The headmistress, Mme Laignel, wrote in her report to the Minister of Education that Simone Weil seemed 'to give her lessons with great sureness of method' and that 'the children took a keen interest in her instruction'. The rector thought she was a little out of her element at Bourges. In his view, 'it would be better . . . to send her to an industrial area, as she herself wishes'. The inspector, for his part, was more censorious: 'The general appearance of Mlle Weil is none too distinguished and by all present accounts shows a lack of grooming. This young teacher fulfils her obligations satisfactorily: the results would be better were the pupils to take part more fully in the class-work and if the lectures were presented more clearly and in a less monotonous tone of voice. In the town, Mlle Weil's attitude has provoked astonishment. She wishes to apply for a post in the north of France; she would like to live in a working-class milieu.'

The head-mistress complained that Simone Weil neglected minor administrative duties incumbent on the staff and that she seldom mixed with her colleagues. Since she was favourably disposed towards her young staff-member, her complaints are significant. In bourgeois circles, she did not pass unnoticed, nor was she viewed in a favourable light—in fact, she was taken for a communist. Observing her solitary evening walks, her neighbours assured one another that she was obsessed by some great idea. (Probably she was preoccupied only by one of her violent headaches.) Sometimes they saw her pushing the prams of workers' children through the streets; instead of admiring her kindness, they were scandalized by her behaviour.

In the homes of her pupils, Simone Weil was not appreciated by their parents, nor did she do anything to win their sympathy. She took the greatest interest in girls who came from poor homes; for the daughters of the rich, she did nothing, for she thought 'they were not gifted'.

To Simone Weil, teaching meant awakening in her pupils the profound sense of life, making them feel how disturbing were the great issues of the day: that, at least, was the task she urged upon her colleagues. It is not surprising that before long she was given to understand that the ideas nearest to her heart were 'unacceptable' in Bourges. All the same, she took pleasure in raising the most controversial issues. Thus, a good many teaching hours were consumed by impassioned discussions—in a hostile atmosphere.

Some of her pupils reported that Simone Weil argued for the superiority of free unions to marriage, the former being in no sense contractual and the union between man and woman existing by virtue of their love, without any social support. Probably those making the reports were misinterpreting a paradox and turning it into a scandalous statement; whatever the case, their teacher could not escape controversy. The accent on the role of society and its nefarious intrusion into private lives is reminiscent of Rousseau and Alain. Simone Weil also invoked the authority of Plato and dictated to her class a text from *The Republic* (VI, 493), presumably of her own translation: 'Each of these mercenary individuals whom the crowd calls sophists and believes to be rivals of one another do not, in actual fact, teach anything but the crowd's own opinions, which the crowd is wont to express when they get together; and they have as much right to call that wisdom as an animal trainer has to describe as wisdom his acquaintance with a big, powerful animal's moods and passions which enables the trainer to approach it, to touch it when it is enraged, or to calm it down . . . If, having learnt all this by dint of time and practice, the trainer were to esteem this to be wisdom, to make an art of it, and apply himself to teaching what he knows, not knowing which of his opinions nor which of his passions is worthy or shameful, good or bad, just or unjust, basing his words on the opinions of the great beast, calling good what is pleasing to it and bad what irritates it, with no capacity at all for justifying these words, naming good and beautiful the things that are only necessary, in ignorance alike of the essence of goodness or of necessity, and how they differ—would he not be a strange sort of teacher?'

The text was related to questions with which Simone Weil was preoccupied at the time: How can the individual avoid becoming a slave to the social order? Is there nothing in man that is not at the mercy of external circumstances—neither impulses, feelings, nor actions? But the capacity to recognize this subjection of his, she told her students, 'proves that man has, at least, a negative insight' into the nature of true freedom. To her, we are all victims of an illusion—we are like Spinoza's angry child, who believes that he is freely willing revenge. True consciousness comes when we awaken ourselves to an awareness of our enslavement. This awareness is what Simone Weil calls 'attention', and she associates it with the true nature of genius.

Her pupils' notes echo their teacher's concepts and experiences: 'Those who are prey to a vice cannot bear to think about the beauties and delights of life; they cannot concentrate on thoughts which take them away from their vice. *Extreme suffering* must be analysed in the same way.

'Christ at Gethsemane knew what sufferings were in store for him, and what was the purpose of his passion and death; and did he not say: "My God, my God, why hast thou forsaken me?"'

Speaking of training, during her course in psychology, she observed: 'A reprimand always, even when it is not explicit, carries with it the threat of dismissal. Whenever a human being is reprimanded, there is a natural reaction of ill-humour. In a mine, in a factory, the manager's reprimand provokes a reaction which has to be repressed, and which cannot be expressed in words or actions; for the worker can permit himself only the movements necessary for his work. These repressed actions are inevitably a source of physical pain. Humiliation is at once a physical and a moral pain; no circumstances mitigate this subservience, and that is what makes this discipline so important. *Money* is a *means of brainwashing*.' And yet again this laconic observation: '*Labour and feelings*—love varies from trade to trade. For example: there are differences between the love of an engineer, the love of a peasant, and the love of a miner.'

To disconcert, to awaken from the habit-ridden paths of customary thinking, she would, socratically, throw unexpected questions to her pupils: 'Have you ever wanted to kill someone?' She would prick their patriotic pride with such barbs as her comment on the liner *Normandie*, then under construction: 'How many workers' houses could have been built for the price of this boat?' Their replies that the beauty and scale of the liner would enhance the prestige of France among foreigners met with her derision. She prodded them on: 'If one were to sell a factory at its just price, and this were shared out, there would be an appreciable amount for everyone.' One pupil retorted: 'But the next day, there would be no machines to work with.' 'Which proves,' said Simone, 'the stupidity of my remark.' Her fallacies, taken at face value by the hearer, were often meant to bring the truth from his own mouth, even at the risk of her appearing somewhat naïve in his eyes.

Despite her monotone delivery and lack of fire, by such methods and the topical character of the examples chosen, Simone aroused her pupils' interest. They liked her on the whole (though there were some dissenters) and called her their 'Little Weil' ('la petite Weil'). They responded to her game of subtle provocation by passing on to her reactionary articles, cuttings from *L'Espoir Français*, or by slipping into the drawer of her desk various documents which they thought would displease her, such as a review of the JOC (Young Christian Workers). They did not realize that, to their teacher, the expression of contrary views aroused by the 'gadfly' of her sarcasm, would be less displeasing, if not positively gratifying, than the sloppy thinking they displayed in their compositions, the 'short papers' she assigned to them. A look at her should have been enough to convince them of her indifference to the opinions of others: all the year round, with her only skirt, which had pockets, she wore either a red or a green pullover. Proper young ladies wore gloves in those days, but not she. At a prize-giving ceremony, she appeared in an old overcoat, very much the worse for wear. That her imperviousness to the impression of others might derive from an inner strength her students could only surmise when they saw the confidence with which she opened her copy of Homer and translated extemporaneously whole passages in true unrhymed verse. They came to trust her for her independence, which was but an aspect of her objectivity, and to admire her for her humility. The harsh and unqualified comments she sometimes made could not dispel the favourable climate she had created. She seemed genuine, a rare virtue indeed.

In turn, she expected from them an authenticity in their writings which could only come from personal experience. Everyday life was the real source she wanted them to draw from. One day she asked them to 'describe any sort of object, in terms of a single sensation, form, or colour', a process familiar to present-day readers of Robbe-Grillet. The prize was won by an essay describing an eraser. These attempts at disciplined writing—very different from the standard topics for classes of philosophy, such as the nature of the soul or the essence of morality—were carefully corrected and returned, the sheets crumpled, smelling of tobacco, sometimes with cigarette holes burnt in them.

That was all there was to her classes: no lessons were learnt, no home-work checked. Most of the year was taken up with psychology; for a while they dabbled in ethics, but logic and metaphysics were neglected. Surprisingly, there were only three failures at the examination, either because Simone Weil's unorthodox methods were at last paying off, or because her students, mainly from a bourgeois milieu, had always had the benefit of the best educational opportunities.

Their teacher hardly seemed to know them or their names and made no distinction between them, except for her preference for those who were not rich. In class, she called for an answer by pointing her finger at her quarry: 'You . . . you.' Such a lack of personal contact explains why no one could fathom or foresee the direction in which her thoughts were moving. The trend emerged only upon reading her posthumous publications.

The only girl to benefit from Simone's personal attention was not a pupil of hers, but of her friend Alexandre, her comrade from Normale. This child had decided to end her studies for the sake of her health. Simone went to see her and asked her not to give up the future to which her abilities entitled her, but to take a temporary rest. She spoke to her gently, very quietly, lapsing into reflective silence from time to time. Her manner of receiving a confidence and giving advice has been likened to that of a good father confessor.

For the most part, however, it cannot be said that Simone Weil's pupils at the Bourges lycée felt the same affection and enthusiasm for her as her pupils at Le Puy and Auxerre. Of this she must have been painfully aware, if she made the comparison. Sometimes she tried to establish less formal relations with them than were required by her professional duties. She attempted, for instance (though without success), to induce some of her pupils to spend the holidays with her on a farm, to join in the work of the harvest, and she took them to the festival of the Fifth Centenary of the Abbey of Noirlac. The day of the oral examination, she took one of her pupils to see Charlie Chaplin's *Modern Times*, a film she loved, as she writes in one of her letters to Auguste Detœuf: 'You have seen *Modern Times*, I suppose? The eating-machine—that's the best and truest symbol of the factory workers.'[2]

Simone Weil's estrangement from her Bourges students was matched by her alienation from the local working class. She lunched in October at the 'fixed-price' restaurant where she could talk to the waitresses: they told her that they earned three hundred francs per month and lacked nothing; they were uninterested in her arguments about the hardships of the worker. Often she invited workers to share her lunch, but none of them shared her ideas or even understood them.

She stuck to her beliefs, nevertheless, and to her way of life. During her year of industrial bondage, she had increased the frugality with which she always lived and was loath to abandon habits which she might some day have to resume by necessity or choice. Most of her salary was not spent, but given away. When she ran out of money, she helped in some other way. She is said to have lavished care, for example, upon a disabled beggar who was at the hospital.

One October day, while supervising her lycée pupils during a recreation period, Simone Weil met a young woman called Mme Coulomb. They were both trying to solve a rebus in the magazine *Marianne*. Gradually, their conversation turned to mathematics. Simone Weil, who was then reading Euclid and trying hard to understand him better, translated the texts from the Greek and commented upon them. Before parting, Simone told her new friend that she would very much like to see her again and to meet her husband, too: a meeting was quickly arranged.

The Coulombs were a young married couple, and Simone always had a soft spot for young couples. She enjoyed their company, spent many evenings with them, and even invited them to her attic, where she offered them vodka in her tooth mug. Except when she had headaches, she seemed tireless, especially after midnight: then she would talk freely about herself, her family, her brother, a faculty member of whom she was so proud, and who was then at the University of Strasbourg.

On Thursday afternoons, a time of the week when classes are never taught in France, Simone would go for a walk in the surrounding countryside with her new friends. Once they set out in search of the château of the *Grand Meaulnes*, the mysterious domain which Alain Fournier, in his novel of the same title, sets at some unspecified and perhaps mythical location in the Berri. Another day, Simone asked a peasant to let her drive his plough, which she immediately overturned. He was furious, and would not be placated with a cigarette; Simone walked away sadly, and did not recover her customary cheery mood for some time. Usually, however, she had a ready laugh, and the spells of silence or sadness brought about by headaches or by such slight heartaches as that noted above were all the more apparent in that they contrasted with her usual good humour. One evening, at nightfall, she told her friends that a Spanish coal-trimmer had once kissed her in Barcelona during a trip she had made with her parents. Coulomb jokingly asked if the man were drunk. Simone burst into tears.

The personal content of these conversations is proof of the sincerity with which Simone spoke to her friends. They say that she was anti-marxist, anti-bourgeois, anti-fascist, and in opposition to society as a whole; that she belonged to no party, not even the political groups with which she had worked, nor to any religion. Regarded superficially, her attitude seemed negative. Beneath the surface seethed a deep unrest. She spoke of Christ, whom she loved, but she could not make up her mind whether he was God or man. Undecided she might have been, but she was not indifferent. And she talked on unceasingly, touching on all topics, trivial or sublime, while she chain-smoked or drank black coffee.

René Hervé, an armaments manufacturer whom she met in 1936 through the Coulombs, was once subjected to her stream-of-questioning conversation for several hours. He was about to leave for America with the Georges Bonnet mission. She wanted to know all about the manufacture of guns, the speed of their production, and other related matters. He was first taken aback and then intensely bored by her incessant questioning and refused to see her again.

Sometimes, Simone discussed music with her friends, urging upon them records of Gregorian chant with a proselytizing zeal. She seemed to realize that this medieval plain-song was as much prayer as it was music and she attended mass in the cathedral to listen to it.

On one hand, she used to try to communicate to others the meaning of religious problems; on the other hand, as though by discretion, she pretended to know nothing about them.

The circle of Simone's acquaintances at Bourges was small and not entirely congenial, in spite of her friendship with the Coulombs and her very slight contacts with workers (who were unnerved by her, surprised, and unresponsive). Sometimes she travelled the 160 miles to Paris for the weekend, where she often saw Boris Souvarine, who had a very high opinion of her. She was, he thought, the most intelligent woman he had known since Rosa Luxemburg. Through Boris Souvarine, Simone met a former Russian official who had recently found refuge in France. He was doubly interesting to her: first, because he came from a country about which there was so little information; secondly, even if he was now reduced to earning his life as a worker, nevertheless he still had, on the new life he led, the perspective of a member of the managing class. The interest was not mutual.

'As a woman,' he said, 'she was really not attractive. I found her ugly, really ugly; that was the first impression. She was very short-sighted, always peering about.' He realized, however, that her greatness came from the power of her thinking—which had its shortcomings in that it disconcerted working-class circles. With her insatiable curiosity, she would always give the impression of conducting an investigation, much to the embarrassment of his wife and children, whom she would question about what he was reading or doing in his absence. He did not feel in her the warm convictions so often felt by others—'the quality of heart which humanizes such behaviour and renders it acceptable to others'.

At this time, Simone Weil began to take part in the meetings of the Cercle des Jeunes Patrons (association of young factory-managers), founded by Auguste Detœuf. They exchanged several letters, and she planned to go into his factory for an indefinite period as a worker, to collaborate with him in his attempts to reform the factory from within. Before making this decision, she sought to reach 'a full understanding' with him. Detœuf felt that personal dignity was an intrinsic quality of the soul which did not depend upon circumstances or appearances; it was not a mere attitude which could be expressed by gestures; its preservation was a question of strength of character. To Simone Weil, personal experience had proved the fallacy of such views. Furthermore, Detœuf thought that Simone had an ingrained repugnance to discipline, obedience, and manual work. But she was capable of submitting herself wholeheartedly to any discipline demanded by the nature of the work provided that the subordination required be meaningful. Was Detœuf fully aware of the more than dutiful responsiveness which was expected from the factory worker? Simone undertook to enlighten him on this point in her letters, and she distinguished three degrading aspects of factory discipline.

First, it is not the duration of work—no matter whether eight hours or twelve—that reduces the worker to servitude, but obedience to a machine that constrains the worker engaged in piece-work to stereotyped motions, which reduces time to 'the dimensions of a few seconds'.

Second, the discipline of the assembly-line has nothing in common with that obedience which, in a healthy man, 'gives a goal to his activity': discipline is brutally imposed on the worker who, subjected to the tempo of production, is taxed to the limit of his strength. The overworked labourer is thus, body and soul, at the mercy of any order he may be given; if he is obliged at any moment to accelerate the rhythm of his work, he endangers his health, and his vitality and his spontaneity may be exhausted. Constantly in fear lest some order from his superiors may compel him to increase his rate of output, the worker unconsciously adopts an attitude of servility.

Third, the obedience expected of the worker is devoid of humanity; it 'makes no appeal, in respect to motive, except to self-interest in its most sordid form—at the level of pennies—and of fear'. To allow oneself to be swayed by these considerations, is to become debased; to reject them, is to condemn oneself to starvation.

Simone Weil carried on her fight for the improvement of the working class at all levels. Julien Loeb saw her in Paris at a meeting of the Union of Socialist Technicians, where she supported a programme of united action—which shows that her position was then well to the left of the socialists. At Bourges, she attended the local 'Comité de Vigilance', a watch-committee of anti-fascist intellectuals. The president, a teacher named Wim-bée, describes how she used to sit, sunk deep in her chair, as though lost in an interminable reverie, suddenly rising to uphold the most intransigent theses, which she would document at length with references to Marx, to the revolt against Robespierre of the 9 Thermidor (28th July, 1794), and other historical sources. To some, she seemed to live in a world of abstractions. Pichon, the secretary of the departmental union of the CGT, met her several times in his official capacity and at his house, where they had endless discussions about Marxism.

Coulomb reports that, having spent a year in a factory, Simone Weil also wished to learn about the life of the peasantry. She asked her friends at Bourges if they knew any peasants in the neighbourhood who would let her work among them. They arranged a meeting with the relatives of one of her pupils, a family in Carron de Gron in Cher. Simone Weil explained that she wanted to look over their farm. They said that theirs was not a farm of the kind she meant; it was only a little family concern. The family worked it all themselves, without help: haymaking, harvesting, baling, feeding the cattle, ploughing, tending the chickens—hard and not very interesting work. 'That is perfect; that's work after my own heart,' Simone Weil said. 'What I want is to live the life of the poor, to share their work, live with their troubles, eat at their table.' 'In that case, come to us, if you've set your heart on it,' they replied.

And so, one cold March morning in 1936, Simone Weil arrived without warning—afraid, as she said, that they might alter the routine of the house on her account. They gave her some coffee with milk, without sugar; she drank it without a word. Afterwards, she asked what work there was to be done. They told her to *dépâter* the beetroots, a local word for unearthing them. She then had to cut them at the stalk; hard work for a woman. When that was done, she prepared the cows' fodder, piled up the manure, drew water for the trough, and even tried to milk the cows (which, she confessed, was difficult). Next, she helped the woman of the house prepare the midday meal; in this way she could watch the latter and prevent her from adding anything to the ordinary fare. 'She ate very little,' the family said. 'But what a lot of questions! How do you manage? What are your returns? Do you like the life? Tell me about it . . .' And when her hosts were astonished that she should submit herself to such hard work, she answered crisply: 'To be somebody, you must have spent a year at least at all kinds of hard work, and not talk about it by guess-work.' The two peasants still recall how she asked them to outline 'their desires'; but the embarrassment that this question aroused in them was dispelled when she went into raptures about their being content with so little and explained how much she was edified by their frugality. She was not sad by disposition, but what she said seemed both sad and obscure to these good people.

Simone Weil was not inefficient and quickly adapted herself to everything. She was determined to learn to plough. To convince the father of the family to teach her, she said that she was afraid she would one day have to do hard labour. It was only much later that he understood what she had meant when she said: 'The important thing is to be nothing. Unbelievers are closer to the truth than believers. Everything is illusion.'

Simone Weil did not live at Carron de Gron. She went whenever she had free time. She did indeed ask the family if she could stay with them, and even proposed to pay them for it. But this she offered on the condition that she should be free at any hour of the day or night to go out and mingle with the lowest classes. They refused: 'Anyone who knew the country would know that that was not possible: after she left, life would have been impossible for us.'

A month had scarcely gone by when the mother of the family went to see Coulomb at Bourges. She found it very hard to come to the point: she was very sorry, but she did not want to have Mlle Weil any longer. She never washed her hands before milking the cows; she never changed her clothes; and, worst of all, in the fields she never stopped talking about the future martyrdom of the Jews, poverty, deportations, and about the terrible war she foresaw in the near future. When they offered her a fine cream-cheese, she pushed it away, saying that the little Indo-Chinese were hungry. Later, this woman wrote: 'My husband and I used to say: the poor young girl, so much study has driven her out of her wits; and we were sorry for her; while really it was we who were out of our depth. But what could we do? All the intellectuals we knew put barriers between themselves and the peasants. Simone Weil threw down these barriers and put herself at our level.' And that was just what bewildered these poor people. They were small peasants who worked hard all day long and who were happy in their way. On the other hand, they did not believe they could do anything about the troubles of the world, and Simone Weil's lectures made them feel 'neurasthenic'.

Simone Weil did not hold a grudge against them. She didn't expect otherwise: she was not surprised at their reaction and remained no less interested in the problems of peasant life. In any event, if she could not get employment, there was still the direct contact with nature. Whenever she could, she went out into the country, equipped with a large-size rucksack loaded with camping equipment—a somewhat haphazard collection, but apparently quite adequate.

Among Simone Weil's philosophy pupils at the Bourges lycée was the daughter of the director of the Foundries of Rosières, Mlle Magdeléna. They got into more than one heated argument over social and political issues.

The Rosières factory, situated in open fields, was surrounded by a whole town of workers. In Simone Weil's time, there were about a thousand workers in the factory and two thousand inhabitants in the workers' town. A real little town, it catered to all the needs of its inhabitants. They also had the benefit of family allowances and of various health services. All this had been provided through the efforts of the management of the factory, and all the responsibilities also fell upon them. If a child failed to get a certificate for its studies, the factory, inasmuch as it subsidized the school, bore the blame. Then the directors found themselves to be responsible in the eyes of the public for factors over which they had no control. The chief engineer, a man named Bernard, had visited the United States in 1933; he brought back a number of ideas which had been introduced into the factory—for example, the question box and the house organ. The latter, a little paper, was supposed to lift the worker out of the narrow framework in which he lived, for literally everything in this small world appeared to be a creation of the factory. The paternalistic atmosphere was somewhat stifling.

A remarkable characteristic of the factory was the extremely low rate of work accidents: the lowest in France for factories of similar products. In 1926-1927, the brother of the present director had written a thesis on the prevention of work accidents at Rosières. The Magdelénas were legitimately proud of this distinction, but Simone Weil paid no attention to it. It was probably in her view only a negative advantage.

After having visited the factory as one of a group, she declared to Bernard that she simply could not agree that wages should not be the same for everybody. 'If you were allowed to decide the matter,' he asked her, 'what would you do?' 'The first thing I'd do if I had a free hand? I would post the directors' salaries in the factory.' Then she, in turn, questioned Bernard: 'But what do *you* do all day?' A simple question—which he thought too simple.

Such were the opening gambits to the correspondence between Bernard and Simone Weil.[3] She had been granted permission to undertake a project which was regarded as experimental among the workers. The idea was to give them a voice and a social consciousness; the factory journal *Entre Nous* was to be the organ. In this way an educational effort was to be initiated within the factory.

To begin with, Simone Weil wrote a leaflet in which she asked the workers for their help in running the little paper. The workers, she argued, would be reading something written by one of themselves; it would do them good 'to see in print things which were perhaps stirring in the depths of their hearts without being able to find expression in words'—perhaps also some things that they felt bound to keep quiet about, things they didn't dare say. The managers would read the paper too, she said; it would sometimes be in their power to remedy, at least in part, some of the grievances that would be brought to their notice. They have shown much ingenuity, the directors of Rosières, she wrote, 'in the making of cooking-stoves . . . Who knows if they might not also be able to show ingenuity in the organization of more humane working conditions? Good will is surely not lacking on their part.'

This article of Simone Weil was not published. Bernard rejected it, and she did not try to defend it. Had Bernard been a Catholic, she wrote to him, she would have been tempted to show him that the spirit behind her work was the Christian spirit pure and simple. In doing so, she would have been perfectly justified, but the argument would not have carried any weight. Bernard had told her that it was no easy matter to educate workers. It is so, indeed, Simone agreed. However, 'the first pedagogical principle is that to educate anyone, either a child or an adult, one must first increase his dignity in his own eyes'. The main obstacle to a true working-class culture consists in the humiliating conditions of life which prevail in the factory. 'This fact,' Simone Weil writes, 'is, in my view, the point of departure for any effective attempt at action among the working masses.' It was precisely this point of departure that was not conceded; Bernard reproached her for having stirred up class-consciousness in her article. This reproach Simone Weil considered to be baseless: what does exist among the workers, she believed, is a common consciousness of class, half-submerged and repressed. To be able to furnish a means for the expression of this repressed tension while avoiding all demagogy would be invaluable; far from stirring up class-consciousness, it would, on the contrary, reduce the bitterness of it: 'What can, on the contrary, revive class-antagonism, are those unfortunate phrases which, through some unconscious cruelty, place an indirect emphasis upon the reader's social inferiority, and such distressing phrases are numerous in the files of *Entre Nous*. Simone spoke to Bernard about her intention of perhaps applying for a job as a worker at Rosières. In view of this, she declined his invitation to visit him at the factory.

For his part, Bernard evidently took the opportunity to point out how hazardous were the generalizations she had drawn from her personal experiences. Simone Weil replied to him in a letter dated 31st January 1936. She defended herself against the charge of having attributed to the directors of the Rosières factory an overwhelming debit; what she had called a debit was a reference to their function, and was not meant personally. On the credit side, she placed, above all, the employers' intentions, admitting also that at Rosières there had been certain achievements. Nevertheless, she expressed her conviction that 'of these, there are far fewer instances, and they are of much less importance than one could believe when viewing things from "on high".' Harsh words, which she tried at once to soften: 'As for me, who have deliberately and almost despairingly chosen to place myself at the point of view of those below, I find comfort in being able to speak with an open heart to such a man as you. It helps one not to despair of men, even if one despairs of institutions.'

The bitterness she felt was entirely on behalf of her unknown comrades in the Rosières factory, for whom she wanted to be able to do something.

When Bernard told her of a meeting of the co-operative at which no one had dared open his mouth, Simone Weil was deeply troubled. She could not conceive of human relationships on any other basis than that of the strictest equality. She would have liked the Rosières employers to arrange regular conversations between managers and workers in which factory problems could be discussed in a spirit of frankness and with perfect clarity on both sides. Such interchanges, she believed, would be an immense intellectual stimulus for the workers and might provide a starting-point for popular articles of cultural significance. 'The search for a true method of popularizing culture—something completely unknown up to now—is one of my dominant preoccupations,' she wrote on 3rd March 1936. In this same letter she repeats that she is ready to enter once again 'body and soul', and for an indefinite period, 'into the monstrous cog-wheels of industrial production'.

Simone's next letter, dated 16th March, expressed the concepts that she had formulated concerning the internal reform of factories: among them, that such reform is completely independent of any political system. But reform and reformism are not synonymous. Simone Weil wanted to see as radical a transformation as possible, but not a revolution. Revolution, she believed, would simply accentuate the inequality that already existed in the balance of forces—the present managerial class would merely be replaced by a State trust which would be supported by the police, the army, and the prison system. What was needed was 'a progressive transition from total subordination to a certain blend of subordination and collaboration, the ultimate goal being complete co-operation'. As to the concrete forms that this goal would assume, Simone Weil had as yet sketched out only a few ideas which she hoped to develop in the future.

She was not, however, without some feelings of compunction towards her correspondent. If (which, after all, was probable) her correspondence should remain without effect, then she would have done no more than 'communicate to him her own sad preoccupations,' she wrote. 'This thought gives me pain. You are relatively happy, and to me happiness is something precious and worthy of respect. I do not wish uselessly to communicate to those around

132

me the lasting bitterness that my experience has stamped upon me.'

In her letter of 30th March 1936, Simone deplored the distrust that had been shown towards her and the opposition to her plan for working in the Rosières factory. Bernard, she felt, placed no trust either in her or in her assessment of the moral welfare of the workers. She realized, however, that she was herself the cause of this lack of confidence, at least to a certain extent, and confessed to him: 'I have written to you with extreme ineptitude, expressing all my ideas in their harshest form. But it was done consciously. I am simply incapable of using artfulness, for any purpose whatever, towards people whom I esteem.'

Inviting him to go to see Charlie Chaplin's *Modern Times*, she added wistfully that 'there, at last, is someone who has expressed a part' of what she herself had felt as a worker. And, by way of an apology of sorts: 'Don't suppose that my concern with social matters makes me lose all joy in life. At this time of year especially, I never forget that "Christ has risen". (I am speaking metaphorically, of course.) I hope it will be the same for everyone at Rosières.'

In her opinion, she writes in a postscript, work itself should be educative as far as possible.

In response to Bernard's renewed request that she should write something for *Entre Nous*, she stated that she was not at all sure she could write 'well-behaved prose' and subject herself to the conditions that would necessarily be imposed on her. She recalled a project that she had long been brooding over: that of making the great masterpieces of Greek thought accessible to the proletarian masses. Throughout her year in the factory, she had often mused over the fact that great Greek poetry was a hundred times nearer to the people than the whole of French literature, classical and modern, if only they could understand it. She made a start with *Antigone* and thought with a certain pride that, if she wrote such articles and they were read, the least literate of the factory-hands at Rosières would come to know more about Greek literature than 99 per cent of college students. And if this project succeeded, she might even go on to write a series of articles on the creation of modern science by the Greeks, 'a marvellous story, and generally unknown even to men of culture'.

Delighted to find common ground at last with her, Bernard consented to publish her article on *Antigone*.[4] It was a sheer masterpiece of lucidity, succinctness, and fervour. The reader might be tempted to apply to Simone Weil the heroine's statement: 'I was made for fellowship in love, not fellowship in hate.' The typical Sophoclean 'character is a proud and courageous being who fights alone against an unbearably painful destiny; he is bowed down by the weight of solitude, misery, humiliation, injustice; at times his courage is at the breaking point, but he holds fast and never lets himself be degraded by misfortune. Thus do these tragedies, although full of pain and suffering, never leave one with an impression of sadness, but rather with an impression of serenity.' However, it is the success of this attempt at popularization that must be evaluated. Testimonies on this point, collected fifteen years later, are very mixed. They suggest that, on the whole, for the educational task undertaken by Simone Weil to have been appreciated—and above all for it to have attracted generally favourable attention, she would have had to continue it for a fairly long period. Unfortunately, this work was summarily brought to a halt by the countrywide strike of June 1936.

The strike caused a serious rupture between Simone Weil and Bernard: 'You can be in no doubt, I think, of my feelings of joy and inexpressible relief at this splendid strike,' she wrote to him. 'I beg you, Mademoiselle, to accept my regrets at not being able, without deceit, to convey to you anything but my courteous regards,' was his cold reply.

Just at this time a general inspection took place at the Bourges Lycée. To her colleague, Mme Cognard, who announced to her the arrival of the inspector, Simone Weil replied: 'Oh well! What does it matter! The strike at Renault is of far more interest to me than any general inspection.' Her article on 'The life and the strike of the Metal Workers' was published on 10th June in *La Révolution Prolétarienne* under the pseudonym of S. Galois.[5] It was an impassioned piece of work, and was composed of almost word-for-word extracts from her factory journal and was charged throughout with intense enthusiasm. 'When one has certain images imprinted in one's mind, in one's heart, in one's flesh itself', one understands what a strike movement signifies: hunger, fear, oppression; a suffering that has been slowly accumulating over the years. All this is relieved from the moment when the workers feel that the pressure upon them is weakening. A strike loosens the grasp that held them prisoner. That is the whole story of the strike; nothing else. 'To hold themselves erect. To have their say. To feel themselves men, for a few days. Quite apart from their claims, this strike is itself a joy. A pure joy. A joy unalloyed.'

The strike movement undoubtedly aroused grave problems. In the eyes of Simone Weil, the key problem was 'the relationship between moral and material claims. . . . In the midst of the demands of the movement, one hardly dares to suggest a voluntary limitation of claims'. It had to be done, nevertheless: for those who know how to take advantage of it, the moment, Simone Weil saw, was favourable to setting up at least an embryonic control over the productive process. 'There would then be, at last and for the first time, in consequence of a working-class movement, a durable transformation of the balance of forces.'

However, Simone Weil had to restrain her excessive enthusiasm. In her correspondence with Detœuf, she made a rather different assessment of the strike movement, recognizing that it was basically one of despair. Despite a show of good intentions, she said, the bosses had done nothing up to that time to relieve their workers from this despair. The workers, then, could not be blamed for whatever might have been unreasonable in the strike movement. When things were stabilized again, the situation would be favourable, for a while, for introducing real reforms into the factories. It would be a disaster at the moment, however, if the workers had to return to work with the feeling that they had given in to force. For this reason, whatever concessions the bosses might have to make, Simone believed that they would be wise to give the workers the impression that they had won a victory. But this seemed hardly likely; and Simone Weil notes the following conversation, overheard in a train. The speakers were two business men, 'white-haired, rather fat, looking very respectable'. What they said, she believed, could have shown the employers to be almost guilty of provoking civil war: '. . . we are completely disgusted, *so disgusted that we are accepting no more orders, even if we get them . . .*' 'The swine . . . *they'll pay for it.*' Detœuf explained that it was necessary to allow for exaggeration in such comments. He also warned her that if there were no other alternatives to the present conditions of the small and medium-sized employers except the bureaucratization of industry, she might soon see 'a whole nation dying of hunger and exposed to all kinds of peril'.

While this tug-of-war was going on between labour and management, Simone Weil arrived to survey the scene of combat, the mills in which reigned the deathly silence of unattended machines. She visited the Renault plant in which she had worked, but with a feeling of exhilaration: the motionless giants were no longer being fed their customary share of toiling men's sufferings, humiliations, wrongs. She could stand erect and speak to everyone she met as an equal. Yet her comrades had not yet been liberated from their inferior status and given a hand in shaping their own lives: the Communist Party had officially recommended a return to work, the employers had made a few concessions that some Union officials thought acceptable, but the workers knew nothing of the negotiations. And her comrades knew nothing about it all. For her part, Simone thought that the problem that concerned them most was not being raised—that is the problem of authority. If the bosses' task is to command, the subordinates' to obey, should the latter have to suffer from the arbitrariness of orders imposed upon them. Should they not be able to relate these orders to the encompassing necessity of the work to be performed?

Hers was the ideal of a humanist, not of a Marxist, or even of a revolutionary. If there was to be a revolution, Simone believed it had to come from man himself, the individual, in proportion to his own deepest needs and expectations.

Precisely, at this point, there was a revolution brewing in Spain (later the Civil War brought it to a head and to an end). Simone Weil had visited Spain, and she had loved the spirit of her people. She wished she enjoyed the gifts of a novelist, she once told Aimé Patri in a night-club in Barcelona, doubtless to capture the sights, the sounds, and the soul of the inhabitants. The anarchist movement which attracted her had its real roots in the Spanish temperament with both its shortcomings and its greatness:

'The National Confederation of Labour, and the Federation of Spanish Anarchists,' she wrote later to George Bernanos, 'were an astonishing mixture, which admitted anyone and which as a consequence, was teeming with immorality, cynicism, fanaticism, cruelty; but also with love, a spirit of fraternity, and above all the vindication of honour, which is so admirable amongst humiliated men.'[6]

In those two movements, she had observed that the militants 'animated by an ideal prevailed over those who were impelled by a desire for disorder and a taste for violence'. If, as has been said, every Spaniard is born an individualist and an anarchist, how well this applies to those remarkable men of industrial Catalonia, who found solace in Plato, Aristotle, the Arab philosophers and Saint Theresa of Avila! And what of those young fishermen who brought Goethe's Faust, Part Two, aboard as they set out to sea? Were not these the very prototypes which Simone Weil had sought in vain in France? They blended culture with mysticism, lived on the fringe of society, knew pride with a prome thean zest, sought beauty and adventure in spirit.

Then came the Civil War; Simone was in Paris. What should she do? Formulated in purely logical terms, the dilemma which confronted her was without issue: as a pacifist, she should not fight; as an anarchist, she had to join her fellows in combat. Yet this was not a war like the others, certainly, and other pacifists had volunteered. Thus Simone solved the problem with her heart: 'I was in Paris in July 1936. I do not like war; but what has always horrified me the most about war is the situation of those who find themselves in the rear. When I realized that in spite of myself I had to take part morally in this war—that is to say, I could not help wishing, every day, and at all hours, for the victory of one side and the defeat of the other—I said to myself that, for me, Paris was the rear . . .'

Under pretext of being a journalist with a certificate from a Paris trade union, she left by train for Barcelona with every intention of joining up. This was in the beginning of August

1936. When her old circle of comrades at the university learnt of it, there were peals of laughter. But she was out of their reach.

She would share the perils of those most endangered by the fighting, without actually taking arms, thus escaping from the 'rear', while upholding her pacifist creed. She had a plan which satisfied this two-fold requirement—or so it seemed. And without entering into any of her deeper motives, she unfolded her extra-ordinary project to Julian Gorkine, member of the revolutionary government of Catalonia, in his office at the Executive Committee in Barcelona. She offered to cross into Franco's zone in search of a well-known trade-union leader called Maurin, who had disappeared in enemy territory.

Furthermore, she explained, she would find out about the state of mind prevailing there. Though her concern for Maurin, a most appealing, mystical, ascetic, Greco-like figure, seemed genuine enough, Gorkine read a deeper purpose in her plan. 'But, my poor Simone, with your face, your reactions, your enthusiasm, you'd give yourself away in twenty-four hours.' Simone insisted. Gorkine was immovable: 'Nothing in the world will make me change my mind.' The argument raged for an hour. At last, deeply disappointed, Simone left.

In the streets she saw a city much like the one she had known in time of peace. The only difference was the presence of a reinforced police and militia. Simone stayed a few days. Her services were accepted by the anarchist-syndicalist elements of the CNT. Towards the middle of August, she joined her new comrades-in-arms who were stationed in Aragon on the banks of the Ebro, some nine miles from Saragossa. Arriving before the column's leader, the famous Durruti, Simone asked him for something to fight with. He told her simply: 'Take a gun; there are plenty of them.' Weapon in hand, the pacifist-turned-soldier sent a postcard to her friend Vidal to express her exaltation at feeling the revolution at her finger-tips. But she was not yet 'hypnotized' by this contact with force. She knew then, as she was to state later in her *Cahiers*, that it was equally important for her to avoid both 'fear and the itch to kill', yet this involved a self-detachment which could not be attained easily: it meant 'a heart-breaking effort, that could not be sustained for long'.

# Wounded (18th August, 1936)

On 17th August, she wrote to Souvarine that she had not yet heard a single shot fired, except at rifle-practice. At that instant, an explosion shattered the reigning silence. There was a general rush into a field of maize. Simone lay on her back in the mud and pointed her rifle towards the sky. But the plane was too high up. It dropped a little bomb and then passed out of sight.

For all her good will and her morale, Simone Weil was no asset to her battalion. Her clumsiness had been noticed, and during field exercises and manoeuvres, everyone was careful to avoid the line of fire of her rifle.

On 18th August, great preparations were made for crossing the river. An Italian officer had managed to procure two machine-guns. For Simone Weil, eager for active participation, it must have been a dramatic moment. The river was crossed without incident. The group came across a farmhouse which was chosen as head-quarters for the day. Berthomieux ordered Simone to remain in camp, to do the cooking, for which she had neither salt nor vegetables. While she remained alone, the others sallied forth to re-connoitre the neighbourhood. The atmosphere was tense with danger. It is well known that 'they' do not take prisoners. Nor do 'ours' either. Outside, the sky was blue and nature was both exuberant and beautiful.

Simone Weil was afraid: if she were found, she would be shot; moreover, she would deserve to be, for morally she regarded herself as an accomplice.

At night-fall came the drama, long-awaited for, but in a different guise than expected. While cooking, Simone upset a basin of boiling oil over her left leg. The captain sent her back to the base, thinking he was now rid of her. Half-an-hour later, wearing a make-shift bandage, she was back at her post. But the next day she had fever. She was then sent to the Terramar hospital, in a converted palace, at Sitges, a seaside resort near Barcelona. A former barber, promoted to medical orderly, took very inadequate care of her, hurting her needlessly, and leaving part of the burn exposed to the air, contrary to recognized practice in those days. Furthermore, he would not change the dressing more than once a week. At last a doctor took her in charge, but his attentions left so much to be desired that he was suspected, in that constantly charged atmosphere, of being pro-fascist.

On her hospital bed, Simone suffered more from what she heard about the war than from her own pain. Here she was told about a young boy whom she later referred to as 'this little hero' and whose death was for ever to haunt her. He was fifteen years old and had been captured by the anarchist-syndicalist militiamen. He claimed that the enemy had forced him to enlist. A medallion of the Blessed Virgin and a Phalangist card were found on him. His captors brought him to Durruti, who lectured him for an hour on the beauties of the anarchist movement. And then Durruti, whom Simone spoke of as 'nevertheless, in some respects' a remarkable and admirable man, gave the prisoner twenty-four hours in which to choose between death and joining the ranks of his captors. When this time had elapsed, the youngster said no—and they shot him. Such crimes, wrote Simone Weil later in her *Cahiers*, are 'as flat as dreams, both with respect to the executioner and the victim'. Like dreams they cannot be real, and yet they are, in all their cruel unreality!

In a village that 'both reds and whites had captured, lost, recaptured, and lost again, I don't know how many times, red militiamen . . . found in the cellars a few haggard, famished and frightened creatures'. Among these derelicts were three or four youths, and the militiamen reasoned as follows: since these boys, instead of coming with us the last time we retreated from here, stayed on to wait for the fascists, then they must be fascists too. The boys were shot forthwith, and food was given to the others. What was this but to kill 'without even knowing whether those that one kills exist—except as things to kill'?

To these reports, Simone could add tales drawn from her own experience. She had herself narrowly escaped being present at the execution of a priest. The unfortunate man had argued in his defence that he was the father and support of a family. While his fate hung in the balance, so did Simone's resolution as she was trying to decide whether to remain as a silent spectator to watch the outcome, or to interfere at the risk of being shot herself. What she would have done 'had not a happy accident prevented the execution', she would have found it very hard to say.

Another time, two anarchists had boasted to her that they had taken part in the capture of two priests. One of the prisoners was killed on the spot in the presence of the other who was then told that he was free to go. When he had taken twenty paces, they shot him. 'The one who told me the story,' Simone Weil later wrote to Georges Bernanos, 'was very surprised not to see me laugh.'

In truth, 'the crimes in Spain were in fact committed in all earnest, and yet they seemed to be merely caprice'. This inference could be drawn from a hundred instances, the most obvious of which were the conversations in which Simone Weil had never heard anyone 'express, even in private, any repellence, disgust, or even disapproval of all the blood spilt for no purpose'. All those she saw in Spain seemed inured to elementary feelings of humanity, whether they had come 'to fight, or just to observe' (these latter more often than not were tame and inoffensive intellectuals). She concluded that if crime provokes no repugnance it must correspond to a natural tendency in man as a social being.

While Simone Weil was concerned with these victims of wanton revenge, her family in France were worrying about her. Through Julian Gorkine, they were able to trace her to Sitges. Their intervention probably saved her from further disastrous consequences of the inadequate hospital care she was receiving. Her wound healed, and she came back to France with a crutch to convalesce. All told, she had spent less than two months in Spain. But the real measure of her stay is better stated in terms of gained personal experience. The sympathies she had always lavished on groups working in the interests of the lowest classes of society, had been dealt a severe blow. Such groups, she was forced to admit, 'are of such a character as to discourage all sympathy', and this was so now of the Spanish CNT. She commented ironically upon her paradoxical affinity for Bernanos, a 'royalist, and a disciple of Drumont', who had come to Spain on Franco's side, and her estrangement from her comrades of the Aragonese militia. For Bernanos had not surrendered as they had to the implacable logic of circumstance.

On leaving Spain, Simone said that she would like to go back yet she did not. The inner compulsion that had at first driven her was lacking now. The Civil War, she knew, did not represent the first claims of the starving peasants, but rather the strategic struggle between the opposing hegemonies of Russia on the one hand and Italy and Germany on the other: 'Such a climate destroys at once the very purpose of the struggle. For this purpose cannot be expressed except by reference to the public good—the good of men—and men are of no value here.'

In the light of such statements, the enthusiasm she showed after her return is puzzling. She did not mention her feelings of disgust, but openly flaunted her red scarf and militia uniform. She even went to Bourges, wearing her army cap and red scarf. Others were less warlike. But she reacted, it seemed, as a child would to a game of warfare, making inquiries, with apparent seriousness, as to the possibility of stealing cannons from the arsenal at Bourges to send to Spain.

The contradiction between her attitude in the autumn of 1936 and the one reflected in her letter to Bernanos in the spring of 1937, which the above quotations have expressed, is easily resolved. Time had slowly washed away the surface residue of illusions. Now she knew the bitter truth: 'One sets out as a volunteer, with the idea of sacrifice, and finds oneself in a war which resembles a war of mercenaries, only with much more cruelty and with less human respect for the enemy.'

This might be considered the main benefit she derived from her summer in Spain: the taste of a defeated purpose. Several years later, she confided to her friend Simone Deitz: 'It was a good thing I had that accident!'

Taking advantage in a way, of her absence, the *Feuilles Libres de la Quinzaine* had published an article about her by Jamet which was a mixture of criticism and praise. The worthy Jamet let the full brunt of his criticism fall on a letter that Simone Weil had written to him on 23rd August 1935: 'Revolution is not possible, because the revolutionary leaders are incapable. It is not to be wished for because they are traitors.'[7]

Unable to let these words pass, he challenged them, though the course that the Spanish Civil War was soon to take would show that they were prophetic. He wrote: 'So that is what S. Weil thinks. It's sad. But why isn't it hateful? Because she is

Simone Weil, and she has a right to this view: she, the saint, who gives all. The heroine of tomorrow, of any time. The spirit that is willing to do everything for the workers, except lie . . .'

Back from the Spanish war, Simone Weil accepted neither praise nor reproach: 'I regret . . .' she wrote to the editor of *Feuilles Libres* protesting against the publication of her words out of their context: 'I regret . . . that you have let slip in such inadmissable epithets, which would be suitable only in an obituary. Indeed, they ought to be forbidden among us, even in obituaries. They should be confined to children's church magazines and military rhetoric. For free men, there is only one virtue worthy of praise: that is for each man to do what he considers to be right and reasonable. And that rarely wins outside appreciation. Emphatic terms should only be used in those milieux where brainwashing is practised.'

After her accident in Spain, Simone Weil's poor health grew markedly worse. Teaching would have taxed her beyond her strength. Four times that year she asked for leave of absence. 'She is not cured of her anaemia,' Doctor Weil wrote to the Minister of Education as late as 15th December, 'and she still suffers from violent headaches and excessive general fatigue. Besides, her left leg, injured by a very extensive burn for which she was treated at Terramar Hospital in Sitges (Spain), is still very painful.' As late as March of the following year, during her stay in Montana, Switzerland, she was still suffering from the effects of this wound.

Simone's sick leave had to be extended to the first term of the school year 1937-1938.

# PART THREE

## THE YEARS OF METAPHYSICAL
## AND RELIGIOUS SPECULATION:
## AGONY OF THE SOUL AND THE BODY

1936-1943

# From the Political Evil to the
# Divine Revelation

## 1936-1938

'Christ Himself came down, and He took me.' Simone Weil, *Waiting on God*

### The Political Evil

SIMONE WEIL had suffered through two singularly harsh trials. Her year as a factory worker had bitterly disappointed her. Whatever good she might have derived from the ordeal had thus far escaped her. This became apparent only after she had succeeded in freeing herself from the ideologies that hindered the growth of her spirit. The two months in Spain had been the first stage in this process of purification; here she had seen the beast in man at work. The crimes she witnessed closed to her the last door open towards a more comfortable way of life: that of liberty from commitment, a free-ranging intelligence which boasts of its emancipation when it is in fact the prey of illusion. Up to now her behaviour had often been characterized by unhampered choice; from this point on she showed an increasing self-effacement, despite the vigour of her contributions to causes that now became marginal in her real life.

On 27th October 1936, Simone published an article in the periodical *Vigilance*: 'Shall We Shine our Trench Boots?' In labour circles, she wrote, we were getting accustomed to singing the *Marseillaise*. And now something else is in the air. The question is whether to take up arms on the side of Russia to destroy German and fascist militarism in Spain. Not in order to transform an international war into a civil war; quite the contrary. The talk is of 'international civil war'. And those who would not strive at all costs to prevent such an extension of the conflict are accused of advocating 'the politics of the "unprotected backside" '. Let people enlist for Spain then: they will find guns enough down there! But they will say it's not a question of war, but just of taking a firm stand until the fascist powers retreat. A singular lack of logic, remarks Simone Weil. For the fascist states will never shrink from the disasters that a war would provoke. And then?

'Between one government that does not shrink from war and another that does, the second will be generally at a disadvantage in international negotiations. The choice is between prestige and peace. No matter whether the rallying-cry is the Fatherland, or democracy, or revolution, the policy of prestige is the policy of war.'

The alternatives were to lay wreaths on the tomb of Poincaré (one of Simone Weil's whipping boys) or—and this went for both sides—to cease trumpeting defiance. If civil war must of necessity become international war, there is but one valid conclusion to be drawn: civil war must also be avoided.

The editors of *Vigilance* had a good card to play, of course, in calling attention to Simone's having spent the summer in Spain.

On the surface, Simone Weil's thesis gives no reply to the essential question: 'Is it possible to stop the imperialist expansion of the totalitarian powers by renouncing prestige politics?' However, her answer is implicit: there is no way of side-tracking an imperialist expansion. Simone Weil seems to have been unaware of the implication: to prevent the shock of two rival expansions which would mean war, the only way to resolve the tensions of 1936 was simply to give way to the side that was most aggressive politically. This veiled solution of the problem posed by German and Italian foreign policy was so far from corresponding with the views of the readers of French newspapers that they never even considered it.

Three articles on French colonialism were written in the same vein: 'A Few Historical Remarks about Morocco' appeared in *Syndicats* on 4th February 1937. The French occupation of Moroccan territory, according to this article, was the primary cause of the war of 1914. Because she was frustrated in her colonial ambitions, Germany had recourse to force of arms, Simone declares. Now that once again Germany contests the colonial clauses of the Treaty of Versailles, she writes, we hope that she will not meet so determined an opposition as that which drove her to suicide in 1914.

On 10th February 1937, again in *Vigilance*, Simone took up the same theme in an ironic tone: 'Morocco, or of Prescription in Matters of Theft'. Isn't Morocco an 'essentially French province'? It seems almost incredible that Germany should show some inclination to wrench the Moroccan people from the traditions inherited from their ancestors, those fair-haired Gauls with blue eyes. What, then, is the history of French Morocco?

France had, in fact, annexed Morocco as the result of a treaty concluded with England in 1904; England got Egypt; France took Morocco. 'As France is always loyal, this partition was written only in the secret clauses of the treaty. The published clauses had actually guaranteed with due solemnity the independence of Morocco.' As for the treaty of Algeciras of 1906, the only problem it presented to France was how to violate it. 'Indeed, this treaty was wholly devoid of legitimacy, since it did not grant Morocco to France. This point should be clear to the meanest intelligence.'

What was there in common between the violation of the pact of Algeciras and that of the Treaty of Versailles? 'These two cases have nothing in common. The pact of Algeciras was unfavourable to France; it was therefore dead from the start. The Treaty of Versailles was to be eternally binding for the opposite reason.' Peace, according to the ironic conclusion of Simone Weil—who did not seem to appreciate the literal truth of such a statement at that time—depends upon the economic, political, and military inferiority of Germany.

On 25th March 1937, in *Feuilles Libres de la Quinzaine*, Simone published a second article, also full of irony, on the North African problem. The Popular Front administration had been in power 'for three quarters of a year', but it had scarcely had time to pay attention to the millions of workers who lived in despair throughout the whole French empire. They were far away, those poor people; and the gravity of injustice diminishes, as is well known, in proportion to the distance. It seemed that these 'natives' were a species apart; they were accustomed to suffering. And, what was more, the handful of agitators and hot-heads who protested about them were in the pay of Hitler. Up till then there had been nothing spectacular in their suffering: 'All the little ten- or twelve-year-olds who were starving and overworked, who perished of exhaustion in the mines of Indo-China . . . had died without bloodshed. Such deaths didn't count; they were not real deaths.' For the bourgeois, social issues only began to matter when they gave rise to 'news sensational enough to displace crime from the front page'. So long as the colonial tragedy did not make the headlines, the French appeared incapable of paying it any attention. And it wasn't so much the government that was to blame: a government only does what it is told to do. It is public opinion that is guilty, guilty of a lack of concern. If there were deaths, they were 'deaths which were not on the agenda'.

She concluded with a prophecy: 'When I think of an eventual war, the fear and the horror which such a prospect inspires is mingled in my mind, I must confess, with a thought that is to some degree consoling. It is that a European war might perhaps be the signal for the great revolt of the colonial peoples to punish our indifference, our cleverness and our cruelty.'

'Though this isn't a promising outlook, it does in a way fulfil the need for immanent justice.'

But the colonial question did not preoccupy Simone Weil completely. She had not been back from Spain long when she resumed her studies of the current French social crisis, to which she had devoted so much time and thought before her departure. On 23rd October 1936, in *Le Libertaire*, she published an analysis of the statement of the CGT which had just called upon the workers to keep calm. While forbidding herself any easy dis-agreement over the issue—'It is all too easy to be perpetually an extremist'—she had to confess that the statement of the CGT disturbed her in a good many ways. She believed it would be disastrous if the trade-union movement showed signs of weak-ness after the great upheaval of June 1936. It was necessary to bear in mind two possible dangers: the first would be to continue carrying on indefinitely a sterile agitation without clear objectives; the second, to surrender the power and dignity that the working class had only barely recovered by the strikes in June. Nothing would better serve the ends of both the communists and the fascists than agitation. 'It is in the interests of the Communist Party to keep the factories in a constant state of upheaval, as a means of blackmailing the government in the matter of foreign policy.' But the working class ought in no way to allow itself to be used as the 'bargaining counter' by one side or the other. As for the second danger, according to Simone Weil, both the procedures of conciliation and arbitration were dangerous: this was the lesson to be learnt from events in Germany. 'Compulsory arbitration, by delivering the whole of social life into the hands of the State, prepares the workers to accept what we regard as the greatest of all evils: the totalitarian State.' In addition, it was equally erroneous to suppose that workers could ever, under any circumstances, agree that the right to work and rights of property could be treated on the same level. But this was what had been implied—how could any working-class organization dare to suggest such a thing?—by the statement of the CGT: 'Work stands for men toiling. Property stands for things, for stone, wood and metal. The ever-enduring claim of the working class is that we should one day, at last, pay more respect to men than to things.'

In *Le Libertaire* of 4th December, Simone Weil published a report on the recent metal workers' congress. 'To anyone who knows what a factory is like and takes part in a congress of this type, it is astounding to discover how little relationship there is between the daily life of the workers and what is discussed in their own organization.' All the real problems—sometimes urgent problems—disappear by sleight-of-hand; they are not even spoken of. There are no discussions of compulsory arbitration, the pace of work, factory discipline, and, above all, the control that should be exercised by the workers. 'Faced with such grave problems, the metal workers' congress showed itself not only incapable of resolving them but even of stating them.' What was behind this? 'The ruthless domination of a political party which

is pursuing quite other ends than the welfare of the workers.'
Also, it might be added, the inertia of the workers themselves.

There was nothing new in all this: Simone Weil still clung to
old habits of thought, even while they were losing their hold over
her. This can be seen in the article she published in *La Révolution
Prolétarienne* of 10th February 1937. It was about the congress of
the Union des Syndicats of the Paris region, the first congress to
be held since the merging of the two hitherto rival organizations,
the CGT and the CGTU. Much is to be hoped for and much is
to be feared from this merger, Simone Weil wrote. To all intents
and purposes, it was a congress of the CGTU. The atmosphere
was at the same time that of a political meeting and of a religious
ceremony: there were ritual crowd movements, prearranged
applause, organized uproar—'the whole show was stage-managed
on Moscow lines'. And yet, the three days' session had been
concerned with other things besides singing the *Internationale*.
'They dealt with the union problems listed on the agenda. . . .
It had been possible . . . to abstain from taking part in the ritual
demonstrations without being threatened with a fist in one's face.'
The congress was held in the same hall where, three years
before, a militant communist had 'charmingly promised to put
a bullet through a minority-member who had committed the
crime of not raising his fist during the singing of the *Internationale*.'

But though it had been possible to speak with some freedom,
the real issues had not been raised. In their progress reports
the leaders had had the temerity to insert one sentence asserting
that the spearhead of fascism had been liquidated in the USSR,
and another affirming that the new Soviet constitution was the
most democratic in the world. The comrades of *La Révolution
Prolétarienne*—Hagnauer, Fronty, Delsol, Guigui and others—
had valiantly challenged this assertion. Charbit had enlarged
upon the dilemma: either the crimes laid to the charge of those
condemned by the Moscow trials had actually been committed
by them, in which case the scandal was greater than anything
to be seen in the capitalist countries; or else the charges were
false, and in that case the Moscow trials were proof of a tyranny
unequalled in contemporary history. In the course of this inter-
pellation, M. Le Hénaff is said to have let fall some ominous

words: Let the Russians dispose of their own traitors and let the French deal with theirs. Observing that nothing is more elastic than the definition of the word 'traitor', Simone Weil observed: 'I am sure we would be well advised at all costs not to take a walk in the Bois de Boulogne.'

Simone Weil could find no words to describe the baseness and brutality with which the Russian delegate spoke about the last recent batch of political prisoners who had been shot. 'This apology for murder was greeted by the delegates rising to their feet and singing the *Internationale*, as prescribed. . . . Have we ever seen anything like it ? . . . The working-class movement was not made to howl for anyone's death. In the glorification of a sentence of death there is something deeply repugnant to the conscience of the working class.'

The syndicalist elections took place; as it was foreseen, they confirmed the grip that the Communist Party had over the movement. The operation had been very cleverly carried out: discussion had been prolonged to the late hours; the voting took place at the end of that cunning manoeuvre—'a small point, this, but very indicative of the prevailing atmosphere'. What conclusion could be drawn? The CGT was in danger: 'There can be no doubt that a CGT subjected to the Communist Party would be a mere appendage to the Russian State, a means of blackmailing the government; strikes would be started or stopped without any regard for the welfare of the workers; so that the CGT would become the principal factor of sacrosanct unity, of chauvinism and war. Now is the moment when all this is beginning to come true.' A severe judgment—a solemn verdict upon French trade unionism!

It was whilst all this was going on that Simone Weil was commissioned to make a report to the CGT on the state of affairs in the north.[1] She observed, first of all, that the strike in June had eased the situation, allowing the workers to return to their 'natural rhythm of work'. This element of progress had its negative counterpart: the quality of work, and of professional discipline, had clearly deteriorated. The workers' delegates, for their part, had taken all the credit for recent reforms and had escaped from that allegiance which they normally owed to their union mandates. It seemed to Simone Weil that the CGT should bring all its weight to bear on questions of work discipline, output, and the censuring of such delegates. Up to a point, at this time, there was agreement between the interests of management and of the working-class movement. Simone Weil warned that such agreement must not blind one to the nature of the relations which tend to unite owners and workers, but that it could be used to consolidate the reforms recently made since management considers them as a lesser evil than continued social strife.

While the crisis of authority was disrupting union effectiveness, factory workers were struggling with a similar problem. Just these words—'A Crisis of Authority'—were chosen by Simone Weil for the title of an article that appeared in *Syndicats* on 11th February 1937. She conceded that, without doubt, management has the right to exact obedience in all production matters. But since June 1936, she noted, the character of authority had changed: a restraint had been placed upon it. No longer could the worker be treated simply as a material more pliant, more flexible and more malleable than the material he handles. In the past, management had bowed before the blind forces of technology, but never allowed any person to question orders. The exercise of authority had been all too easy. Now, management had to consider the degree of difficulty involved in carrying out orders. In other words, the human factor had to be taken into account. Whatever hardships the worker incurred in the name of obedience now had their counterpart on the managerial level, where the efficacy of a plan was restricted in proportion to administrative inability to apply it judiciously.

In an article entitled 'Guiding principles for a New Administrative System in Industrial Enterprises',[2] Simone Weil tried to define the nature of the compromise that would weigh workers' rights against the material interests of production. She foresaw reforms which have since become standard operating procedures. In her insistence on the rational organization of man-power through the enlightened co-operation of all workers in the productive process, she even seems to be ahead of our own time.

On 23rd February 1937, Simone Weil lectured before an audience of workers on the subject of 'rationalization'. All that remains are a few notes taken down by a listener. The great problem of production, as she saw it, was respect for the dignity of the workers: 'A factory ought to be organized in such a way that the raw materials that it processes will turn into products neither too scarce nor too expensive, nor in any way defective, and also at the same time so organized that the men who go to work in the morning do not leave physically or morally the worse for wear in the evening, either at the end of a day, at the end of a year or after twenty years.'

This principle was overlooked by Frederick W. Taylor, the American management expert of the mid-nineteenth century. Attempts to improve on his methods had not ameliorated the situation. On the contrary, since they all aimed at increasing productivity, they had resulted in a rhythmic acceleration of work at the expense of that personal attention and creativity which had given a certain value to the worker's activity.

At the same time as Simone Weil was writing about problems of labour and management, she was also concerned with the question of war and peace. This was the theme of her article entitled 'Let Us Not Have Another Trojan War' which appeared in *Les Nouveaux Cahiers* of 1st and 15th April 1937 and has been recently republished in *Selected Essays* under the heading 'The Power of Words'. It is a brilliant piece, and even more striking in its style and its relentless and implacable logic than 'Reflections on war' or 'Are we moving towards a proletarian revolution?' For in it she unfolds, with new method, rigour, and logic, a theme familiar to philosophers such as Pierre Charron, who in this respect belonged, like Pascal, to the tradition of Montaigne: 'Let us call to minde that the greatest alterations of the world, the most generale and fearfule agitations of States and Empires, armies, battels, murthers have risen from light, ridiculous and vain causes, witness the wars of *Troy* and *Greece*, of *Silla* and *Marius*, *Cesar* and *Pompey*, *Augustus* and *Antony*. The Poets signifie as much, when they set all *Greece* and *Asia* on fire for an Apple. The first occasions and motives arise of nothing, afterwards they grow and increase: a testimony of the vanity and folly of man.' [Charron, *Of Wisdome*, I, xxxvi, London, 1651.] Never before had the metaphysical falsehood implicit in war, been so implacably exposed.

Simone Weil wrote that the most threatening conflicts of the moment had a common trait: *no definable objective*. Though this might reassure superficial minds, she said, it constituted the real threat. History shows that those conflicts which have no objective turn out to be the most bloody and ruthless. This paradox was one of the keys to history: there was no doubt in Simone's mind that it was the key, also, to our own epoch.

The lack of any precise objective led to a measuring of the importance of the conflict solely in terms of the sacrifices it demanded; 'and since . . . the sacrifices already made continually exact further sacrifices, there can be no reason for terminating' the struggle—unless the human forces are exhausted, as they were in the Trojan War. Yet, after a lapse of three thousand years, Poincaré produced the very arguments that had induced the Greeks to take up arms: that the wrongs endured by their dead comrades had to be avenged. The Greeks spoke of their gods; we speak of plots against our economy and other such phantoms, while the true explanation of the mysterious impulse which hurls men into the most unnecessary catastrophes lies in the nature of man himself.

Could anything be more agonizing than the unreality of nearly all the conflicts that arise in modern society? 'You have only to put initial capitals to words devoid of meaning, and however little the circumstances warrant it, men will shed torrents of blood . . .' If such catastrophes are to be avoided, ideas must be clarified: words that are meaningless must be discredited; others must be defined by strict analysis. Such an effort could save many human lives. But our generation shows no capacity for it. 'Our science is filled like a shop with the most refined intellectual mechanisms for the resolution of the most complex problems, but we are almost incapable of applying elementary methods of rational thinking.' We take as absolute, black or white, good or evil, without respect to shades of meaning, words like 'nation', 'security', 'capitalism', 'fascism', 'authority', 'democracy'. And so our world is peopled with myths and monsters.

What can be cited as an example? The most tenacious myth, without doubt, is the belief in the reality of the antagonisms between nations. Anatole France said that men believed they were dying for their country when in fact they were dying for some industrialist. That was far too rosy a picture, Simone Weil declared: 'One does not even die for anything so substantial, so tangible, as an industrialist.' Is it the clash of national interests that accounts for war? Obviously not. If nations go to war because of conflicting interests, a compromise less costly than war would eventually force itself upon them: 'But when political and economic interests have no meaning apart from war, how can they be peacefully reconciled? It is the very concept of "nation" that needs to be suppressed. Or rather it is the manner in which the word is used; for the word "national" and the expressions it gives rise to, are utterly without significance, and their only substance is millions of corpses, orphans and cripples, despair and tears.'

Do we need another example? Take then the apparent opposition between fascism and communism. On analysis, we find two social and political conceptions, almost identical to one another. 'No two nations are more similar in structure than Germany and Russia.' And yet these two nations threaten each other with destruction for reasons of principle and talk about an international crusade, each pretending to regard the other as the beast of the Apocalypse. The phantom of Helen that drove Greeks and Trojans to slaughter one another is, for Simone Weil, substantial reality compared with the pretended opposition between communism and fascism.

In *Les Nouveaux Cahiers* of 15th April, Simone Weil continues the attack on such 'murderous myths', which, even in terms of the opposition between democracy and dictatorship, have far less substance than the words which express them. Many Frenchmen, for example, believed that the defeat of Germany would be a victory of democracy over dictatorship. 'In their eyes, freedom resides in the French nation, and tyranny in Germany, pretty much as the contemporaries of Molière said that a "dormitive virtue" resided in opium.' So it was too with the Spanish Civil War: one side was seen as wholly good, the other as wholly bad. And yet 'the mere fact that any hooligan could carry a gun meant that hundreds of crimes were committed daily on both sides'. Still, the very idea of an armistice remained repugnant. Both right and left wanted to fight it out to the end. To bring an end to the bloodshed was unthinkable: 'it would be displeasing to the dead,' as spake Minerva in Homer, or Poincaré in 1917. The reader of Simone Weil's article comes to wonder if it is the cold and insensate logic about death that carries with it an almost universal appeal to the living? Does the equanimity with which it settles their differences seem the shadow of the justice which they are pursuing?

But surely, Simone Weil argued, the class war was not purely a figment of the imagination. It had a better basis in fact and was, of all man's divisive forces, the most serious, having something vital, legitimate, and essential about it. She termed it 'the eternal struggle of those who obey against those who command, when the mechanism of social forces tends to crush human dignity of those at the lowest levels', and explained that it was an everlasting struggle because, whether they know it or not, those who command always tend to trample under foot the human dignity of those who are in their power. With rare exceptions, the function of command cannot be fulfilled without disrespect to the humanity of those who have to obey. For in the exercise of power, men are treated as though they were things; things that offer no resistance; not as human beings but as a kind of material that those in power find pliant and malleable. In the last analysis, the supreme sanction of authority is death: when a man is threatened with extinction, he is more malleable than inanimate matter. He condones his own servitude.

Yet, class warfare is as unreal as that of states. The terms upon which it rests are unreal. What is capitalism? For the worker, it is an abstraction to which he attributes all the sufferings that he has ever observed or endured. 'It seems to follow that a man of true character cannot help but devote his life to the destruction of capitalism or, what comes to the same thing, to revolution; for this negative meaning is the only one given today to the word revolution.'

For the worker, the struggle against the boss is mixed up with his sense of dignity; for the boss, the conflict with the 'ringleaders' is part and parcel of the faithful discharge of his function. Both beat the air. Genuine problems are side-tracked. Insofar as it is legitimate, the manager's authority 'consists exclusively in indicating what work should be done; in co-ordinating, as effectively as possible, the tasks necessary to doing it; and in controlling, by recourse to certain constraints, the effective performance of the whole'. But the worker confuses his struggle against managerial authority with 'the irrepressible protest of the human being crushed by too hard a life'. And the manager believes that a subservient and respectful atmosphere, which actually is unnecessary for the effective carrying out of his orders, is essential to maintaining his authority. When he notices any kind of revolt among his personnel, he closes his eyes to the 'physically and morally unbearable' conditions which have brought it about. This dogmatism of both sides gives rise to the belief in the myth of 'capitalism' that renders any solution impossible.

And yet, these empty notions that have caused so much bloodshed do correspond to one human group or another. 'All the absurdities that make history seem like a long delirium are rooted in one essential absurdity, that of the nature of power.' Myths take on a shape and substance when they are related to power; they become living, breathing, man-devouring monsters. Helen symbolized the might of power to the Trojans and could not be returned without an avowal of weakness. And in Spain where two virtually identical ideologies were in conflict—in a virtual collusion to shed human blood it seemed—the search for peace had been banned as by mutual consent, since all initiative for broaching the subject would have marked a difference between partners in pride, as between the one strong enough to be merciless, and the other one weak enough to want mercy.

In every society, whether this be a cultural entity, as in Greece, or a national entity, as in Spain, there is an inherent contradiction which shapes its discords. They arise from the discrepancy between the forces at the disposal of opposing groups and the prestige that is related to success or the promise of success. These forces are limited, measurable, definable, and should not be expended beyond reason. They are, in spite of their opposition, a principle of social stability, since they find their own point of equilibrium in what is called 'the balance of forces'. But prestige s a kind of metaphysical parasite whose claims are limitless, immeasurable, undefinable. 'Every gratification of prestige to

159

one is an assault on the prestige or dignity of another.' In practice, power and prestige are inseparable in the minds of men. Society is thus divided into groups whose mass or whose means measure their power but whose affinity for prestige is infinite. This contradiction renders impossible both logic and peace: 'Not only does this cloud of vacuous entities hide from us the nature of the problem, but it also prevents us from realizing that there is a problem to be solved and not a fatality to be endured . . . The *tracking down of such myths* in all spheres of political and social life is a task of great urgency in the interest of public health and welfare.' The objective precludes all appeasement predicated on the *status quo*. The struggle must go on. Did not Heraclitus say that struggle was 'the condition of life itself'?

This indictment of war as a conflict based on a play on words, and on sleight of hand by which limited means and aims take on a vested interest in infinity, marks a dividing line in Simone Weil's life. In her forceful, ironic article she castigates power, nationalism, and patriotism in a clearer voice than ever before, while over-stepping the issue of pacifism. She reaches her true depth as a political analyst: the past is used as a clue to the present, from which, in turn, it derives its meaningfulness in historical perspective. Paradoxically, these reflections that breathe with Simone's usual prophetic fire, also convey an impression of serenity, as of one seeing things from afar . . .

### The Divine Revelation

Early in 1937, Simone Weil visited the winter resort of Montana, in Switzerland. From there, she crossed the border into Italy, taking the passport she had used in Spain, which bore the stamp of the Anti-fascist Spanish Militia. This act of bravado, however, passed unnoticed. In her letters at that time, and in recollections, she traced her route and her experiences from Pallanza, through Stresa, Milan and Bologna, Ferrara, Ravenna, Florence and Rome, to Assisi, and back to Florence.[1]

She was in Milan on the day following the announcement of a wage increase of 10 to 12 per cent. This good news, heralded by the press, left no trace in the faces of passers-by, Simone observed, as she walked through the workers' quarters. 'I read in their eyes, alas, what I used to read in the eyes of my fellow-workers, and what had been in my own at the most painful moments': a sense of servitude, a feeling of oppression which weighed upon all.

However, the peasants of Italy remained true to tradition: the noble Umbrian peasants—'a handsome race, so healthy, so vital, so joyful and so gentle' whom Simone admired in Assisi; or the young men who came in from the country to the market at Ravenna, with their inborn dignity and simple bearing.

At the same time, she was by no means indifferent to current political issues. In Florence, she went to the headquarters of the Fascist Party; introducing herself as a socialist, she met one of the minor officials of the organization who was very cordial and asked for her address. All during the next year he showered fascist pamphlets on her family in Paris. Elsewhere, she had been able to speak openly with a young fascist, Lucien A., 'one of those characters full of repressed enthusiasm and lofty, unavowed ambitions', who told her candidly that her 'normal and legitimate place in society' was 'at the bottom of a salt mine.'

'A mine would seem less stifling to me than this atmosphere, this obsessive nationalism, this worship of force in its most brutal form—namely, collectivity . . . this disguise for the deification of death.'

Like other tourists, Simone had come to Italy to enjoy looking at its masterpieces of art. She spent hours in contemplation before *The Last Supper*, observing how Leonardo da Vinci had created an effect of perspective and depth by directing the lines in the ceiling and those which link the hands of the apostles towards a single invisible point in the hair of Christ: 'This convergence . . . exists only in the two-dimensional space which the picture constitutes, not in the three-dimensional space that it gives the impression of. . . . There is, therefore, a twofold composition: one in the two-dimensional space; the other in the three-dimensional space; the eye is led from all directions towards the face of Christ by an unperceived, hidden force, which gives it an almost supernatural serenity.'

In Florence—'her' city, in which she had lived 'a prior life'—

she was kept inside the Medicis Chapel by the springtime rain and her fascination with Michelangelo's reclining figures. His *Dawn* suggested the bitter awakening of a slave, anticipating a day of crushing work; his *Night*, a slave seeking in sleep not a restoration, but a refuge from despair. Simone related this feeling of oppression to the period during which these sculptures had been made, the beginning of the reign of Alessandro de' Medici (the despot killed by Lorenzaccio of Musset's tragedy). And she pondered the nature of the ties which link artistic creativity to political freedom, as she reflected on the turbulent history of Florence: 'We may conclude, on the whole, that the epochs of creative initiative, of ebullient intellectual life, are also periods of great liberty and even civil disorder; that in the wake of such periods, only strong authority can favour their further development by bringing about stability and by compelling thought to concentrate itself and find expression through roundabout ways, a situation no less favourable to art, which thrives on transposition.'

In Rome, at the Vatican, she observed how, in the Greek sculptures which pre-date Phidias, 'the stone seemed a liquid substance which has overflowed in sheets and settled afterwards in a perfect balance. The kinship between flow and balance arises from the fact that a liquid is rendered motionless by equilibrium alone, whilst a solid is maintained by its internal cohesion.'[2] She was also deeply moved by the liturgy, which attained that 'union of all arts sought by Wagner'.

It is in Assisi, however, that Simone Weil found her native element: 'I have been struck with awe in these mellow fields, so marvellously Franciscan and evangelic, impressed with fervour in these chapels, and by the host of blessed memories they awakened . . .' But why is it that 'everything in Assisi and in the neighbourhood is Franciscan, except what has been done in honour of St Francis', exclusive of Giotto's frescoes? It seemed to Simone that Providence had taken a hand in shaping 'these happy fields and these humble and touching oratories' as a mirror for the Poverello's sun-blessed spirit of joyful detachment, in whose spiritual wake she herself was caught: 'As I was alone in the little twelfth-century Romanesque chapel of Santa Maria degli Angeli, a rare wonder of purity in which Saint Francis often prayed, something stronger than myself compelled me, for the first time in my life, to go down on my knees.'[3] In these terms, she later described to Father Perrin, a Dominican priest with whom she was to become friendly, how an aesthetic impression was transmuted into a religious experience.

The impact of this journey on her artistic temperament was no less enduring: it gave rebirth, she acknowledges in one of her 1938 letters, to her 'vocation for poetry, which had been repressed since adolescence for several reasons'.

More than a year later, in the summer of 1938, Simone Weil returned to Italy, to Asolo, a small, picturesque old city on a hill near Treviso, north of Venice. At the approach to the town, by the road which climbs up from the valley below, the Chapel of Sant'Angelo is one of the first buildings to catch the eye. The tourist who wishes to visit it must ask for the key at the presbytery of the parish church, on the town square. Upon entering the chapel, he may be disheartened by the sight of pieces of coloured plaster that have flaked from the frescoes on to the ground and benches. Simone Weil was shocked by this neglect, already obvious in her day, and wrote an article that underlined the main reason for her concern: beneath the crumbling fifteenth-century fresco, on the right-hand wall, 'an extraordinary Romanesque fresco' was coming to light.

'This fresco is made up, essentially, of two large standing figures, of a monumental aspect, which strike one especially by a quality which gives the fresco a character of its own in all Italian Romanesque art; this is due to the fact that the faces are completely alien to any Italian or European type. They are broad, rather than long, the cheek-bones are very prominent, the eyes are distinctly narrow; flat nose and thick lips almost suggest a Negroid type. All this imparts to the figure on the left an indescribable effect of barbaric majesty and terror, while the figure on the right has an altogether more serene dignity and seems to represent a woman.'[4]

She supposed that these two barbaric figures must date from some time in the tenth century, when Magyar hordes had occupied Asolo, driving out the bishop. 'Standing in that grim presence one could not but wonder what spiritual life could have been like in this city, deprived for fifty years of its natural ruler, burdened by the memory of so dreadful an invasion and given up to all the terrors of that harrowing tenth century.' But the aesthetic character of the work impressed her no less than the ethnological problem it suggested: 'It is impossible to express the impression of grandeur, of fierce strength and beauty, made by this fresco of unforgettable faces even when placed alongside the most famous masterpieces of Italian art.'

Simone Weil brought the matter to the attention of 'several important townspeople', but to no avail. She had been the first to notice the second fresco. The article she wrote was belatedly published in the June number of *Il Ponte* in 1951. It had stimulated an investigation, described in the same issue, which was conducted by Cesare Favola of the Gallery of Florence. He reports that more extensive damage was clearly disclosing three levels of frescoes where Simone had only discovered two. In the centre, at the earliest level (which dated, like the church, from the thirteenth century), stood the 'Magyar'-like, but truly Gothic figure, with the narrow eyes; to the right, a handsome youth in the dress of a deacon whose face alone could have been visible in 1938; to the left a recent flaking revealed, on the second level, the face of a woman painted in the fourteenth century.

How was it possible for Simone Weil to have placed a tenth-century mural on a thirteenth-century wall?

In his Introduction to *l'Attente de Dieu* (1948 ed.), Father Perrin tells of a brief exchange between Simone Weil and one of her friends, an historian. Simone argued: 'But Herodotus has said that . . .' The friend interrupted: 'You should criticize his statement; look into its background and question its meaning.' Simone asked indignantly: 'Why should I criticize Herodotus!' 'Because he is open to criticism.'

Less than a factual recording of events, history was, for Simone Weil (as for all true disciples of Alain), the treasure-house of wisdom and experience of the ages—and above all, for her, the repository of a tradition of spiritual life: a poem of mankind had been registered on the crumbling walls of time which our devout restoration, in the inner cell of individual memory, or in the social pattern of our lives, allowed a brief but magnificent respite against the 'terrors' of our 'harrowing . . . century'.

Precise evaluation of fact, whether in the history of art or in the history of religion into which Simone Weil was soon to enter, was too shallow a concern for one viewing the shadows of eternal ideas on the walls of the world's cavern, not as a silhouette carefully to be delineated, but as an image of the truth itself to be contemplated.

Yet pictures do appear on walls, less as a projection—except in terms of individual non-historical consciousness—than as a coating for the aging plaster and the supporting stone and mortar. But Simone's telescopic sights were set for the whole of things, and not for the careful scrutiny of detail, which plagued her as something she neither had the patience to resolve, nor the heart to neglect. Hence both her vast vistas, encompassing aeons of cultural drift and change; hence her tremendous erudition which accumulated true and proven data, as well as the hypothetical, without the practical possibility of discrimination.

Simone Weil returned to teaching in October 1937. She had been appointed to the lycée of Saint-Quentin, a town of 50,000, situated some sixty miles to the north of Paris, famous for its large Gothic church and its museum of Latour's pastels. Since it is almost within commuting distance from the capital, Simone could go there easily on weekends.

Fragmentary and inadequate though they are, the notes taken by Simone Weil's Saint-Quentin pupils reveal astonishing changes in teaching methods in comparison with those from her previous teaching.

Subjects were presented differently. At Le Puy, Auxerre, Roanne, and Bourges, Simone had followed the official programme of studies even if she only covered it partially. Now, inexplicably, she departed from it. She applied, for example, the favourite teaching precept of Alain: to pass from the concrete to the abstract. Not that she had ever neglected concrete examples or experimental data. But instead of choosing her teaching material from philosophical work, she drew now upon literature: Balzac's *Le Curé de Tours*, Saint-Exupéry's *Vol de Nuit*, etc.

Simone's class read Balzac's *Colonel Chabert*. Their attention was directed to the following phrase: 'the kind of humility which

165

gives a false appearance to gestures of unhappy men'. It prompted a series of conclusions on the kind of behaviour which circumstances impose on a man and how his freedom is thereby violated:

'The way a man behaves depends more on his situation than on his nature.

Analogy with Homer: Zeus, who hurls thunderbolts, gives mixed gifts, sometimes to good purpose, sometimes to bad.

But he to whom Zeus gives none but disastrous gifts is exposed to every sort of outrage.

An ill fate pursues him all over the divine earth.

He wanders abandoned by both gods and men.

For the immediate reaction to human wretchedness is contempt.'[5]

For this reaction, there was a remedy, according to Simone Weil:

'The Christian revolution consisted in not despising the weak. The God of the Christians is weak.

According to Valéry, goodness consists in not blaming the unhappy for their unhappiness, and this is very difficult.'

Considered in the light of what Simone Weil was to write later in *Waiting on God*, her thought seems to take a prophetic turn. If there were no other traces of Simone's stay at Saint-Quentin, statements such as those in her pupils' notebooks would be enough to prove that she had taught there. 'Whenever the soul is assailed by the terror of the supernatural, numbers have considerable power.' Obviously, numbers are reassuring, and the positivists use them to dispose scientifically of the anxieties of the soul.

'[One must] attain to the greatest possible range of one's thoughts.'

'What situations are most favourable to the forming of eternal thoughts?'

'If it is true that society is founded only upon relations of force and if it is true that the soul is subjected to outside pressures, nothing is more injurious to man than society.'

' "The Great Beast" [society in its evil aspects] thinks that the earth is round.'

'A village voted that the earth was round.'

'How will the soul be saved after the Great Beast has acquired an opinion about everything?'

The 'social' thinking of Simone Weil had taken definitive shape:

'A genius is he who ordinarily has thoughts which are beyond the influence of the Great Beast.'

'A genius is a man who has known how to remain as intelligent at eighty as he was when he was two.'

Other works were studied during the course of this school year: *The Iliad* (which inspired initially the ideas later given form in an article on 'the poem of force'), and the Platonic dialogues, 'Theaetetus' and 'Gorgias.' On the reading list, too, were *The Last Viking* by Johan Bojer and *The Life of the Eskimos* by Jan Welz, from which dramatic episodes were drawn by the teacher to illustrate certain immemorial truths, much as Saint-Exupéry does in his novels: 'When, in a situation that is weighing heavily upon him, a man assumes the part of a spectator, he is sublime.' Why did Simone choose such minor works to make a point such as this? She could have drawn from the wealth of French literature the classic example of a man transcending conflict: Augustus of *Cinna* pardoning his would-be assassins, because he sees his act from the vantage-point of posterity. But then Simone did not like Corneille's conception of Roman *grandeur d'âme*.

Similarly, it is Guillaumin's *Life of a Simple Soul* which suggests the following words that might have been inspired by *The Imitation of Christ* by Thomas a Kempis: 'For joy to be had on earth without changing the laws of necessity, it is not the great things that must be changed, but the little things, which for the soul are precisely the great things.'

That year, Simone Weil did not wait until the third term before giving written essays to her pupils. Topics such as the following were given from the beginning:

'Society and the individual.'

'Imagine what would come to pass in the mind of a man born blind, after operations had removed the cataract from one eye, and then from the other after an interval of a fortnight (a question taken from Alain's recollections of Lagneau).'

Simone Weil's methods of teaching in class were not, however, appreciated by her superiors who, without seeming to have known her very well, nevertheless described her in official reports.

'Perhaps her method is not sufficiently scholastic for very average children,' wrote the head-mistress of the lycée. The inspector of schools found that she 'lectured without appearing to think of the pupils, who were writing without having the time to think'. Yet her superiors were well aware of Simone's intrinsic worth. The head-mistress explains her shortcomings in performance through her 'very mediocre state of health, which endangers practical results'.

In fact, headaches did interfere with Simone Weil's teaching, preventing her from giving undivided attention to her classes. Later, she described her suffering as a 'pain situated around the central point of the nervous system, at the point of junction between soul and body, which goes on even through sleep, never ceasing for a second'.[6] This crippling torment affected her to a point where she had to discontinue her courses.

'Yet a moment came when I felt threatened, through exhaustion and the aggravation of pain, with such a hideous decay of the whole soul that for several weeks I asked myself with anguish if death were not for me the most imperative of duties, even though the thought that my life would end in horror was unbearable to me . . . Only a resolution of conditional death, at a given time, brought back my serenity.'

In January 1938, she was given sick-leave until June. The many neurologists she consulted brought her no relief. She then became convinced that she was suffering from an abscess on the brain and saw herself lapsing into a state of slow mental decay from which desperate measures alone could save her. In a doctor's waiting-room, she said to her father: 'If the doctor recommends an operation, let him operate at once.' But this specialist was no more able than his predecessor to reach a diagnosis or prescribe an effective treatment.

In the early spring of 1938, impelled by aesthetic rather than religious motives, Simone Weil, still agnostic, went to the Benedictine monastery of Solesmes, which was famous for its plain-chant. Her headaches persisted. They accompanied her throughout the services, which she attended for more than eight hours a day. Each sound, each word of these long ceremonies struck at her exacerbated sensibility like a blow on a raw nerve. The effort she made to concentrate on the religious rites, which seemed at first beyond her strength, brought about a helpful division between spirit and flesh—the first wholly rejoicing in the beauty of the liturgy, the second cast aside, left behind, thrust in a suffering heap of pain thrown in a corner. Through this division, she came to understand 'the practical possibility of loving divine love in spite of pain and suffering'. And whilst she meditated (almost unceasingly during the ten days of her 'retreat'), into her soul, now liberated from its bondage of pain if not from pain itself, the image of Christ entered, 'once and for all'. [7]

Of equal significance was her meeting with a young Englishman. 'From the angelic radiance which seemed to clothe him as he was returning from communion', she wrote, she conceived 'for the first time the idea of the supernatural power of the sacraments'. Yet the full benefit of their encounter was derived from a more intellectual association: it was he who introduced her, in the course of their conversations, to the English metaphysical poets of the seventeenth century—George Herbert, John Donne, Richard Crashaw—to whom she responded immediately.

Back in Paris, she shared her new poetic interests with her mother. Her own preferences are stated in a list in her own hand at the end of her collection of Herbert's poems: 'Love', 'Discipline', 'Bitter Sweet', 'The Cellar', 'Dialogue', 'Justice', 'Denial', 'Affliction', 'Redemption'. Of these, 'Love' was her favourite; and she used to recite it by heart, sometimes with her mother, or else by herself.

> *Love bade me welcome; yet my soul drew back,*
> *    Guiltie of dust and sinne,*
> *But quick-ey'd Love, observing me grow slack*
> *    From my first entrance in,*
> *Drew nearer to me, sweetly questioning*
> *    If I lack'd any thing.*
>
> *A guest, I answer'd, worthy to be here:*
> *    Love said, You shall be he.*
> *I the unkinde, ungratefull? Ah my deare,*
> *    I cannot look on thee.*

## 'Christe Himself came down . . .'

*Love took my hand, and smiling did reply,*
*Who made the eyes but I?*

*Truth Lord, but I have marr'd them; let my shame*
*Go where it doth deserve.*
*And know you not, sayes Love, who bore the blame?*
*My deare, then I will serve.*
*You must sit down, sayes Love, and taste my meat:*
*So I did sit and eat.*

As with the Gregorian plain-chant at Solesmes, Simone was at first conscious only of the aesthetic quality of Herbert's work: 'I used to think that I was merely saying beautiful verse; but though I did not know it, the recitation had the effect of a prayer. And it happened that [in the autumn of 1938] as I was saying this poem . . . Christ Himself came down, and He took me.'

In the stillness of the senses, the imagination being mute and the body held in the thrall of suffering, Simone Weil was brought into 'the presence of a love similar to the one expressed in the smile on the face of a beloved one'.

Yet she had always denied the possibility of 'a real contact, from person to person, here on earth, between a human being and God'. There could be no solution to the problem of God, she had said. However, without the wishful causality, the spirit of anticipation, which lead to illusions, she had felt the touch of the divine: 'Christ Himself came down, and He took me.'

A world of boundless dimensions opened up before her, the 'breadth, and length, and depth, and height'[8] of which cannot be recorded, but which Simone attempted to suggest in the language best suited for these metaphysics of love. Thus, to be 'taken into the arms of Love' is a metaphor for a spiritual event which known reality cannot directly signify:

'Space seemed to be torn open. Leaving the wretched body abandoned in a corner, the spirit was lifted to a point outside space, which was not a point of view, from which there was no perspective, and from which this visible world was seen as real, without perspective.

'In relation to what it had been in the egg, space became an infinity to the second or rather to the third power. The instant was motionless.

'Although a few sounds may be heard, all space is full of a dense silence which is not an absence of sound, but a positive object of sensation, more positive than a sound: the secret word, the word of Love which from the beginning has held us in his arms.'[9]

This atmosphere of familiarity between Creator and creature is restated in many passages, though they relate to later experiences in which 'the visible world' is not only seen 'as real', but described in full:

'He came into my room and said: "Come with me and I shall teach you things of which you know nothing. . . ."

'He led me out again and took me to an attic from which, through the open window, the whole town could be seen, some wooden scaffoldings, the river where boats were being unladen. He made me sit down.

'We were alone. He spoke. Occasionally, someone entered and joined in the conversation, then left again. . . .

'At times he would fall silent, take some bread from a cupboard, which we shared between us. This bread really tasted like bread. I have never again found that taste.

'He poured out, for me and for himself, wine which tasted of the sun and of the soil upon which this city was built.'[10]

In this unbounded world, where the second and the third power of infinity were surpassed, a sequence of events unfolded, inside a city, by a river, beneath a sky lit by a sun that was not of this world.

However, when the familiar landmarks of everyday occurrences entered again into the field of perception, when the vision of things not seen disappeared, the soul reflected on its experience. In a perspective of time, and with words misapplied for such use, the supernatural event was measured and interpreted according to previous beliefs.

In terms of duration, the experience had been brief, perhaps instantaneous. It carried no message, but impressed a conviction: the certitude of love. God and man could not communicate, had been Simone's belief. Yet now, they had entered into communion!

Therefore, she qualified her belief: God could not communicate anything to man, except Himself:

'He had promised to teach me, yet he taught me nothing. We spoke of all sorts of things without plan and without order, as old friends do.

'One day he said: "Now, go." I fell down before him, I clasped his knees, begging him not to drive me away. But he put me out on the stairs. I went down knowing nothing, my heart broken. I wandered about the streets. Then I discovered that I had no idea where that house was . . .

'I know well that he does not love me. How could he love me? And yet something deep within me, some part of me cannot help thinking, with fear and trembling, that perhaps in spite of everything, he loves me.'

Both in its surrounding circumstances and in its characteristic features, Simone Weil's experience bears the stamp of an authentic mysticism: the suffering which preceded it robbed her of her self-will; she was bereft of foreknowledge or initiative; the ecstasy she felt bore no relation to known feeling, except analogically. Yet the interpretation that she gives is uniquely hers, down to the poetic transcription and the underlying philosophy. She follows therefore in the tradition of a long line of great thinkers and spiritual authors, among whom is Pascal.

The prominence of the aesthetic factor is further emphasized in her three poems of metaphysical inspiration: 'The Sea', 'To the Stars' (both as yet unpublished), 'The Gate', all written after the revelation of Christ. They constitute chronologically the first literary expression of this mystical experience. In treatment, the first two poems reflect the long-lasting admiration of Simone Weil for Valéry, the last one, her recent discovery of Herbert. In theme, they are closely connected: man's relation with nature is used as an allegory which illustrates his relation to the supernatural.

In the first poem, the sea is described as teacher. By its obedience to necessity, it resolves the conflicting claims of change and permanence:

> *Gentle sea . . . silently submissive sea,*
> *Straying sea whose waves for ever are in chains . . .*

Indifferent, yet constantly wakeful, it oscillates, yet stays in its place, evoking the notion of limitation which Simone Weil later defined in her *Notebooks*: *Limit—something which is always exceeded, but imposes a compensatory oscillation.*[11]

As if responding to the call of justice, the sea weighs in its invisible scales both its own waters and all things that float. The sea mirrors the sky as truth itself, and draws at the horizon the geometer's straight line of rectitude. The all-encompassing sea brings to man the realization of law permeating creation and of God's love permeating law:

> *To him who is sinking, speak thou before he perish,*
> *Enter even into his soul, O our sister sea;*
> *Deign to cleanse it in thy waters of justice.*

'To the Stars' described in the second poem, Simone Weil addressed a stoic's song:

> *Since it must be, we will follow you, our arms bound,*
> *Our eyes turned towards your pure and bitter radiance.*

The unfeeling and silent stars have uprooted the human heart from its yesterdays and sent it against its will into the future. Cries are of no avail. Divine grace will respond only to silent waiting and blind submission:

> *Suddenly in the heart, they are there—the divine fires.*

One must shed all that pertains to life, except life itself, and go through a kind of death: such is the moral which Simone draws in her third poem: 'The Gate'.[12]

The soul wanders along a road unfriendly to strangers, eager for the rest it will find at journey's end. The road leads to a gate, which is closed, and the soul cries out in anguish:

> *Open the gate; we will walk among the fruit-trees.*

But the barrier remains shut. For the soul dreams of flowers, fruit and water. To such desires the gate is for ever closed. The weary traveller waits in silence, looking at the immovable obstacle opposed to his longing. He turns as if to leave, having forgotten the pleasures he sought, discarded the illusions which led him on, and lost his dream. The gate will open when all hope has been abandoned, for love alone obtains what is impossible:

> *But when the gate swung open it let such a silence pass us by*
>
> *That neither fruit trees nor flowers in bloom appeared;*

*And space alone remained in its immensity, void*
*And empty, yet full of light, which overwhelmed the heart*
*And washed with tears the eyes which dust had almost blinded.*

It is plain from all the evidence previously cited that Simone Weil's experience had little in common with the conversions from sinner to saint we read about in the *Vitae Sanctorum*. Her first contact with the Divine did not result in a change of heart, but in an illumination of the soul; nor was it a negation of the past, but a new orientation towards the future, the sudden flowering of a plant which had been patiently growing since childhood. Simone Weil's interest in certain aspects of Christianity went back as far as 1935. There is nothing to indicate that, on the purely human level, any new element intruded into her life in 1938.

And yet, if the event is viewed with the hindsight of all the subsequent developments of her thought, it was like the bursting through into a new world, a new dimension, like a chrysalis out of its cocoon.

## Pacifism

In the spring of 1936 a group of writers had founded the *Nouveaux Cahiers*. Among them were Simone Weil's old friend Detœuf, and some new ones: Denis de Rougemont, Vigneaux, Laffay. Simone followed attentively the activities of this group, who called themselves 'people . . . belonging to the class called management' and explained that they sought 'to clarify their mutual ideas about the necessary reforms'.[1]

Meeting every Monday, members of the group 'invited people from different walks of life' who tried to approach current problems in a co-operative spirit. The first issue of their review appeared in March 1937. Projects for study multiplied rapidly: workers' housing, regulations for hiring and laying off, educational reform, training of personnel, etc. Personalities who were famous or were soon to become so took part in these meetings: Jean Paulhan, François Perrin, Jean Wahl, to mention only a few. Members of the group defined the 'spirit of the *Nouveaux Cahiers*': 'Its spirit is that of a group in co-operative search of positive conclusions shielded from the mass-passions.'

174

## Anti-racism and anti-Zionism

It was a programme perfectly congenial to Simone Weil, whose name often appears in the minutes of the weekly meetings. Her contributions are distinguished both by their rigorous intellectual attitude and by the strength of her opinions which reveal her pacifism and her political convictions. Having followed her development thus far, it is possible to see the extent to which her politics and her pacifism were consistent and complementary, well-articulated links in a whole philosophy. But the opinions she expressed must have disconcerted anyone unfamiliar with her ideas.

During one session when they were discussing the new racial form assumed by 'pan-Germanism', Simone Weil urged them to distinguish between two 'quite different aspects' of racialism: 1. *The idea that all groups of the same race or language as Germany fundamentally belonged to Germany.* 2. the very different idea, *that the German race is superior to any other race.*

Only the second of these ideas appeared to her to be repulsive; so monstrous in fact that it could not be anything but a theme for internal propaganda, intended to keep the people open-mouthed before 'the mirage of a great future'. At this time, the fact that Hitler's government had the practical intention of implementing this theory in international politics had not yet become evident. If the bellicose speeches aimed at German audiences and the pacific speeches meant for foreign consumption were in contradiction, it did not necessarily mean that the latter were lies. 'In short, if the actual intentions of Hitler's administration are less reasonable than he says in speeches designed to be read abroad . . . might they not be much more reasonable than one would think from his speeches to his own people?' Hitler, Simone Weil believed, had to be given the benefit of the doubt.[2]

In perspective it seems that, for love of peace, Simone Weil was viewing political trends in the light of her own wishes—that Hitler should prove, in the end, no danger to Europe. On the other hand, she always remained faithful to her principles in her judgments of political movements. For example, her anti-nationalist principles forbade her to feel any sympathy with the Zionist movement: '[She] saw yet another danger in the creation of a Jewish state in Palestine: why create a new nationality? We suffer already from the existence of young nations, born in the nineteenth century and animated by exacerbated nationalism. (One recalls what Lamartine said about the unification of Italy: let us not allow another Prussia to arise to the south-east of France.) What could be less advisable than to create a nation today, which, in fifty years, may become a threat to the Near East and to the world? The existence of an old Jewish tradition in Palestine is the best reason for creating a Jewish homeland elsewhere than in Jerusalem.'[3]

Within the *Nouveaux Cahiers* group, a special committee was given the job of studying the problems of teaching. Composed of Laffay, François Perrin, Isembert, de Tarde, and Simone Weil, it met frequently at Simone's house. She still professed great admiration for Alain, but she had no intention of being influenced by him any more. She often saw Detœuf, whose friend she had become.

According to Laffay, she could not conceal her admiration for Christian thought. She saw the Catholic Church as a symbol, a framework which created in the believer a state of mind favourable to the reception of truth. Yet she treated dogma with a certain off-handedness: 'It's all a question of interpretation.' To her friends, she seemed to be indulging an intellectual caprice. But her fundamental sincerity could not be denied.

Later, she herself wrote about this period of her life: 'Yet, I still half refused, not my love, but my intelligence. For it seemed to me certain, and I still think so today, that one can never wrestle enough with God if one does so out of pure concern for truth. Christ likes us to prefer truth to him, because before being Christ, he is truth. If one turns aside from him to go towards the truth, one will not go far before falling into his arms.'[4]

She 'turned aside' to apply herself, among other things, to the political problems of the hour. Early in 1938, these were reaching a crucial point. In March, the German army invaded Austria. Léon Blum, whose government was shortly to be out of office, gave Czechoslovakia the most formal assurance that France would honour its obligations towards her. This commitment endangered the peace, Simone Weil thought, and she expressed her concern in a violent article published in *Feuilles libres de la Quinzaine* on 25th May 1938. 'With regard to the Czechoslovakian problem,' she wrote, 'many people mistakenly refuse to face up to the implications of the most acute form it may very well take.' With hindsight it is obvious that this is precisely what Simone Weil was doing herself. What would actually happen, she asked, if Hitler had decided to gain a decisive success in Central Europe? Before answering this question, all the factors of the case would have to be carefully weighed.

Every international situation could be viewed as a question of rights, balance of power, foreign commitments, perils of war or chances of peace. On the question of rights, the oppression of the Sudeten Germans by the Czechs was a fact, even if the severity of this oppression was open to question. The Sudeten territories should therefore be returned to Germany. Strategically, this would place Czechoslovakia at the mercy of her powerful western neighbour, whose satellite she would become. If such dependence was unjust, no less unjust was the present fate of the Sudeten. Would not such a relative domination, brought about peacefully, be preferable to the wartime subjugation which a blind resistance would entail? Czechoslovakia could still preserve her culture, her language, her national characteristics. The racial ideology of Nazism, Simone argued, had nothing universal about it. 'Its only universal principles are anti-communism and anti-semitism. The Czechs can outlaw the Communist Party and exclude the Jews from the more important posts, without losing anything of their national life.'

Moreover, is it really for France to redress another's wrongs? 'In preventing the *Anschluss* for twenty years, France herself violated, in the most flagrant way, the historic right of nations to self-determination.' And if France was really concerned about rights, if she really wished to act according to principles, 'heaven knows there is no lack of peoples to emancipate in Africa and in Asia, without the risk of war'.

As for the balance of power, it was obvious that Germany had force on her side, 'for if there is to be a hegemony in Central Europe, it is in the nature of things that this will be a German hegemony'. And though it was anything but agreeable to have to say so, a German hegemony would be no whit worse than a French hegemony. Besides, it is the fate of little nations to fall under the domination of greater nations. Simone observed that many people said that it would be madness for Hitler to risk a European war for the sake of Czechoslovakia. But, she asked, is it not just 'as great a folly for England and France to run the same risk to defend her'?

In conclusion, Simone Weil admitted that Hitler was not merely seeking economic concessions in the economic field; this was not his real objective. His régime needed 'periodical and brutal' reassurances of the existence of a new Reich and of its invincible power. 'It is improbable that he can be turned back upon that road except by force of arms.' But if it came to that, how many young people and mothers in France would think it just or reasonable that French blood should flow for Czechoslovakia?

This article reflected the same rationalization that had dictated Simone Weil's commentaries on the Moroccan question. Yet once again, there was no alternative but to submit to force as the lesser evil, in a domain of which force is constitutive—that is, the domain of politics. Let us not make bad worse by deceiving ourselves on this point, Simone Weil seemed to say. If we resist force, we are making use of force. Evil cannot justify evil. And since the object of the evil is good, if we give it free rein it will attain its object even in the midst of its very excesses, which will, however, be less brutal than if it were thwarted in its aims.

In rereading the article, a partial consolation can be found in the thought that such an ultra-rational demonstration contains in itself the likelihood of a recoil. The pacifist position of Simone Weil was on the point of collapsing.

This pacifism had found expression in some other declarations. On 25th March 1938, in *Feuilles libres de la Quinzaine*, she signed a petition in favour of an 'immediate negotiation' with the fascists: 'One is bound to say, however distasteful it may seem, that the policy of Mr Chamberlain—inasmuch as its aim is to put a stop to the deadly armaments race—is actually *the only one* that, through an effective negotiation, makes an attempt at a pacification of Europe.' In its vigour and sobriety, this text expresses its point in a language which seems familiar. Did Simone Weil have a hand in drafting it? In another instance, she would not sign a petition, with which she was in full accord, unless she were allowed to redraft it.

The same issue of *Feuilles Libres*, 25th April 1938, announces a 'mass meeting of pacifists' at the Château de Moncel, in Jouy-en-Josias, near Paris . . . a meeting which would 'gather together some of the most significant figures of the pacifist movement. Maria Montessori, Simone Weil, Wilfred Wellack' were scheduled, from the 16th to 29th August to deal with 'certain aspects of the problem of war in relation to present preoccupations'.

After writing the article on Czechoslovakia, Simone Weil spent a month and a half in Venice and Asolo. On her return from Italy, she applied herself, in an article for *Essais et Combats*, to the task of pointing out 'New Factors in the Colonial Problem of the French Empire'. It is interesting to consider side by side with this the article published on 10th March 1938, in *Vigilance*, 'These Palpitating Limbs of the Fatherland'—a biting satire on the old colonialist concepts of the French colonial empire as an extension of Metropolitan France. All colonialism, she said in substance in *Essais et Combats*, tends automatically, by a sort of inertia, to keep the colonial power and the colonial people in the relationship of conquerors and conquered. The illusory peace which is the outcome of this balance of forces strangely resembles a state of war. There is nevertheless a difference: one side is deprived of arms.

This humiliating and intolerable situation would come to an end if there arose in the colonial power a wave of opinion opposed to the frightful injustices that are committed in colonies. In 1931, Louis Roubaud had published, in *Le Petit Parisien*, a series of articles full of shocking revelations on the situation in Indo-China. But the French public was as self-righteous as ever about their generosity and as blind as ever to the wrongs inflicted by their country on distant people.

On the other hand, could a victorious rising of indigenous peoples put an end to colonialism? The price they would have to pay for such independence, Simone observed, would be altogether prohibitive.

Was there, then, no other solution to the colonial problem? There remained, in her opinion, a third possibility: 'That is, that it would be in the colonial power's own interests to emancipate progressively its own colonies.'

In Europe, peace was being maintained only at the cost of the Munich concessions—concessions whose consequences were painful for those Sudeten Germans who had not been taken in by the Hitler régime, sad for Czechoslovakia, bitter for the democracies. But to the Asian and African countries, Munich had given great reason for hope. The Munich pacts had the effect of revealing that France no longer had the power to defend its far-flung empire. On the other hand, even if French settlers in the colonies were suddenly to adopt the most humane measures, this would not of itself create, in the Empire, the change of feeling necessary to the security of France.

It was necessary to set the colonial people 'effectively, and soon, on the path that would lead them from the status of subjects to that of citizens'. However, it was perhaps already too late for this. 'If, for instance, it is true that out of the millions of inhabitants of North Annam and Tonkin, some nine families out of ten had lost at least one of their members as a result of the repressive measures of 1931, those millions may not easily forgive it.'

Yet this policy of frank co-operation is the only one that offers France 'the sole chance of keeping her rank among the Great Powers, which almost all politicians consider indispensable to her security'.

From a more altruistic point of view, this policy would be of great advantage to the indigenous peoples themselves: 'The freedoms thus gained would make it possible for them to protect themselves against any kind of oppression and open the way towards a complete emancipation.'

No doubt, she wrote, 'those who are accustomed to thinking of everything under the dual categories of "revolutionary" and "reformist"—the former, in this Manichaean system, designating the good, and the latter all that is evil'—will reject this solution, alleging that it is tainted with the vice of reformism. A 'reform' of this kind would nevertheless be infinitely preferable to a victorious insurrection, for it would permit the colonies 'to achieve at least a partial liberty without being obliged to fall into a frenzy of nationalism . . . and into an excessive industrialization founded on the indefinitely prolonged poverty of the mass of the population; into an exacerbated militarism, and the submission of the whole of their social life to the State, such as characterizes the totalitarian countries.' Such, to Simone Weil, were the almost inevitable consequences of a victorious uprising. As T. E. Lawrence wrote: 'Those whose objective is liberty desire to live to enjoy it rather than to die for it.'

But Simone Weil was under no illusion about the kind of welcome to be expected for the solution she foresaw. There was nevertheless a chance of success: 'This is where information may play a very important part. So long as information about colonial rule had no other result except to put in question the benevolence of France, it was in danger of meeting only with indifference and above all with general incredulity. . . . But as soon as security is in question, it has a chance of being taken seriously . . . The opinion of a country, irrespective of class distinctions, is very much more sensitive to what threatens its security than what impugns its justice.'

On 19th March 1939, German troops entered Prague. This event dealt the death-blow to Simone Weil's pacifism. There was no doubt that it brutally exposed the fallacy of the extreme views that she had expressed at the moment when the Czechoslovakian crisis had been about to enter its decisive phase. The change in her attitude towards war was, however, by no means sudden. The Munich agreements had not allayed her apprehensions; she had not been able to approve of them, which is astonishing considering that the Munich policy was the expression of her own ideas. But her moral conscience was against the Munich agreement. The invasion of Czechoslovakia marked a new stage. It set in motion a process whose direction could be foreseen with complete certainty. To Simone Weil, all that was to happen seemed from that moment inevitable, to such a point that her freedom was reduced to nil, and but one response could be made, which was not the one she would have chosen. The drama was analogous—though of infinitely greater dimensions—to the one that had taken place within her in July 1936. The following passage, written in 1941, in the *Notebooks*, alludes to the pity which Arjuna must overcome in order to fight the war in which he will have to slay his own people:

'Give free play to one's faculties for action and for suffering. Parallelism between Arjuna and Christ.

'He will fight because he cannot stop this war, and because, if it takes place, he cannot do otherwise than take part in it. (It has already begun.)

'*Do only that which one cannot not do.* Non-active action . . .

'Non-violence is good only if it is effective. . . .

'To strive to become such that one may be able to be non-violent.

'That *also* depends upon one's adversary.

'To strive to substitute *more and more*, in the world, *effective* non-violence for violence.'[5]

It shows how Simone Weil managed to extricate herself from the contradictory position in which she had become entangled: first, by affirming that there are certain inward necessities from which escape without moral treachery is impossible, so that what cannot be avoided must be done; second, by admitting that pacifism can succeed only if the enemy is capable of responding to the non-violence which opposes him: non-violence is morally requisite and permissible only when it is effective.

This way of resolving the problem still leaves a conflict between the two following points: if pacifism is morally permissible only when it is effective, this is because there are principles which should be defended—principles so legitimate that, beside them, pacifism has a very relative value. On the other hand, if war is necessary and if one cannot help but kill, the use of force, even for legitimate ends, remains no less perilous and pernicious.

Under the stress of impending war, Simone Weil's pacifism was mitigated by events, as it had been previously during the Spanish Civil War. In either case, she had not readily abandoned her philosophy of non-violence. But she realized that its prescriptions were too easily reached to satisfy the demands of every situation. Such an about-face brought its penalty of suffering. Her inner torment sharpened her perceptions and weaned her from her idealistic defeatism.

Shortly after the invasion of Czechoslovakia, Simone Weil wrote an essay that was not published until ten years after her death.[6] 'Everyone feels only too acutely that Europe now finds itself in a tragic situation.' The most certain sign that a great tragedy was imminent was that everyone's conscience became obsessed by problems of politics. 'Tragic moments generally paralyse intelligence; and yet they impose upon us, more than any others, the duty of clearly evaluating the entire situation, both for the sake of safety and of honour.' Hence these 'Reflections in View of An Assessment.'

Some people were far from being in agreement about the nature of the danger, which nevertheless jeopardized the very survival of the nation. The thesis of integral pacifism could not be validly sustained in the existing situation, not because it was necessarily wrong, but for the simple reason that pacifism could have no concrete effect upon the situation, and could not be included among the decisive political factors. Others made out that all attempts at universal domination must necessarily meet with defeat. Charles V, Louis XIV, Napoleon were, after all, defeated. Ancient Rome did succeed in dominating the world; but since Rome is commonly regarded as the great civilizing power, this example is scarcely impressive.

'. . . for my part, since I believe that the Roman conquests, with their atrocious material and spiritual annihilation of whole populations, have been history's great disaster, I readily concur with the general opinion that for Germany to exercise universal dominion would be a catastrophe. The Roman precedent at least compels us to ask whether the danger is purely imaginary or not.'

After noting that the concept of 'limited war' had disappeared, Simone Weil went on to pronounce every major war 'a total catastrophe, which would demand from everyone his utmost efforts, which would impose supreme sacrifices, and which would probably end only after the complete exhaustion of the vanquished and the almost complete exhaustion of the victors. . . . It follows from this that there can no longer be any objectives in war.' The peace that came after a total war would be a further catastrophe. The conqueror, for reasons of security, would have to eliminate the danger which had made him go to war; he would have to annihilate the conquered nation.

Another consequence of total war: negotiations would no

longer be able to keep wars within national limits. When the very
existence of a country is at stake, negotiations are merely a phase
of the war; to gain concessions becomes impossible. 'The dividing
line between concessions that one can and therefore ought to
make, and those that one cannot make, is non-existent.'

In the intermediate state between war and peace—that of
Europe in the spring of 1939—what reasons were there to hope
that France might come out on the right side, that is, the side of
peace? It would be a mistake to count the personality of Hitler
among those reasons. There were no grounds for looking upon
him as a 'maniac with delusions of grandeur'. Hitler saw the way
to universal domination opening before him: to resist that appetite
for domination, he would have to be either a saint or a little man,
and he was neither. 'Clearly then, he is not a man who will
fall short, even by an inch, of exploiting the opportunities open to
him. . . . The sole question is, whether with time there may come
a change in circumstances which would cause men to stop
believing in the possibility of universal domination as a real and
imminent danger.'

The example of Rome—the republican Rome of the second
century B.C.—was to some extent deceptive. Rome reached its
apogee under Augustus; the empire preserved its conquests, but
it conquered little else. 'It no longer constituted a school
for world leaders; it merely maintained a mechanism whereby any
lunatic, until he was assassinated, could quite easily play the part
of master of the world.'

The history of Russia afforded an example nearer home and
even more striking; there one saw an instance of a conquering
power that owed its collapse to an internal régime of dictatorship
and corruption.

Not only was there hope for a progressive weakening of
Hitler's Germany as an outcome of its own domestic administration, according to Simone Weil, but also it was possible to say
that this decadence was already under way. The prodigious
dynamism which made the Nazi régime so terrifying bore the
seeds of its decay. 'In such a régime, all that might ensure the
permanence of its strength is sacrificed to whatever might bring
about its development: thus once its development has reached a

certain limit, paralysis ensues.' Machiavelli proved that a revolution or a conquest has to build on the support of those who had
fought it.[7] Hence, there is a constant purge in the ruling elements.
Conscientious citizens, who are the true backbone of the nation,
are constantly humiliated, bullied and often enough destroyed.
'The example of Russia suggests that this is a mechanism which
becomes more and more inevitable with the passage of time. And
it must in the end lead to impotence.'

This progressive weakening is especially obvious in the
economic and technical spheres. The working masses are
enslaved by the State. The incentive to improve production does
not make sense any more; quality of workmanship is in constant
regression. From the political point of view, it is clear that
totalitarian régimes rely upon the enthusiasm of the crowd. But,
a condition of unflagging enthusiasm cannot be maintained. And
once it has died, people become painfully aware of the full extent
of servitude to which they are subjected. 'For one feels free,
under such a régime, only to the extent that one feels enthusiastic.'

But, Simone Weil concluded, it would be foolhardy to risk war
upon the belief in a more or less imminent change of government
in the enemy country. 'Another temptation would be to allow the
power of Germany to expand till it reached its natural limits,
whatever these might be, and never to take the risk of war in order
to slow it down or arrest it, hoping that in time the internal factors
of decay in the régime would bring about a turn in the tide after a
minimum of damage. The temptation is great, for it would be a
wonderful thing indeed if a Napoleonic adventure, for the first
time in history, were to run its whole course from success to
collapse without the intervention of war.'

But the risk was too great; greater than twenty-one centuries
ago, when Rome achieved world domination: 'Then, thank heaven,
there were the barbarians, who, by the end of a few centuries,
forcibly introduced the vitality and diversity from which a new
civilization could spring.' We no longer have barbarians; we have
suppressed them; we have colonized them. 'If for several generations Europe and her territorial possessions were subjected to
such blind tyranny, one could not measure what would be lost to
humanity. For, contrary to what is often believed, force does

185

destroy spiritual values and can abolish all traces of them. Indeed, if this were not so would there be other than mediocre spirits to concern themselves with politics?'

Thus Simone Weil resigned herself to resist the German conquest. The history of the Roman conquests was an invaluable justification for her. The analogy was a last hope. It both explained and concealed the intellectual reversal necessary in view of world conditions in 1939. Moreover, Simone Weil had to examine the obligations of man towards society, foster-mother as much as 'Great Beast'. It was an examination that her conflict with the Church was partially to frustrate, but that nonetheless was to bear its own fruits of truth.

On the political level, the words of Herodotus which Simone Weil quotes can be applied to herself: 'The most detestable of human sufferings is to understand too well and to be unable to act.' The awareness of impotence is the heaviest of all human burdens. It cannot be shared, for few possess the intelligence necessary to understand, and because those who could share, prefer, through an optimistic force of habit, to place their faith in what they do not know . . . but imagine to be possible.

It was to this situation that Simone Weil alluded when she said jokingly to her family: 'I am Cassandra.'

## 2

# Pacifism in Collapse

### 1939-1940

> You are a child to think that a city is defended by its beauty.
> The Secretary to Violetta, Simone Weil, *Venice Preserved* (ii, xiii)

SIMONE WEIL had not recovered sufficiently in health to resume her teaching activities for the school year 1938-1939. Later, she analysed the state of her spirit at this time: '(As in the case of my headaches in 1938), not to be able to conceive that the affliction could cease, because the thought of being delivered from it would force one to conceive the pain more clearly. Prostitutes, who do not want to escape from their condition, etc. Warriors who by dint of suffering reach the point where they do not want peace (*Iliad*).'[1]

She had given up all hope of being cured when, in 1939, she consulted Dr Vernet. He ascribed her headaches to an unusual form of sinusitis, and the treatment he prescribed produced a marked improvement. Nevertheless, her headaches recurred at intervals, although they were less intense, until her death. This suffering, at once physical and mental, became charged with all the significance which, at a later date, Simone attached to the notion of 'affliction' or *malheur*.

In July 1939, she applied for further sick leave of a year. She left for a six months' holiday, taking two cases of books with her. In Geneva, with her parents, she spent about ten days looking at the pictures from the Prado Museum, then on exhibition at the League of Nations. It was on this occasion, perhaps, that she added to her list of those 'few painters . . . who speak to one's soul—da Vinci, Giotto, Masaccio, Giorgione, Rembrandt and Goya'[2]—the name of Velasquez. She had meant to go from

Geneva to the Swiss Alps. But war broke out at the beginning of September, and she returned to Paris with her family.

For a little while, Simone was without any clear motivation. It was wartime, but as yet there was no real war. Flag-waving patriotism irritated her, and in a sense prevented her from thinking about the catastrophe which had become certain.

The activities of the *Nouveaux Cahiers* group continued: its meetings took place as before.[3] One important project emerged from these discussions. It was concerned with giving working-class children possible access to higher education, and so a claim to careers in keeping with their gifts. The promoters of the project thought it necessary that a minority from the ranks of the people should be enabled to rise to positions of leadership. How could the son of a peasant or a worker who had the necessary talent expect to rise above the sphere in which he was born without external assistance? Simone Weil opposed this project with all her might. Since her stand on individualism had always been clear, her friends found her present attitude rather astonishing, to say the least. But she had profound reasons for dissenting. It seemed to her that this project approached the problem from the point of view of the community; it was a pragmatic approach that left the personal worth of the individual altogether out of account. According to her, the value of an individual has nothing to do with his value for society, except indirectly. It is not enough to help only those who are intellectually gifted to better themselves, but to improve, as a whole, the conditions of the working class. She then proposed, in place of the project that she attacked, a reform that would extend education to all. Why, for example, should we not raise the school-leaving age to eighteen? Her friends ascribed her point of view to her sense of social justice. They could not foresee the far more comprehensive ideals which she was to reveal later. This argument is of special interest, for it is the key to many passages in *The Need for Roots* and illuminates the general position that Simone Weil was to take up in regard to the education of workers and peasants.

On 1st January, 1940, in the *Nouveaux Cahiers*, Simone Weil published her 'Reflections on the Origins of Hitlerism.' This paper was the outcome of a careful study of Polybius and Appius.

This was valuable reading, for it furnished her with arguments in support of a thesis already familiar to her: the striking analogy between ancient Rome and the Hitlerian régime. If the resemblance was not obvious, she said, this was only because French children were taught how to read from Corneille and the *De Viris*. The conquests by which we are threatened rightly inspire us with horror. But those which we ourselves accomplish are wrongly esteemed as admirable and beneficial.

One of Simone Weil's most eloquent articles, its denunciations are directed at her chosen enemy, her favourite adversary: 'Rome, the unique object of my resentment.'* When this new Camilla spoke of Rome, she thought of all that she most hated: nationalism, colonialism, *la raison d'Etat*, the 'Great Beast' etc. She spoke of Rome as the ancient Christians spoke of Babylon—as the cesspool of the universe.

Yet, occasionally, some unconscious admiration for the marvellous Roman administration, maybe an echo from her reading of Montesquieu or Bossuet, gives eloquence to her style, even in the course of her indictment: 'The Romans conquered the world by their seriousness, discipline, organization, consistency of views and method; by the conviction that they were a superior race, born to command; through their premeditated, calculated and methodical use of the most pitiless cruelty, cold perfidy, and the most hypocritical propaganda, all used at once or one by one; by their unshakable resolve always to sacrifice everything to prestige, regardless of peril, of pity, or of human respect; by their skill in undermining the souls of their adversaries with terror, or lulling them to sleep with hopes before enslaving them by force of arms: in short, by such skilful employment of the grossest deception that they deceived even posterity and still deceive us now. Who would not recognize these characteristics?'

Simone's purpose was to describe Rome as it appeared to those whom it crushed: 'Carthaginians, Iberians, Gauls, Germans and Britons'. To them Rome appeared in two guises, both assumed for their subjugation: one manifesting 'a kind of genius', and the other 'a limitless brutality'.

'The Romans knew how to manipulate at will the feelings of

*Camilla, in Corneille's *Horace*, IV, sc.5

189

men. This is how one becomes master of the world'. And for that, they had the indispensable duplicity: 'Cardinal de Retz said that when a man has coldly resolved to do evil, he can keep up appearances; whereas if a man lets himself be drawn into evil, without willing it, he almost invariably provokes a scandal'. It was this cold-blooded resolution to do evil that explained the Romans' reputation for perfidy: they always knew how to keep up appearances. Examples are too numerous to be quoted, but they include: the conquest of the seventy towns of Illyria by Paulus Emilius, the history of the Iberian wars, and above all the destruction of Carthage.

'Roman history demonstrates a combination of the most horrible cruelty combined with an equal amount of perfidy.'

'When cruelty is the result of a caprice, of a morbid sensitivity, of anger, or of hatred, its consequences are often fatal to the person who gives way to it. Cold-blooded, calculated cruelty, methodically applied, cruelty which no emotional instability, no considerations of prudence, respect or pity can temper, and from which there is no hope of escape, either through courage, or dignity or energy, or by submission, supplications and tears—this is an incomparable instrument of domination. As blind and deaf as the forces of nature, and yet as clear-sighted and far-seeing as human intelligence, such a cruelty is so monstrous a combination that it paralyses the mind with a sense of fatality'.

This sort of cruelty is effective to the point of producing the contrary impression upon the minds of its victims: it 'gives rise to feelings which seem to be due only to clemency. It stimulates confidence . . .'

The 'cruel' paradox does not stop here, but goes relentlessly on its way: everything Roman was subordinated to prestige; the maintenance of prestige was the cardinal point of Roman politics. Driven to its logical conclusions, the politics of prestige necessitated the application of the following principle: no one, neither friend nor foe, should be allowed 'to feel himself in a position to bring any pressure whatever to bear upon the will of the people which claims dominion; and the futility of energetic affirmations, of weapons, of treaties, of past services, of submission or of petitions' had one after the other to be demonstrated. Mercilessly applied, this principle left no way out for the oppressed. Because he abstained from exercising the full extent of his powers, the oppressor appeared to display virtue and forbearance.

No nation can generate the energies required to act in this way without having the conviction 'that it has been chosen from all eternity to be the sovereign master of the others'. Since the Roman people considered themselves the natural rulers of the human race, all who refused to obey them were rebellious slaves. Thus no logical intermediate course remained between disobedience and total submission to the power imposed upon the world by the very nature of things. For the Romans, a conquered enemy was necessarily a slave to be chastised. 'According to Herodotus, the Scythians, when at war with a band of bastards, their wives' children by their slaves, suddenly put down their weapons and seized their whips, and so put their adversaries to flight; such, in war and in politics, is the power of opinion.'

No doubt, to make it appear that the master is always right, he must dispose of considerable astuteness, the unparalleled skill developed by the Romans in keeping up appearances, which quenched all the fires of indignation in other peoples and banished all compunction in themselves. Unlike the Greeks, cynicism was unknown to them.

Moreover, nothing was more persistent in this system than its methodical use of propaganda. By exalting Rome in his own soul above all else, each Roman became a natural propagandist at the service of his country.

But in the arts of dissimulation practised by ancient Rome the essential thing was 'the observance, in all action directed towards other nations, of a rhythm calculated sometimes to lull them into an apparent security, sometimes to paralyse them with anxiety or stupor, but never allowing them to lapse into an intermediate state.'

Doubtless, Rome appeared more formidable to her neighbours than Hitler, whose principal weakness was that he could not destroy Carthage (in this context, England). But that circumstance in no way diminished the analogy between his system and that of Rome. He had added a Teutonic zeal to the purely Roman traditions. 'Neither his objective, which is to impose peace by

enslavement and subdue nations by force to an allegedly superior
form of organization and civilization, nor the political methods
by which he pursues it, are different from the Roman.'

This article was the second part of a work in three sections
of which sections I and III, having been suppressed by the censor,
could not be published.  Simone Weil gave a reading of Part I
to a group of friends and acquaintances, however, at the home of
Marcel Moré.  Among the listeners was Gabriel Marcel, the
philosopher.

It is hard to evaluate a work like this.  Five centuries of
human history generally believed to have been organized for peace
are presented as having been orientated towards violence.  In this
context, it is true to say that philosophy remakes history by
constantly improving on its appearance or, as we may believe in
this case, by reading a new meaning into it, closer to the truth
of reality.

But although she consulted Appius and Polybius, Simone
Weil also devoted time to other matters; at the end of 1939 she
read the *Bhagavad-Gita*.  And in consequence she went on to
study Sanskrit.  During all this time, she felt the need to continue
her pursuit of classical literature, seeking mystical enlightenment in Plato, seeing the whole of the *Iliad* suffused with a
Christian light, convincing herself that 'Dionysius and Osiris are in
a certain sense Christ himself.'[4]

As for her attitude towards the war, Simone Weil felt bound
to admit to a friend  some time later, that Hitler's entrance into
Prague had induced her, not without inward struggles, to abandon
her pacifist position.  It was then that she recognized, tardily
but once and for all, that her first duty was to fight against
Hitlerism.

The sincerity of the position she took can be in no doubt.
At the beginning of 1940, she drew up a 'Memorandum on the
Formation of a Front-line Nursing Squad',[5] addressed to a senaotr
who, she hoped, would undertake to have her project backed by
appropriate legislative means.  It prompted her to write in her
letter of 30th July, 1942 to Maurice Schumann, that she had
been 'close to achieving her aims but that events had overtaken
her'.

## Pragmatics of mercy

Simone Weil's scheme was very characteristic of her. She envisaged the formation of a corps of nurses to work at the very front line. As she wrote in the letter to Schumann, 'many soldiers' lives' could thus be saved 'considering the number of deaths caused on the battle-field by lack of *immediate* care in cases of shock, of exposure, of haemorrhages'. The nurses would have to be completely mobile, always to be found in the most dangerous positions.

Such a new experiment could only begin, she realized, with a small nucleus of women prepared to make the supreme sacrifice. They would have to have heroic courage 'without being sustained by the combative spirit, but, on the contrary, devoting themselves to the wounded and the dying'. The prospect of running such risks would eliminate all candidates with weak nerves and thus exclude from the start those prone to break down in the face of danger. No doubt, she said, there would be a large toll of victims. But, 'in any military operation, the death of two or three humans is regarded as an almost negligible factor'. And why, anyhow, asked Simone Weil, should a woman's life be regarded as more precious than that of a man, 'especially if she has outlived her prime youth and is neither wife nor mother'?

The project was based on the moral factor, which played such an important role in warfare. It appealed to the imagination, on which the psychology of soldiering, as understood by Hitler, relied so heavily. Doubtless, we should not follow literally such a model, 'first, because we are fighting in another spirit and with different aims, and also because any copy falls short of the original, and only the new can grip the imagination'. Therefore we should innovate with such a project, whilst retaining the pragmatic outlook of our foe.

It should be said that, in a sense, 'such groups necessarily presuppose a *religious* inspiration; not in the sense of adherence to a particular church, but in a sense far harder to define, for which, however, no other word will serve'. There may be particular circumstances in which an inspiration of this nature is more important than strictly military factors. The Germans were impelled by an *ersatz* of real faith. Perhaps Simone Weil considered the allied victory was conditional upon the existence of an inspiration of this kind, but a true and authentic one. 'An inspiration is dynamic only when it expresses itself, and this not by words but by deeds.' The courage of which our soldiers would have to give proof would be of a wholly different character from that of the SS. 'Theirs is of a brutal and base kind; it proceeds from the will to power and destruction.'

In conclusion, Simone Weil suggested that the presence at the front of a group of devoted women who do not fear death would have the moral value of a symbol and would make a profound impression also on the soldiers of the enemy and on international opinion. Who could say what it might also mean to our own soldiers? 'It is neither possible nor desirable to transform our soldiers into fanatical young brutes like the Hitler *Jugend*. But it would quicken their ardour to the utmost to have the image of the hearths they are defending appear as a living reality before them.' Even in scenes of the most appalling brutality, they would be reminded of the gentleness of their home life; and this evocation would not soften and weaken them, rather it would exalt them. 'The ancient Germans . . . whom the Roman armies could never subjugate . . . had the custom of setting a young girl, surrounded by a bodyguard of the pick of the young warriors, in the front of their line of battle.'

It might not be easy to recruit such remarkable women, but for the purpose of an experiment, ten would be enough. 'These women certainly do exist. They can be readily found.'

This extraordinary project had the merit of revealing the true nature of Simone Weil's idealism—a sort of moral need never to shelter herself from any struggle; a restless will to act, immediately, upon any idea that seemed to her to be good; a tendency to meet and to out-do violence and suffering by total sacrifice.

God never remains insensitive: He gives of Himself,—but through a chosen medium—to those who give of themselves. For Simone Weil the mystical was the chosen way of God. And we find in the prologue of *La Connaissance surnaturelle* an account of a visit from God which may well have occurred at this time of Simone Weil's life:

'He entered my room and said: "Wretched one, who understands nothing and knows nothing: come with me and I will teach you things of which you have no idea." I followed him.

'He brought me to a church. It was new and ugly. He led me up to the altar and said: "Kneel down." I said: "I have not been baptized." He said: "Fall upon your knees before this place and with love in your heart as you would before the abode of truth." I obeyed.

'He led me out again and took me up to an attic room from which, through the open window, one could see the whole town, some wooden scaffoldings, the river where boats were being unladen. . . .

'It was no longer winter, yet nor was it spring. The branches of the trees lay bare, without buds, in a cold air full of sunlight.

'The light grew stronger and more resplendent, then faded until only the light of the moon and stars came in at the window, and once more dawn would break.

'At times we would stretch out on the floor of the attic, and I was overcome by the sweetness of sleep. Then I awoke and drank in the light of the sun. . . .

'One day he said to me: "Now go". . . . I understood now that he had been mistaken in coming for me. My place is not in that attic. It is anywhere, in a prison cell, in one of those middle-class rooms filled with curios and red plush, in a station waiting-room. Anywhere, but not in that attic.'

The above experience was related to well-known facts. Such terms as 'the prison-cell', the bourgeois room 'filled with curios and red plush', and the 'station waiting-room' had a relevance for Simone Weil in February or March 1940. Considered in this perspective, 'the new and ugly church' should refer to the Church of Saint Antoine de Padoue, on the boulevard Lefebvre, built during the time of Napoleon III and mentioned in the *Journal d'Usine* for Easter Sunday, 1935. The river 'where boats were being unladen' was the Seine.

However, the text describing this event was not written until late 1940 or 1941. It is difficult therefore to decide between those close to Simone Weil who place this occurrence in Paris in February or March 1940, and those, equally close, for whom it took place in Marseilles, in the following year.

In order to give her account an impersonal character, as if she were speaking for someone else, she referred to herself in the masculine: 'Je n'ai pas été baptisé'. Thus strengthened by this visit from her God, Simone Weil courageously supported her remoteness from the front lines.

The front lines came to her.

On 10th May 1940, the German armies began their triumphant offensive on the western front.

Simone Weil was in Paris at the time. In spite of the ominous advance of the Germans and the rout of the Allied forces, she decided to stay in the capital. She was hoping that it would be defended, as it had been in 1870. But it was declared an open city on 13th June. The sight of the placards bearing the announcement broke her heart. She left at once. 'I go without thinking of my return,' she wrote to a friend. 'I have always thought that one day I should go away like this.'

She followed the retreating front up to Nevers, hoping once again that a line of defence would be created along the Loire. But the Germans reached the Loire on 16th June. The news of the armistice on 18th June shattered her last illusions. She then resolved, as she wrote later to Jean Wahl, to go to England as soon as possible. With this goal in mind, she crossed—whether legally or not—the frontier from Nevers into unoccupied France, walking all the way in spite of an injured ankle.

She went to Vichy where she stayed with her parents for two months, the time needed to cure her injury.

To her, the armistice was cowardice, collective betrayal; the whole nation was responsible for it, including Paul Reynaud who, according to her, ought never to have resigned. 'As for me, the armistice truly distressed me from the outset. But despite this feeling, I believe that every Frenchman, including me, shares responsibility for it as much as Pétain; for at that moment, judging by what I saw, the nation as a whole welcomed the armistice with relief; which means that the responsibility is national and indivisible.'[6]

She was to find at Vichy several of her former friends from the university, some of whom, as Aimé Patri has told us, had subsided into 'bleating pacifism' or had turned traitor; others held anti-semitic views or were preoccupied with their careers. These encounters and the disgust they aroused in Simone Weil convinced her beyond all doubt that it was time to make her position completely unequivocal. She wrote: 'The criminal error that I committed before 1939 with regard to pacifist groups and their actions came from my disability brought on, through so many years, by the crushing weight of physical pain. Since I was incapable of following their actions closely, of meeting and talking with them, I was unable to perceive their disposition towards treason.'[7]

Simone Weil never cared for half measures and did not mince her words. No doubt her physical condition had prevented her from taking an active part in the pacifist movement. But this, she maintained, did not exempt her from indirect responsibility for the activities of the group. Thus she had fallen by default into a 'criminal negligence towards the country'. The reasons for such weakness must be sought in her poor state of health, and also in her inveterate tendency to force herself on. Rather like a seminarist who 'dares not look at a woman' because he is struggling with 'the most violent temptations of the flesh', she had blindly reacted against inaction. Having more than once given way to lassitude and inertia in little things, in this great problem she had wanted all too readily to escape the inconsistencies of abstention.[7]

During her stay in Vichy, Simone Weil worked at the composition of a play, which she was never to complete, but to which she often referred in later years.

Was it to Thomas Otway's *Venice Preserved* that she owed her interest in the historical novel of the Abbé de Saint-Réal, *The Conspiracy of the Spaniards against the Republic of Venice in the Year MDCXVIII*? The English work is not mentioned in her notes, nor is *Das gerettete Venedig* of Hugo von Hofmannsthal. She seems to have ignored Antoine de la Fosse's *Manlius Capitolinus*, where the action is set in ancient Rome. But she derived some subsidiary elements from the English and German plays and freely adapted the original theme: Spain, who controlled much of Italy in 1618, sought absolute domination.

Since Venice alone stood in the way of this grand design, the Marquis of Bedmar, Spanish Ambassador to the Republic, conceived a plot to seize the city. He entrusted its execution to Renaud, a French nobleman getting on in years, and to Pierre, a captain with a great reputation. After having won over to their cause the mercenary troops of Venice, the conspirators planned to capture the city by surprise, at night, on the eve of the Pentecost, the day when the Doge marries the sea. *Venice Preserved* tells of the failure of this conspiracy. In a little over twenty-four hours, from dawn to dawn, the danger threatening the city was dispelled. Venice was defended by her beauty—saved, paradoxically, by her vulnerability—because the heart of one of the conspirators was touched with pity. *Venice Preserved* is also the story of the conspirators and of the errors which were their undoing. In spite of his subordinate Renaud who tries to dissuade him from it, Pierre entrusts the command to his friend Jaffier, who is too soft-hearted for the role. When Jaffier reveals the plot to the Ten, he exacts from them a promise—later betrayed—of safeguard for his friends. Such is the drama.

The decisive factor, which is never mentioned in the play, is the supernatural: it inspires Jaffier with the humane feelings upon which the safety of the city depends; it wrecks the designs of the enemies of Venice; its intervention outwits fatality. Yet this supernatural is not equivalent to Providence, a tutelary deity of the city. It is no more than an incidental motive in the dramatic action, an invisible element, but one whose existence cannot be doubted, for without it the impossible could not have befallen. Venice would not have been saved.

The major themes of Simone Weil, which were not to be made explicit until later, are here to be found only in their germinal state. The conspirators are exiles in the service of Imperial Spain, in other words 'the uprooted hirelings of a social order'. Their chosen victim is a city, a human environment endowed with a past, 'with roots'. Venice, no less than Violetta, the living symbol of the city, has the beauty of all that is fragile, the frailty of 'apple-blossoms'.[8] Through this aesthetic quality, their objective reality reveals itself to Jaffier. In philosophical terms, one might say that the town suddenly appears as a 'value' or, in the words of Simone Weil, a '*metaxu*', i.e. a bridge towards transcendence. An object of contemplation, it has assumed the incorporeal nature of an ideal; it no longer resists evil. The agony and death that Venice was about to suffer falls instead upon the hero who has spared it. Everything is determined by the inevitable law of compensation: the sum total of evil on earth being always the same, one victim is exchanged for another. For evil and pain are a false currency which is passed from hand to hand until it reaches someone who receives it but does not pass it on. Through such a one Venice was saved! Unwittingly, however, he had transferred to his comrades the defiling coin of disaster which he would share with them.

The dramatic action is marked by a vigorous rhythm. The aspiration of the conspirators gives life to the whole of the first act. In the second, they are still exalted by this initial dynamism, all but Jaffier, for Jaffier is not one of them in his inmost heart. In the third act, they share in his immobility. Each of the three acts, in its turn, is characterized by inimitable and contrasted 'moments'. Such, in the last act are, the desperate pleading of Jaffier which no one hears and the subsequent efforts of his guards to make him speak when he is silent, episodes which manifest, one after the other, the unreality of the world in the eyes of the sufferer and the unreality of suffering in the eyes of the world. If a being or a situation ceases to reflect the idea, sad or joyful, that one of the characters has formed they immediately lose for him their own identity and no longer exist as such.

Each character is thus shown clinging to a position in which he is alone, in which all communication with anyone else has been withdrawn. He has even his own specific form of expression, as it were, his own language. Thus the effects of contrast, due to the variety of themes and dramatic conflicts, are re-enforced by the diversity of speech-patterns, each of which corresponds to a different way of being: the mercenaries, earthly creatures, speak in prose; Violetta, the potential woman, in blank verse of 11 syllables (5-6); the Utopian Jaffier in blank verse of 13 syllables (5-4-4), extended alexandrine, etc. Each person is a symbol: 'Violetta is happy innocence', Jaffier is the 'perfect hero'. Renaud is ambition incarnate, Pierre is the perfect friend, etc. Each bears a destiny of which he is only partly aware, but which is the inevitable outcome of his character.

When the curtain rises, the conspirators, gathered together in the house of a courtesan, are discussing the firm friendship between Pierre and Jaffier, which surpasses even the love that both feel for young Violetta, daughter of the secretary to the Ten. Renaud, the politician of the group, explains that it is necessary to subjugate Venice in order to ensure Spanish supremacy, and he alludes incidentally to the sack of the city. While he is speaking, he notices Jaffier's pale face and troubled expression. This sign of weakness arouses his suspicion. A good conspirator should never draw back, or express love. Anyone who shows pity should be 'suppressed'. 'What is one human life when we are about to change the world?'

In the second act, Pierre, in order to blunt the vigilance of the Ten, is obliged to leave the city; he is happy to prove his faith in his friend, against the suspicion of Renaud, by entrusting him with the supreme command:

> *This city is yours; tonight you shall clasp it*
> *In a mortal embrace, its body obedient.*
> *You shall possess it; how fine it is to be the ruler.* (II 4)

Pierre's disinterestedness is beyond Renaud's comprehension: according to him, 'human beings without exception seek to wield all the power they can.' But now that Jaffier is the chief agent of the conspiracy, he silences his doubts and unfolds the plans he has conceived for the coming night, in which acts of rape, abduction, murder and pillage will all play their parts. The aim is to tear the vanquished population loose from every attachment to the past, and thus transform it into a pliable being, without a future and almost without memories, which will no longer dare think for itself, for fear of recollecting horrors of which it still dreads the consequences or the repetition. Conquerors, says Renaud, these men of action 'compel others to dream their dreams. The conqueror lives his dream, the conquered lives the dream of another . . . Weapons make dreams more potent than reality.' (II 6)

Jaffier listens in silence. Then, left to himself, he ponders again the remarks of Pierre and Renaud:

> *The town, the sea, the people will be mine. . . .*
> *Now it will arrive; the moment when suddenly*
> *My hand clenches and then shatters it.* (II 16)

To Violetta, his *inamorata*, he had said that she was right when she declared that Venice was an invulnerable citadel. And the young girl's father had been quite wrong to tease her: 'You are a child to think that a city is defended by its beauty!' (II 13). In fact—although during the second act this is not apparent to Renaud's watchful eyes—Jaffier has decided to reveal the secret of the conspiracy to the Ten. In return, they have promised him, under oath, to respect the life of his friends. Guilelessly, he relies upon those deceitful words, to the very moment when, from a place of concealment, he sees that his accomplices, captured on his information, are being led to torture. He hears Renaud cry out, in his frustrated ambition:

> *I would have known how to govern a realm large as the world;*
> *I was born for that, for that all my soul thirsted.* (III 3).

He hears Pierre lamenting for the absence of his friend:

> *Dear God, if I could only hear his voice,*
> *Suddenly touch his hand, if his eyes rested on me!*

But he can do nothing for his former comrades: the Ten have betrayed him. All his indignation, denunciations and tears are wasted upon men such as his guards; in an astonishing moment of insight, he predicts that the future will bring to Venice the destruction from which he has spared her. To his indifferent guards, he is just a prisoner who takes too much of their time: 'Because of him,' they complain, 'we shan't see the festivities.'

At that moment they perceive the signal announcing the execution of the condemned prisoners. Jaffier sighs: 'At last it is over. Now I would like to sleep.'

Compelled to leave the city, he refuses the gold the Ten have sent him in reward for his betrayal: he stops, he has heard the cries of a handful of mercenaries who are still fighting back their assailants. His keepers are delighted; they won't have to lead him out of the city. 'Look how he smiles! Has he suddenly gone crazy?'

Pushed into the fight by the guards eager to find a valid excuse to kill him, he seizes a sword which they have placed within his reach and rejoins the fight:

# Letter to a Minister of Education

*Now disgrace has gone.*
*To my eyes soon to be sightless, how lovely the city is!*
*I must depart from the land of the living, never to return.*
*Where I am going there is no daybreak—there is no city.*

While he thus fulfils his destiny, Violetta, who has known nothing of the events of the previous night enters the deserted scene:

*Day beautifully rising, like a smile suddenly suspended*
*Over my city and its thousand canals,*
*To all human beings receiving your peace*
*How sweet it is to see the light.*

In November 1940 Simone Weil wrote a letter to M. Carcopino, Minister of National Education, which was soon to be made famous by Boris Souvarine.[9] It was related to a body of regulations set up by the Vichy government which curbed the rights of Jews, in particular as to the professions which they could practise. The most noteworthy rule perhaps was the one which closed the teaching profession to all persons of Jewish descent, presumably to protect the young against the 'bad influence' they might exert in the realm of civic responsibility. Simone Weil informed the Minister that the sick leave she had renewed for a year in July 1939 had come to an end the previous July. In August, she had asked for a post, preferably in Algeria, but her letter had not been answered. She asked for an explanation of this silence. Certainly she had read in the press the 'Statutory Regulations for Jews'. That was certainly the explanation of the Minister's silence. But she knew nothing about the definition of the word 'Jew'. It was a point which had never entered into her course of studies; this was the explanation of her ignorance of the subject.

It was true that the Statute contained a definition; anyone who had three Jewish grandparents was to be considered a Jew. But such a definition made it no easier to solve the problem. It was of no use to project the question backwards two generations. If the word 'Jew' designated a religion, she was bound to admit that her maternal grandparents were free-thinkers. Although her paternal grandparents seemed to have gone to the synagogue, she then had only two Jewish grandparents, and not three as the Statute stipulated.

# *What is a Jew?*

Was it to be understood that the word designated a race? In that case, she thought there was no reason to believe that she had any connection whatever with the race that inhabited Palestine two thousand years ago. When, moreover, one knows the ruthless way in which the Roman armies behaved in Palestine, one is forced to admit that only the Jews who were then living outside Palestine could have managed to ensure the preservation of the race.

Insofar as she was concerned personally, if there was any tradition that she regarded as her patrimony, it was the French tradition, Hellenic and Christian. The Hebraic tradition was utterly alien to her.

But if it seemed to the Minister that she came within the scope of the law, she did not wish to cause any difficulty in accepting it. 'I am ready to submit to it as I am to any other law, whatever it may be. But I should like to be officially enlightened at this point, since I myself have no criterion by which I may resolve the question. Otherwise, I wish to have the benefit of the rights accorded me by the contract implied in my rank as an agrégée.' Needless to add, this letter remained unanswered.

Simone Weil left Vichy in October to live in Marseilles.

# 3

# The Years of Intense Speculation

## 1940-1942

'Blessed are they who suffer, in the flesh, the suffering of the world itself in their epoch.' Simone Weil, letter to Joë Bousquet

THE YEARS 1940-1942 were extremely fruitful ones for Simone Weil. This was the period of her life during which she delved deeply into the various philosophies that later influenced her own thinking. This was the time of her intense mystical contemplation. And these were the years in which she met Father Perrin and Gustave Thibon, who were to become the source and the springboard of many of her most important ideas.

## Speculation

At the beginning of 1940, Simone Weil began to acquaint herself with Indian philosophy. She read through the *Bhagavad-Gita*. Such a concentrated text, so heavily charged with theology, however, could not be fully grasped after just one reading. So she constantly returned to it and sought to augment her understanding by reading also from the Upanishads. Her comprehension of Indian philosophy may seem impressive. Yet, her study of it falls short, in scope or depth, from that which she had devoted to other matters, such as Platonism or Marxism. Her acquaintance with the basic scriptures of Indian theology was relatively superficial. It is most remarkable, however, that by sheer insight and congeniality she often came close to restating principles found, for instance, in the *Samkhya Karikas* of Ishavara Krishna, the philosophical system upon which the *Bhagavad-Gita* is mainly based. The same applied to her intuitive rediscovery of some Buddhist tenets. And, while thus forever broadening her fields of interest, she went back, again and again, to the Greek texts, classifying her cumulative discoveries under two headings: unification of religious thought and religion of science.

The influence that these studies had upon Simone is evident in her writings of 1940 to 1942. On arriving in Marseilles, she had attached herself to a group of thinkers and writers who expressed their views through the *Cahiers du Sud*. In December 1940 Jean Lambert submitted to the editorial staff 'The *Iliad*, or The Poem of Force', a study which Simone had entrusted to him. Her intention was to translate the whole of the *Iliad* for publication, but the project came to nothing. While she was working on it, however, she made notes of reflections prompted by the text and found a thread of Stoicism running through them. 'The true hero, the real theme, the central motif of the *Iliad*, is force,' she concluded. This great poem was for her no mere document of the past; once she had discerned that force was central to contemporary events as it is to world history, she understood why the *Iliad* was, more than a document, a mirror of reality.[1]

'Force is that which makes a thing of anyone subject to it. When force is exerted to the utmost, it makes a man a thing in the most literal sense of the word: it reduces him to a corpse.' Not all force is lethal, however; a man remains a living being, for he has a soul. And yet, at the same time, he exists as a thing. An unnatural state, for the soul was never made to inhabit an object. 'This thing continually yearns to be a man or a woman, and yet never succeeds in being one. This is death drawn out to the length of a life, a life that death has frozen long before extinguishing it.'

Every abuse of force is unjust, and calls for punishment. The law of retribution is found in the *Iliad*, it is formulated in terms comparable to those used in the New Testament. 'By its very blindness fate itself establishes a kind of blind justice.' The man who resorts to violence inevitably oversteps himself and, for that reason, exposes himself to a misfortune which strikes him down, sooner or later, with mathematical certainty.

Simone Weil believed that this applied to our own time, to our own culture. But the western world not only does not know

how to arrest its headlong plunge down the slope of violence;
it has forgotten the very meaning of the words which, in other days,
set bounds to the exercise of brute force and thus protected man
from the retribution that follows all reckless adventure. 'The
ideas of measure, balance, and limitation that ought to determine
the conduct of life have now no more than a subsidiary function,
in technology. We are "geometers" only in regard to matter;
while the Greeks were "geometers", first of all, as an apprenticeship in virtue.'

This sense of balance applies to the notion of fatality which
consists essentially in the appreciation of man's bondage to force,
and through force to matter. He is beholden to the might which
shakes the spears as deadly shafts of light in the array of battle
just as he is to the crashing quake of the avalanche or the onrush
of a torrent. Whether as the battering-ram or the door splintering
beneath its onslaught, he belongs to one or the other side of the
active-passive relationship. In the turmoil of war, assailant and
assailed are pawns in the hands of necessity. Man is the prey set
upon by a predatory beast which is his brother: the same natural
compulsion throws both into these opposite roles. This cruel
game absorbs man's faculties to a point where he becomes
quite unaware of the reason for his fighting. All he knows is that
he is the killer or the thing-to-be-killed.

But according to the *Iliad*, there were during the Trojan War
a few redeeming moments in which pity bridged the gap between
enemies and established on a kind of transcendental level a
conscious equality. Such flashes of insight created a higher
brotherhood between men which paralleled their subjection to
necessity. 'Whatever, deep within the soul, and in human relations, escapes the dominion of force, is loved, but loved sorrow-
fully, because of the threat of destruction that constantly hangs
over it.'

In their perception of this universal dereliction of man to fate,
the Gospels are 'the last marvellous expression of the Greek
genius, as the *Iliad* was the first'. They reveal in a God the truth
about man, the real *conditions d'existence* of the humanity he fully
assumed: they show him trembling before death, accursed before
heaven and earth. Without this feeling for the misery of man's

condition there can be neither justice nor love. Without this understanding, a person lives in a world apart, pleasantly removed from those beset by misfortune, to whom he attributes a special vocation for unhappiness; or else he assumes, with a cruel naïveté, that affliction can strike a being without leaving an actual impress on the deepest fibres, the very soul, bringing about a change in outlook, in personality.

The Greeks knew the truth about misfortune. So did the writers of the Gospels. But the Hebrews and Romans thought they were a people elected, set apart, and this conviction of theirs corrupted the message of the Gospels: 'From the earliest times it was believed to be a sign of grace when the martyrs joyfully endured suffering and death—as though grace could do more for a human being than it could for Christ. . . . Unless protected by the armour of a lie, man cannot endure force without being pierced to the soul. Grace can prevent this blow from corrupting him, but it cannot spare him the wound.'

It was in this article on the *Iliad* that Simone Weil assumed a position that was to remain virtually unchanged through later years; in fact, in her opinion, it was a position that could not be denied without self-deception. The idea was that force cannot be separated from suffering nor suffering from life. Simone Weil rejected all systems and all religions which to her mind did not accept as fundamental the suffering inherent in the human condition.

As for grace, its function, according to Simone Weil, is to engender stoicism in the depths of misery, enabling man to maintain his dignity intact, the dignity of a being who would be self-sufficient in nature. Thus man can transcend the 'absurdity' of his suffering, for grace enables him, paradoxically, at once to bear and to rise above his condition, with the understanding that such grace is a sign of a supernatural order.

Thus formulated, this interpretation of Simone Weil's ideas develops her thinking somewhat further than she did in 1940-1941. It is clear, however, that even at that time, she had already imprisoned herself in concepts of her own making.

At the same time as Simone Weil was analyzing her reflections

on the *Iliad*, she was also to speak of God, of grace, of the supernatural, and of Christianity with an assurance that may appear
surprising, especially since it reveals, above all, an absence of
inner conflict. On 30th March 1941, the Young Christian
Workers' Movement (Jeunesse Ouvrière Chrétienne) held two
meetings in Marseilles, one in the heart of the workers' quarters.
Simone Weil attended these meetings and was deeply impressed
by what she heard there. In the April number of the *Cahiers du
Sud*, she wrote that the group did not seem to be a 'youth movement in the ordinary sense of the word: there was no mob-
emotionalism, no mesmeric effects whatever, no slogans, no
obsession with power, no flattery of youth'. . . . : 'It is the pure
Christian spirit, without any adulteration, that is expressed in
the JOC. Politics do not enter into it, nor religion itself except
in action. These young people have felt that, over and above the
economic system and the employers, it is matter itself which
weighs them down and oppresses them every day—matter that
they handle hour after hour, under order, despite fatigue. . . .
They are more subject to matter than others, but, from the
moment they achieve self-awareness, they feel more keenly than
others that they are subject to it, and that is an immense
superiority.' Their exaltation at the thought of the incarnation
of Christ, above all that he was a workman, is therefore understandable. 'Among them, Christianity has an authentic ring; it is
that which used to give to slaves a supernatural liberty. In the
hard and brutal life of a factory, the spirit always appears as
what it really is, something supernatural, a miracle, a grace.'

The linear direction of Simone Weil's studies during this
period is confirmed in the few pages that she published in the
*Cahiers du Sud* of May 1941. In a review of an article by Brion,
she suggests that Oriental and Occidental thought ought not to
be considered as opposed. Every Taoist formula can be paralleled
by a text from Heraclitus or Protagoras, from Plato, from the
Cynics or the Stoics, from Christian teachers, or even from
Jean-Jacques Rousseau. The Chinese texts that Brion cites
evoke for her familiar thoughts; as Plato says, the reader remembers
having known it 'on the other side of the sky'. The same is true
of the plastic arts. Brion speaks of the great importance of the void

Marseilles' office of the *Cahiers du Sud*, magazine for which
Simone Weil wrote articles

Gustave Thibon and the author

in Chinese painting; Simone Weil points out that it is reminiscent of Giotto, 'in whose art a blank space in the centre of a fresco often has so powerful an effect'. She believes also that Greek science is nearer to modern science than is generally supposed and, in a sense, much better integrated: 'In Greece, the notion of balance had orientated all scientific study towards the good.'

For Simone Weil, there were, basically, two types of philosophy: that of Aristotle and Hegel, of the builders of systems 'whose value can only consist in a certain poetic beauty, and, above all, in the marvellously penetrating formulas that abound in the works of some of them'; and that of Socrates, whose thought is constantly orientated towards salvation and calls for an 'effort of detachment which surpasses the intelligence'.

Simone's own philosophical writings are much closer to the 'Socratic' than to the 'Aristotelian', as she defines them. The bases of her religious thought are revealed in two essays: *'L'Amour de Dieu et le malheur'* (The Love of God and Affliction)[2] and *'Formes de l'Amour implicite de Dieu'* (Forms of the Implicit Love of God). The former contains numerous passages parallel to some found in the *Cahiers* and *La Connaissance surnaturelle*, which belong to the same period. Its theme is the familiar Weilian one: *Malheur*.[3] An 'admirable word, without its equivalent in other languages', Simone admits that it is hard to define precisely. For *malheur*, as she used the term, is not just a synonym for suffering; *malheur* takes possession of the soul and brands it to the depths with the mark of servitude. It no doubt implies long and frequent physical pain. It implies social degradation. After branding a person, as with a red-hot iron, with scorn, disgust, and self-loathing, *malheur* leaves him writhing on the earth like a half-crushed worm.

The principal effect of *malheur* is to render God absent for a time, more absent than one who has died. A kind of horror then overtakes the soul. While God is absent, nothing is lovable. Yet if, in these empty and desolate shadows, the 'unhappy one' ceases to love, 'God's absence becomes final'. The soul must go on loving, and that is impossible if the supernatural help of divine grace is not present. If the soul perseveres in love, God reveals Himself.

What is the metaphysical explanation of this state of abandonment? The created universe wherein we live is the infinite distance 'placed by divine love between God and God'; like the whole universe, 'we are a point in this distance'. And yet a mechanism, blind but of a mathematical precision, governs creation at every level; it is the mechanism of necessity. Nothing is free from it, not matter, nor animals, nor human beings.

However, blindness is not the only characteristic of necessity. Creation is complete passivity and obedience. For that reason, matter is a model to us: a perfect model because of its perfect obedience. It thus deserves to be loved. In the beauty of the world, sheer necessity becomes an object of love.

There is also the *supernatural* interpretation of *malheur*. 'The infinity of time and space separates us from God.' *Malheur* defeats the creative act and, by a supernatural mechanism as inevitable as that of nature, brings us back to God, yet only if we so wish. Affliction, then, is that 'marvel of divine technique'. It is a simple and ingenious device enabling the immensity of a 'blind, brutal and cold' force to enter into the depths of the soul of a finite creature. The weight of necessity falling from the infinite distance, separating God from the creature, directs all its quickening force upon a single point, the centre of the soul, and pierces it. 'By the rent eternity enters.'[4]

The man who suffers such a thing has no part in his affliction. 'He struggles like a butterfly pinned alive into an album. But through all the horror he can continue to want to love.' Far from such love being impossible, there is no obstacle to it; one might almost say no difficulty. 'For even the direst pain, so long as consciousness endures, does not touch that point in the soul which consents to a right direction.'

To go on living it is enough to know that love is an orientation, not a state, of the soul. If a person does not know this, he falls into despair. If he does know it, he keeps his soul directed towards God, while it is being pierced by the nail which impales it at the very centre of the universe: a centre which is situated not in the middle of, but beyond both time and space. This centre is God. 'According to a dimension which does not belong to space and is not that of time, but is wholly another dimension', this nail fashioned by divine love has pierced through creation, traversing the screen that separates the soul from God. 'Through this wonderful dimension, the soul, without leaving the place or the instant in which the body it inhabits happens to be, can pass through the entirety of space and time and come before the presence of God Himself.' The soul thus finds itself at the point of intersection—which is that of the two parts of the Cross.

'The tremendous greatness of Christianity,' says Simone Weil, 'comes from the fact that it does not seek a supernatural remedy against suffering, but a supernatural use of suffering.'[5] No doubt: 'human misery would be intolerable if it were not diluted in Time. We should prevent it from becoming diluted *in order that* it may be intolerable'.[6] For only extreme anguish has redemptive power. It must not be sought out; it must be endured: 'Death is what is required, not suicide.' *Malheur* is necessary so that 'the human creature may un-create itself'.[7]

Simone Weil's attitude is lucid, even logical, once the theological ideas on which it is based have been discerned. She conceives of creation not as participation in the divine plenitude, but as a withdrawal, a *diminutio* of God or, more expressly, a theft, a sort of metaphysical original sin, which consists in existing as a being really distinct from God. This being so, why did God, Who is Love, create? What He created becomes a breach of the original purity, goodness, and integrity.

Simone Weil's concepts might have delighted a Valéry, but it is hard to see how such metaphors can avoid leading to something very different from traditional Christianity. Like the great system-builders (whom she had, however, no wish to emulate), Simone Weil was not afraid of contradictions. She knew that no philosophy can contain the whole of reality, and that any genuine philosophical quest ends in unanswerable questions. She therefore respects mystery, and makes no impossible attempts at conciliation.

What she says about *malheur* and the love of God presupposes that in the human soul there is an innately supernatural element identical with God, which reveals itself when exceptional anguish has destroyed the illusion of being something that is not God. This is the extreme position which she sometimes formulates, not without qualifications. It follows necessarily from her theological postulates; from it she could not escape without undermining the very basis of her 'system'. It is possible to observe here how closely she approaches to the position of the Arab philosophers of the Middle Ages, for whom the degrees of Being apprehended in the human soul culminated in the identification of the 'active intellect' with God.

According to Simone Weil, affliction is a form of natural redemption, a sacrament on the natural plane and salvation on the supernatural plane at one and the same time, within the reach only of an individual in whom extreme suffering and genius are present together. There is no necessity for the Incarnation of the Word. Christ has become an example, a paradigm, a living doctrine, but he is not the source or the necessary condition of salvation. This she had to say in veiled terms of the utmost reticence; but she could not avoid saying it without changing the very core of her teaching.

'L'Amour de Dieu et le malheur' was followed by 'Formes de l'Amour implicite de Dieu.'[8] In Simone Weil's eyes, as she writes in the latter article, love of neighbour is the first of the forms of implicit love for God. When two men have dealings with one another and neither has the power to command the other, mutual understanding between them is essential; they regulate their relations with each other according to ordinary justice, which alone has the power to bring two different wills to agreement. But when one is strong and the other is weak, there is no longer any need for rules; the weaker gives way and the stronger treats the weaker as though he were inanimate matter that could be manipulated at will. If, on the other hand, the strong would treat the weak differently, it would be either an act of charity or of supernatural justice. The supernatural virtue of justice is present when he who is stronger acts towards the weaker as though they were equals. For the weaker of the two, thus treated, virtue consists in his not thinking that there really was, after all, equality in the relationship of forces but in his realising that generosity is the sole cause of the treatment he has received from his superior. That is what we generally call gratitude. The virtue of gratitude—the pre-eminent Christian virtue—reproduces, to the extent that it is possible in the creature, the original generosity of the Creator: 'Creation is, on the part of God, not an act of self-aggrandizement, but of withdrawal, of renunciation. . . . In the creative act God denies Himself, even as Christ enjoined us to deny ourselves.'

In Simone Weil's view, every religion is 'true' which has a firm grasp of the voluntary self-effacement of the Creator, of his apparent absence and his presence in the secret of the world. For her, too, charity was a form of creative attention, the interchange of compassion and gratitude that occurs like a flash of lightning between two beings, one of whom is provided with, the other deprived of, a full human personality.

We want the faculty of free consent to exist in the other who has been deprived of it; we transport ourselves into him, we ourselves consent to suffer. That is to renounce oneself: 'By denying oneself one becomes capable, after God, of affirming another by a creative affirmation. . . . This is a redemptive act.' The afflicted one, for his part, shows supernatural gratitude when he rejoices at being the object of a supernatural compassion.

Unfortunate men and benefactors alike have both recognized that it is good not to dominate everywhere, even when the power is there. Love of neighbour is a love that descends to man from God. God makes haste to come to the poor. 'Wherever the afflicted are loved for their own sake, here God is present.' The sufferer will become aware of the presence of God only with time. But God is there even if the soul has been unable to call the divine presence by its name of supernatural justice. He is not present, though his name be invoked where the unhappy are presented only as an occasion for the just to do good. In this case, the sufferer is still treated according to his natural condition; that is, as a thing.

In Simone Weil's thinking, then, such expressions as 'to love one's neighbour in God' or 'for God' are deceptive. When we are dealing with those who suffer, it is no time to think of God. There are moments when a person must turn his thoughts away from God's creatures so as to give all his attention to Him, and there are moments when one must forget God and be absorbed in the care of His creatures. Thus, 'the presence of

God in us is conditional upon so profound a secret' that it is hidden even from us. Modesty is here 'the condition of the nuptial union'. 'It is not we who love the afflicted in God'; it is God who, without our knowing it, loves them in us. He who gives bread to the hungry for the love of God will have no thanks from Christ, for he has already received his recompense. The love of one's neighbour cannot, therefore, be love for God, except implicitly.

In the relationship between man and his neighbour, the neighbour stands in the place of God. If then a man thinks of God when he is doing good, the relationship he is cultivating is idolatrous. For him, God is not in the neighbour, but in some idea of God that the man made up—a false image, an illusion. Love of neighbour is therefore incompatible with self-love.

Simone Weil presents here a metaphysical insight into her own past experience and a foretaste of the vigorous language which she later employs in her *Cahiers d'Amérique* where she expresses herself without fear of being misunderstood: 'As for me, I have no debts. I am a debt. My being is a debt. God cannot remit this debt without making me cease to be—cease to be whilst still living here below. And by selling what remains after the annulment of my person, so that it may serve to nourish other creatures.'[9]

The love of one's neighbour is, then, a form of self-annihilation. Each person must sell himself to the world as a slave; identify himself with the world as it is—the world of men with its crimes, its greatnesses, its contradictions. Love of neighbour or love of the neighbour's necessity is a voluntary bondage whereby one gives oneself as food for others and thereby becomes others.

Simone Weil had not misinterpreted the traditional concept of Christian charity, of a love through which the intrinsic value of every human person is revealed and made manifest to everyone. But she maintained, together with this concept and in permanent conflict with it, the belief that charity must be an attachment to the world in its wholeness, with all its pains, burdens and miseries —a notion almost identical to the *amor fati* of the Stoics.

For Simone Weil, this system of living on two levels presented a painful contradiction. She lived the charity in which she

214

believed; guided only by her logic and her thirst for the absolute, she drove herself to inward annihilation.

In the second part of her study devoted to the love of the order of the world, Simone Weil openly expresses herself as a Stoic. But, in contrast to what she wrote about love of neighbour, what she has to say here reveals nothing new. There are only ideas that had always been active within her and which owe their synthesis simply to the urgency with which the problem of the acceptance or rejection of baptism then presented itself to her— a problem discussed later.

Love for the world-order, she wrote, proceeds from the same renunciation as love of neighbour; this, too, is an image of the creative renunciation of God. The Creator brings the world into being, 'by deciding not to dominate it, although he has the power to do so'. Instead, he leaves its government, on the one hand, to 'the mechanical necessity attached to matter' and, on the other, to 'the autonomy essential to thinking persons'.

Man does not have to give up command over matter or over his neighbour, for he does not possess the power to command. But in creating man, God has given him a fictitious image of such a power—a kind of 'imaginary divinity'—so that, although only a creature, he also can dispossess himself of his 'divinity'. For there is in man—and this is the key to the understanding of human psychology—a propensity for dreaming that he occupies the centre of the universe. To renounce this central position— to renounce it not only with the intellect, but also with that part of the soul which imagines it—is to awaken to reality, to the eternal; it is 'to see the true light' and 'to hear the true silence'. But not only must man 'give up being, in imagination, the centre of the world', he must give up being something; he must consent to be nothing, to know he is nothing, knowing that he is an illusion.

For Simone Weil, love of beauty of the world is almost absent from the Christian tradition. Such absence was hard for her to understand; it was an important deficiency. For 'science, art and religion are connected together through the notion of *order of the world*, which we have completely lost'.[10] Christianity has no right to call itself Catholic so long as the universe has no

215

place in it, she says. For the beauty of the world is a sacrament; it is the radiance of the tenderness of Christ smiling through matter; it is a real presence; it is also the mediation between God and all the efforts to achieve beauty that are made by men in their partial and often criminal activities.

'The beauty of the world speaks to us of the love that is its soul just as would the features of a human face that were perfectly beautiful and did not lie.'[11] Even as God comes instantly into any soul that opens itself in love for those who suffer, so does he hasten to love, through the soul that perceives it, 'the tangible beauty of his own creation.'

Christianity will never become truly incarnate, Simone Weil says, until it assimilates within itself that attitude of the Stoics who felt a filial piety for that *civitas terrena*, that homeland here below which is the universe. On that day when, through a misunderstanding that is hard to comprehend, Christianity cut itself off from Stoicism, it condemned itself to a separated, abstract existence. For the notion of necessity it substituted Providence. But the universe is empty of natural finality and the absence of finality means the reign of necessity. The world of nature is the domain of causes, not of ends. Those who believe they can discern the special designs of Divine Providence in human and natural events are behaving like those professors who devote themselves, at the expense of a great poem, to what they call the explication of the text.

According to Simone Weil—whose more considered thoughts on this subject are to be found in her *Intuitions préchrétiennes* (*Intimations of Christianity*)—Providence is the reign of *particular ends*, whilst necessity is the rule of a *general end*.[12] According to traditional doctrine, on the contrary, Providence rules *particular ends* and the *general end* at the same time; necessity is subject to it. Simone Weil, when she wanted to emphasize a truth, was in the habit of distorting the commonly accepted terms to her own purpose; thus she achieved effects by contrast. Her liking for antithesis, which is at the same time so modern, so 'existentialist', and yet so ancient, had already been described by Pascal when he wrote about 'those who make false windows for the sake of symmetry'. But with Simone Weil, more is involved than merely a figure of speech. Providence is rejected because science rejects particular ends; science actually rejects all ends; it admits nothing but causes.

Then what is the knowledge that admits finality? It is the knowledge of love. For love can have but one end, and that an invisible one, which yet is made manifest by the essential attribute of the beloved object: beauty. Beauty, diffused throughout nature, signifies that finality is unique because it speaks of God transcendent.

Seen under the aspect of beauty, necessity is infinitely lovable since it speaks of God. Providence, on the contrary, is not lovable because it does not speak; it tells us nothing, it cannot explain anything, for it rests on imaginary finalities which science has destroyed, exorcized. Providence is a myth. It is a myth in two respects. Regarded as the determinant of particular ends, it is a fiction. Seen as 'the wise persuasion of love', it is the inspiration of the work of God, the theme of the universal poem.

If man's soul is truly oriented to love, the more he contemplates necessity, the more he presses against himself, his very flesh, the hardness and metallic coldness of necessity, the nearer will he approach the beauty of the world. In rain and in sunlight, which make no distinction between the just and the unjust, in the circular motion of time, the absence of intention or finality is evident, and for that very reason are these things resplendent with pure and supernatural beauty.

The universe is our home. We have a celestial home, it is true, but, in a sense, that is too easy to love. We are in danger of loving, under this name, a fiction which over-simplifies everything. It is above all necessary then, to love our home on earth; that is what God has given us to love; for He wanted man to find love difficult. In the world, men are all strangers, uprooted. Besides, in imitating the beauty of the universe, in responding to its lack of finality, of purpose, and of discrimination, man necessarily renounces his own will. That is what God wants. That which is in man, the image of God himself, is the faculty of renunciation.

The love of our earthly home is the love of God, but only by implication. God must be conceived of as impersonal rather than personal, in the sense that He is the divine model of a person who transcends himself through self-renunciation. To conceive of God as the All-Powerful—or indeed to conceive of Him as a human person under the name of Christ—is self-exclusion from true love of God.

To sum up Simone Weil's thesis: we must identify ourselves with the universe, that is, with necessity. But in itself, such identification is of no use unless we presuppose that through this attitude man induces God to give himself to man in a mystic union. Simone Weil did presuppose this: that by wholly submitting itself to necessity—from which God is absent—the soul pierces through necessity and penetrates into the domain of mystical experience.

Psychologically, Simone Weil's idea of God can be explained only upon the basis of experience: her theology is not a set of dogmas.

While Simone Weil was associating with and writing for the *Cahiers du Sud* group in Marseilles, she also developed an interest in the *Cahiers d'Études Cathares*.

On 23rd January 1941, Simone wrote Déodat Roché a letter, which was subsequently printed in the April-June 1949 issue of that magazine. The letter expressed a long attraction to the Cathari, while admitting little knowledge of them. What particularly interested her, she explained, was their teaching of the Old Testament, which 'so justly maintained that the adoration of power led the Hebrews to lose their notion of good and evil'. The account of the cruelties of the Hebrews had always kept her apart from Christianity; indeed, she said, how could these have failed to influence Christian thought during the last two thousand years? 'The influence of the Old Testament and that of the Roman Empire whose tradition was carried on by the Papacy, are, in my opinion, the two main causes of the corruption of Christianity.'

Simone Weil believed that 'Catharism has been the last living expression in Europe of pre-Roman antiquity', and she linked the Catharist movement to the tradition of which the 'works of Plato constitute the most perfect literary expression'.

In her opinion Catharism was truly a religion; that was what made it a sort of miracle: 'The most exalted thought thrived in a human milieu and not only in the minds of a few individuals.'

Pointing to her enthusiasm for the vanished civilization of the *pays d'oc*, some have suggested that Simone Weil might be called 'gnostic'. The proofs used to support such a suggestion, however, are found in a direction of her thoughts rather than in any definitive formulation of her ideas; thus they seem to indicate little more than a tendency.

The fact of the matter is that while she was attracted by this mediaeval remnant of Gnosis and Manes, she was able to disengage herself from 'modern Catharism' because she knew that: 'One cannot, in fact, be a supporter of that which doesn't exist. For example, one cannot be in favour of the re-establishment of the Carolingian dynasty on the throne of France, or an adherent of the Catharist religion, or of the Order of Templars.'[13]

Nevertheless, Simone Weil's contact with the *Cahiers du Sud* and *Cahiers d'Études Cathares* groups inspired two major essays. The special issue of the *Cahiers du Sud* (1942) in which these articles appeared was called: *The Genius of Oc and the Mediterranean Man*; they gave the publication its chief claim to fame. More than one reader, who knew nothing of the identity of 'Émile Novis'—the anagram that Simone Weil had taken at the editor's request, because her own name was Jewish—was struck by the surprising difference in tone of these articles.[14]

In 'The Agony of a Civilization', the first of the two articles, Simone takes a fragment of the epic in *langue d'oc*—the 'Song of the Crusade against the Albigensians'—as a theme for reflection. The war had just destroyed the Albigensian civilization, a war that was ended by a purely military decision and brought the triumph of intolerance in its wake. Intolerance might be called a mediaeval failing. But if it had won the day, that 'was only because the swords of those who had chosen intolerance had reaped the victory'.

Such is the might of arms, writes Simone Weil. 'Contrary to a very widespread prejudice, a purely military decision can influence the course of human thought for long centuries, and over vast areas.' That is what happened to Europe, which was never able to recover the high degree of intellectual liberty that it had enjoyed before the crusade. Before the war, the *pays d'oc* was a region within which ideas could freely circulate without clashing with one another. It had, therefore, the very atmosphere most conducive to intelligence, for ideas are not made for strife. Under the force of arms the very concept of spiritual liberty perished and did not revive.

The Mediterranean has always been the natural melting pot for traditions coming from the North and from the East. The concern for religious orthodoxy, by raising an obstacle to spiritual relations between the West and the East, transformed this sea-way into a means of transport through which the weapons and the machines of Europe were able to destroy the traditions of the East. After the tenth century, however, there reigned on the shores of the Mediterranean an atmosphere of stability favourable to the development of a civilization enriched by diverse gifts—Catharism. The Cathari were the heirs of Platonic thought, of the initiatory doctrines, of the mysteries of pre-Roman civilization, of the rites and wisdom of the Druids. What extraordinary fruits that astonishing synthesis might have borne, Simone Weil writes. How can its potential fecundity be estimated? A tree is judged by its fruits—but in this case, 'the tree was cut down'.

Yet the Cathar civilization was once complete. It was 'a civilization of the city that was developing in this land'. More than two centuries before Joan of Arc, the Cathari had a keen sense of their fatherland—a fatherland which, of course, was not France and which derived its name from its language, the *langue d'oc*.

Very different were those countries from which the conquerors came. In their lands, there had been neither freedom nor class unity. The only political system known to the invaders was feudalism, 'a régime in which obedience was a commodity to be bought and sold'. The *Song of the Crusade* describes both the felicity of the peoples living in the *pays d'oc* and the brutality of the crusaders. All the inhabitants of Béziers were massacred according to plan. This first shock of terror shattered the Cathari, who then suffered defeat after defeat. Accustomed to obey by duty, they found themselves suddenly compelled to obey by terror. There were spasmodic revolts, but these soon disappeared. The loss in spiritual riches cannot be reckoned, Simone Weil laments. The Church had been trying to ensure religious unification; she obtained it by the simplest means: by the suppression of heretics, on the one hand, and, on the other, by offering forgiveness of sins and eternal salvation unconditionally to all crusaders who might fall in the fray. By thus promising impunity in this world as well as in the next, it opened the door to every sort of excess. In addition, by appealing to the secular arm and to the force of arms, the Church fathers encouraged an ever more unscrupulous resort to cruelty.

Simone Weil urges as a duty, a duty of pity, that modern man should cherish the few and fragmentary remains of the now-vanished civilization of the Cathari: 'Nothing is more cruel to the past than the commonplace which asserts that spiritual values cannot be destroyed by force; on the strength of this belief, civilizations that have been destroyed by force of arms are denied the name of civilization. It can be done without fear of being contradicted by the dead, but it kills a second time what has already perished, and thereby associates the holder of the opinion with the cruelty of arms. . . . The spirit of the civilization of the *langue d'oc* in the twelfth century, insofar as we have knowledge of it, fulfilled aspirations that have not disappeared and which we cannot permit to disappear, even if we cannot hope to realize them.'

Simone Weil picked up the same themes, with greater vigour and with certain ramifications, in another article in the same issue of the *Cahiers du Sud*: 'What Was the Occitanian Inspiration?' She began by rejecting the notion of progress: 'The idea of progress is the idea of the gradual coming to birth, in the course of time, of the better from the less good. Science demonstrates that an increase of energy can come only from an exterior source of energy. . . . Spiritual things are controlled by an analogous law. We cannot be made better except by the influence upon us of what is better than we are.' That is why, when we are looking for someone to provide what is lacking in us, we always have to address ourselves to the past; for the future, which exists only in our imagination, is even less real than the present.

Should we deduce from this that Simone Weil has seen an equivalent to the supernatural in the arts? Or, the view that art unfolds along lines parallel to grace, so that grace finds itself represented there, with all its own modalities in time and space? According to Simone Weil, art is definitely one of the channels of grace. Wherever art is absent, grace is also lacking; wherever art is inferior, grace is degraded. Pure art alone is the indicator of an authentic contact with the supernatural. The periods in which it has flourished are those in which God took delight. To these He was drawn by a means of mediation as essential and as powerful as that of His own son—beauty, which is the visible form of His love.

Among the Greeks, Simone writes, beauty was incarnate in religion, in the mysteries, in philosophy, in art and science. All served as links between heaven and earth, 'bridges' built over the infinity between man and God. However, bridges are meant to be crossed, not to be dwelt upon; the great mistake is to try to take up one's abode on them as humanism did when it domesticated Greek art without understanding its vital role, its supernatural function.

The Cathari, on the other hand, in the twelfth century, knew how to make use of 'bridges'. Not only had they inherited from the Greeks this knowledge, but also their sense of mediation, measure, balance, and therefore justice. They were able to contemplate force, to be exposed to it without being drawn to it, without being attracted to or giving themselves up to it. It is to their wisdom that we must return, if we wish to understand our own destiny. If we contemplate it steadily, with desire, it will enter into us.

Such, in brief, is the moral that emerges from her article on 'Occitanian inspiration': the logic of its exposition, the importance of its central doctrine of 'bridges'. In her *Notebooks*, Simone Weil calls such 'bridges' *metaxu*, from the Greek word meaning 'intermediary'.

In essence, the Occitanian inspiration was, for Simone Weil, identical with the Greek. For it recognized the just measure of force without *hubris* or uncontrolled passion. 'That knowledge belongs only to supernatural courage'; for it implies not only the scorn, but also the abhorrent rejection of force. The refusal to use force finds its positive counterpart in the plenitude of love.

We have been told about homosexuality among the Greeks; but 'what the Greeks thus honoured was none other than *impossible love*. Hence, what they honoured was chastity.'

'When Christianity and the high purity of manners introduced by the Germanic tribes had placed between man and woman that barrier which was lacking in Greece, they became for one another objects of Platonic love. The sacred tie of marriage was an obstacle equivalent to that provided by identity of sex. The authentic troubadours were no more disposed to adultery than Sappho and Socrates were to vice; what they needed was impossible love.' Such love, when it attains its fullest measure, is nothing but the love of God 'through the person loved'. Thus in Greece as in the *pays d'oc*, 'human love was one of the bridges between man and God'.

In the Romanesque churches, there is neither power nor force, says Simone Weil. But 'there is a certain taint of power and pride in the upward surge of Gothic spires and the height of the ogival vaults'. The Gregorian chant is another example of this rejection of force. It 'slowly rises until, at the moment when it seems to be gaining assurance, the ascending movement is broken off and goes down; the ascending movement is always conditioned by the descending. The source of all this art is grace.' The same is true of Occitanian poetry; it is the Pythagorean poetry.

'The Pythagoreans said that harmony or proportion is the unity of contraries *qua* contraries. There is no harmony if the contraries are brought together forcibly, nor is there if they are mixed; the point of unity has to be found. Without ever doing violence to one's soul, without ever seeking either consolation or suffering, to contemplate the thing, whatever it is, that arouses emotion, until one arrives at the secret point where sorrow and joy, by virtue of being pure, are one and the same thing; that is the essential virtue of poetry.'

Public life in the country of the *langue d'oc*, eliminated as far as possible every element of force, that is, 'everything that is collective, . . . all that issues from the social animal'. Obedience to a leader simply as a man, that is, to a being without power, is perfectly pure; a man can at one and the same time swear allegiance of his person to a leader, yet preserve intact his pride and dignity. On the contrary, obedience to a man regarded as the embodiment of collective power, 'whether with or without love', is necessarily degrading. No doubt in the Toulouse of the thirteenth century there were blemishes, but the inspiration was pure: 'Among those who attacked it victoriously, inspiration itself was defiled.'

This need for purity found 'its extreme expression' in Catharism; it resulted in its destruction. The Catharist religion seems to have carried spiritual freedom to a point where there were no dogmas—an absence which wasn't without its drawbacks. It was undeniably necessary for the Church, outside the Cathar country, to preserve Christian dogma in its integrity, like a pure diamond. As far as the Cathari were concerned, they 'pushed their horror of force even as far as the practice of non-violence and the teaching that all that belonged to the domain of force, that is, all that was carnal as well as all that was social, proceeded from evil. That was to go quite far, but no further than the Gospels. For there are two sayings in the Gospels which go as far as it is possible. One is about the eunuchs who make themselves eunuchs for the sake of the kingdom of heaven. The other is the word spoken by the devil to Christ when he showed Him all the kingdoms of the world: "All this power I will give thee, and the glory of them: for that is delivered unto me; and to whomsoever I will, I give it".'

Simone Weil dreamed of undertaking a big work, under the title *The Descent of God*, which, according to her publishers, was to be an annotated anthology of the 'most beautiful non-Christian texts upon the love of God'. She had made this 'the theme of her talks, at some intimate meetings in the crypt of the convent of the Dominicans of Marseilles'.[15] The work would have brought out the undercurrent of spirituality in Greek thought, which Simone Weil believed to be its essence.

She undertook, at the same time, the dozen other studies now included under the title: *The Greek Source*: 'Zeus and Prometheus'. 'On the Theaetetus', 'God in Plato', etc.[16] All these can be regarded as products of the same inspiration, but the last is of central importance. In it, Simone Weil asserts without hesitation

Dilapidated house in which Simone Weil lived in Saint-Marcel
d'Ardèche, August-September 1941

Simone Weil, Marseilles, winter 1941-2

that Plato's thought faithfully represents the Greek mentality, that his spirituality is the Greek spirituality. The problem was simplified, as far as she was concerned, by eliminating Aristotle from the true Greek tradition and casting him into outer darkness.

Despite his normative rôle, however, Plato was only the least among the best. What was he, in fact, asks Simone Weil, but the 'heir of a tradition of mysticism wherein all of Greece was bathed'? 'Plato is an authentic mystic and even the father of Occidental mysticism.' He was but the popularizer of a mystical tradition who happened to write works which survived him. The *Banquet*, for instance, was not solely his work, since it was derived from a religious tradition.

Once this method of approach is defined, each Platonic theme takes its place naturally within the frame of the 'Weilian' theology; and the greatest pages of Plato take on a renewed meaning.

In a commentary on the *Gorgias*, Simone Weil writes: 'The image of "nudity" is linked with that of "death" . . . This double image is the purest mysticism.' This is so because truth is, and must remain, hidden. Truth being at the basis of justice, the latter's existence is conditional upon that nakedness which comes from death. 'It is evident that this justice is impossible to human nature and is supernatural.'

Man is prevented by numerous attachments from giving himself to justice. First, there is the flesh, then society. 'Numerous passages of Plato speak of the peril of the flesh.' The 'adulterous union with the flesh'[17] is the first refuge of man from God. His second refuge comes to him from the world: 'the Great Beast . . . the social animal'. The implication is that society is intrinsically bad and must not be submitted to except in the domain of what is necessary. Such a negative attitude is not always rewarded by success. Simone Weil sadly observed that even the Apostles abandoned their Lord. And so does modern man: 'at every instant, even at this very moment'.

Grace is therefore indispensable, but it is of no avail without love which is the disposition of the soul to receive. 'THERE IS NOT, NOR COULD THERE BE, ANY OTHER RELATIONSHIP OF MAN TO GOD BUT LOVE. WHAT IS NOT LOVE IS NOT RELATIONSHIP WITH GOD.'

The intellect directed to the discovery of truth quickly loses all contact with its object if it is not illuminated by love. If God is truth, and if God can only be apprehended by the heart (as Pascal would have us say), truth is not in the man who does not love. 'The love of God,' Simone Weil said, translating the *Republic*, 'is the sole source of all certitudes.'

A gulf divides the mysticism of Plato from the intellectualism of Aristotle, but there is nothing to distinguish it from Christian mysticism. The 'image of the cave' is of universal application. It describes the conversion of man: 'We are born chastised.'

'We are born and live *in falsehood*.

We are born and live *in passivity*.

We are born and live *in unconsciousness*.'

The process whereby the soul, born in the night, can attain the contemplation of intrinsic beauty has been abundantly described by Plato. At the end of the ascent of the spirit, 'the whole soul must detach itself from this world, but it is only the supernatural part which comes into contact with the other world. When the supernatural part has seen God face to face, it must turn back towards the soul to govern it, to bring the whole soul into the waking state . . . The natural part of the soul, detached from one world, yet unable to reach the other, is *in the void* while the process of deliverance is under way. It must again be given contact with this world, which is its own, but a legitimate contact which is not attachment.'

In the 'Divine Love in Creation',[18] Simone Weil expresses this concept more precisely: 'Once a certain threshold is crossed, the supernatural part of the soul reigns over the natural part, not by violence but by persuasion, not by will but by desire.' Individual redemption is attained through a separation between the natural and the supernatural. God does not intervene. It is a natural redemption, a redemption accomplished without Him. Grace is a latent dynamism which must release itself in the heart of man. That force which separates nature from supernature becomes the weight which, after separation, draws what is above downward to what is below, for a new incarnation which will give a new dignity of being to the lower part. The order to be followed is irreversible: man must first 'disincarnate' himself in order to be reborn according to a new kind of generation.

# Metaxu

Upon the mystical path man meets with certain types of help. These are the *metaxu*, the intermediaries: they at once eliminate sensory differences and signify God.

'The function of the intermediary is . . . to keep the middle way between ignorance and true wisdom, between temporal becoming and the fullness of being . . . Moreover, it must *draw the soul towards being, bring forth thought.*'[19]

In the sphere of thought, the use of *metaxu* enables man to rise above 'logical' contradictions; 'for wherever there appears to be contradiction, there is a correlation of contraries, that is, a relationship'.[20] Our intelligence is impelled and drawn towards what is higher. We are forced to see the unity of the world, and in the world non-being and being are mixed. Yet our intelligence cannot co-ordinate the existence of non-being and the non-existence of being. Thus, the mind raises itself to the consideration of a higher truth concerning opposites. Science, which enables us to discern the watermark of necessity in every page of the book of the world, is one of these *metaxu*. The order of the world itself is another. Together, all form the intellectual way towards God.

Upon the non-intellectual path, the beauty of the world, the visible manifestation of the divine beauty, sets a snare for the soul. This is the 'pomegranate seed' which the soul eats furtively —the assent that it accords to God 'almost without knowing it, and without admitting it to itself. This is an infinitely small thing among all the carnal inclinations of the soul, and nevertheless this decides its destiny for ever'.[20]

It would be a mistake, however, to limit the number of the *metaxu*, and here one can see that Simone Weil is interpreting the Platonic *metaxu* as the cipher of God in the world. From the moment that something created is not an end but a means, it becomes a bridge to God. 'All that separates is also a link',[21] like the common wall between two prison cells which enables prisoners to communicate with each other by knocking out messages upon it.

The plasticity of the term *metaxu*, the variety of its applications, and the lack of any definitive formulation limits its further consideration. Worth further attention, however, is the 'bridge' which Simon Weil studied so long with such particular attention: science.

In the *Cahiers du Sud* of December 1942, Simone Weil wrote a review of Max Planck's *Introduction to Physics*, which had just been republished. She took the opportunity to express her own ideas.

As a result, the article might have been called 'The Relativity of Modern Science'. Under the title, 'Reflections on the Quantum Theory', it disguises an attack on Planck's views from the standpoint of the principle of non-contradiction.

The quantum theory consists in 'considering energy, or rather the action which is a product of energy by time, as a magnitude which varies in a discontinuous manner, by successive leaps . . .' But 'science', when it is 'at the level of representation' cannot accept what is offered here, 'an explanation . . . which is in no way representable', since it contradicts the data of the senses, for which space and time are 'continuous magnitudes'.

Why then have recourse to discontinuous quantities? They were introduced quite incidentally by Planck, when he applied the calculus of probabilities to the phenomenon called dark radiation. The result of the transference of his measurements to the thing measured—the former being discontinuous, since they referred to numbers—was that the latter took on the same appearance, wrote Simone Weil. Thus, discontinuity was introduced into energy 'for the convenience of calculation'. It was not necessary; it was not to be found in the object under study. Energy, represented by formulas which have no respect for its real nature, has become merely a word 'divorced from its concrete meaning. . . . The paper, as they say, will put up with anything'.

In the way in which they used algebra, scientists were no less guilty of an abuse of trust: they made it serve more and more as the sole language of science, as though they did not know that letters were perfectly useless for the representation of notions. In fact 'some statements that are incompatible can find their equivalents in equations which are not so at all'. The result is an obscurity that passes for profundity. 'If a profound thought cannot be expressed, it is because it embraces at the same time several vertically superimposed levels of meaning, and a common language can but ill reflect these different levels; but algebra is even less appropriate for this, for it puts everything on the same plane. . . . It is quite flat; the third dimension of thought is absent from it.' False profundity, however, has attracted the attention of philosophers, who have been seeking, 'with a touching perseverance, for a profound meaning in the conception of the world implied by contemporary science. Quite in vain, for there is none'. One is reminded of Hans Christian Andersen's story of the emperor who walked about naked because no one dared call attention to the fact. Whatever may be said about it, the science of today is without any philosophical significance.

For Simone Weil, Max Planck's book shows that the very first to be taken in by science are the scientists, who think that science is 'a universal floating above the heads of scientists of all times and all countries'. And yet they know that their science is the result of convention. 'The creator of a hypothesis,' writes Max Planck, 'has practically unlimited possibilities at his disposal. He is as little bound by the functioning of the organs of his senses as he is by that of the instruments he is using . . . One might even say that he makes for himself whatever geometry he chooses.' That is why 'scientific theories have disappeared in much the same way as men's fashions of the seventeenth century; suits in the style of Louis XIII disappeared when the last old men who had been young under Louis XIII were dead'. A new theory is accepted, Simone Weil declares, once it has become a mental habit among the new generation.

There is no such thing as science with a capital S, with edicts which have the force of law, she protests. But there are scientists all over the world—just enough of them to people a small village. They live apart from the world, even when they live in the midst of the busiest cities, and they think apart. They have their little circle, their club, where no one can be a member without their permission, where thought is governed by an average opinion which is the result of compromise between persons and generations. This average opinion constitutes the state of science at any given moment.

What Simone Weil tried to do was to demonstrate the

contradiction in ascribing infallibility to a science that is the result of a free postulate. If science is infallible, she says, it participates in truth, and thus it is impossible that it should contradict itself. Moreover, such science becomes necessity, and cannot be abandoned to the scientist's own choice. On the other hand, if science is quite gratuitous, then it depends simply upon the scientist's capacity for invention—and loses its relation to reality. In neither case does science have any moral content. What arises from necessity, like what depends merely upon fancy, has nothing to do with moral good. That is of a wholly different order.

What Simone Weil sought to achieve was to situate science between the two extremes of infallibility and gratuitousness—the establishment of science on the plane of freedom, where choice has a human value because it involves consent to the truth. There the scientist becomes responsible, and his discoveries reflect the moral quality of his intent. There his genius derives not only from natural aptitudes, which are his own, but also from inspiration which he has received from others, a tradition of truth, a responsiveness to values, a responsibility towards the good.

Simone Weil also asked for a general review of scientific knowledge as a first step in the elucidation of the obvious contradictions of modern science. This would help also to bring it down from its esoteric level, relate it to the rest of knowledge, and allow for its formulation in terms intelligible to the average man which would not be an assault on his common-sense. Furthermore, it might put a welcome brake to the drift from truth to pragmatic use which is fast becoming the only criterion of successful research, a criterion which is deadly both to science itself, as Simone Weil pointed out, and she might have added, to a civilization held in the spell of an unbridled and uncontrollable technology.

If science, like art, is a vehicle of truth, literature is the most direct means for the expression of truth, as well as the most dangerous. No writer can be absolved of his responsibility, Simone Weil thought. Writers have definite duties that they may not disregard.

In October 1940 and March 1941, the *Cahiers du Sud* had

published two writings of L. G. Gros, on 'the survival of poetry', and 'the modernity of poetry', both directed against two views prevalent at that time. One of these, from Vichy, attributed to contemporary literature the long-term responsibility for the defeat of France. The other, maintained by magazines in the Free Zone, denied the possibility of there being an uncommitted literature.

Without being in sympathy with the authors of these theses, Simone Weil nevertheless shared their point of view in a letter on the 'Responsibilities of Literature'.[22] Although there is nothing very original about what she wrote, it is of some importance in displaying a fundamental tendency of her thinking, which was more often apparent in connection with other themes.

Not only was the defeat of France attributable to the demoralizing influence of contemporary literature, but it was the indication of an even greater misfortune: 'I believe that the writers of the period which has just ended share in the responsibility for the misery of our times.'

It is not true that there is a gulf between literature and the public. It is pointless to pretend that the best books are little read. It is impossible to exonerate great writers from the influence of their works upon the public. For even if these books are practically inaccessible to the general public, they are more or less directly accessible to those who write for the masses.

However, writers are careful not to judge one another; they tolerate every kind of baseness in each other and never withdraw their mutual esteem: 'These easygoing literary manners, this tolerance of turpitude, gives our most eminent writers a responsibility for the demoralization of a peasant-girl who has never left her village or as much as heard their name.'

But writers have a more direct responsibility: 'The essential characteristic of the first half of the twentieth century is the diminution and almost the disappearance of the notion of value. . . . But writers were, pre-eminently, the guardians of the treasure that has been lost, and some have taken pride in this loss.'

Surrealism is an extreme example of the desire for total licence; of the intoxication into which the spirit plunges when it is rejecting every consideration of value and surrendering to the moment. But 'what is good is the pole towards which the human spirit is necessarily oriented, not only in action, but in all effort, including the effort of pure intellect'. The surrealists chose 'as their supreme value, the absence of all values. Licence has always gone to men's heads'. In the course of history, cities have often been sacked. 'But the sack of cities has not always had a literary equivalent, and that is what surrealism is.'

It is not from a lack of morality, nor even of moralism that contemporary French literature is suffering. But it can no longer see evil as evil nor good as good. For lack of this sixth sense, it has become empty of all true humanity. The principle that Terence proposed to writers, *nil humanum a me alienum puto*, remains a dead letter. We are worse than our ancestors were at the time when Rome was oppressing the culture of the Greeks.

Today, the universal soul is perishing because it has lost 'a sense of value'. 'Goodness', 'honour', 'virtue', 'nobility', have given place to ambiguous terms: 'sincerity', 'gratuitousness', 'wealth'. Words formerly so full of meaning, whose power of suggestion once seemed limitless, wither away with the things they describe. And this is not because the realities with which literature once dealt have disappeared. In one way, it is worse than that. For if the impoverishment of language had followed upon an impoverishment of reality, literature would only have been reflecting the facts. But its retrogression was deliberate; literature has refused to assume the full burden of human destiny.

Destiny oscillates between the two alternatives of choice which Baudelaire defines as those of God and Satan. But art has turned away from its representative function. It has abandoned truth in favour of sincerity, the value of an action in favour of its gratuitousness, liberty of the mind in favour of the commitment of the soul.

To sum up: 'What has happened to words makes it clear that the idea of value has been steadily diminishing, and though the fate of words does not entirely rest with writers, yet one cannot help making them peculiarly responsible, since words are their especial concern.'

Bergson himself did not escape the modern trend, according to Simone Weil. He took part in it and bears his share of responsibility: 'At the heart of the philosophy out of which his first three works originate, we find a notion that is inherently alien to every consideration of value; that is, the notion of life.' In this Bergson places himself far from the Christian tradition with which people have tried to associate him. As for Proust, he describes 'non-oriented states of the soul'.

'Here, the good appears only at rare moments when, either by the effect of memory or of beauty, a presentiment of eternity slips through time.'

Psychology, a science of observation, has spoilt the literature of the twentieth century, she writes. For psychology is concerned with description, not judgment; with reducing everything to a common denominator, not with establishing a scale of values. It places all states of soul on the same level 'without discrimination between values, as though good and evil were external to them, as though the effort towards the good could be absent at any moment from the thinking of any man'.

Simone Weil recalls that 'the human condition' which all writers flatter themselves that they are describing is attached inseparably to concepts of good and evil. Indifference with regard to good and evil is deadly for art. Their opposition gives it all its perspective and relief. Racine never was so great as when he was preoccupied with Jansenist morality and wrote *Phèdre*. Rimbaud never attained Villon's stature, because Rimbaud so rarely knew evil for what it was. Villon could steal, but he knew what it was to steal. He knew that it was neither 'an adventure nor a free act'. 'The sense of good and evil pervades all his verse, as it pervades every work that is not estranged from human destiny.'

Simone Weil was not asking for a 'reform' of literature in the name of morality. She had a profound contempt for moralism in literature. She thought censors were inferior to men of letters. She knew well enough that: 'If present sufferings ever bring about a reform, it will not be accomplished by means of slogans, but in silence and moral solitude, through pain, afflictions and terrors, in the innermost depth of every soul.'

In another of her articles, 'Morality and Literature',[23] written at the same time, she again takes up the theme of the opposition of good to evil; it is apparent that this is central to her aesthetic.

'Nothing is beautiful, marvellous, or perpetually new, perpetually surprising, charged with delightful and enduring excitement, except goodness. Nothing is as desolate, bleak, monotonous and wearisome as evil. Thus it is with real good and real evil. With fictitious good and evil the qualities are reversed. Fictitious goodness is wearisome and dreary. Fictitious evil is varied, interesting, attractive, profound, and most seductive.'

Good and evil, then, present themselves under contrary appearances which reveal their oppositeness. But the irony is that they borrow each other's appearances when they pass from the plane of reality to that of fiction. On the plane of being, good inevitably attracts us; it pleases us, solicits us and we consent to it. We recoil from evil; it displeases us, and automatically provokes refusal. On the plane of imagination, on the contrary, it is evil that is wonderful and good that is disappointing. For then they are elements in a world of dreams, whose possibilities are infinite so long as they are not circumscribed by reality. But good alone belongs to the fullness of being; consequently, to the degree that it is present, it limits the field of imagination.

To illustrate: a man's falling from a ladder in the street provokes a movement of horror. But if a man were to walk upon air, we would never be tired of gazing at him. In the same way pure good is a thing of wonder. 'Necessity which is as strong as the laws of gravitation condemns man to evil, forbids him all but the most limited good arduously achieved, completely mixed with and soiled by evil, except when the supernatural appears on earth and suspends the effect of earthly necessity. But if, in a painting, I show a man climbing up into the air, this would be of no interest. That is something which would be of interest only in reality. Unreality deprives good of all value.'

Men who leap and jump about crazily will attract attention, as long as no one notices that there are burning coals beneath their feet. By contrast, the ordinary gait of a passer-by will be of no interest at all at first sight, but as soon as one is aware of the torture inflicted upon others, it will be something to be wondered at. 'So evil, while it is fictional, derives an interest from the variety of forms that it takes, which seem then to belong to a roving fancy. . . . The simplicity which makes of the

fictional good a colourless and uninteresting thing is an un-
fathomable marvel in real goodness.'

It is upon these premises of universal application that Simone
Weil bases her condemnation of those who want to introduce
morality into art: 'Since literature consists mainly of fiction,
immorality seems to be inseparable from it. Quite wrongly do
we reproach writers with being immoral, unless we reproach them
at the same time for being writers, as people had the courage to
do in the seventeenth century.'

Is it logical then to think that a writer can be moral? The
terms themselves are in contradiction. There are simply good
or bad writers, and those who have pretensions to morality are
to be found among the latter. Does this mean that only an
aesthetic criterion can be applied to literature? Not at all. For
one cannot remove any human activity from the categories of
good and evil: 'All activity is related in two ways to good and
evil, in its origin and in its accomplishment. Thus any book
can be on the one hand either well or badly done, and on the
other hand it may proceed either from good or from evil.'

Genius makes manifest the laws of gravity which it does not
share and which it does not impart to the reader. It perceives
them as we do when we are looking at a precipice, if we are in
a safe place and not subject to vertigo. 'It discerns the unity and
diversity of their forms in the architecture of the abyss.'

There is, then, an ethic of aesthetics which is no less binding
than the universal ethic, to which it belongs as a part is related
to the whole. This inherent ethic of art is decisive, not for talent,
but for genius. It allows a genius the full deployment of his
gifts, but denies him their exercise when he is oriented towards
evil. 'Just as the maturity of genius is its conformity with
the true relationship between good and evil, so the work
which corresponds with the maturity of a demoniac genius is
silence. Rimbaud is at once its symbol and its outstanding
example.'

We may say then that immorality is the very material of art,
except in the case of works of genius. The unique function of
writers who are not geniuses, and in consequence are immoral,
is to establish the environment in which geniuses can appear.

Literature must abandon any pretension to morality. When that which is inherently immoral pretends that its function is to moralize, the result is devastating. 'This usurpation dates from the eighteenth century and above all since the inception of romanticism. It introduced into literature a Messianic turgidity wholly alien to the purity of art.'

While we await the downfall of this literature, there remain the geniuses of the past, to whom we can still turn. The inspiration that comes from the contemplation of their works of art 'tends, as Plato said, to make the soul grow wings to overcome gravity'.

Simone Weil frequently attended the meetings of the Philosophical Society. There she met Gaston Berger, who asked her to write an article on pure philosophy for the *Études philosophiques* of which he was editor. Her 'Essay on the Meaning of Reading',[24] published by him, was the first article of its kind that she had undertaken since 1929, when she sent her very first essays, *'De la perception, ou l'Aventure de Protée'* and *'Du temps'*, to *Libres Propos*.

The whole of life is reading: this was her thesis. How could it be otherwise? 'The sky, the sea, the sun, the stars, human beings and everything around us—all this is reading-matter for us; and what we call the correction of an illusion of the senses, is a modified reading.'

But reading is dependent on two conditions: the text must have meaning, and the reader must know how to read. And there is always the question: are some texts truer than others?

'Where is one to find the norm? To think of a true text that I don't read, that I have never read, is to think of a reader of this true text, that is to say, God: but at once a contradiction appears, for I cannot apply to the being whom I conceive when I speak of God this notion of reading.' God is related to such texts not as a reader, but as the truth. He is the truth of all possible texts and also their meaning.

On the other hand, the morality of his response is determined by the way in which a man reads. The finder of lost property will either give it up or retain it according to whether he reads in this object the desires that he can gratify in keeping it, or the joy of the rightful owner in recovering it.

The interest in elucidating such a notion of reading lies in the fact that it presents the moral problem in concrete terms. The real metaphysical conclusion of this article will be found in the *Notebooks* in which, at this time, Simone Weil was reflecting on the categorical imperative of Kant: 'Act in such a way that the maxim of your action could be elevated to a universal law.' One way of living up to this moral criterion is: 'To read in appearances something that another person, differently situated, differently affected, can read—by making the same effort.'[25] She concludes: 'Do not read. Read the unread.'[26] The true response to the moral problem, here as elsewhere, is a response of mystical character.

## Mysticism

The years 1940-1942 were, for Simone Weil, a time of intense contemplation. Her fondness for the poetry of George Herbert, begun in 1938, did not diminish. It was from his poem 'Love' that she had derived her first mystical experience when, 'for the first time' Christ came to claim her. She had believed she was reciting a beautiful poem; unknown to her, it had been a prayer. She describes anew the experience in a letter to Joë Bousquet, dated 12th May 1942: 'In a moment of intense physical pain, as I was concentrating all my thoughts on an act of intense love (yet not thinking that I had the right to give a name to this love), I felt—without being in the least prepared for it, for I had never read the mystics—a presence more personal, more certain, more real, than that of any human being; a presence inaccessible to either senses or imagination, and analogous to the love that shines through the tenderest smile of a person whom one loves.'[1]

Similarly, as she was to do at St Marcel d'Ardèche, when she was to practise reciting the 'Pater Noster' in Greek, her thoughts were to be removed from her body to be borne away to 'a place outside space, where there is neither perspective nor point of view'. This prayer, she was to confide to Father Perrin in a letter of 15th May 1942, called forth Christ in person, in 'a presence infinitely more real, more poignant, clearer and more full of love'[2] than that first time in 1938 when he had taken hold of her.

These mystical experiences, whether the initial one of 1938 or the following ones of 1941-1942, both related in the letters to Joë Bousquet (12th May 1942), and to Father Perrin (15th May 1942), should not be confused with the revelation described in the 'Prologue' to the *Connaissance surnaturelle*. There are certain indications that the Prologue retraces an experience which took place in Paris during the early months of 1940; however, according to other testimonies, it was at the beginning of 1941 in Marseilles that it occurred. In effect, this text was found on the opening pages of the notebooks she wrote during her stay at Marseilles. The church of the Dominican Fathers, called 'new and ugly' in her description of the experience, was modern enough to have that very ugliness which seems inseparable from all that is new. The 'station waiting-room' and the 'prison-cell' are explained, the first by the travels of Simone Weil and the second by her interest in the prison camps and the trials she attended. And though there was no 'river' in Marseilles, there was the harbour 'where boats were being unladen' and where barges from the Rhône could be seen along the shore. Finally, there is no reason why the vision of Simone Weil should correspond to current reality, and why her account should be accepted as descriptively accurate in all details. It is sufficient that she found herself one day in a Paris or Marseilles street (as she later told, Simone Deitz), wandering about, not knowing where she was, as if she had just awakened from a dream or left another world where she perceived what her eyes 'believed they had seen',[3] but to which only the soul can bear witness. It is probable that not even those who might have encountered her would have noticed an indication of the vision revealed upon her face or in her deportment. She was a young girl like so many others, undistinguished as she walked on the pavement, heeding the traffic. But while her feet trod the pavement, her soul was with the mysterious host in the 'attic' which her physical self had never entered. Brutally she had been thrown 'on the stairs' and had suddenly found herself wandering 'about the streets' not knowing where the house in which she had been 'was to be found'.

In the account of her 'awakened dream' is there *affabulation* on the part of Simone Weil? (Does she use fantasy in attempting to recreate her experience in words?) If so, to what extent? Her text bears the unmistakable stamp of the creative imagination of the author. If a synthesis occurred, what share of the precise facts, the charismatic data, and the symbolic acts emerged?

Simone Weil describes the mysterious host entering her room. He reproached her for her ignorance and promised to teach her. He led her to a church, where he ordered her, though she was not baptized, to kneel before the altar. He led her to an attic, where they were alone. Sometimes he took from the cupboard bread that truly tasted like bread, he poured out wine 'which had the taste of the sun and of the earth'. Sometimes they lay at full length on the floor. He had promised to teach her, but he gave her no instruction. Then one day, abruptly, he sent her away. She tried to find the attic again. But she could not. 'I cannot help repeating, now and then, with fear and remorse, part of what he told me. How can I know whether I remember it accurately? He is not there to tell me.'

At the heart of this silence of God, she recalls, it seemed to her that she heard his love expressing itself without words.

The possible interpretations of this document are far from simple. It seems to be divided into three parts, each amenable to symbolic interpretation, especially in view of the chronological order of events. The first part takes place inside a church; a simple episode of obedience, it is, at the same time, partial and total—total where the heart is concerned, but incomplete in regard to the understanding of the intellect. Outside the church, in the attic, true mystical contact occurs: the soul loses its virginity. Finally, there is the enforced return into the street, into night and solitude, with the memory and the certainty of having tasted love and of having been transfigured by the contact.

The 'Prologue' deserves to be kept for its documentary value; above all, it is significant for the light it throws on the fleeting nature of Simone Weil's mystical experiences. There is, however, a contrast between this experience, as Simone Weil relates it, and the 'system' for which it supplies the point of departure. On the one hand, Simone insists on the pre-eminently personal character of the Being who reveals himself to her: 'Christ is present in person' with 'a presence more personal, more certain, more real than that of any human'. On the other hand, her doctrinal mysticism is based upon the experience of the Divine as such; it is indeterminate; it has no very explicit relation to the tenets of the Christian religion, but has a definite relation to the theological system constructed by the intelligence of Simone Weil. Outside her revelations, the elements of which cannot be translated into precise terms, Christ always remains hardly more than a symbol for her, the human appearance and the historic support of a transcendent love.

The mystical experience of Simone Weil had been preceded by two important factors: first, that suffering, 'located around the central point of the nervous system, at the point of junction between body and soul, which goes on even through sleep, never ceasing for a second'; next, the assurance, the moral and intellectual certainty, that every desire has its own efficacy. Since the age of fourteen, she wrote to Joë Bousquet, she had been sustained by the belief that 'no effort of true attention is ever wasted, even though, directly or indirectly, it should never achieve visible results'.

Her own interpretation of the experience itself is perhaps the most lucid statement available to her readers:

'Man escapes from the laws of this world but only for the space of a flash of lightning. Moments of pause, of contemplation, of pure intuition, of mental void, of acceptance of the moral void. It is through such moments that he is able to approach the supernatural.

'Whoever for an instant can endure the void either receives the supernatural bread or else falls. Terrible risk; but we have got to run it.'[4]

A description of this experience can be found in a very ancient myth, the egg of the world: 'The egg—that is this visible world. The chick—that is Love; the Love that is God himself and who dwells in the inmost part of each man, at first as an invisible seed. When the shell is pierced, when the being has

Ενύπομένη

emerged, it has the same world still for its object. But it is no longer inside it. Space has been opened and rent.'⁵

The mystical experience is of very brief duration because 'my soul . . . cannot abide in God save for short spaces of time', but it is so decisive that it can only be compared to nuptial union with God. 'For each human being, there is a date which no one knows (he himself, least of all) but which is wholly determined; beyond it, the soul can no longer preserve its virginity.' Such an experience presupposes the existence of that *malheur* which is 'the redemptive function itself'. Both body and soul must remain nailed by suffering to a fixed place; an essential requirement is the enforced immobility that *malheur* imposes upon them.

'Thanks to this immobility, the infinitesimal seed of divine love thrown into the soul can grow at leisure and bear fruit by waiting *en ûpoméné*, as the divinely beautiful words of the Scriptures express it . . . . Remaining in one's place, waiting, not motionless, shaken or displaced by any shock from without. . . .

'I am convinced that suffering on the one hand, and the joy of pure and total adherence to consummate beauty on the other, each implying loss of personal existence, are the only two keys by which we can enter into that pure realm, the realm where one can breathe, the realm of reality.

'But both must be without alloy: joy without the least shade of dissatisfaction; suffering without consolation.

'The divine love that a person touches at the very depths of suffering, like the resurrection of Christ through the crucifixion, constitutes the intangible essence and the central core of joy; it is not consolation. It leaves the pain itself untouched.'⁵

Through pure joy and pure suffering a contact with divine love may be achieved at a higher level than that of pure intellectual speculation; yet it is a descending or 'prevenient' contact which cannot come from the soul itself, and must, for this very reason, be regarded as supernatural or mystical. 'The experience of the transcendent: this seems a contradiction in terms, and yet the transcendent can only be known through contact, since our faculties are unable to construct it.'⁶

From her contact with the supernatural, Simone Weil derived

the conviction that she had attained the 'unconditional good',[7] that she had touched upon that sphere reserved for genius from which she previously had believed she was excluded by the limitation of her intellect; it was the certainty of having broken out of the 'egg of the world'. Salvation was for her identified with mystical knowledge; although erroneous from the standpoint of Catholic theology, this was a conviction consistent with her system. More precisely, Simone Weil had exorcized the notion of salvation; she was no longer preoccupied with it. She regarded the hope of salvation as a stage that was unnecessary for one who loved God. It was for just that reason that she could not see anything to be gained by entering the Church and asking for baptism, as Father Perrin thought she would. All the intellectual arguments that Simone Weil had formulated, or was logically bound to formulate, against Christianity crystallized themselves around this issue of baptism.

The first points of Christian doctrine which proved stumbling-stones to Simone Weil were those that testified to the survival, in Christianity, of the Hebraic tradition. She believed that Israel had learnt the essential truth about God—namely, that he is good —from alien traditions. The religion of the Jews was, for her, nothing but an immoderate desire for exclusive election; they were less in touch with divine truths, she thought, than certain neighbouring people who did not 'make an idol of their own destiny'. The preaching of the Gospel was intended for all, as Christ himself said; but it was tainted with patriotism from its source in Judaism and thereby took on a narrow and aggressive character. To preach the message of Christ, Europe cut itself off from Greek antiquity and became spiritually rootless. And it passed its own shortcomings on to the whole world: pervaded by Roman imperialism as well as by fanaticism, it set out to conquer the peoples of Africa and Asia. The history of the Church, wrote Simone Weil, is still blood-stained by this vast effort to enslave others.[8]

This controversial attitude of hers towards Israel was closely wedded to her syncretism; implicit in it are a second group of reasons which kept her away from the baptismal font. In different civilizations, she suggests, there may well have been writings with as good a title to revelation as the Judaeo-Christian. Texts referring to Melchisedech prove that quite apart from Israel there was worship and knowledge of God analogous to that of the Gospels and vastly superior to anything that the religion of Israel had ever been. There may also have been other Incarnations of the Word besides those of Jesus—from Melchisedech, Osiris, and Krishna, for example. Moreover, Simone Weil maintains, there are religions other than Christianity that convey, in much more lucid terms, truths that are only implicitly contained in the Christian religion. If this is difficult to accept, she points out that it is because a religion can be known only from within. But are not the mysticisms of all religions so near to one another as to be almost identical? Is not the teaching of the mystics that which constitutes what is true in each religion? Before Christ, there were men who went to even greater lengths in their love of God than Christian saints; after Christ, there has been no increase in the number of chosen souls. Lastly, a deep understanding of Christianity has been made almost impossible to present generations, because what took place in early Christian times is wrapped in mystery. Surely, she says, despite the 'nonsense' written by Clement of Alexandria, in the beginnings of Christianity there were syncretist efforts of which nothing now seems to be known.

Simone Weil's particular attitude towards Redemption gives rise to a third explanation for her refusal to be baptized. If the Redemption, with corresponding signs and sacraments, had not been manifest on earth from the beginning—not merely since the coming of Christ—then God could hardly be forgiven for the tribulations of so many innocent people. 'A Roman slave, torn out of his own society, subjected to the rule of his master, maltreated and finally crucified, must have died with his heart full of hatred—and consequently have been damned—if Christ did not descend into him. Since Christ came only twenty centuries ago, how could God be forgiven for the suffering of Roman slaves?'[9]

Outside the Church there has been a development of dogma upon the question of possible salvation. Following the example of the Roman slaves, for example, it has been said that Catholic doctrine, as traditionally expounded in regard to the fate of still-born children, is also inhuman.

As a fourth deterrent to baptism, there were the following points of doctrine to which Simone Weil's own religious experience had introduced her, plus the special quality of her asceticism:

1. The importance of *attention* (contemplation). The fact that, for Simone Weil, the desire was necessarily effective compelled her to assert that whenever a man invokes, in all purity of heart, Osiris, Krishna, or any other incarnation of the divine Word, the Son of God responds by sending the Holy Ghost.

'It is impossible that the whole truth should not be present at all times, in all places, at the disposal of anyone who desires it: "If he ask for bread". Truth is bread. It would be absurd to suppose that for centuries no one or almost no one desired the truth, and that, during the centuries that came after, entire peoples desired it. . . .

'Whatever has not always and everywhere been at the disposal of anyone who desires truth, is other than truth.'[10]

A logical development of this thought was Simone Weil's attitude towards missionaries. Missionary action she saw as bad in itself. She would never contribute a penny to missionary funds, for she felt that a change of religion is as dangerous to a soul as a change of language is to a writer. This idea was closely connected with her great theme of 'rootedness', as well as with her pacifism: 'Faith ought to be defended only by innocence and love. Missionaries ought neither to be helped, nor protected, nor avenged by arms, nor by political power.'[11]

Thus, for Simone Weil, desire carried to its ultimate limit calls for mystical experience, direct contact with God; religion, then, is only a form, a means; all religions are of equal value if their foundation is mystical.

2. *The impersonality of God.* Christianity over-emphasized the personal nature of God, according to Simone Weil. If God is thought of as primarily personal, 'one cannot progress beyond a certain point on the way towards perfection . . . To go beyond this it is necessary—by the force of desire—to shape oneself in the likeness of an impersonal perfection'. God is 'an impersonal

Person. He loves, not as I love, but as an emerald is green. He is *I love.*' Necessity is the kiss of God upon his creature.[12]

From this pivotal point the following conclusions were, for Simone Weil, inevitable:

Everything in the Christian religion which reveals a personal love of God for the creature must be regarded with suspicion. (There is in this a somewhat paradoxical but fundamental distrust of Catholic Christology.) Christ may be represented only as a kind of symbol to the second power, an avatar of Divinity, whose dogmatic content is practically identical with that which it assumes in Indian theology.

Up to a point, Simone Weil's theology succeeds in assimilating the Word, the Second Person of the Trinity; but it can also dispense with Christ in his incarnational aspect. She sees no need of him for the salvation of the soul. Since a portion of the soul is eternal, supernatural, it has only to grow, to reveal itself, to take possession, once it has been disengaged by ascesis.

Related to this concept of salvation and the soul is the fact that Simone Weil never speaks, in the Catholic sense, of sin or of free will.

Had the Scriptures omitted any allusion to the Resurrection of Christ, Christian faith would have been easier for her. It was the Passion of Christ, his crucifixion, his victimization, that made her believe in him. We know the eminently supernatural role that she attributed to suffering. Her view of the Resurrection, however, was the antithesis of Christian teaching. In the latter, if the Passion of Christ has a meaning, it is that of redemption and victory. That is just what repelled her.

As for love of one's neighbour, Simone Weil was intensely concerned with depersonalizing it, both in the one who loves and in the one who is loved.[13] She believed it ought to be impersonal, without attachment either to God or to the neighbour as individuals: 'To love someone impersonally—that is to love him in God': it is to love, in him, his capacity for love of God, the uncreated part of his soul, which, in him, is identical with Christ.

Such love, however, must be personal in the sense that it commits the whole personality of the lover, that it is directed to the person who is loved not as a means of doing good, as a material object might be, but as a plenary and complete end in itself.[14]

When God is present and shares in human relationships, they take on a triangular appearance. When he is absent, they are linear and irreversible because they are founded on the association of two egotisms (though the bond of love may be reciprocal), not on the interchange of absolute values. Thus the limitations and contingencies of human love are revealed: '[The corpses in the *Iliad*] . . . far dearer to the vultures than to their wives. Such is human love. One loves only what one can eat.'

The 'other' becomes an object to be consumed. When he is of no further use or 'ceases to be "edible" . . . he is abandoned'. 'In our love we are cannibals', writes Simone Weil. Human love has a taste of ashes:

'It is not true that human love is stronger than death. Death is far stronger. Love is subject to death.

'It is easy to love what is living. It is difficult to love what is dead. . . .

'The death of a loved one is horrible because it reveals the truth about our love for him—because it reveals that our love was not stronger than death.'

Yet, behind what Simone Weil says about human love, behind this *sic transit gloria mundi* theme, there is still faith in unconditional love. 'Love for what does not exist' is not at the mercy of death, no malady can disfigure it, no caprice can depreciate it. In what does not exist there is the security that is lacking in what does exist. The object of unconditional love, being menaced by none of the perils of life, cannot be said to 'exist'. God is such an object. He is the one who does not 'exist'. He is not habitually present in man. Therefore, what we love in man is a God who, for the most part, is not there, but who remains linked with man by the bond of desire: 'To love purely is to love, in another human being, his hunger . . . One should love in all men . . . either the desire for, or the possession of, God.' In other words, the unconditional element. But: 'there is no unconditional good in any man who has not attained mystical union, unless it be the possibility that he may yet achieve it'.

Love is not blind, since it knows what it loves and why it loves. And yet love does not see its object: 'Existence and lovableness (the quality of that which can be loved) are the "conditions" of love. If one loves that which is deprived of one and the other condition—it is indispensable that it be both—one loves "unconditionally".'

The paradox is that what does exist is not lovable since it is swayed by necessity, and what is lovable does not exist because it is God. But if the qualities of one condition are referred to the other, a person may love necessity because God is lovable and may love God because necessity exists. 'Such is the soul's torment,' explains Simone Weil.

'Love is something divine. Once it invades the human heart, it will break it.

'The human heart was made to be broken in this way. It is the saddest kind of waste when it is broken by something else. But it would rather be broken by anything rather than by divine love: for divine love breaks only those hearts that consent to it. And that consent is difficult.'

What sublime distress is offered in the *intentio benevolentiae* that excludes all *intentio unionis*!

In those weighty formulations so characteristic of Simone Weil, it is important not to lose sight of the perfectly logical character, the organic cohesion of her thoughts. Each proposition is balanced by a counter-proposition; each conclusion is clarified by its consequences. Thus, love must be at once personal and impersonal (as above), and the end that consummates it corresponds with its perfectly altruistic character. 'The recompense is indeed total identification with God.'[15]

The encounter between God and the soul takes place beyond their union, in a fusion, a 'fainting away', in which identity is lost in a conclusion that is not even desirable, so far does it transcend all our conceptions.

Simone Weil distrusted everything in Christian dogma that spoke of happiness, peace, or liberation; any source of consolation might also serve as a source of deception. The 'ways' of Providence are always 'ordinary' ways: they are called 'laws', because they arise from necessity. The gratuitous is deceptive when it conflicts with the real. The notion of the miraculous is 'devoid of meaning'.[16] Miracles are not proofs of faith. If they are taken as proofs, they prove too much; for they can be found in all religions. Besides, the age of miracles is past. And if the Church does not modify its teaching on this subject, many will lose their faith, because of the apparent incompatibility of miraculous phenomena with science.

Above all, current notions about miracles corrupt the religious spirit. God wishes to remain hidden. Faith in the miraculous either prevents the unconditional acceptance of the will of God (which Simone Weil regards as the essence of the supernatural disposition) or else compels the turning of a blind eye to the quality and the nature of evil as it exists in the world. Such wilful blindness is, apparently, easy in the shelter of the cloister, but is impossible for those who are submerged in the masses and who are familiar with their frailties.[17]

Is this to say that the intellect has no role in matters of faith? Although the mysteries of faith cannot be objects for the intelligence and its capacity for negation and affirmation, they may become supernaturally intelligible when all the faculties of the soul are subordinated to supernatural love. Intelligence, then, may recognize, after the event and by experience, the advantages of subordination to love.

To sum up: the mysteries of faith are not made to be affirmed; they are to be viewed by the intellect from a certain distance, like the brass serpent. Whosoever beholds, will live. This attentive, loving gaze receives, in return, a shock that strikes a spark of light in the soul, shedding light over every aspect of human life. As soon as dogma is asserted, it loses its meaning.[18]

Is it surprising that Simone Weil formulated so many arguments against Catholic dogma? Not really. It is their relatively small number which is actually surprising. For as soon as the authority of the Church is set aside, possible interpretations of the Scriptures are so varied that it is difficult for anyone elaborating his own concepts to arrive at views entirely in conformity with those of the Church. None the less, Simone Weil's doctrinal divergence, in spite of its relative character, is sufficient in itself to explain her resolution to give no further thought to the question of an 'eventual entry into the Church'. She believed that sacraments are real and efficacious only when they are received at a 'certain level of spirituality', which she had not reached. Below this level, she said, they are merely symbols, the expression of the desire that they may be received one day. Of what use would it be to make a show of belonging to the Church, so long as she did not inwardly feel at ease there? Her natural element was 'the immense and unfortunate multitude of unbelievers'.[19]

Simone Weil's reluctance to be baptized is therefore the expression of what she felt to be a God-given repugnance, an obstacle put there by his hand which he would remove at the right time. To the implicit question that she had put to her 'host', the soul of Simone Weil had received no answer: 'I told him: "I have not been baptized." He said: "Fall upon your knees before this place and with love in your heart as you would before the abode of truth." I obeyed.'

God left many questions unanswered and some promises apparently were not kept: 'He had promised to teach me, yet He taught me nothing.' In order to exclude all 'phenomena of compensation',[20] all help apart from grace, and any ill-effects from the power of suggestion, to which she thought she was susceptible, Simone Weil preferred not to give a name to the faith she had received. She called it 'Catholic', but she thought it would be more truly universal if it were not of the Church and especially if it were not Roman. But obedience must be preferred to love: 'If I had my eternal salvation placed in front of me on this table, and if I only had to stretch out my hand to take it, I would not put out my hand so long as I thought I had not received the order to do so. At least, I like to think so. And if instead of my own it were the eternal salvation of all human beings, past, present and to come, I know I ought to do the same thing. In that case it would hurt.'[21]

At Easter 1942 Simone Weil journeyed to Carcassonne. On her way, she stopped at the Benedictine Abbey of En-Calcat, at Dourgnes, where the austere discipline and splendid Romanesque architecture delighted her.

At Carcassonne, she called on the Roubauds whom she had

known at the university. She wore rough homespun; her bare feet were in sandals. Remote, far from all preoccupations, she seemed to her hosts like a saint of the middle ages. They spent the evening together. Jean Paulhan, the French writer, was there, too.

Simone had come with a school exercise book under her arm. First, she spoke about the political situation. She had never declared herself Jewish, she said, because she thought she ought not to. She also spoke, with a kind of childish pride, about her experience as a grape-picker. She told the story of the Emperor's clothes to the little boy of the family and said that she searched for mystical meanings in folk-tales. Her preoccupation with mysticism was apparent to everyone. When the curfew hour arrived, she left saying: 'I want to be truly useful. I want to go wherever there is the greatest possible danger . . . where my life will be least protected.' When she had gone, she left behind a feeling of uneasiness. Her lack of interest in earthly and secular affairs, the new light under which she had presented herself, aroused a curious emotion. The Roubauds were not to see her again, but in letters that Simone Weil wrote to them she mentioned the vivid memory she retained of the evening they had spent together.

Possibly it was after leaving the Roubauds that Simone went to see Joë Bousquet, whom the First World War had left a bed-ridden paraplegic. She arrived at his house, in spite of the curfew, about two o'clock in the morning. It was their first and last personal meeting, although their letters kept them in touch with each other. Kindred souls through suffering, they were both of a Stoic bent. The rest of the night 'went by in impassioned discussion'. Joë Bousquet tells us that 'at dawn Simone Weil agreed to stretch out on a mat in a little room next door, as usual refusing all comfort. A few hours later, she left to return to the abbey'.[22]

A touching correspondence followed. Simone Weil sent him *Venise sauvée* (Venice Preserved) as well as other poems, in particular, *Nécessité* (Necessity), written in 1941. In the latter, she expressed her *amor fati*—her love for the beauty of the world —in an address to the stars, 'measured in the steps of their dance':

## *Joë Bousquet*

*Rend fleshly things, you chains of pure light.*

. . . . . . . . . . . . . . . . . . . . . . . .

*May we obey you even unto death.*

The interest shown by Bousquet touched her: 'Attentiveness is the rarest and purest form of generosity', for 'it is given to very few minds to discover that things and people exist . . . I do not think, since I came into this part of the world, that I have found anyone whose destiny is not much inferior to yours: with only one exception'—Father Perrin. Joë Bousquet replied that he envied her intuition for goodness and her sense of evil. As for *Venice Preserved*, he comments on her style: 'You are more clairvoyant in verse than in prose. One might say that for you the rhythm of verse is that of consciousness itself.' Simone Weil sent him her scheme for 'the formation of a front-line nursing squad', to which he added suggestions concerning some points of detail. She reasoned that the approval of an officer severely wounded in the first war would lend weight to her project later on, when she could submit it in London.

But the heart of the correspondence between Bousquet and Simone Weil is in the confidences she imparted to him in response to his request: 'I would like to read some of your mystical impressions, and to know that you analyse what you experience'. Her long letter to him dated 12th May 1942 is one of her most often quoted writings: 'Blessed are they who suffer, in the flesh, the suffering of the world itself in their epoch. They have the possibility and the function of knowing in its truth, contemplating in its reality, the suffering of the world. . . .

'But unfortunate are they who, having this function, do not fulfil it.'

In some pages of this letter, she gives the quintessence of her spirituality, the key to her life.


### *In the Folds of Friendship, in the Fields of Labour*

The preceding analyses of Simone Weil's mystical and philosophical writings, like those of the articles mentioned in the following pages, can serve as an introduction to her personal life. Certainly, she lived in the realm of ideas more than in the realm

251

of things. Rather, ideas were the medium through which she best established contact with the physical and material universe that she had always longed to clasp to herself. She was like the workman who feels through his tools that he is in direct touch with the wood or the steel upon which he works. But she did not conceive her thoughts in the vacuum of pure abstraction, nor even in the concrete experience of mystical encounters. They occurred in her life as a by-product of the practical tasks she gave herself or the people she met, just as afterwards they directed her attention to those tasks or people from which new thoughts would arise, less as the reason for her choice (*ratio eligendi*), than as the spontaneous inclination of her active and affective nature. Thus the practical experience is the link, the cement, through which, existentially, ideas are related to other ideas and organized into a vital whole. Her system, if it can be called that, is made up of a life upon which thought feeds and a thought which nourishes life. This interference is both simple and paradoxical. For one sphere will sometimes be the natural complement of the other, as if Simone Weil sought to compensate on one level for her shortcomings on the other, and at different times, the immediate expression of the other. Thus she who was most impatient and who could hardly ever wait to perform something she thought worthwhile was most eloquent in her appraisal of the spiritual role of 'waiting' (*l'attente*). At the same time, the need to relate manual to intellectual labour, for which she seemed to have no temperamental affinity, was both at the centre of her doctrine and the guiding principle of her self-imposed adventurous tasks—much to our loss, for she was to die of it.

At the beginning of June 1941, at the Dominican monastery in Marseilles, Simone Weil met the Reverend Father Jean-Marie Perrin. This monk who was almost blind, 'this friend of God', as she soon came to call him, was an affable man with great natural charm. He was at that time working to help those whom the Allied defeat had exposed to political reprisals: Frenchmen, Germans, foreigners, 'in need of help, shelter, or passports'. To explain her ideas to him, Simone Weil had to seize the few moments of respite that were allowed him by the anonymous crowds who came to seek his aid in the monastery parlour. Simone Weil and Father Perrin were filled with a reciprocal admiration and joy at what seemed to be a profound spiritual communion. Paradoxically, it was most keenly felt at just those points where their doctrinal differences were most marked, differences that were to create difficulties between them in the end.[1]

Simone Weil spoke to Father Perrin about her Oriental studies, the Sanskrit texts that she was then reading. These were the same works that she discussed with Gilbert Kahn in a hitherto unpublished letter of August 1941: 'Having given some little study to Sanskrit texts this year, the spirit I find in them is so exactly the same as in those of Greece that I might be tempted to believe in an Indo-European philosophy anterior to the separation between the two peoples . . . But while that of Greece is nothing now but a memory, India's still exists, so it is said, in a real, though more or less degraded condition.'

Father Perrin not only took an interest in Simone Weil's studies; he encouraged them. He also believed that her sociological theories were akin to certain new Christian ideas about the world of labour which were then gaining currency. It was for this reason that he asked Simone Weil to write her experiences as a factory-worker for a publication he had in mind. She had previously analysed her concept of labour quite thoroughly in the article entitled 'Perception, or the Adventure of Proteus'.

'Labour, in contrast with reflection or persuasion or magic, is a series of actions which have no direct relationship either with the initial emotion, or with the end pursued, or with each other . . . At each moment of a man's labour, his motions are separated from motions accomplished, from motions intended, and also from his desires.

['The circumstances of work can change] without there being any change in the law of labour, which consists in indifference to what has preceded or to what will follow.'

In the article written at Father Perrin's request—'La condition première du travail non-servile'[2] ('The Primary Condition for Non-Servile Labour')—new statements appear. First, Simone Weil asserts that work inevitably engenders servitude. This element of servitude, she declares, would not vanish even in a régime in which social justice was perfect. Insofar as it is a revolt against social injustice, the revolutionary ideal is good; insofar as it is a revolt against the suffering which is essential to the very condition of workers, it is deceitful, for no revolution whatever can abolish labour. The term 'opium of the people' which Marx applied to religion (not without reason, for Simone, when religion betrays itself) applies equally to revolution. Hope of revolution was a form of escapism. 'There is no alternative [to labour]. There is only one remedy. Only one thing makes monotony endurable, and it is the light of eternity: i.e. beauty.

'Human nature will accept the yearning of the soul, not for what might exist or what will exist, but for what actually does exist, in one case alone. That is, in the case of beauty.' Beauty fuses feelings which otherwise could not be reconciled: both desire and contentment in the object of desire. The gaze that turns upwards to the star-studded sky is filled with a longing which this spectacle encourages and satisfies at the same time.

As Kant says, beauty is an end in itself. It is perfect finality, since it is self-sufficing—the only finality here on earth in which the form is one with the end. Thus, beauty is the symbol, the reflection, the *adumbratio* of God. It constitutes the sole link between our attention and its only adequate object, God. 'Since working people are obliged to direct all their desire towards what they already possess, beauty is made for them and they are made for beauty. Poetry is a luxury for other social classes, but working people need poetry as they need bread.'

Marx had rightly discredited the distinction between manual and intellectual work, Simone Weil conceded. But he had never suspected that it was necessary to transcend the distinction itself and to unite manual and intellectual labour by contemplation. Yet contemplation is not a kind of work for workers. No society allows a man who works on a machine to exercise the same kind of contemplation as that of a man who solves a theoretical problem. But there is another kind of contemplation—an attention of an intuitive kind, a direct link with God, which is possible for the worker. If everyone practised it, Simone believed, there would be true social equality: 'The best of them [the workers] ought to be able to find in life itself that fulfilment which artists search for indirectly through the medium of their art.'

Clear recognition of a supernatural destination in each social function is the only effective criterion for social reform. The economic security of the worker, of course, ought to be protected. However, he should be promised neither more nor less than the prospect of passing from a narrowly limited to an ampler state of welfare, for anything else is false. The greatest crime, the sin against the spirit, is to distract the worker's attention from beauty, to allow false hopes to interfere with his natural ability for contemplation. When the worker's capacity for attention is destroyed, his soul is cut off from that which is the root of all supernatural vocation.

In her *Connaissance surnaturelle*, Simone Weil defines labour as 'consent to the order of the universe'.[3] Was this consent to be given in joy and peace of soul, or under constraint, under the pressure of hunger and harsh necessity? In the existing organization of labour, Simone Weil seems to suggest, nothing is to be seen but constraint. The only incentive to work is wholly negative: the necessity to endure, to avoid death. Work provides food— although barely so. It does not provide at all for the nourishment of the soul, whose hunger is no less demanding though it may be less apparent.

From this it is possible to arrive at Simone Weil's central thought: 'Only God is worth concern: nothing else is.'[4] God may be sought in happiness or in pain; above all, in obedience to His laws. Man best expresses his acceptance of the necessity through which God disguises His rule of love by physical work.

Simone Weil had asked Father Perrin to help her find work as a field-hand. She was thinking, of course, of the hardships she would endure with the most under-privileged, but in giving her the help she wanted Father Perrin was guided by quite different and almost opposite considerations. He recognized her deep resolve, but sized up her physical weakness; the wisest course, he believed, was to send her to a friend of his who might keep an eye on her.

Gustave Thibon, Father Perrin's friend, seemed the best

possible Mentor for such a Telemachus: he was both a farmer and a Christian philosopher. A quick-witted, self-taught man, Thibon was at first wary of being saddled with a hare-brained intellectual idealist, but he was persuaded to give Father Perrin's protégée a try. For her part, Simone Weil affirmed her willingness to do any work required of her, without preferential treatment. 'What worries me is not the consequences of doing such work . . . it is whether I shall be able to accomplish it . . . In any case, I hope I shall not be found wanting in the determination to go to the limit of my strength.'[5]

In preparation for her new task, Simone bought an astronomer's atlas with which to study the heavens in her spare evenings on the land. In an unpublished letter written on 30th June to Gilbert Kahn, she announced her intention to contemplate the sky, learn all the constellations as well 'as the Babylonian shepherds', and compare them with existing maps of the stars. The letter goes on to describe her hopes for farm work: 'As to the Babylonian shepherds, I think I am going to find . . . a situation as a farm-hand. This will be a very sudden change in my way of life, but Krishna will no longer be far from me, since he was the beloved of milkmaids. But I believe you don't know Krishna . . . This job will be in Ardèche . . . I suppose that you'll also be going into farming during the holidays? But, I hope, in a less menial condition. Menial conditions suit me, but that's a special vocation.'

In another unpublished letter to Gilbert Kahn, written on 6th August, in which she announces that she is on the eve of her departure, she confides her deepest thoughts: 'I was much interested in your observations on the effect of physical fatigue on the mind. I mean that I sympathized, in the most literal sense, like someone who has suffered and who is about to suffer in the same way. . . .

'I also expect to witness the extinction of my own intelligence through fatigue. None the less, I consider that physical work is a purification—but a purification akin to suffering and humiliation. Yet there are also, far below, moments of deep joy . . .

'Why should I ascribe a great value to this part of my intelligence of which anyone can deprive me, absolutely anyone, with whips and chains, . . . or a mere piece of paper bearing certain letters? If this part is all there is, then I am almost wholly devoid of value, and why should I spare myself? If there is something else which is irreducible, then it is that which has an infinite worth. I am going to see if it is so.'

The following day, Simone Weil set out for 'the house of Saint-Marcel,' in the département of Ardèche, about 150 miles north of Marseilles, 'where three beings live who love one another'.[6] Her first contacts with Gustave Thibon were not promising. The only thing she had in common with her host was a strong will. Speaking in a monotonous and inflexible tone of voice, she measured herself against her opponent in endless discussions. They could not agree on anything: 'With her the respective positions of being and appearance were reversed: . . . she showed on the surface, with a fearsome spontaneity, the disagreeable side of her character, but it needed a great deal of time and affection, and much effort at overcoming her own modesty, for her to show herself at her best.'

Eventually, however, Gustave Thibon was able to perceive the supernatural element which dwelt 'beneath this hard crust'. He was sensitive also to Simone Weil's wonderful combination of genius and grace. He tells us how she looked to him when he came upon her as she was contemplating the valley of the Rhône, and she turned her head towards him: 'I then saw her gaze emerging gradually from the vision, returning to the view; the intensity, the purity, of that gaze were such that one felt she was in contemplation of interior abysses.'

Though they had been brought together for other purposes, the social philosopher and the professional scholar spent much time discussing each other's crafts. One day, they argued about style. Thibon was astonished by the apparent tenseness and harshness of some writings Simone had shown him: 'She replied to me: "Your criticism is certainly deserved. Clumsiness, stiffness, are doubtless defects; but I must confess that of all defects, these are the least displeasing to me, in the things of beauty that are dearest to me: in Romanesque sculptures, Giotto's frescoes, Greek sculptures of the beginning of the fifth century; in Homer, the Gregorian chant, in fact in all that comes just before the full maturity of classical art. Not that I wish to make any comparison!" '

Such statements confirm what many readers have said of Simone Weil: that she does not belong to this century, that she is a figure out of the Middle Ages astray in the modern world . . .

As though she belonged to an even earlier period than the Middle Ages, Simone Weil tried to live like an anchorite at Saint-Marcel and to sleep under the stars. Mindful of his responsibility, Thibon tried to talk her out of it. They struck a compromise, and she 'camped out' in a half-ruined house, close to the Rhône. Each day, she went up to her work, which she performed awkwardly, but her perseverance triumphed in the end over her natural clumsiness. Though she took her meals with the Thibons, she refused to eat anything that city-dwellers had to do without. Sometimes she ate nothing but the berries that she gathered in the hedgerows by the roads.

Food rationing regulations had the full force of law for Simone Weil. Indignantly, she refused a morsel of bread that a village baker offered her one day. Though there was no necessity, she thought, to follow the Vichy government in political or ideological matters, it had the right to obedience in everything else. Dying of hunger was no sin. So strong were Simone Weil's sentiments that on 10th October 1941 she wrote to Admiral Leahy to beg him to stop the food supplies that the Americans were sending into unoccupied France through Vichy. This is an astonishing letter, written in very correct English, though with a visible effort that shows her national origin. To Gustave Thibon she explained that these deliveries of wheat were immoral, because most Frenchmen were Gaullists; therefore they should not benefit from 'material advantages which they received from a government they condemned in their hearts'. In a similar tone is the reproach that she addressed to a militant of the extreme Left who to escape from the Gestapo accepted help from the Dominicans of Marseilles: it is not permissible, she said to him, to accept help from those whose faith you condemn.

In the evening at Saint-Marcel d'Ardèche, when work in the fields was done, Simone sat on a stone bench and taught Greek to Gustave Thibon. As she used to do with beginners in Greek, she started with the text of the *Pater*. After having gone over it word by word, they promised each other to learn it by heart. 'I do not think he did so,' she wrote later to Father Perrin. 'Neither did I, at first. But a few weeks later, leafing through the Gospels, I told myself that since I had made a promise to myself and the object was worthy, I should do it. And I did.'

Having done so, she was struck by the 'infinite sweetness' of the Greek text, and took to reciting it at every moment. A week later, the grape-harvesting began; she said the *Pater* in Greek before starting for work; she repeated it often as she laboured in the vineyard. And she forced on herself the habit of saying it every morning with complete concentration and perfect attention:

'The effect of this observance is extraordinary and surprises me every time, for although I experience it each day, it exceeds my expectation at each repetition.

'At times the very first words tear my thoughts from my body and transport it to a sphere outside space where there is neither perspective nor point of view. Space opens. The infinity of the ordinary perceptual space is replaced by an infinity to the second or sometimes the third power. At the same time this infinity of infinity fills from end to end with silence, a silence which is not an absence of sound, but which is the object of a positive sensation, more positive than that of sound. Noises, if there are any, may not reach me except after crossing this silence.

'Sometimes also, during this recitation, or at other moments, Christ is present in person, but with a presence infinitely more real, more poignant, clearer and more full of love than that first time when he took possession of me.'[7]

Like the repeated visits of the Beloved to the Sulamite in the Canticle of Canticles, Simone Weil's encounters with Christ in 1938, 1940 and 1941 reflect a deepening mystical relationship.

To the image of Simone Weil created by such marvellous events, certain 'frailties', writes Gustave Thibon, supply a counterpoise: her liking for tobacco (her only vice), for example, and her attraction to uneducated or backward people. Since teaching meant for her a communication of wisdom, though not her own, rather than a communication of science, which was her own, she found herself unable to resist any 'soul's need for instruction'. Thus she applied herself with great zeal to inculcating the rudiments of arithmetic in a village urchin. And for a young refugee girl from Lorraine in whom she thought she saw the signs of a true intellectual vocation, she annotated the Upanishads. Thibon recognizes that her pedagogical gifts were such that she could have adapted any subject to any kind of mind.

The season of the grape harvest arrived: Simone Weil was able once again to fulfil her wish to share as a stranger in the lot of the agricultural labourer. Her boss, a landowner at Saint-Julien-de-Peyrolas, who had employed her from 22nd September to 23rd October 1941, stated in a testimonial dated 24th October that he was satisfied with her work. And well satisfied he might have been, for she fulfilled her share of the work, and wished to do more, in spite of the fatigue she felt. Sometimes she would lie down under the stumps to rest her tired body while she went on gathering grapes.[8]

Her poor health was apparent, nevertheless, and her migraines often impaired her strength and appetite. She seemed content with such minor nourishment as onions and raw tomatoes, and would have eaten little else were it not for the insistence of her employer, in whose house she lodged. He also recalls that in the evening, on returning from the fields, she worked in her room at her writings or correspondence until late into the night: the light under her door shone at all hours. This round-the-clock performance of alternate physical and intellectual work offers at least one explanation for her headaches.

The impression that hell was a vineyard in which one harvested unceasingly came quite naturally to her as the days of unendurable unending toil went on.

Yet the grape-harvest could not last for ever, she knew. On 18th October 1941, a week before it was over, she wrote to Xavier Vallat, Commissioner for Jewish Questions, to inquire about some money which was due to her. In this text, still unpublished, she asks why her letter of November 1940 to the Minister of Education has been left unanswered. She assumes that the silence is due to the 'presumption of Jewish origin' arising from her name. (In fact, there is in her dossier in the Ministry of Education this note: 'Isr. [Jewish]—does not return to the Occupied Zone'.) Yet the indemnity 'provided for in such cases by the Statute Concerning Jews' has not been paid to her, much to her 'satisfaction at having no part in the financial difficulties of the country'. 'The government has proclaimed its desire that Jews should go into industry, and preferably go to work on the land. Although I do not regard myself as Jewish, since I have never entered a synagogue, have been brought up without any sort of religious practice whatever by agnostic parents, am not attracted in the least to the Jewish religion, have no link at all with the Jewish tradition, and have been wholly brought up, since earliest childhood, in the Hellenistic, Christian and French tradition, I have nevertheless obeyed.'

For, she relates, she has become a grape-picker; she has cut grapes 'eight hours a day, every day for four weeks, in the employ of a viticulturalist of the Gard'; and her employer has honoured her with the statement that she was really worth her keep. Ho paid her the even greater compliment of saying that she might be married to a peasant; a declaration that no countryman would make lightly to a young woman from the town: 'He is unaware, it is true, that solely by the fact of my name, I bear the ancestral blemish which it would be inhuman, on my part, to transmit to my children.' One week of harvesting remained: after that, she wrote to Vallat, she hoped to enter into the service of a rural market-gardener: 'One could not . . . be more completely obedient.'

Although she regarded the Statute concerning Jews as unjust and absurd—how could anyone really imagine that 'a graduate in mathematics could do harm to children learning geometry?'—nevertheless she wished to express some gratitude to the Vichy government. It had excluded her from the social status of intellectuals, only to bind her to the earth, and hence to the whole of nature:

'For nature and the earth can be possessed only by those into whose bodies they have entered, through the daily suffering of limbs, through back-breaking fatigue. Days, months, seasons —the celestial vault, which ceaselessly revolves above us—

belong to those who have to pass the space of time each day between the rising and setting of the sun, moving from one fatigue to another. It is they who accompany the firmament in its rotation; they live each day and do not dream it.

'The government, whom you represent in regard to myself, has given me all that. You, and the other present leaders of my country, have given me what you do not possess. You have also given me the infinitely precious gift of poverty, which you do not possess either.'

From the administrative point of view, so eloquent a letter required no reply, except to place its author under the supervision, albeit remote, of the Vichy police.

*La Vie intellectuelle* of July 1953 published an article by Simone Weil, entitled 'Christianity and Life in the Fields'. Its date of completion is unknown, but internal evidence suggests that it was written later than 'The First Condition for Non-Servile Labour'—that is, after June 1941—but before her departure for Saint-Marcel d'Ardèche. (There is no direct allusion to grape-harvesting.) It is pertinent at this point, however, because it synthesizes Simone Weil's conclusions resulting from her varied experiences of work in the fields. And the themes she deals with echo throughout her later works.

Boredom, Simone Weil said, is the moral leprosy which corrodes the rural life of France. On the other hand, work is said to be a form of prayer. 'Only fitting associations of appropriate ideas, implanted in the centre of the mind by intense emotions, enable the thought to dwell upon God, without even interior speech, during the motions of work.' The Church ought to arouse those associations and images which make contemplation possible without detracting from the superficial attention which must necessarily be given to the work itself.

Christ constantly referred to the life of the fields and the problems of agricultural workers. Little heed is paid to this. 'Most of these agricultural parables have no place in the Sunday liturgy. This liturgy has no connection with the succession of the seasons . . . The cosmic element is so absent from Christianity as it is generally practised that it is all too easy to forget that the universe was created by God. But the peasant cannot get into contact with God, unless he does so through the created universe.'

Simone Weil suggests two major reforms: first, the village priest should comment at Sunday Mass on some passage of the Scriptures related to agricultural work in progress. Texts and analogies could be found for every event, either seasonal or accidental. For 'what must be done in the largest possible measure, is to transform daily life itself into a metaphor of divine significance, into a parable'. Such is the experience which the sower and the stock-breeder constantly witness in the country: the seed is received into a passive element, whence it draws its substance until it flowers into a life of its own. The soul, in the same fashion, is the receptacle of the divine word.

The second reform would be to make the Eucharist 'the heart and soul of everyday life in every vineyard and wheat field'. The priest can make 'the flesh and blood of Christ come into being on the altar with the consecration of the Host. But the peasant's prerogative is no less sublime'. He sacrifices his flesh and his blood throughout his interminable hours of labour; they pass into the corn and vine; these become eventually the body and blood of Christ.

This analogy suggests many images, many parallels to her fertile mind. If it is true that Christ incarnates himself in the Host in order to be absorbed by men, it is also true, she says, that the energy of the sun 'is crystallized in plants (and thence in animals) to be absorbed by us'. Thus what man eats is an image of the Incarnation and of Holy Communion.

Lastly, she writes: 'Christianity will not permeate society until every social class has its special, unique, inimitable link with Christ, and there ought to be correspondingly, special bodies for the priests.' The members of the JOC speak of Christ the worker; the shepherds have the image of the Good Shepherd; mothers can think of the Virgin Mary. The need, then, is 'to find and define, for each aspect of social life, its specific link with Christ. This link ought to be the inspiration of each group of Catholic action'.

'Thus, just as religious life is shared out among orders which correspond with various vocations, so would social life appear to be an edifice of distinct vocations uniting in Christ. And in each vocation there must be certain souls as wholly devoted to Christ as a monk can be; which would be the case if those who want to give themselves to Christ were no longer to enter automatically into religious orders.' It is possible that this passage on the Eucharist and the conclusion of the article are of a later date than Simone Weil's stay with Gustave Thibon, as distinct from the first part of the article. The influence of Father Perrin is evident throughout.

When Simone Weil left Marseilles, she wrote to her friend Kahn that she hoped to keep her job as a farmhand for a year, 'unless something unforeseen happens'. It did happen. Less than three months after her arrival, she received a letter requesting her immediate return to Marseilles to go through the formalities necessary to obtaining an American visa. It put an end to her brief but significant career in the fields.

Simone's second winter in Marseilles was spent in a small apartment 'on the Catalans', as it is called locally. From her room she had a view of the sea, the 'gentle, straying' sea of her poems. On the walls she hung some photographs of statues and 'the ambiguous gaze of Titian's *Three Musicians*'; through her windows, in her room, 'the blue light, the flashing movements of the sea and the confused mass of the bodies on the beach and their thousand and one cries'.[9]

As Father Perrin has written, 'the weeks and months at Marseilles flowed quickly by'[10] for her. Sometimes she interrupted her work by taking long walks out of the city to the east with a friend, Dr Bercher, in the lovely mountains of Marseilles-Veyre between Goudes, Cassis, and Baumettes. One day, when the two friends had climbed the slopes of Saint-Michel d'Eau-Douce, they passed over a little crest and found themselves facing the astonishing rocks which rise like something from a Greek landscape to form the eastern wall of the ravine of Canelongue. The splendour of the sight impelled Simone Weil to exclaim: 'To think that they could take all this from me!' She was thinking of an interrogation which she had just undergone.

Standing there, on the height, Simone told her friend how

the military magistrate had asked her point-blank what her feelings were towards England. She had replied: 'My feelings towards England are those of the utmost sympathy.' The magistrate wanted to know whether she was engaged in pro-English propaganda. She answered negatively. He said to her: 'Knowing the risk you run, you still openly profess pro-English sentiments. And over and above this you actually disseminate them.' 'If you ask me what my opinions are,' Simone Weil replied, 'I do not hide them from you. But I don't express them to anyone who does not definitely ask me to.' The magistrate then reached the actual reason for the interrogation: a study proposing the recruitment of a front-line nursing-squad which she had tried to send to England, and which had been seized by the police. Simone had continued to work on this proposal, by getting information from veterans of the 1940 campaign. On learning that whole units had disintegrated without even being attacked, she realized even more clearly than before the defeat, the decisive character of morale.

The officer brandished the document at her, saying: 'That's a tactical idea, that is what it is. A tactical idea! So you've passed through the Staff College?' 'No more,' Simone Weil replied, 'than many who are concerned about war.' With that the interrogation ended: the judge merely got her to sign a statement of her declarations.

At a later date Simone described this whole scene in a letter to Maurice Schumann. After pointing out that she had had the good luck to be arrested on a day when her health was not bad enough to deprive her of presence of mind, she wrote: 'On the contrary, I think it was I who made them feel rather unwell, by looking straight into their eyes for a whole morning.'

In fact, what the magistrate did not seem to know at that time was that Simone Weil's intentions were far graver than her actions. She was eager to join the *résistance* and even became a member of a supposedly clandestine group (actually a trap set by the Germans to catch potential underground workers). Being a small fish, however, she passed through the net.

On occasions, Simone Weil distributed copies of *Témoignage chrétien*, a resistance newspaper. One day some members of the *résistance* (genuine ones, this time) gave her important documents to carry. In getting down from a tram with her case in her hand, she stumbled. The case that she had forgotten to close crashed to the ground, scattering all its contents. She was not at all disturbed; she picked the papers up.

Eventually she got herself mixed up in matters that bordered on illegality, especially through her criticism of the internment camps that were being built by the Vichy government.

Simone Weil had always championed the people of the French colonial empire. Whenever there was the opportunity, she struck up an acquaintance with those who came to Paris. In 1938 the condemnation of the Algerian Messali Hadj shocked her profoundly. During this year, she met some Annamite students in Paris, and she told them how much she had been horrified by the repressive measures taken by the French in 1930-1931. The youngsters apparently knew nothing about the incidents she described. Their ignorance only increased her interest in their problems.

At the outbreak of the war, Mandel, a Minister who had a reputation for administrative energy, had drawn thousands of Annamites to France for work in munition factories. They had had no choice but to live in deplorable sanitary conditions. After the 1940 armistice, the Annamites flocked to Marseilles where there was no work to give them and they were soon confined in camps. In the winter of 1940-1941, some were put to work sweeping snow from the streets. As with the unemployed of Le Puy, on the Michelet square, Simone Weil tried to get to know them. 'There was never a more pitiful sight,' she said later to Dr Bercher, 'than those poor creatures, standing in the thick of the snow, in threadbare clothes, completely at a loss what to do.' She visited them in their camp, now the Baumettes prison, which was then under construction. They had neither heat nor light. One Indo-Chinese told her that he had enlisted in the labour force in order 'to see France', but he had seen nothing. He wrung her heart when he said: 'I live in darkness and I am sick to death of it.' One of the punishments inflicted in the Baumettes camp especially infuriated Simone Weil because she considered it degrading: those guilty of infractions had half their head shaved.

As a result of her visit to Baumettes, she made a number of futile attempts to bring about the removal of the former colonial administrator who was in command of the camp.

Father Perrin informs us, moreover, that Simone Weil often went to the Palais de Justice to observe the trials; it was there that she gained her first-hand knowledge of the way justice was actually dispensed, later revealed in an indignant article entitled 'Human Personality, the Just and the Unjust', as it is already in the 'Forms of the Implicit Love of God'.

'Nothing is more frightful than the all too common spectacle of an accused person who, in the situation in which he finds himself, has no resource in the world except words, but is incapable of wielding them because of his social origin and his lack of culture; who is abject with guilt, suffering and fright, inarticulate in speech before judges who do not listen, but interrupt him with ostentatious displays of their refined language.'[11]

Meanwhile, Simone Weil and Father Perrin were engaging in conversations that had as their core a 'continual return to the question of baptism.'[12] There is absolutely no evidence that Father Perrin ever put Simone under any pressure. He compared her to 'the bell that calls to the church in which it does not enter', an image in which she found a poetic justification for her attitude of 'waiting, ἐν ὑπομένη'.[13] His most overt attempt at influencing her consisted in his writing to her that the day of her baptism would be one of great joy for him. His entire apostolic effort was restricted to keeping her 'in a state of availability' towards the will of God and to making her 'acquainted with the truth'. As she afterwards wrote to him: 'You have given me no other advice but this of availability, for which I am infinitely grateful to you.' And again: 'You once said to me at the beginning of our relationship some words which went to the bottom of my soul. You said: "Be very careful, because if you were to overlook something important through your own fault, it would be a pity." '[14]

It was their discretion that impressed Simone Weil most in persons like Father Perrin. She told Dr Bercher: 'They've got something all right . . . In order to lead another person into their conception of things they assume that this is precisely the conception at which he himself has arrived.'

When she first met Father Perrin, the question of baptism had not even occurred to Simone Weil. Strongly attracted as she was to Christianity, she had no desire to belong to the Church through formal baptism. She found herself 'at the intersection of Christianity and everything that is not Christianity'.[15] In reply to Father Perrin's queries, she offered the following well-defined arguments:

1. Complete liberty is necessary to intelligence; intelligence is never duty bound to believe in anything whatever, for belief is not a thing we can will.

2. In the absence of such liberty, oppression of the individual by society tends to become authoritarian. That explains the 'malaise' of the intellect in Christianity.

3. The faculty of attention can be directed, however, and its orientation can be controlled by the will.

4. Since it imposes a certain discipline of attention, the Church's jurisdiction in matters of faith is not harmful. It may even be necessary, in that it preserves the essence of dogmatics as a focus of attention.

Nevertheless, Father Perrin seems to have believed that Simone Weil was on the threshold of joining the Church. In his defence, it can be said that his conversations with her were of short duration; that she spoke of Christ and the supernatural, the Eucharist and grace, with an accent of passionate sincerity which took on the colour of their Catholic meaning; and that her person radiated such an 'aura' of asceticism, detachment and purity that any meeting with her was bound to produce a deep impression on him. And at this time Father Perrin had not read, of course, '*L'amour de Dieu et le malheur*' and '*Formes de l'amour implicite de Dieu*', two essays that would have revealed more clearly to him the true basis of her religious thought. So he encouraged her to think of herself as virtually a Christian. In the course of their discussions, he treated her as though she already were of the same faith as he.

On her part, Simone did not dare to dissuade him from what must have been for him such a favourable opinion of her. 'When

I talked to Father Perrin, I was paralysed by pity,' she later confided to Simone Deitz. 'I could not tell him everything. He could not see.' Tears would well up in Father Perrin's eyes which were permanently irritated; he would dry them on his white scapulary. Simone would then stop speaking: though she knew better, she had the impression it was she who made him cry; she could not stand the sight of tears. And so she was forever hindered from saying anything which might have pained him.

Father Perrin had to be away from Marseilles during the last months that Simone Weil was there. Perhaps it was then that she wrote to him: 'As for the existence of a compact mass of dogma beyond the reach of thought, I feel that this compact mass is something infinitely precious. But I believe that it is offered to our attention rather than to belief.'[16]

The adherence that she accorded to dogma was only such as might follow from deep attention to those aspects of it which were beyond her or which repelled her and from a deep confidence that by meditating upon them, she would finally come to penetrate them. It seemed to Simone Weil that she should not deny herself the possibility of penetrating the mystery which still veiled from her eyes a great deal of revealed truth. For she had come to learn through experience how passages in the Gospels, formerly unintelligible, could become suddenly flooded with light after long and loving consideration.

In her struggles, in her suffering, and in her waiting, she derived a paradoxical comfort from meditating upon her remoteness from God, who was the object of her devotion. 'What greater joy can exist for us . . . than to think how infinitely distant He is from us.'

Few people rejoice for such reasons. Those who do are exalting detachment into an absolute value. As Simone Weil always had the courage to maintain a barrier between herself and friendship on the human plane, similarly she maintained a barrier between herself and the Church on the plane of faith. She took comfort in the thought that the Father was distant: 'For one who loves can there be a greater joy than to be able to say: whatever may happen, he whom I love is completely safe? Only one who loves God has this joy.'

269

She did not believe that God had completely abandoned man, however. Beauty was the sign of his concern, and also the proof of his remoteness: beauty vouchsafed to man by a Providence more ineffable than that which we commonly understand it to be. Providence, as usually understood, does no more than slacken that marvellous adjustment of necessity which, in its essence, said Simone Weil, is the magnificent signature of the divine: 'Everything of beauty in this world is a trace of that wise persuasion which has subdued necessity. All the blind acts of destruction which occur are evidence that this vanquished necessity is still sovereign and that God does not dwell here below, but in the heavens.'

To her, obedience was to necessity as a good copy is to the original: the effort made to subscribe to a perfectly accomplished work which has no need of our assistance: 'God entrusts his creation to necessity. Were this not so God would be here below, in the world, and not in the heavens. His presence would then annihilate creation. Or rather, God would not be Good itself.'

We willingly conform ourselves, then, to an order of which the most faithful servitor, inanimate force, is ever glorifying God without knowing it. And we should rejoice, always, because God is out of our reach, and that He is spared any contact with our defilement. 'He is in the heavens and whatever evil we do, whatever evil we undergo, we know that no evil can befall God.'

But if in our misery there is need for more immediate consolation, some reason for reassurance, it is given from God: '. . . if we are cruel enough to wish to have that which we love with us in our distress, we can have that sorrowful comfort too. There is a point in space and time where God is, nailed to a Cross, bereft of divinity, in the guise of a slave.'

Rejected by her Father in heaven, but reunited with her crucified God, Simone Weil waited for an insight shed into the mysteries, still veiled from her sight, which prevented her from attaining the Faith. Thanking Father Perrin for having understood her so well, Simone Weil sent him, just before leaving Marseilles, two texts which were discussed above: '*L'amour de Dieu et le malheur*', and '*Formes de l'amour implicite de Dieu*'. After reading these, he was better able to understand her, but he had no time to tell her so before she was gone. Certain signs indicated to him that he would not see her again. The fact that she had entrusted him with her manuscripts seemed a premonition. In making her farewells, she summed up, in a few phrases, all that she expected from the future, all that she hoped for:

'Good-bye, I wish you all possible good things, except the Cross; for I do not love my neighbour as myself . . .

'Every time that I think of the crucifixion of Christ, I commit the sin of envy.'[17]

Gustave Thibon was leaving Marseilles at the same time. To him also, Simone Weil entrusted some MSS. He remembers still the indifference of manner, whether studied or natural, with which she handed them to him. Standing on the station platform, she plunged her hand absent-mindedly into her satchel, took out a dozen large notebooks, held them out to him with as little concern as she might offer a packet of cigarettes, and immediately began to talk of something else. Later, from Oran, she wrote: 'If you don't hear of me for three or four years, consider yourself in complete possession of them,' In any case, she said, what did it matter? 'Nothing that concerns me will be of any kind of importance.'[18]

On 17th May, just as Simone Weil was embarking for Morocco on the S.S. *Maréchal Lyautey*, she said to a friend: 'Don't you think that the sea would be a beautiful baptismal font?'[19] On 26th May, she despatched her last letter to Father Perrin, from a refugee camp in Casablanca. In it she recapitulated her favourite theme: since, by leaving Marseilles, she had dedicated herself to affliction, she was happy in the thought that henceforth the mercy of God would be made known to her: 'If, still persevering in our love, we fall to the point where the soul cannot keep back the cry: "My God, why hast thou forsaken me", if we remain at this point without ceasing to love, we end by touching something which is not affliction, which is not joy, something which is the central essence, necessary and pure, something not of the senses, common to joy and sorrow, something which is the very love of God.'[20] For her, all is joy: 'What we love is perfect joy itself. When we know this, even hope becomes superfluous, it no longer has any meaning.' Such joy is thwarted only by compassion. Compassion alone, wrote Simone Weil, can lead to doubts of the love of God. And the suffering of others—that of strangers, of those indifferent to us, of those who live in the most distant centuries—is unendurable. 'I feel a certain reassurance when I remember that Christ wept when he foresaw the horrors of the sack of Jerusalem. I hope he forgives compassion.'

To Father Perrin, Simone Weil acknowledged an infinite debt of gratitude. He alone had never, for a moment, used his friendship to cause her pain. 'My position towards you is that of a beggar, reduced by destitution to continual hunger, who has come again and again throughout a year into a prosperous house asking for bread, and who, for the first time in his life, has suffered no humiliation there.'

In her gratitude, she says, she owes him the truth about himself—about his faults, however slight these may be. First, she reproaches him because of his lack of openness of mind. 'You think that I have the right to the name of Christian,' she tells him, then points out that he cannot believe in her special brand of Christianity, nor in the supernatural validity of the 'implicit faith' which has always been living in her. But it is 'the love of those things which are outside visible Christianity', Greece, India, and the sight of what was hidden in the human heart, in hearts empty of religious belief, which kept her 'outside the Church'.

She deplores the imperfection of Father Perrin; in particular, 'his attachment to the Church as to an earthly fatherland'. For here below there is nothing but 'the universe itself with all the rational creatures it has contained, contains now, and will contain . . . that has the right to our love'.

Nothing is to be loved for itself, she says, no one is to be loved more than another; but all are to be embraced within the same universal—that is, 'catholic'—love. Friendship was the only legitimate exception to that duty.

He who will love like that will be the saint for whom our age is waiting. He will have other virtues than his forerunners. He will have those needed today, the most indispensable of which is genius.

'Only a kind of perversity can compel God's friends to deprive themselves of having genius, since to receive it in superabundance they need only to ask their Father for it in Christ's name.

'. . . The world has need of saints who have genius, as a town stricken by the plague needs doctors. Wherever there is need, there is obligation.'

Her sense of responsibility towards her world weighed heavily upon Simone Weil. It was for this reason that she confided her thoughts to Father Perrin; fearing that her inadequacies would render them less meaningful to others, she implored him: 'I see no one but you whom I can beg to give them favourable attention.'

Simone Weil felt too exhausted to express her ideas fruitfully. She knew she was but 'a damaged instrument'. Yet, she could not bring herself to ask God 'to repair the mutilations of nature'. 'Such a request would seem to me an offence against the infinitely tender Love which has made me the gift of affliction.'

Simone Weil took leave of Father Perrin before entering into the night. Theirs had been one of the great friendships of her life, the only one as yet so fully documented. Simone Weil turned from its intimacy again to become part of the crowd, one of those who pass unobserved: 'I am the colour of dead leaves, like certain insects.'

# 4

# New York

'I go without thinking of my return . . . I have always thought that one day I should leave like this.' Simone Weil, letter to a friend

SIMONE WEIL'S decision to go with her parents to America was not made wholeheartedly. She had many reservations: leaving brought with it at least as many tribulations as she might be escaping by not staying in Marseilles, from her point of view. For she was not fleeing from privation, nor the danger that threatened her as a Jew, nor even any of the more direct perils of war. Rather, it was her relatively easy life in Marseilles, her comparative comfort, and above all the fact that she had no opportunity to play a part in the conflicts that were rending the world—these were the factors that influenced her to go. Her ultimate plan was to return by way of America and England to the Occupied Zone, where she might be given a task equal to her need for sacrifice in fellowship with those less fortunate than she.

With her parents, Simone Weil was sent to the camp of Aïn-Seba at Casablanca. There 900 refugees, most of them Jews, slept on the ground in blankets, all together. The food was poor and meagre, and unhappily for the orthodox Jews, it was cooked entirely in pork fat.

In the morning the rabbis, Polish for the most part, came to say their prayers in the vegetable-garden. Their high-pitched voices, their continual swaying forward and back, was a surprise and a delight to Simone Weil who had never witnessed the *hassidim* ritual.

She kept busy writing, monopolizing all day long one of the eighteen chairs available. At this time she was at work on part

274

of the text published under the title *Intuitions préchrétiennes*. Whenever she left her chair for a moment, her parents sat on it, for fear that someone else might take it.

From Casablanca after 17 days in the refugee camp, Simone Weil embarked for New York. The crossing, on the Portuguese ship *Serpa Pinto*, took a month. On board, wrapped in her huge French cape, with her dark blue beret tilted over her emaciated face, Simone aroused the curiosity of all the passengers. She spoke to no one except the young Jacques Kaplan, a recent *baccalauréat* graduate, whom she drew into endless discussions. He said: 'She was very pleasant, very protective, very sarcastic. What especially struck me was the astonishing contrast between her and normal people—or, rather, ordinary people. She couldn't bear the cabin-class passengers, because they openly enjoyed comforts that those in the steerage were deprived of. She took an interest in me because being a "scout", I volunteered to take charge of the refugee children in the hold.'

Simone showed special affection for a young mental defective on board, whom she decided to visit in New York. Throughout her life, retarded children had appealed to some instinct deep in her. 'Natural' afflictions, which seem so pathetic in the very young, reminded her of her own sufferings, the sufferings of the little girl who had felt crushed by the 'mediocrity of her natural faculties'.

The *Serpa Pinto* docked in New York about the 8th of July 1942. Scarcely had Simone Weil disembarked when she realized that she had been mistaken in imagining an 'easy' journey from New York to London. The innumerable obstacles in the path of her plan wore her down. Her efforts seemed fruitless. Her gaiety, her mischievousness, and her smile disappeared. Had the tension and frustration continued it might have broken her completely, for she tried relentlessly, without sparing herself, to find a way out of the trap she seemed to be in.

Her torment was aggravated by an article about the troubled situation in Marseilles which she read by chance in *The New York Times*. More and more she regretted having left France. For two days she stayed in her room, eating nothing. She wrote to Dr Bercher:

'I am depressed, and seriously so. But what's the use of going on about it? I was so much happier when we used to go walking together . . .

'I am trying to bring off my little schemes . . . That's why I haven't looked for a job here. I hope to leave New York before long, unless some unforeseen obstacle prevents it.

'While waiting, I sometimes go to the libraries. Among other things, I continue to rummage in the odd corners of theology. And I explore Harlem. Every Sunday I go to a Baptist church there. I'm the only white person in the church. After a service of two and one half hours, when the atmosphere is "established", the religious fervour of the pastor and the congregation explodes into dances much like the Charleston, exclamations, cries and spirituals. That's really worth seeing. A true and moving expression of faith, it seems to me.'

One Sunday, Simone took her friend Simone Deitz there. After the service had continued for three hours, she noticed that her companion was sharing in the general exaltation. The faithful were crying out, clapping their hands and dancing. Simone Deitz felt that she too was being swept away by the contagious, rapturous enthusiasm, and wanted to leave. 'Better to imitate them,' said Simone Weil, 'than to get up and interrupt the fervour of the faithful.' They stayed to the end.

Every day she attended Mass at the nearest Catholic church, *Corpus Christi*, on 121st Street. The Mass was read in English, to her intense satisfaction; she had always thought Latin deplorable.

From New York, in an almost desperate effort to get into the Resistance movement, she wrote several letters to Maurice Schumann who was the spokesman for the Free French in London.[1] As documents, they are among the most revealing left to us by Simone Weil.

She began her correspondence on 30th July 1942. In her first letter she explained to Schumann that she had heard him praised in France. Whenever she had listened to his broadcasts on the Free French Radio, she continued, the memory of their happiness, years ago, while attending Chartier's class at the Lycée Henri IV, came back. She spoke of the drama that was going on within her.

Never would she have left Marseilles had she known how hard it was to get from New York to London. In France, she had had at least some responsibility for the circulation of *Témoignage chrétien*; there had been the consolation of suffering with her country. If she had taken upon herself to leave France it was only because she hoped thereby to play a bigger part in the efforts, perils, and trials of the war.

She wrote of her two plans: one, to bring into being her project for a front-line nursing squad; the other to forge a link between Occupied France and the Free French. These projects she still cherished, but to realize either of them she had to leave New York.

'I am appealing to you as a comrade to help me out of the moral situation in which I find myself; a moral situation which is too painful to bear.

'Many people fail to understand why this moral situation is painful; but you will certainly understand. We had much in common in the past, when we did our studies together.'

This letter reached Maurice Schumann in the course of time, but Simone Weil could not be sure it would, so she wrote him a second letter on the same day, to make the most of 'the offer of Captain Mendès-France' to act as courier. She told him of the joy she felt when she learned that he was working in London as a contact with the French Resistance. But it is certain, she said, that 'this liaison is inadequate. André Philip has clearly said so, and he is quite right'. From the moral and strategic point of view, a better contact was essential. How could it be arranged? By sending agents into France from time to time. A woman could be just as suitable as a man for missions of this kind. She herself had already had the chance of proving her coolness in the face of imminent danger; she said that she would gladly undertake a mission of sabotage, or serve as a messenger, passing on instructions. Having left France only in mid-May, she explained, she still had a few contacts with clandestine organizations—notably, the organizer behind the publication of the *Cahiers du Témoignage chrétien*, who was constantly in touch with the leaders of the other underground groups in the Free Zone.

Schumann's reply was evidently a great encouragement to

Simone Weil, for in answer she wrote: 'I am overjoyed to see
that we really are very close to one another. We were so in our
young days, and we are perhaps still more so now, after a parallel
development.' Feeling that he would be sympathetic to her
religious views, she confided to him that she wholly subscribed
to the mysteries of the Christian religion, with what seemed to
her to be the only legitimate form of adherence to religious
mysteries. 'This form of adherence is love, not affirmation.'

Her next letter continues in the same personal manner. Apart
from the general culture which they had in common, there was
also, no doubt, the experience she had gained through personal
contact with proletarian circles. She had been a factory-worker.
What she wanted was 'any task that does not require technical
knowledge and which involves a high degree of efficiency, pain
and danger'.

'Pain and peril are indispensable to my mental make-up. It
is fortunate that this is not so with everyone, otherwise all
organized activity would be impossible without it; but for my
part, I cannot change; I know this from long experience. The
suffering that is spread over the whole surface of the earth
obsesses me and overwhelms me to the point of annihilating my
faculties, and I cannot recover them and free myself from this
obsession, unless I take upon myself a large share of danger and
suffering . . . .

'I beg you to arrange for me, if you can, enough useful suffering
and danger to save me from being consumed by useless regrets.
I cannot go on living in the situation in which I exist at the
moment. It is driving me nearly to despair.'

She did not think, she said, that it would be impossible for
him to find the kind of task for which she asked. There could not
be such a flood of requests for difficult and painful missions. She
might be given some provisional job, perhaps, to begin with.
But her hope for dangerous service must not be taken from her.
Danger was as necessary to her as bread. 'It is unfortunate to
have a character like this. . . . But it is something too basic in
me to be modified. The more so, since I have the certitude that
it is not only a question of character, but also of vocation.'

Simone Weil did not reveal to her correspondent the real

nature of her suffering. Every frustration affected her physically. Whenever she encountered an obstacle to her return to France, she suffered a violent attack of neuralgia. For days, she shut herself up in her room without eating, stretched out on the floor in the sleeping-bag that served her as bed. When asked about her headaches, she replied: 'There's nothing surprising in that, when one is a misshapen piece which God cut out so badly.'

Whenever the obstacles to her departure seemed to diminish, she promptly got better. She resumed her studies on folklore and the quantum theory at the public library; she could then enjoy the almost Mediterranean luminosity of the atmosphere of New York, seeing from her flat on Riverside Drive, the brilliant colours of the sunsets over the Hudson. In the evenings, she strolled through the streets of nearby Harlem.

Her friend Simone Deitz recalls, that at times while she was out walking, her movements would become graceful. Her carriage seemed to harmonize with the aesthetic character of the landscape she was contemplating or the truth she was discovering; her bearing lightened, became more airy, as if her whole being responded to beauty. Then, when her attention was distracted, she would lose her lightness of step and the peculiar charm of her appearance.

She always wore the jumpers her mother had knitted for her, a dark woollen skirt, in which green predominated, or a grey-and-red checked skirt which reached to her ankles. She had shoes without laces like moccasins, with flat heels.

As each phase of Simone Weil's life had corresponded with a friendship that marked its character, so in New York in the ante-room of the French Consulate she found Simone Deitz, with whom she had first become acquainted in Marseilles. Like herself, Simone Deitz wanted to go to England. Simone Weil asked her point-blank: 'Would you like to be my friend?'

Such a friendship exacted a state of perpetual availability: it meant listening to Simone Weil for hours, each person serving as a springboard for the other's ideas. Simone Deitz used to arrive at Simone Weil's apartment (number 6G, 549 Riverside Drive) at 9.30 a.m. and leave at six in the evening. Their conversations were often about God, more frequently about more general topics.

Simone Weil explained to her friend (who had become a Catholic) the reasons why she did not join the Church: 'When one can accept only a part of the demands of Christianity, one must have the courage to deny oneself baptism. And it is impossible for me to believe either in Limbo or in the Communion of Saints.' 'The Credo makes no mention of Limbo,' replied Simone Deitz. 'The Credo does not contain the whole dogma,' Simone Weil answered. 'A Catholic must accept all the ideas that are implied by the formal content of Christ's teaching. For Christ espoused the Church. He came to her—not she to Him, as He comes to us—not we to Him. In espousing the Church, He guaranteed her doctrine. Every believer owes complete adherence to His teaching.'

But Simone then understood the doctrine of Limbo according to its most rigorous interpreter: St Augustine, who thought that infants who died without baptism went to Hell. On the other hand, she accepted in principle the dogma of the Communion of the Saints, but restricted its scope: she believed in it only for other people. Where her 'self' began, grace stopped short: it was as though God recoiled with horror. *Her* debt to God was too enormous.

Simone Weil found it quite natural that she herself should undergo what she so indignantly protested against on behalf of others: she was scandalized that unbaptized infants should suffer exclusion from the Communion of Saints, but that she should share that fate went without saying. And the paradox did not stop there: she did not in fact believe that unbaptized innocents were for ever deprived of divine grace; but that it was so with herself was somehow due to her vocation—the effect, as it were, of a peculiar predestination. Her suffering was necessary, because it seemed an appropriate price as an infinitesimal and symbolic counterbalance, for the happiness of others. To every blessing had to correspond an evil that was equivalent if not proportional; not according to direct causality, but as a consequence of the universal order which was governed by an obscure balance between good and evil. Therefore Simone Weil had assumed the only evil that could be assumed, she thought, without sin. Like the Christ who remains in agony to the end of time, so, for all eternity, she would be an object of the wrath of God—and no one else would be able to share with her this supreme reprobation, this uniquely elected iniquity. Such was the logic behind attitudes of which she could not have been wholly conscious herself.

A born teacher, Simone Weil taught Greek to Simone Deitz. She also began with her a work on the folklore of the American Indians. She wished to discover the material form of their gods, to compare it with that of the Egyptian deities. She also tried to establish a connection between Irish folklore and Greek mythology. A number of notes on these themes can be found in her New York journals. In the course of her researches, Simone Deitz came by chance on the life of Milarepa the Wise, the Tibetan ascetic, magician, and poet of the eleventh century. Relegating other projects to secondary importance, Simone Weil decided to undertake a work of exegesis on this text and began to study Tibetan.

But she was not exclusively preoccupied with past centuries. Current politics interested her more, and she expressed opinions that were not widely held at that time: 'If we are going to do to the Germans as they have done to us, it would be better that we should be beaten.'

In her imagination, she was living in the future; in her heart she shared the sufferings of the present world and tried to relieve them by immediate action. According to Simone Deitz, she sent President Roosevelt her project for a 'front-line nursing squad'. In this she still emphasized the urgency of giving immediate attention to the wounded in order to reduce mortality caused by accidental hæmorrhages. Within ten days the White House answered that the recent development of blood plasma—which could be administered easily—had already improved first-aid measures.

Simone Weil believed that a first-aid diploma might be a help in obtaining a visa for England, so she took a course in first-aid in Harlem (which she chose for social reasons). She was too nervous to pass her first examination, although Simone Deitz, upon whom she practised bandaging and artificial respiration, found her light-handed enough. Her proverbial clumsiness seemed to have left her. At the written examination, Simone was much amused by the question: 'Is iodine a disinfectant or a plant?'

Such questions gave her a poor opinion of American education.

Suspecting that Simone Weil was not eating enough and was not taking meals regularly with her parents, Simone Deitz invited her to eat with her own family. She would take what was given her, especially if care was taken to draw her into an interesting conversation. At dinner, when steak was served in her honour, M. Deitz directed the conversation to the topic of comparative religion. Hoping to provoke Simone Weil's indignation, he pretended to extol the moral superiority of Judaism to Christianity while he surreptitiously slipped another piece of steak on to her plate.

Meanwhile Simone Weil's theology was becoming clearer; this cost her an almost intolerable metaphysical anguish and interior suffering. With remorseless integrity, she developed every principle to its ultimate conclusion. Intellectually, this was a work of construction: the theses were interlocking and logically faultless.

At the beginning stands the 'Weilian' concept of the Creation, as of the nature of an abdication by God, who ceased to command wherever he had the power. He emptied himself of his divinity. The God of the Christians, she says, is a supernatural deity, a God who withdraws; but this movement of withdrawal is Love. For the individual, the withdrawal of God is not a very comforting reason for existence. 'We are then a joke of God.' Or, worse still: 'What is creation from the point of view of God is sin from the point of view of the creature.' In the act of creation, God automatically created the possibility of sin; for it is not freedom but existence to which sin is indirectly attached. 'God gives up— in a sense—being everything. That is the origin of evil.' Does not the fact of existing outside God involve a metaphysical sin, a 'sin committed *before* any sinning? Outside of time, transcendental'? A sin prior to all action? A sin which consists in existing as a creature? It was to this thoroughly Hinduistic conception that Simone Weil was irresistibly drawn: creation and original sin are nothing but two aspects, for us different, of the act of abdication by God the Creator. 'God asked us: "Do you wish to be created?" and we answered "Yes".'[2]

## 'Creation is abandonment'

Among the unresolved questions that this theology raises, there is this: Does the metaphysical choice between being and non-being have to be made afresh by each of us? In being born we participate in Adam's theft. How can we logically explain this inherent contradiction of the creative act?

'We stand towards God as a thief who has been enabled by the generosity of someone whose house he has entered to steal his gold. This gold, from the point of view of the rightful owner, is a gift; but, from that of the thief, it is a theft. He must go back to the owner and return it to him. It is the same with our being. We have stolen a little piece of being from God to make it ours. God has given it to us. But we have stolen it. We have to restore it.'[3] Since all comparisons are dangerous, the central point of this doctrine remains unresolved: 'Why is creation a good, seeing that it is inseparably bound up with evil? In what sense is it a good that I should exist and not God alone? How should God love Himself through the wretched medium of myself? That I cannot understand. But everything that I suffer, God suffers too, for that is the effect produced by necessity, the free play of which He refrains from violating.'[4]

The intellect which finds itself up against unanswerable questions is humiliated, and in this humiliation creature and Creator meet, on the level of a mutual embrace, on the level of necessity and suffering. Through the Creation, God has identified himself with necessity; his image is that of the sun shining on just and unjust alike, with apparent indifference. 'Creation is abandonment. In creating what is other than He, God has necessarily abandoned it.'[5] He has abandoned his power to the Prince of this world and to necessity. We are abandoned, thrown adrift in time.

In this universal 'dereliction'—to make use of one of the terms of the philosophy of existence—there survives only an infinitely small speck, a seed of supernatural knowledge that is not 'abandoned'. On the one hand, God has emptied himself of his divinity by creating us; he has invested us 'with a false divinity'.[6] But, on the other hand, while sin says 'I', the only creative act of the creature is renunciation.

Could anything be clearer? Or is it possible to go still further?

# 'Moral death'

The creature must redeem the creation by unmaking it. 'This act is the end of the act which has created us. In this very moment, God, by his creative will, is keeping me in existence so that I may renounce it.'[6]

This doctrine leads logically to inferences that Simone Weil avoided: first, that evil or sin is at bottom nothing but illusion; second, if existence is accompanied by the illusion of being, then what is death? According to Simone Weil's system, death would be the door to a needed and unavoidable liberation. For death undoes the Creation! What will the renunciation of man's only apparent existence then entail for him? Will it amount to a liberation from or an identification with God?

But what concrete forms should supernatural renunciation take? First and before anything else, waiting: a waiting until and unto the complete exhaustion of the body. The cross is offered us, not joy. A Simone Weil will not refuse the cross. This leads to a study of her ascesis.

*The end to be attained:* to disappear; to annihilate the 'ego' that holds a screen between God and creation, that is to say, in reality, between God and God. As we know, this means a kind of moral death; for to consent to be only a creature is to consent to be nothing. Salvation is 'that consent to death which makes an inert nothingness of us. The saints are those who, while still alive, have really consented to death'.[7] And since man is void, to know the void, to annihilate oneself, to attain to nakedness of spirit or moral death is not only a condition of the love of God; it is its all-sufficing condition. For moral death is love of God.

*Means:* 'moral death' being the aim, Simone Weil's ascetism is negative, and the only road towards self-annihilation is to seek the void which she defines with this striking formula: *Void, when there is nothing external to correspond to any inward tension.*[8] To what reality do the two terms of this definition allude?

*Inward tension or desire:* it is possible to postulate as did Plato's Socrates that all men aspire to the good. But there are several kinds of desires. One may desire food or drink; sleep or quiet; to see a dear friend or to shake him by the hand: and 'so long as one's heart is set on all these frivolous objects, one's inmost soul

284

does not dwell in goodness'[9]—these desires are always sufferings for they are ever unsatisfied. But a man can, like the prodigal son, waste his energy on the things of this world, spend it vainly, profligately, at a pure loss, without really gaining anything. Then he realizes at last that what he obtains is valueless; and if the energy is really spent, it exhausts itself without renewal. At the end of this wasteful process the prodigal son can understand that *desires become reality when we remove from them the cloak of imaginary satisfaction*.[10] The inner tension of the soul having been thus frustrated of its object, the soul touches the void.

*Nothing external:* the void, when at last it is attained, produces in man 'an anguish, a desperate revolt'. Although the void is the supreme plenitude, man has not, so to speak, any right to know this; 'and the proof is that Christ himself, for a moment, completely forgot it'.[11] In a moment of perfect praise, he cried out: 'My God, why hast thou forsaken me?'

'Thus to cry out during our brief and interminable, interminable and brief, stay on this earth and then disappear into nothingness, is enough: how can one ask for more? If God grants more, that is his business; we shall know this only later. I would prefer to suppose that even in the best of cases, he grants nothing but that. For that is the plenitude of satisfaction—if only from now until the moment of death, there could be no other word in my soul but this uninterrupted cry in the eternal silence.'[12]

Such an awaiting, such a cry, does 'imply the very tension of desire, but without the reality of desire, a tension which has been accepted for ever and for ever'.[13] To the source of desires one should go so that the energy they deploy should not be wasted on the search for their object. In so far as it is a tension, this energy is real and true; but in its object, desire is deceitful.

Yet, when desire is frustrated, there is an unutterable wrench for the soul; a necessary laceration which is the condition of truth. 'I am in the truth if I tear my desire away from all the things that are not good things to direct it solely towards the good, without knowing whether it exists or not.' But though it is heart-rending, this desire of desire is also possession. Whilst the desire for earthly things is sometimes effective and sometimes ineffective, the desire for good is always effective: 'The desire for gold is not gold; while the desire for the good is a good.' The argument seems simple, but there is no simplicity, when one tries to see right into the depths of it.

'That God is the good is a certainty. It is a definition. That God in a certain way—unknown to me—is reality, that also is a certainty. It is not a matter of faith. But that each of my thoughts whereby I desire the good brings me nearer to the good, that is an article of faith. I can only experience this through faith. And even after having experienced it, it is even then not an object of affirmation but only of faith.

'As the possession of good consists in desiring it, the article of faith in question—which is the unique article of true faith—has for its object the fecundity, the capacity for self-multiplication of every desire for good.'

To believe is then belief in the supernatural efficacy of desire. That is the most important of all Simone Weil's assertions—and it reveals her spiritual evolution, for that evolution was her passage through the various stages of waiting.

We know that Simone Weil regarded waiting—a spiritual variant of what she termed 'attention'—as the very foundation of the life of the soul:

1. First, waiting allows a creature to wear God out with patience.

2. Why should God feel compelled to yield himself to the patient man? Because waiting is 'the extreme of passivity. It is obedience to time. Total submission to time obliges God to send eternity.'

3. Waiting is a higher form of attention; it is then an ability to 'read' what is supernatural in things. For Simone Weil, one had only to draw aside the curtain of irreality by knowing how to read reality. This superior form of reading is the mystical experience in essence; in its negative phase, it is the practice of the void.

4. Thus, what she called 'attention' is that which gave her system its coherence. It seems as if Simone Weil's inner life had overflowed spontaneously into her writings. The reality of her experience could *not* be expressed. Thus, with painstaking heroism, she had formulated a *system* only to find that it was still-

born.  Then she had to detach herself from it—a long undertaking which took place in two stages.[14]

The negative character of her asceticism is, by now, familiar: a man must submit himself in all things to necessity; he must not wish to change.  For the things that are outside man's power, the meaning of the Lord's prayer was clear: Thy will be done, and not mine.  But for the things within man's power?  Never regard them as such.  'Read obligation as a necessity', a necessity not only external, but internal.  A man has to accept also internal necessity.  Accept what he is, at a given moment, as a fact—even shame; even the past sin and the deeds to come; and this even in the little things, like going to bed, reading, smoking and eating.  'I have never disturbed, I will never disturb, the order of the world.  Henceforth, what does my fate matter?'[15]

And why?  Because to yield to necessity instead of mastering it is the only way to renounce one's will.  And 'obedience is the only pure motive, the only one which does not in the slightest degree seek a reward for the action, but leaves all care of reward to the Father who is in secret and who sees in secret.'  And obedience is pure only when it is obedience to necessity.  'Do not act *for* something; *act only because* you cannot do otherwise.'[16]

In the second stage, this extreme deprivation does not depend upon the will.  'We should do only those virtuous actions which we cannot prevent ourselves from doing, that is, to perform those acts which we cannot not do; however, through well-directed attention, we should strive to increase the number of those things which we are unable not to do'.[17]

This concerns the problem of action, or of what Simone Weil calls the 'transubstantiation' of energy in the decisions we have to make, at every instant and in every situation, between good and evil.

'The contemplation of a possible evil (possible in the full sense of the word), for a long time, without accomplishing it, brings about a sort of transubstantiation.  If one resists with a finite energy, that energy exhausts itself in a given time, and when it is exhausted one yields.  If one remains motionless and attentive, it is the temptation that exhausts itself. . . .

'The transubstantiation of energy consists in this: that, for evil, there comes a moment when one cannot do it; and for good, a moment when one cannot not do it.'[18]

But in the course of this transubstantiation of energy, some energy escapes; exerting itself in another direction, it ceases to nourish life—the soul, so to speak. Thus, Simone Weil is not content to affirm the inefficacy of purely voluntary efforts. She wants us, moreover, to liberate ourselves. And by what means?

'We have to desire that it be done in us, desire it genuinely. Truly desire it; with no attempt to accomplish it; simply think about it. For every attempt to accomplish it is in vain, and is dearly paid for. In such an undertaking, all that I name "I" must be passive. Attention alone, attention so complete that the "I" disappears, is required of me. It is necessary to keep what I call the "I" deprived of the light of attention, and to turn that light back upon the inconceivable.' In other words, 'to attempt this liberation by means of my own energy, would be to act like a tethered cow that drags at its halter only to fall on its knees'.[19]

Simone Weil thus reveals to herself that her life and her thought are not in step. She is torn asunder by the conflict that opposes the desire of her soul and the demands of her proud intelligence. When she speaks of the void, of affliction, of necessity, she is exhausting herself in a supreme effort to redeem herself all alone. When she speaks of *reality*, of *reading*, of *waiting*, and of *attention*, she knows, indeed, that she has to receive everything: that every attempt to achieve self-liberation is both vain and costly.

Let us remember, however, that she believed that prolonged waiting in an outward and inward void will necessarily be followed by mystical experience. For waiting is tension. It is also passive. It directs the soul's attention into the void that underlies the *natural* objects of desires, and leads into the *supernatural* reality that underlies the emptiness of natural desire. Attention is a form of reading and an ascesis. Simone Weil thought, in other words, that she had resolved the ontological contradiction that she saw between the supernatural and the natural orders, and had resolved at the same time the psychological contradiction between the demands of an intellect (which were such that she had to be wary of pride), and the needs of a heart (which were such that she had to be secure against illusion).

Yet her formula of passive tension proved explosive. When her ascesis had reached its goal, there remained in her experience a residue which could not find its place in her system. And what the system did not contain was the most precious part of herself, her hope, her real waiting, her person.

Since childhood, Simone Weil had believed that, if waiting were sincere and thorough, it could not be frustrated. Such a belief is necessarily founded on an intimate conviction that God is Love. That belief not only survived her intellectual manipulations, but had now become cut off, separated from them, by a gulf of suffering, from which death alone could entirely free her.

We catch a glimpse of this internal conflict between a mind that is reasoning about renouncing and abdication, and a heart that is seeking love in a special, but self-assigned vocation, in this letter which she sent to Father Perrin: 'I cannot cease from wondering whether, in this epoch when such a great part of humanity is engulfed in materialism, God does not wish there to be men and women who have given themselves to him and to Christ, and yet remain outside of the Church.'[20]

And why? She gives two principal reasons for this: first, Christianity must contain in itself all vocations without exception, since it is Catholic; so must the Church. But, in her eyes, Christianity was Catholic *de jure*, not *de facto*; so many things were outside it, so many things that she loved and did not wish to abandon, so many things that God loved, or else how could they exist? Over the immense extent of past centuries, before the last twenty, there were all the countries inhabited by non-white races; all the secular life in the countries of the white races; all the traditions condemned as heretical, like the Manichaean and the Albigensian; all the values born with the Renaissance, often degraded, but not quite bereft of beauty. And as Christianity is Catholic by right but not in fact, she believes she is in the right to stay outside the Church in fact and yet belong to it by right; what is more, it was a matter of duty for her, so strict an obligation in her eyes that she could not free herself from it without self-betrayal. If she did, she would deprive all the values that she had just mentioned from membership in the Church.

Second, she believes that it is her vocation to 'remain in a

# Dr von Hildebrand

certain sense anonymous, ever ready to be mixed into the clay of common humanity'.[21] This was, no doubt, a compassionate attitude. But it was more than that. To submit herself to necessity, to suffer evil, to immerse herself in the mass of mankind, was obedience to necessity. And so we return again to the cardinal theme of Simone Weil's thought:

'To consent to being anonymous, to being human material (Eucharist), to renounce prestige, public esteem—that is to bear witness to the truth: namely, that one is composed of human material, that one has no rights. It is to cast aside all ornament, to put up with one's nakedness. But how is this compatible with social life and its labels?

'It is, as always, a question of relationship to time. We have to discard the illusion of being in possession of time; to become incarnate.

'Man has got to make an act of self-incarnation, for he is disincarnated through the imagination. What comes to us from Satan is the imagination. . . .

'To humble oneself is supernatural'.[22]

During her stay in New York, the tension in which she lived and her preoccupation with the arrangements for her departure did not prevent Simone Weil from extending her circle of acquaintances. She was always pleased to meet others when she was in circumstances favourable to her search for truth.

It was thus that she introduced herself, on the recommendation of Father Perrin, to Dr von Hildebrand, then professor of philosophy at Fordham University. She discussed with him the problems of faith and her difficulties with the dogmas of the Church. She expressed, in particular, many reservations about the Old Testament.

Then she began to eulogize Pagan antiquity, whose God, she thought, had never been cruel. 'The Greeks believed that "the supplicating Zeus" dwelt within any unhappy person who implored pity,' whereas Jehovah, on the other hand, is 'the God of armies.' Pagan antiquity, she told him, was far more Christian in spirit than Judaism.

In Carcassone, Simone Weil had consulted Dom Clément, a

priest with whom she had left a small questionnaire (now published in the *Pensées sans ordre concernant l'amour be Dieu: Thoughts without order on the love of God*). It opens with the following question: 'To have faith in the mysteries of the Trinity, of the Incarnation and of the Eucharist, but never to see the possibility of adhering to the Christian conceptions of history—how can one legitimately think of entering the Church?' It was in this document of only five paragraphs that Simone Weil first expressed the essential elements of 35 questions which she presented to Father Couturier in New York, later to become her *Letter to a Priest*.

Father Couturier was one of two priests whom Simone Weil consulted just before she finally succeeded in leaving New York for London. The other was Father Oesterreicher.

To Father Oesterreicher she seemed like a soul in torment, an unhappy soul, an utterly sincere being, whose thinking had all the signs of a deep inner conflict. Her vehement discussion with him lasted a whole afternoon. Simone Weil expounded upon the themes that are to be found in her *Letter to a Priest*, but in the heat of argument she expressed them with an extremism that is not in the work itself. She maintained that the mysteries of Christianity were not only contained in the works of the ancient Greek poets and philosophers, but were better expressed there than in the New Testament.

After two conversations with Father Couturier, she sent him the pages which were later to constitute the *Letter to a Priest*. The priest did not have time to comment on them, for his correspondent left the next day for England.

The *Letter* repeats the ideas with which we are already familiar. It maintains that the non-Christian cults, although differing from Christianity, have an absolute value; that Israel and its religious tradition had falsified the true Christian spirit; that the Church had too narrow a conception of the faith.

But in the *Letter* these ideas are fragmented and advanced as 'opinions' which, although admittedly hazardous, nevertheless give a reader the impression of arguments *pro domo*. Through the cumulative effect of a logical enumeration of ideas and of a tone that sometimes rises to the style of an indictment, the *Letter* tends to make the reader suspend his judgment as it grips his attention. But Simone Weil's intention was not to oppose the Catholic faith with irrefutable arguments. She demanded only the right to freely examine all propositions not admitted by the Church. Nevertheless, what she wrote, without meaning to, is a pamphlet against the Church; she appears, in fact, to be seeking to undermine its historical foundations, destroy its authority, and invalidate its faith.

She requested a clear answer (an answer which, however, she must have foreseen) 'upon the compatibility or incompatibility' of her views 'with membership in the Church'.[23] For, although she did not believe that the propositions she maintained were the only legitimate ones, she could not behave as though she had not thought of them, or as though she had not entertained and even believed them, to the degree that they warranted belief.

It is needless to enumerate here the 'thirty-five opinions' that she could not bring herself to give up in order to purchase the right of access to the Sacraments. The whole letter is again based on the postulate that revelation cannot be unique: 'The Catholic religion contains explicit truths which other religions contain implicitly. Reciprocally, other religions contain explicit truths that are only implicit in Christianity'.[24]

The essence of Simone Weil's syncretistic outlook can be found, condensed, in three paragraphs of a letter that she wrote at about this time to Jean Wahl, whom she had known at the École Normale.[25] It is difficult not to use the term 'syncretism' in regard to a theology which was born of the fusion of different religious currents, since Simone Weil did consider each established religion as a unique revelation. She believed in the existence of a *religio perennis*, whose tradition was sometimes lost by the prevailing culture of the time, but which was always assured of ultimate survival, and whose simultaneous presence in several different traditions was most assuredly conceivable:

'I believe that an identical approach is expressed very clearly and with scarcely any marked differences in the ancient mythologies; in the philosophies of Pherekides, Thales, Anaximander, Heraclitus, Pythagoras, Plato and the Greek Stoics; in the Greek poetry of the Golden Age; in the folklore of all

races; in the *Upanishads* and the *Bhagavad-Gita*; in the texts of
the Chinese Taoists and in certain Buddhist trends; in the surviving sacred writings of ancient Egypt, in the dogmas of the
Christian faith and the writings of the greatest Christian mystics
(above all Saint John of the Cross), and in certain heresies,
especially in the Catharist and Manichaean tradition.

'I believe that this thought is the truth, and that there is need
today for a modern and Western expression of it. This means
that this truth needs to be expressed through the one tolerably
good medium that we can properly regard as our own; namely,
science . . . There are a few texts which indicate with certainty
that Greek geometry owed its origin to religious thought, and
it seems clear that this thought was so close to Christianity as to
be virtually identical with it.'

The very brevity of this letter indicates a dogmatic and
exhaustive systematization, presented in a synopsis. The author
is not in the least hesitant; she blithely recites her profession of
faith. She knows what she must believe and to what extent she
must believe it. She cannot help but declare in her innermost
heart that 'her vocation is to be a Christian outside the Church'.

In this position where she could neither participate in the
Sacraments of Christ, nor claim an open brotherhood in his blood,
she wished nevertheless to share in his sufferings. Had he not
thirsted for the coming of his hour? She prayed for a physical
consummation modelled on his own:

'Father, in the name of Christ, grant me this:

'That I may be like a total paralytic—wholly prevented from
making any movement of the body, or even any attempted
movement that corresponds to any prompting of my will. Let
me be incapable of receiving any sensation, as a being completely
blind, deaf, and deprived of the other senses. Let me be wholly
incapable of making the slightest connection between one thought
and another, even the simplest, like those defectives who not
only cannot count or read, but have never been able to talk.
Let me be insensitive to all sorrow and joy, incapable of any love,
for any being, or for any object, or even for myself, like an old
man in his dotage.'[26]

Would this wish be agreeable to the Father? Had he not

already granted his servant gifts of charity, faith and wisdom? Were the natural endowments of the senses, the heart, and the mind that had led her to truth not enough? And yet was not this request for the withdrawal of what had been given his inspiration? If that was the case, he could now grant what had been asked; it would be well received. Freeing his servant from all ties with the world of feeling and thought, he could lift her out of herself and ravish her in his love, consume all that was hers and not his alone, transform her into his Son, and like his Son, she could be given as bread to the hungry.

Such was Simone Weil's prayer: to become a cripple, paralysed and deaf, defective, 'as an old man in his dotage', worthless, but for the love of him who seeks his friends among 'the poor, and the maimed, and the halt, and the blind', the rejects of the earth. She no longer feared that 'hideous decay of the whole soul . . . through exhaustion and aggravation of pain' that had brought her to the brink of despair three years before. Others, in their last comatose moments, have passed through stages of mental and physical decay but few have felt in advance a supernatural purpose in this prelude to death. Yet Simone yearned that her hour should come: 'Father, since you are the good and I am the mediocre . . . delay no longer your visitation upon me, nor my departure: Tear away from me this body, this soul and make them wholly yours; do not let anything of me survive into eternity beyond this wrenching away of myself, or let there be nothingness.'

When she left her parents on 9th November 1942, Simone Weil said to them simply: 'If I had several lives, I would devote one of them to you. But I have only one, and I owe it elsewhere.'

She knew her prayer would be answered.

# 5

# London

THE END

'Love is something divine. Once it invades the human heart, it will break it.' Simone Weil, *La Connaissance surnaturelle*

DURING HER SIXTEEN-DAY VOYAGE on the Swedish boat *Valaaren*, according to information supplied by a fellow traveller, Simone Weil was in excellent spirits. After disembarking at Liverpool, all passengers were directed to the war-time detention camp known as the 'patriotic school'. Here, too, Simone managed to maintain her good humour. She saw Simone Deitz who had crossed on the same convoy. She played volley-ball and took part in practical jokes. One night, for example, after everyone had gone to bed, she disguised herself as a ghost.

The camp had been established primarily for the screening of spies. Simone's detention was prolonged: as a veteran of the Spanish Republican Army, she was suspected of communism. Her reputation as a pacifist was held against her. Maurice Schumann was informed of her detention, and obtained her release finally on the 14th of December.

In London, Simone lodged for a while in the barracks of the Free French Women Volunteers. Later, she stayed with friends. At the end of her first month in London, she realized that, in spite of the many applications she had made, her plan for returning to Occupied France within the near future was impracticable. She tried to content herself with a job that had been offered her in the Ministry of the Interior. 'I regret more and more,' she wrote to her parents, 'the decision I made in May [to leave Marseilles].'[1]

On a freezing Sunday evening in January 1943, Simone

arrived at the home of Mrs Francis, a widow, in the Notting Hill neighbourhood—31 Portland Road, Holland Park—where she had taken a room. The area had been bombed in the morning. From Simone's emaciated appearance, Mrs Francis assumed that her new tenant was very poor. She said of her: 'I think she had the saddest face I have ever seen.' Simone was shown to her room which had not been warmed. She was asked if she wanted the gas-fire turned on, and said no. She took off her shoes and lay down on the bed. Mrs Francis could do no more; she left the room.

The two Francis children soon became Simone's friends. David was fourteen; his health was so poor that he spent most of his time in bed. As a result, he was far behind in his studies. John, who was four years younger, went to school. Simone Weil took a great interest in his education. He showed her his homework, which she commented on and corrected, then left in the hall when she went out at odd hours. Simone asked John innumerable questions about his school, for she wanted to compare the English and French educational systems. After he had completed his homework, she would tell him stories: *Beauty and the Beast*, *The Emperor's New Clothes*, and others. One day she gave him a copy of *Hansel and Gretel*.

In both youngsters she tried to create a revulsion from the radio, for she could not bear having to listen to the news. She was protective towards them, and tried to persuade Mrs Francis not to scold them. John, who would sometimes come and curl up at her door, without saying a word, was the object of her special care. Simone believed that he was suffering from thyroid trouble. One day, having made an appointment for him, she took him to a doctor who gave him some pills to take regularly. The child, much interested, asked her: 'Will they help me to spell, Miss Simone?' 'Miss Simone' laughed heartily. It was the only time that Mrs Francis ever saw her laugh.

For the first two weeks, she had a ground-floor room in Mrs Francis's house, looking out on Portland Road. Then she moved to a room at the top of the house, overlooking Princedale Road. She thought it a pretty place, 'with the branches of the trees full of birds, or at night, a sky full of stars, just outside my window', she wrote to her parents. A pigeon delighted her by making its nest there. Simone spent her evenings and nights in her room, writing well into the early hours of the morning. Mrs Francis worried about her health, for she had a terrible cough. She begged her to rest and to eat. But Simone could or would not. How could she feel like eating, she complained, when the French were dying of hunger? She did, however, drink black coffee. Once Mrs Francis brought some to her during an air-raid alert. Simone did not want to accept it. 'You must not disturb yourself,' she said. 'You have two boys.'

During air-raids, Simone sometimes came down into the kitchen, but she showed no sign of fear. She invariably refused, abruptly and adamantly, to allow anyone to 'look after' her in any way. Mrs Francis managed to clean her shoes from time to time, but eventually this upset her, so she hid her shoes. She would not let Mrs Francis tidy her room. But how indeed could the poor woman have done it, despite her good intentions? There were papers on the bed, all over the floor, on the chairs—papers strewn about everywhere. Simone warned her landlady that if her papers were disturbed by any cleaning of the room during her absence, it would only give her days of trouble and additional labour. So the room, like its occupant, was left alone.

Simone Weil worked frenziedly. Her thinking had matured under tension. Her *Letter to a Priest* had disengaged her from Father Perrin's hold upon her; she was alone once more, alone upon heights to which no one else would follow. While climbing the precipice of philosophical speculations and following a continuous path, she had found at each succeeding stage the same themes, the same problems, and the same answers. Now that she was approaching her goal, however, everything seemed to simplify itself. The centre alone was immobile: the circular pathways drew steadily closer together. The end was near.

All this is clear from her last papers. Never had she dealt with such a wealth of difficult subjects with so sure a hand. Quantitatively as well as qualitatively, these papers demonstrate the writer's complete possession of her remarkable faculties.

At the Ministry of the Interior, she worked for the Commissariat of Action upon France, and her immediate superior was

Closon. André Philip, Secretary of the Interior in the de Gaulle cabinet, gave her the job of writing a report on all documents of a political nature which came from France. These documents were the work of committees located mainly in the non-occupied zone. While the Resistance was fighting the underground war, they were making plans for the peace time that would follow liberation; they were 'organizing the peace'. Once the Germans were gone, what was to be the country's next constitution? What changes were to be made in legislation? Education? The status of workers, etc? The Third Republic had been destroyed, and few regretted it. The Vichy government was a transient thing.

Following André Philip's directions, intellectuals from the whole social and political spectrum, united in their faith in victory, in their hopes for the future, were secretly getting together (but with a relative measure of freedom of communication) in Lyon, Grenoble, Aix, Arles, Montpellier. In remote corners like Chambon-sur-Lignon in the Auvergne farmers formed a 'Course on Biblical Studies on the Epistle of St James'; in actual fact, a training group for the *résistance*. Others concentrated on an ideological frame for a future state which they envisioned as free from previous ideological and constitutional faults. All were dreaming of a new society. (Such hopes were to be blighted after the Liberation by party division, internecine blood-letting, and political jockeying for power.)

In America at the same time, General Marshall, with an improvidence since then much deplored and heavily paid for by the loss of freedom in all Eastern European countries, was urging that no efforts or talents should be diverted from the total war effort by idle speculation about post-war contingencies. Agreements based on America's basic trust in her comrades-in-arms, and little else, were to be sealed at Teheran and Yalta.

Yet, 'there's a divinity that shapes our ends, rough-hew them how we will'. Just as the American pragmatic approach was later to prove unsound, the long-term view of the French, with its basic reformulation of the whole structure of a nation, was hardly more effective in bringing about the better world towards which it was directed. Despite the difference in fundamental attitudes between the intellectual French and the energetic Americans, they had a common fault: they were working for a goal narrowly definable in time and space, which was to begin with the Liberation or the Armistice, and which was to cover a field strictly commensurate with their plans.

No satisfactory parallel can be made between an individual and a nation. Simone Weil, who was a prophet when she thought in terms of larger units such as a people or mankind, was a mere child, impetuous, obstinate—and generous—when she planned for herself. The discrepancy was not based on any divorce of her speculative and practical faculties. It is related to the strange ability she had to think of the particular in terms of the absolute which served her in good stead in her writings, in which she dealt with essences, but which in life, with its countless options between greater and lesser good, resulted in her choosing always to accomplish the greater good, irrespective of her own capacities: working in a mill; fighting in Spain; joining the underground. Even the terms used are illusory. Joining the underground was not and could not be a practical goal for her, because it was impossible. She was not wanted. To send her to France would be to execute her. André Philip asked the *résistance* movements in France whether they could use her. They answered: 'On no account!' She had three marks against her. She seemed so obviously Semitic that the Gestapo would have arrested her promptly. She was patently absent-minded. She was awkward and clumsy. In her favour, she had her dedication and her courage; no one doubted that she would not speak under torture. Strangely enough, in spite of her emaciated appearance, she had succeeded, by dint of long walks or the other extraordinary exertions of which she boasted, in conveying to André Philip the idea that she had stamina and physical resistance above the average. But everything considered, she was a liability, since she was bound to draw attention and thus endanger the whole group. Yet these considerations could not sway her purpose either because they were sometimes not mentioned to her, as in the case of her Semitic appearance, or because at other times she would not listen. She could be quite candid about her motives: 'I want to share the suffering of the French people. I wish to be with them in their hunger and their want. I cannot stay here when Christ is suffering elsewhere.' No Secretary of the Interior was ever asked in such terms for a perilous mission behind the enemy lines.

She had hoped to see her project for a 'front-line nursing squad' implemented in some way. André Philip took it to de Gaulle, who read a few lines, discarded it as lunacy ('Mais elle est folle!'), and showed no inclination to meet the author. The English army, according to André Philip, was more interested, but nothing came of it for Simone Weil.

The work she had to do instead of the work she preferred brought her into contact with the committees working for the France of tomorrow, instead of the groups fighting the underground war. She knew that the former were the ideal recruiting-ground for the latter; it added to her conviction that her efforts were being wasted. Whenever she completed a report, she herself took it to André Philip. He told her, in complete good faith, that the work she did contained both long-range and immediate applications. In the latter category was her suggestion that a Supreme Council of the Revolt be created in France, so that the impetus to liberation might come from within the continent. This was the only other idea of Simone Weil's to be brought to de Gaulle's attention. He liked it, and it was carried out. A Lycée teacher of history at Lyon, a *résistant* named Georges Bidault, became director of the Council.

After each of her futile efforts to persuade André Philip to send her to France, Simone's chagrin was immense; she fell sick with her splitting headaches and could not come to work for the next day or two. But then another report would come from France, and she would meet the work as a challenge: she used to digest the data and put her reflections to paper in an almost continuous session lasting two or three days and nights, all of which she spent in her office. Sometimes her comments would be returned to the interested committees in France, who would send comments in their turn. And between these men who figuratively (and sometimes literally) wrote with a gun at their side and the would-be underground agent, an exchange of ideas took place about such abstruse matters as might have graced a discussion in the groves of Academe: the notions of justice, of sovereignty; the impersonal nature of man or of good; and other matters of more transitory quality, such as the organization of the *résistance*, the future constitution, freedom for colonial peoples, the threat of the Americanization of Europe. Whatever the topic, it was always envisioned by Simone Weil *sub specie aeternitatis*. Thus, what she wrote in 1943 has kept to this day its freshness and its vitality.

One of these papers deals with the problems that political parties will create in a society, either through their mutual antagonism or the dictatorial powers for which they strive.

Political parties received short shrift in Simone Weil's hands. She was merciless towards anything that could be called 'collective'. She entitled her article 'For the General Suppression of Political Parties'[2] and argued that they must all be suppressed in the name of justice and the common good. Such groups, she claimed, whatever their doctrine, are dedicated to the brainwashing of an always increasing portion of the public. While the truth is one, these groups divide it, unjustly appropriate it, and make it a bone of contention. The more a truth becomes particular the more it appeals to passion at the expense of reason:

'A political party is a machine for manufacturing collective passion.

'A political party is an organization so contrived as to exert a collective pressure upon the thought of every one of the human beings who is a member of it.

'The primary and, in the last resort, the only object of every political party is its own growth, and that without limit.'

These three characteristics turn every party into a more or less totalitarian enterprise. To allow such organizations to exist is to grant to limited groups the monopoly for spreading light and putting into practice a political programme which is supposed to ensure the good of everyone. To create a party is to go back upon the very principle of republicanism, whose ideal is to act according to the general will.

Simone Weil's view of political parties is not original. Spinoza and then Rousseau expressed similar concepts long before. To

Rousseau, Simone Weil's arguments would be beyond question. He did not look upon the general will as an absolute good or a self-justifying process, as so many have done in his name. He used it as the corner-stone of his political theory mainly to express his distrust of individual wills. His was the paradoxical belief that, in the general will, the individual passions which are natural sources of diversity and error, neutralize one another; whereas in the individual, the will is the immediate ally of his passions. The general will is like a body of water made of individual molecules whose individual movements are erratic; but since they collide with one another and neutralize one another, they exert a uniform pressure and present a horizontal surface which shows a perfect equilibrium.

The will of the majority, then, does not necessarily coincide with justice or the public good; yet it is closer to justice than are individual wills, insofar as it is further removed from the passions. In practice, therefore, there is a rapprochement between general will and justice. Everything harmful to this rapprochement, said Simone Weil, should be eliminated. Anything which ruffles the calm waters of general opinion by dividing it into separate currents, whatever sets the even mirror of justice boiling and heaving, is bad. That is why political parties are bad. They represent evil in its pure state: they recommend means to men, as though they were ends. They propose themselves instead of the good, as ends. Furthermore, the doctrines of political parties can only be fictitious, yet parties are all doctrinaire. One constantly hears people say: 'As a monarchist, as a socialist, I believe that . . .' Once he is a party member, the individual feels himself excused from acting as a citizen. He takes the party line either as a justification for not thinking about the problems of the hour or as a screen to hide his selfish refusal to act and to think according to the public good.

The rise of the political parties is a contemporary disaster, whose origin, according to Simone Weil, can be traced back to the Middle Ages, when the Church's intolerance sowed the seeds of future political divisions. 'It must be confessed that the machinery of spiritual and mental oppression that is characteristic of the parties was introduced into history by the Catholic Church in its struggle against heresy.' The French Revolution, after 1789, provided the soil in which the seed has grown. Since then, modern man has suffered this evil without being able to exterminate it.

Every party is a little church, no little church should be tolerated. 'The suppression of the parties would be an almost absolute good.' Instead and in place of them, Simone Weil recommends the creation of 'reviews of ideas': these would constitute centres of attraction and engender 'circles of affinity', the fluidity of which would defy collective passion. To advertise oneself as of one review would be prohibited. An election candidate would be judged solely on the basis of his programme and his personal integrity. As for the inevitable 'clandestine parties', their members 'would no longer be able to make public profession of their servility of mind', or to engage in party propaganda.

The creation of groups presenting a social programme and enrolling militants would not be permitted. Such measures, so simple as to seem paradoxical, would have the beneficent effect of freeing peoples' minds from the obsession of 'for' and 'against' which confront us with artificial dilemmas in every direction. 'Do you agree or not?' is asked even of pupils at school after a quotation from some great author, notes Simone. In art and literature we have coteries with their leaders and doctrinaire programmes. One is either a 'Maurassian' or a 'Gidean'.

'Almost everywhere—and frequently even in purely technical problems—taking sides, assuming an attitude for or against, has been substituted for thought. . . .

'It is doubtful whether we can cure this disease which is killing us, without first suppressing the political parties.'

Two articles on the future constitution were written by Simone Weil. In the first, she posed the problem that had to be solved before anything new could be built. Entitled 'The Legitimacy of the Provisional Government',[3] it included the following statement: 'Legitimacy is not a treasure which has been stolen from the French people, either by the enemy or by a conspiracy organized from within. The French people, as a whole, from the leaders to the labouring classes, has opened its hand and let the treasure fall to the ground without even looking down to see where it was rolling. The passers-by trod it underfoot.'

It was therefore 'an abdication of the nation as a whole' that took place in July 1940. And the conduct of General de Gaulle, who picked up the treasure, 'put it away, and let the public know that he appointed himself its guardian until the day when the owner would be in a position to reclaim it', was absolutely irreproachable. 'Legitimacy is not a first principle; it derives from justice.'

The stage now being set for a new régime, let not this legitimacy to which it is heir lead it to overreach its attributions. This was the thought which she carried into her next article, 'The Project for a New Constitution'.[4]

The project which had been submitted to her laid stress on the words: *La souveraineté réside dans la nation*—'Sovereignty resides in the nation'. The first word signals caution. If sovereignty has any meaning in itself, she declared, it loses all content when it is made into the attribute of 'nation': never in all known history, nor in prehistory so far as can be made out, has there been a sovereign nation. 'Moreover,' she said, 'it is not to be desired that the nation should be sovereign; justice alone should be.' Force alone is sovereign in fact, alas! and justice is only transcendent.

'Justice is the sovereignty of sovereignty. That is why, through justice, the weak one has access to one who is very powerful, as by royal ordinance. . . .

'Instead of "Political sovereignty resides in the nation", I would propose: "Legitimacy is constituted by the free consent of the people to the authorities taken as a whole to which they are subject". That at least, it seems to me, has some meaning.'

Simone Weil also passionately rejected the phrase, 'representatives of the majority and of the opposition', which had been used to specify the members of the future 'High Court of Political Justice'. 'The complete monopoly of the parties over public life is what has done us the most harm. To consecrate it officially in the very text of the Constitution would be strange indeed.'

Of the articles written by Simone Weil at this time, a large group might come under the general heading of the relation between civic rights and civic duties, although their relevance to this topic is sometimes rather vague. However, this theme was at the very core of the preamble of the new constitution, and it proved to be the most delicate of all the tasks confronting her and the intellectual groups with which she corresponded, for it entailed the formulation of the philosophic or humanistic principles upon which it was to be based.

Each one of the constitutions of the three French republican régimes which had waxed and waned over the previous century and a half had been directly related to the principles embodied in the *Déclaration des Droits de l'Homme* ('Declaration of the Rights of Man') voted by the Assemblée Constituante of 1789. The general impotence of the executive branch under republican régimes and some lack of integration between the rights and the duties of the individual as stated in the *Déclaration des Droits de l'Homme* led many political scientists and political philosophers to re-evaluate, in the enforced leisure of these a-political times, the hallowed dogmas of the past.

There were those who claimed that Marxism was the answer to the current malaise. They maintained that a new leaf had to be turned, and that much, if not everything, of the Marxist doctrine could be profitably assimilated into a new constitution and a new economy. To this school of thought Simone Weil responded with an ironical query: 'Is there a Marxist Doctrine?' This question became the title of an essay.[5]

The founding father of communism had but one merit in Simone's eyes: he understood (she congratulates him for this understanding) the need for a science of society. But he had been incapable of creating one, even though 'his mind, of a range inferior to that which the exposition of a doctrine requires, was capable of ideas of genius'. Two of these ideas, which were original and which had been allowed to lapse into oblivion— 'the truth is too dangerous to touch; it is explosive'—attracted Simone Weil's special attention: 'Marx first, and if I am not mistaken he alone—for his researches have not been followed up —had the double insight to take society as fundamental *human* fact, and to study in it, as a physicist does in matter, relations of force.'

But upon these principles he grafted an 'inhuman system' that completely dishonoured them and is no more than an expression of the mechanistic scientism of his time . . . 'a system according to which the relationships of force which define a social structure entirely determine both the destiny and the thoughts of men. Such a system is merciless. Force is all; no hope is left for justice. There is not even the hope of conceiving justice in its true reality, since thoughts only reflect relationships of force.'

It is on this very point that Plato reveals his greatness, argues Simone, for having also intuitively realized that force is sovereign in societal matters, he had nevertheless reversed the Marxist proposition in advance. 'He did not say that the good is automatically produced by necessity, but that the Spirit dominates necessity by persuasion'—the Spirit alone. 'Man cannot serve as basis for a certitude.'

The world such as Marx sees it is the result of necessity, in which there is no room for the good, for the good is nothing but necessity. Thus it is matter, which is the *locus* of necessity, which becomes the sole support of the good. For the materialist 'matter must ultimately be considered as a machine for the production of the good'.

Marx is not always wrong. He was 'right to regard the love of liberty and the love of domination as the two motive-powers that keep social life in continual flux'. Unfortunately, he underestimated their scope, limiting it to the particular case of the oppressed and the oppressor, which alone received his attention. Simone Weil regards this as an over-simplification on his part. In fact, she says, everyone is at once oppressed and oppressor, in variable proportions according to his position in the social hierarchy. She therefore concludes: 'The only real contribution Marx has made to social science is to have shown the need for it. That is much; it is immense; but we are still at the same point. Such a science is still needed.'

Though Marx's thinking was questionable, his intentions were not. He duped himself as he did so many others. He saw that man was steeped in the material universe to the point where he could neither obtain nor even think justice. Then Marx created 'a dream in which social matter takes over the two functions of which it has deprived the individual: that is, not only the doing but the thinking of justice'. Such is the very basis for his 'dialectical materialism'. 'Marx attributed purely and simply to society considered as matter that movement through contradictions towards the good, which Plato described as the movement of the thinking creature being drawn upwards by the supernatural operation of grace.'

In Plato and in Marx, Simone Weil observes that the same good—justice—reveals itself at the end of two contradictory approaches. Marx says that, thanks to the movement which makes the lower classes succeed to power, a day will come when the class at the very bottom of the social ladder will find itself right at the top. Then class distinctions will fade away, he predicts, and there will be justice. Possessing justice, men will know it 'as it really is'. But so long as it remains absent it is impossible to know what it will be, for the thoughts of men are conditioned by the surroundings in which they live.

Like the bourgeois on whom he passed judgment, Marx codified the morality of a new social group. What is more, he gave it a mystique, or rather a myth—the great myth of force in the hands of the weak, of those who remain weak despite their number. This identification of force with weakness, for its paradoxical character, would have some truth if it were true that numbers amount to force. Indeed, they do create a force—but an anonymous force which belongs to the one who can get possession of it, as the strength of a horse is not its own to dispose of, but the carter's, to use as he will. Power is not in the hands of the masses, but in the hands of a group outside it. Ambiguity towards the so-called power 'of the people' was supposed by Marx to be characteristic of the bourgeois state. He exempted the popular state of the future from it.

Weakness, Simone Weil agrees, may be a force while still remaining weakness—that is the Christian paradox, the scandal of the Cross, the property of the supernatural, whose force is non-existent in the eyes of the world and whose weakness is its force. Such force does not reside in the masses (where, however, it may penetrate), but in certain souls. As for Marx, however, he 'admitted the contradiction of force in weakness, but without

admitting the supernatural which alone legitimizes the contradiction. Similarly, Marx sensed a truth, an essential truth, when he
understood that man does not conceive of justice unless he has
it . . .'

According to Simone Weil, therefore, the Marxist doctrine
is no more than a correct intuition draped with a prodigious
illusion. But, unlike many of her contemporaries, she does not
reject materialism to find a moral consolation within personalism.
The individual could not be measured or defined by his environment; but neither could he be referred to solely as a person.

In her next article (entitled 'Human Personality'[6] in Richard
Rees's translation, but more accurately in manuscript: 'Collectivity.
Person. Impersonal. Right. Justice'.), Simone Weil pursues her
analysis of man, this elusive creature to which the state ascribes
duties and recognizes rights. What is this fundamental unit,
this impermanent speck, this walking, talking, suffering monad?

As usual, Simone Weil is not concerned with abstract defini-
tions, but with the living object whose experiences are the only
clue to its nature. Does man feel himself to be a person in such
a way that this term, when he uses it, wholly and fully corresponds
to what he thinks of himself?

If a man suffers violence, if he is wounded and loses his sight,
the person in him suffers no diminution. Thus it is wrong to
speak of the rights of the human person, for such a person is
situated beyond everything that men may wish to preserve.

'Only one thing would restrain me from seeking my own
satisfaction or my own profit by hurting my neighbour . . . it
is the knowledge that if someone were to put out his eyes, his
soul would be torn by the thought that harm was being done to
him.'

'This profound and childlike and unchanging expectation of
good in the heart' has nothing in common with that other demanding, domineering side of the personality, which wants to extend
the limits of its power, and speaks of its rights, like a boy who
cannot bear to see his brother with a bigger piece of cake than
he has himself.

'That depth of heart which cries out in surprise when a wrong
is inflicted upon it' does not have, as a rule, the means to express

itself. There must be silence, before such a cry can be heard. But everything—social structure, laws, the moral climate of our times—is directed against such silence and conspires against this cry. Political parties thirst for expansion, not justice; men in power take their orders from their party, not from their conscience. No one is listening to this cry which arises from the depth of the heart of our neighbour, and which, like a petitioner trembling with fear before an Oriental potentate, begs for our audience.

Far from suppressing the personal in us—which would be too good to be true—the tyrant only hurts what is impersonal: 'Far from its being his person, what is sacred in a human being is the impersonal in him. Everything which is impersonal in man is sacred, and nothing else.'

Blake's horrible saying: 'Sooner murder an infant in its cradle than nurse unacted desires' would be justified if it were true that 'the fulfilment of the human person' is the goal of our action. The gratuitous act (in the sense in which it has been described by Gide) cannot be judged in moral terms; it gives the sure measure of the man who accomplishes it, or, it might be said, he accomplishes, perfects and carries himself with it on to the most personal plane of all—the irrational.

In the realm of aesthetics, just as in that of ethics, nothing is of value but what is or deserves to be anonymous. The author of the *Iliad* and the architects of the Romanesque churches have disappeared. Their works dwelt with beauty, their thoughts dwelt upon truth. 'What is sacred in art is beauty,' and what is beautiful is anonymous, like everthing impersonal, like perfection.

'Our personality is the part of us which belongs to error and sin. The whole effort of the mystic has always been to become such that there is no part left in his soul to say "I".

'But the part of the soul that says "We" is infinitely more dangerous still.'

For this part is not, properly speaking, ours. It belongs to the 'collective'. It has no rights because the right of all cannot reside in one alone. 'The soul which says "We" ' is well aware of this fact, since it seeks to be one with the crowd from which it expects, as the part claims from the whole, what it cannot find in itself. Hence the disregard of the crowd for the individual, from whom or to whom it can, at will, add or subtract its ephemeral personal dignity. Therefore, 'the reason that prevents the person from feeling sacred is that, in fact, the person is not.'

The notion of 'rights', moreover, is improper. A right is not a rule for the establishment of justice, but the legislation of property, of commerce, of exchange. Rights, in ancient Rome, were powers that masters held over their slaves. There is nothing natural about rights, even though the eighteenth century Encyclopedists said so. The Greeks never spoke of rights.

Justice is not of this world, asserts Simone Weil. That is why justice should rule the world. Antigone understood this very well: justice and charity are cut from the same cloth. Expressions like 'What you are doing to me is not just' and 'You have no right to . . .' are not equivalent. Justice is what is expected of a man, that which he is measured against; his rights are what he expects from the world, in the form of legislation, privilege, or custom, in the form of assistance towards the fulfilment of his personality.

Those favoured by an arbitrary distribution of liberty cannot appreciate the suffering of their brothers because they do not share in it. Nor has it been given to the latter to understand their own misfortune because they are shut up inside their misery. The outcasts of fortune never understand their lot. 'Thought revolts from contemplating affliction, to the same degree that living flesh recoils from death.'

But 'that which is indispensable to the good, and is impossible naturally, is always possible supernaturally.

'Supernatural good is not a kind of supplement to natural good. . . . In all the crucial problems of human existence the only choice is between supernatural good on the one hand and evil on the other.'

And there is some evil in all those notions which are alien to pure goodness—'democracy', 'rights', or 'personality'. They are of no use to the poor; they are lying words, promising what they have not. 'On the contrary, the fulfilment of an obligation is a good, always and everywhere. Truth, beauty, justice, compassion are good, always and everywhere.'

These ideas are essential to open up the world beyond us.

## The piercer of walls

There are men who can not only think them, but realize them; minds which have access to the truth, souls that have access to goodness; geniuses and saints. 'Real genius is nothing other than the supernatural virtue of humility in the domain of thought.' Is it necessary to say then that genius has nothing to do with talent nor even with intelligence, which do not belong to the realm of what is good?

The writer uses the medium of words, the artist the plastic forms. All lovers of beauty, they try to make us grasp the riches of the world of truth which they have glimpsed. But there is a natural limit to their means of communication, as there is a limit to their creative faculties. They are capable of handling only a restricted number of relations, the relations of sign to thing signified and of sign to sign which constitute the language, the means of expression of their art. Yet the true object of art is the whole, an enduring complexity which arrests the mind as if it were faced with an enigma. It would be necessary to see through this complexity, upon which truth depends, in order to reach the perfect expression of what is but which cannot be reached. Like a prisoner beating against the walls of his prison, the spirit eager for truth batters against the limitations of language.

'He will beat his head against the wall until he faints. He will come to again and look with terror at the wall until one day he begins afresh to beat his head against it; and once again he will faint. And so on endlessly and without hope. One day he will wake up on the other side of the wall.' He will find himself 'there at the beginning of wisdom', where intelligence ends, having passed through his 'own annihilation', that wall of affliction that must be pierced if we are to know the truth of affliction.

He who pierces the wall is not without reward, for in attaining the truth he also attains beauty. 'Because affliction and truth require the same attention to be understood, the spirit of justice and the spirit of truth are but one. . . .

'To the degree to which affliction is hideous, so is its true expression supremely beautiful.' Pure love enables us, by dint of sympathy with other beings and things, to break the yoke with which the laws of language weigh us down. Beauty, become

311

more approachable, can then minister to her two sisters, justice and truth, which are dumb; she can lend them her voice.

'Why am I being hurt?' the oppressed and unhappy man cries out to justice, whose tongue has been cut out. 'Why has that other man more than I have?' demands the person whose right has been transgressed. God does not answer the former, for he 'has power to deliver from evil only the eternal part of the soul'. But all the oppressive apparatus of human justice bestirs itself to assist the latter.

'We have lost all idea of what punishment is. We are not aware that its purpose is to procure good for a man. For us it stops short with the infliction of harm.' Punishment is legitimate for one reason only—a reason that we have forgotten. It is justified only if the criminal asks himself; 'Why am I being hurt?' —if, by suffering, he discovers (before it is too late) that eternal part of his soul without which he cannot have access to pure good.

'Suffering and violent death are a treasure which Christ appropriated and which he frequently offers to those whom he loves—we think so little of it that we throw it to those who are the vilest in our eyes, knowing that they will make nothing of it, and having no intention of helping them to discover its value.'

Having delivered this severe indictment of 'Personalism', and analysed the social and aesthetic implications of such a school of thought, Simone Weil next turned towards what could be termed 'the problems of the hour'. That these problems are also those of all time, at least in their source, does not come as a surprise.

In an article entitled 'A War of Religions'[7] she attempted to point out the roots of the current ideological malaise. The French title of the essay is explanatory: '*Cette guerre est une guerre de religions.*' If this premise is accepted, Simone Weil argues, an investigation into the nature of religion will have to be made, for the weapons used in a conflict must be related to the cause of the conflict.

The first question in such an investigation, implied though not stated, must be: 'Is religion necessary?' Simone Weil's answer is without doubt, for to her what is man-made is patently insufficient. Human justice, she declares, is of no help to man, no more than morality, which 'creates an atmosphere in which he cannot breathe'.

Morality, she says, weighs upon us—morality is hateful—it tinges all our actions with the colours of good or of evil and prevents us from living happily. We must therefore escape from the grip of the moral alternative. But where can man flee to escape it? He will turn, she predicts, to irreligion, idolatry, or mysticism.

To be irreligious is to deny the moral problem altogether; the atheist recognizes only one cult, the worship of self, which he can develop as he likes in absolute licence.

Idolatry 'consists in the mapping out of a social area into which the pair of opposites, good and evil, may not enter; inasmuch as he belongs to that area, man is no longer subject to those opposites'.

Mysticism offers transcendence, the union with the absolute good.

The principle of irreligion is desire; yet desire is not enough, for it presupposes an orientation. A desire without an object is an effort without direction. 'When direction ceases man becomes mad, in the literal, medical sense. So this method, being based on the principle that all objectives are equal, leads to madness.' There are civilizations and cultures which have gone mad in this sense. Idolatry—let us say nationalism, which is its truest form—liberates the individual from responsibility for personal evil when he pays the price of collective evil; eventually it leads to the downfall of the social organism which gave it birth.

Mysticism would enable man to escape from the moral alternatives if it were possible, practicable, accessible.

None of the three methods of emancipation from the opposition of good and evil is available to slaves or enslaved people. There are, however, some beings capable of living the 'spiritual poverty' of St Francis. Among the fragments that Simone Weil wrote in London, are a few detached leaves in praise of poverty:

'The love of poverty is not at all ascetic; it gathers and savours in their fullness all the joys, all the pleasures that offer themselves. . . .

'In poverty there is a poetry for which there is no equivalent. It is the poetry that emanates from miserable flesh, seen in the truth of its affliction.'[8]

To these 'poor in spirit', the mystical way remains open. Would it be possible to make of them a sort of religious order, without cowls or monasteries, and convert the masses to 'spiritual poverty?' This is no doubt in the realm of dreams, but thus would be born a faith such as would uplift a people and be more decisive for victory than the force of arms.

As proof of this Simone Weil refers to 'that halting of the German troops at the Channel' which was the 'supernatural point in this war'. 'If a faith were to arise in this miserable continent . . . victory would be rapid, certain and secure.' It would generate a spirit of resistance which would spell the destruction of the enemy's communications. And is it not by the control of the means of communication that wars are won?

Basic to any vision of a liberated future, however, were the conditions under which a successful war of liberation could be fought. It was to this topic that Simone Weil addressed herself in her 'Reflections upon Revolt'.[9] She declares, first of all, that the purpose of revolt should be twofold: against the occupying power, and secondly against the conditions that brought about the occupation. And it should be long-term; that is, a reformation. 'The spirit of reform was not compatible with the state of dreaming, unreality and passive waiting that existed all over the country.'

How will it assert itself today?

'Action itself is the most powerful of appeals to action and the most irresistible stimulant.' Will action be sufficient to awaken all men of good will? Some of them are cool heads who are not attracted by lost causes. These men and women must come forward, however; they are indispensable. For the real heroes, like General de Gaulle, fulfil a useful mission for too short a time. They are the symbols of today, but not the leaders of tomorrow. Peace removes them from their privileged status.* Their ideal must be shared by those who are well equipped for

*In view of Simone Weil's theory, it is interesting to note that it was the crisis in Algeria that faced France with the immediate prospect of a civil war which brought de Gaulle back to power.

peace. Otherwise, the movement that carries France to liberation, being neglected by the wise, will fall into the hands of the fanatics, and the country will be in imminent peril of civil war.

It was imperative that with the utmost speed a 'Supreme Council of the Revolt' be created which would place in the hands of France and Europe the initiative for their own liberation. Coming from without, such a liberation would throw the country open to 'communist or American influence' and imperil Europe's own tradition. Without the 'systematic organization of the revolt on the Continent, carried out with the help of the English naval and air forces', it is doubtful whether the French could recover their own soul.

This last proposal of Simone Weil was, as has been said, carried out. But it is most significant that such a practical suggestion should be followed by a demand for reflection. The situation in France was desperate and called for immediate action. Still, the enterprise to be undertaken had to be analyzed, its deeper motives and hidden causes had to be probed. A struggle led in the name of justice could not be vindicated without further proof. To the title of her 'Are We Fighting for Justice?'[10] Simone Weil replied in the negative. Justice is not a dynamic concept and cannot be proposed to man as a motive for his actions, she argued. For when a man is fighting, he is fighting for himself. He may disguise this fact from himself for social or political reasons. But he cannot fight otherwise. In the conflict in which we are engaged, we will not consider as obstacles those whose strength is not great enough to keep our own in check. They become instead a kind of dough to be kneaded into shape. Their very weakness cancels their value in our eyes. For us, they are without dignity and do not deserve attention. Beings without opacity, as transparent as glass, they are only means to our ends, never our partners.

'This cannot be helped. Were it otherwise, nothing could ever be done, and if nothing were done we would perish.

'By the same token, action is stained with sacrilege. For human consent is sacred. It is what man owes to God. It is for this that God comes seeking, like a beggar, among men.'

In the absence of consent, there can be neither obedience nor

315

love, there is only oppression and violation. That is why God, of whom Plato said 'he was good', took great care not to exercise in full His sovereign power. Upon matter, He imposed its own mechanism of unbreakable laws. To man He surrendered freedom —His freedom.

God went further still: Christian teaching adds that 'he emptied himself', that he 'came in the condition of a servant' (Philippians II, 7). Impelled by the folly of love, he 'had need of the free consent of men'. 'Men who are mad with love for their fellow-men grieve to think that all over the world there are human beings serving as means to the power of others without having consented to it.' They 'want to see the power of free consent blossoming out' over the world. 'The aim of justice is the exercise upon earth of the power of consent.' Like a wretched, famished man to whom each restaurant represents the 'plenitude of reality', these men who are 'crazy for justice' for their fellow-men 'suffer stomach pains'. They hunger and thirst for righteousness, and for them alone 'are all human beings real'. They bring freedom, they create a climate of obedience by consent. 'Freedom is the flavour of true obedience.' But such free obedience will not exist in a political climate of constraint; nor will it germinate in a parliamentary democracy whose sole standard or value of exchange is money, and for whom it is the only end of work. In such a world neither is there any room left for enthusiasm. It has been banished and will only reappear momentarily, in periods of national fervour, as a means of binding together the public into a coherent whole.

Where is freedom to be found? It has been in exile for too long. It will have to be discovered and invented all over again. Meanwhile, the world has gone astray and 'humanity is mad for want of love'. 'The fragile possibilities for beauty, happiness and fulfilment upon earth' stand at our doors as beggars craving for compassion. Our fear of them is such that we will not open to them without the much needed 'folly of love' which must take the place of 'greatness', 'glory', and even 'honour'. Pity alone remains!

Internal politics, however, can never be studied in a vacuum.

From the broader perspectives of past and present history, they
tie up with the present problems of mankind. Thus, from
France in bondage, to the under-developed parts of the world
which she herself held in bondage, the link was obvious. Simone
Weil emphasized this point in her article 'On the Colonial Question in Relation to the Destiny of the French people'.[11]

As Hitler has treated us, she writes, so we have behaved
towards our colonies. We have deprived the indigenous population
of their traditions and of their souls, and have reduced them to
the state of human matter. This analogy should lead us to apply
ourselves to the practical solution which is the least harmful.
According to Simone Weil, this might take the form of a system of
internal independence which would allow the colonies that are
weak but have long traditions to achieve their own nationhood,
with the support of a foreign military protection against outside
interference.

'The next idea which can throw light on the colonial problem
is that Europe's situation makes her a sort of geometrical mean
between America and the East.' The colonization of the East has
almost deprived it of its soul, says Simone Weil, but the Americanization of Europe which will follow the war will be no less
dangerous, as Europe stands in grave peril of losing that part of its
soul which understands and is culturally related to Oriental civilization. Our small Western subcontinent needs periodic contacts
with the East if it is to remain spiritually what it is. There is something in its heritage which is alien and contrary to the Orient: this
element has reached a pure state and a double potency in America,
from which it now threatens to devour the world.

'The fate of the human race is at stake . . . The Americanization of Europe would lead to the Americanization of the whole
world.'

By the disaster into which she has fallen, France has been
moved to grope towards a deeper meaning which she has tried to
find in her own past. But this past is closer to the Orient than it
is to what Europe has become today. France should therefore
substitute cultural exchange for political or economic tutelage and
so establish a life-giving contact with her liberated colonies, from
which she will draw the strength to make a future for herself.

A past that is so necessary for survival should be nurtured with the greatest care. For once it is lost, it can never be found again; it can only be preserved. 'We have only to look at the United States,' Simone Weil remarks in another context, 'to see what it is to have a people deprived of the time-dimension.' She thus repeats a familiar anti-American cliché, but she gives it a meaning which is her own. If the faculties of man were such as he likes to think they are, there might not be any disadvantage in starting from scratch, ignoring what came before, and counting upon vital resources of will and intelligence to foresee, without the help of memory, and to overcome, without the benefit of centuries of experience, every obstacle on the road to progress. 'That is what people used to think, and what nobody actually thinks any longer, except the Americans, because they have not yet been exposed to the shock of misfortune.' One treasures what one is about to lose; but one cannot prize what one has never known. 'On the other hand, if man is in need of help from outside himself, and if it is agreed that this help is of a spiritual kind, then the past is indispensable, because it is the storehouse of all our spiritual treasure.'

A religious man will call on grace, at this juncture, to put him in contact with the spiritual values. Yet that state of attention 'which is the necessary condition of the receiving of grace' will not arise without the well-spring of the past from whose treasures a compelling radiance emanates.

'There is no religion without a religious tradition, and this is true even when a new religion appears.

'The loss of the past is equivalent to the loss of the super-natural.'

Whilst 'the Americans have no other past than ours', the East clings to its own traditions, and Europe serves as a middle ground and a pivot for both. This perfect equilibrium has been strained, and may soon be destroyed.

To save the day, new relations must be established with the East, for our own sake as much as for the cause of justice. Let us give a new meaning, Simone Weil suggests, to the word 'protec-torate'—a meaning that will convey the idea that 'populations not organized into nations' and at present in certain respects dependent upon the organized states 'will be sufficiently independent in other respects to feel that they are free'.

Such a policy offers two advantages. It can relate to and apply equally well to the weaker countries of Europe, which suffered so much from aggressive hegemonies. And, furthermore, it can checkmate American cultural imperialism. Since they have no colonies, the Americans have no colonialist prejudices. And since they very naïvely apply their own democratic criteria to anything that does not touch themselves, they regard the colonial system without any sympathy. It is foreseeable, therefore, that they will soon give a serious shake-up to a Europe benumbed by her ancient practices. But by taking the side of the populations that France has subjugated, American policy, without knowing it, is providing us with the best means to help us resist America's own colonizing influence in the near future. America does not understand this point of view. But 'it would be disastrous if we failed to understand it also'.

What is worth underlining in this essay is not the prophetic tone nor the severity of her remarks addressed to America: its most significant feature—which it shares with the majority of the preceding articles—is the use Simone Weil makes in it of the idea of the supernatural.

In London, Simone Weil renewed her acquaintance with Maurice Schumann. Since the talks she had with him were the natural outcome of her previous correspondence from New York, it seemed only natural also that now her conversations would be supplemented by a new series of letters.[12] The theme remained the same, or at least seemed logically related: as in America, Simone relied on Schumann to speed up her passage to England, now she called upon him to help her realize her wish to be sent on a mission to France.

She must have understood that she was more convincing on paper than in conversation. Yet there is in her letters a spontaneous outpouring of her thoughts which is a testimonial of her innate trust in Schumann and in their deep friendship.

She had noticed some admiration on his part for her patriotic fervour. But she stiffened under praise and changed the subject.

Was she not born with 'mediocre intellectual powers?' Her sufferings, her headaches, had further reduced them. 'But there are treasures of divine compassion for those who desire the truth.' 'Although the thoughts that flow from my pen are far above me, I cling to them as to what I believe to be the truth; and I think I have had, from God, the command to prove by experiment that they are not incompatible with an extreme form of warlike action.'

Since she had been thinking about war as far back as 1914, the divine imperative could not be shaken off as a passing impression: it 'had continually become clearer and more imperious'. Even if erroneous, beliefs cannot be disregarded and imaginary calls to duty retain their obligatory character.

'I am quite sure that if anyone, believing even mistakenly that he had received a command from God, fails to carry it out from lack of energy, of faith or of ability to persuade, he commits a crime of disobedience.

'That is my situation at this moment.

'That situation is in my eyes infinitely worse than hell— assuming the truth of all that theology affirms upon that point.'

While the very damned in hell suffer in submission to God's will, Simone Weil was racked by the thought that her state was more pitiable than theirs who at least are in obedience. And she launched 'desperate appeals' to her correspondent.

But it seems that she feared he might misinterpret her eagerness as a sign of a lack of maturity. She was not naïve. She intended to show, quite truthfully, that she understood all that what she was asking for might entail, especially for a woman. She was able to visualize disaster, and knew what it means to be brave in the face of danger. On the one hand, she had taken 'the resolution to take part in any serious act of sabotage' she might chance upon. On the other hand, 'from the moment of the armistice' she had fully 'recognized the obligation of undertaking inwardly, in view of certain eventualities, the renunciation of [her] own dignity before the enemy'. Again and again she returns to this theme of her personal dignity, for which she refuses to concern herself, when the hour of torture comes. In her insistence, she recalls to mind the early Christian maiden, persecuted yet resolved to place her faith above the physical integrity of her honour. If she had to carry secrets in her hands, she would consecrate to these the whole of her energy, forgetting about herself. And if she were put to torture, she would husband her strength in such a way that the false confessions she had prepared in advance would appear spontaneous. 'On account of my physical weakness, death would come to me soon enough. A moderate amount of ill-treatment would put me definitely in the state where thought becomes vacancy.'

Whatever the methods employed by the Nazis to extract information from their victims, Simone Weil counted upon the mercy of God. 'It is beyond doubt that there are treasures of divine compassion for those who give up everything, even their honour, and pray only for the grace not to do evil.'

'Because of the physical deficiency of my nature, no intermediate degree is possible for me between total sacrifice and cowardice.' So much self-abnegation might have inclined Schumann to think he was dealing with a martyr or a saint, but Simone Weil is careful to avoid that impression: 'I can explain to you very clearly what my situation is in relation to sainthood.' She does not talk of it as the Christians, for whom it seems to be 'a beautiful thing of which they know they are deprived, which they love and admire, but which they would not for an instant dream of reproaching themselves for not possessing.' It ought to be, she says, a pattern of life to which anyone could easily raise himself. 'But a conspiracy as old as Christianity which has grown in strength from century to century, strives to conceal this truth, as well as several others no less uncomfortable.'

'Among the motives and reactions of man which seem to be essentially bound up with human nature, and ineradicable except by a supernatural transformation, many are in fact only linked to the reserve of vital energy possessed by every normal man.

'When circumstances cause this reserve to disappear, these motives and reactions disappear too . . . when they have vanished, all is over. The process is irreversible, like growing old.

'It is the existence of such irreversible processes that makes such a tragic thing of human life.

'The end of this process is a state which has some superficial resemblance to the detachment of the saints. . . . Only, this state, being the result of an entirely mechanical process, is without value.

'Discernment is easy. Saintliness is accompanied by an uninterrupted flow of supernatural energy, which takes effect irresistibly on all around it. This other state is accompanied by moral exhaustion, and often—as in my case—by an exhaustion that is moral and physical at the same time.'

Nevertheless, Simone says, she makes sanctity the rule of her life, 'not in the hope of acquiring it, but simply to pay homage to it'. For herself, she desires only to be 'of the number of those to whom it is prescribed to think that they are unprofitable slaves, having done only what they were commanded to do'.

But she had received a command which was unprofitable to the cause she was serving: 'Philip has taken me into his service, apparently on the presumption that I may be able to furnish ideas that he could use. If what I am writing does not lead him to change his opinion when he reads it—which may well happen— he must be sure to put me in the only position that can stimulate a mind like mine to generate ideas—in contact with the object.' She must go soon, she says; otherwise she will no longer be equal to the effort required. As for her reasons: 'One is moral, for the painful sense of being out of my proper place steadily increases and will end, in spite of myself, I fear, in clogging up my thinking. The second is intellectual: it is evident that when it expresses itself concretely, my thinking will come to a halt for want of a purpose. The third is physical, for fatigue overtakes me.' Moreover, she cannot 'eat the bread of the English without taking part in their war effort'.

Her letters to Schumann include the following confidences:

'Putting aside whatever it might be granted me to do for the good of other human beings, for me personally life has no other meaning and has never, at bottom, had any other meaning but that of waiting upon truth.

'I suffer an ever-increasing agony in mind and in the depth of the heart, from my incapacity to think, at the same time and in truth, of the misery of men, the perfection of God, and the relation between the two.

'I have the inner certainty that if ever this truth is granted me, it will only be at the moment when I myself will be physically placed in a state of affliction, in one of the extreme forms of the affliction of our time.

'I am afraid this may not happen to me. Even when I was a child, and believed that I was an atheist and a materialist, I always had within me the fear of failing, not my life, but my death. That fear has never ceased to grow more and more intense.

'An unbeliever might say that my desire is egotistic, because the truth received at such a moment can no longer be of use to anything or anyone.

'But a Christian cannot think in those terms. A Christian knows that one single thought of love, lifted up towards God in truth, even though it be mute and without echo, is more useful even to this world than the most resounding action.

'I am outside the truth; nothing human can take me into it; and I have the interior certainty that God will not bring me into it in any other way than that: a certainty of the same kind as there is at the root of what is called a religious vocation.'

Following this allusion to her function as an intermediary between the world and the Catholic Church, Simone Weil adds that she cannot help 'showing the shamelessness, indiscretion and importunity shown by beggars'. For her, no doubt, it is 'hard to depend upon anyone else'. But unhappiness does not define itself by pain and death. 'It is defined first of all by necessity. It is suffered only by accident or by obligation.' One must also have the opportunity to undergo it; it was to find such an opportunity that she had come to London. 'I miscalculated. Or did the cowardice in me calculate all too well? For my nature is cowardly.' She concludes: 'In such need as I find myself to be, my one hope of help lies in you.'

The kinship of interest she found with Maurice Schumann led Simone Weil to speak to him about other matters too. In her last letter she enclosed a text, 'The Theory of the Sacraments', which has the ring of a personal statement.

She starts by affirming that the desire of the soul cannot be divorced from the fulfilment it can find in the actions, gestures, and postures of the body. Since the acquisition of goodness depends on a desire for good, the body must play its part in the improvement of the soul. Yet what is supernatural is beyond reach; the flesh is thwarted, for it cannot reach it. Prisoners of the flesh, we cannot rise beyond limited objectives, nor can we respond to anything that is in essence infinite.

Beyond finite man and infinite God anything that God chooses will serve as bond, if man responds to it. The medium is a mere convention, but its conventional character does not remove its supernatural efficacy. Such is the bread of the host. God's covenant and man's desire have made this the point at which, in the communion, the soul and God meet. The miracle of faith is that it produces reality in response to desire.

Thus the sacrament is attuned at one and the same time to the relationship between human thought and flesh and to the operation of grace. The sacrament is a test: the soul is torn in two: it aspires towards pure goodness, on the one hand; and on the other, it holds fast to belief (achieved through channels of imagination and sensibility, not through the intellectual paths of faith) in the identification of God and host. The higher part of the soul pursues its course towards the absolute good; the lower, mediocre part shrinks with fear, as if confronted by death. Yet the evil alone (in the lower part) is burnt by the touch of goodness incarnate. Once past this crucible, the soul, now whole again, comes to a rest, in a motionless, attentive, and enriching state of 'waiting'.

In her rare moments of leisure, Simone Weil investigated her new surroundings. She noted with satisfaction that the England she had known through books did indeed coincide with the one she was discovering.[13] The qualities of 'humour' and 'kindness', mentioned by Lawrence as distinctive traits of the British, applied perfectly to them, she observed. They had that good humour which emerges in times of stress. In the London pubs the mood of Shakespeare's comedies was still alive. And in the *petites gens* of England shone the kindness so well described by Dickens. With their good nature, their politeness, and their sentimental side, they had seemed somewhat unreal to Simone Weil in his works—because, she said, he lacked the genius to translate observation into creation; but they were real enough in fact.

# Hyde Park

On Sundays, Simone Weil went to Hyde Park, that modern *agora*, not to listen to the orators so much as to watch the audience. Her quick eyes spied 'the naughty little cockney girls' who should have been in church, if they had followed their mothers' orders. But 'they can't see what's the use of prayers', when boys are waiting to be picked up on the streets. In the evening, she sat beside an old taxi-driver while he told her how he drilled with the territorials after a day's work. Simone marvelled at the firmness of purpose and at the courage of the Home Guard made up of the very young and the very old. The London bobbies, she wrote to her parents, 'are utterly delightful'. To her friends Simone Weil described the adventure which befell Simone Deitz who was robbed of her handbag in the Underground while in civilian dress. Two days later the bag was returned untouched by mail, with a note pinned to her military identity card: 'We don't take money from soldiers.'

Simone Deitz recalls their excursions together. One week-end, they camped on the outskirts of London, in the grounds of a convent. Suddenly it began to rain; the tent was soaked through. While Simone Deitz was glad to accept the nuns' invitation to spend the night indoors, Simone Weil stoically elected to remain under the dripping canvas, shivering and sleepless in her wet sleeping-bag, until dawn.

Simone Deitz had agreed to teach Simone Weil how to drive. Her pupil clasped the wheel, peered short-sightedly through her spectacles, and in a matter of minutes fulfilled her teacher's worst expectations. Sometimes she gave free rein to the whimsical side of her nature: once when boating with Simone Deitz, she teased her by rocking the boat until they both fell into the shallow waters of the Serpentine.

In her serious moments, Simone pursued the conversations begun in New York. She taught her friend Tibetan, so that she might be able to read Milarepa the Wise in the text. And she gave her advice based on her own practice: to avoid all loss of time; not to go out; to sleep on the floor or on a table in order to limit the hours of sleep to four or five hours. She herself slept three hours a night, waking at the first streak of dawn. These austere rules were not offered as precepts, for she hated to infringe on matters of personal conscience: 'I particularly do not want to talk to you about religion,' she said to her, 'for fear I might become a screen between you and God.'

Simone attended Mass every day at the church in Farm Street. In her room, thinking no doubt of the words of Christ, 'Where two or three are gathered together in my name, there am I in the midst of them,' (Matthew XVIII, 19), she would ask Simone Deitz to join her in silent prayer.

The English metaphysical poets had always appealed to Simone Weil. Now she quoted them often, with spiritual relish. Her favourites were: George Herbert, in 'Discipline':

> *For my heart's desire*
> *Unto Thine is bent:*
> *I aspire*
> *To a full consent.*

or the American Francis Thompson, in 'Daisy':

> *Nothing begins, and nothing ends,*
> *That is not paid with moan;*
> *For we are born in others' pain,*
> *And perish in our own.*

She recited again and again Herbert's poem 'Love', in an attempt to correct her English accent, which was rather poor. In the field of music she placed the Gregorian above all. She expressed a curious appreciation of Wagner: 'I have such a noise in my head during my migraines that I need something still noisier to drown it.'

Although it was not obvious at first, the war was taking its toll of Simone Weil. Those who had not seen her for a length of time, remarked how much she had changed. When he came over from America in March, Jacques Kaplan, the boy she had met on the ship from Lisbon, found a different Simone Weil from the one he had known: she was worn out and tense; she seemed remote and it was impossible to make contact with her. She would cut off a discussion with a brusque: 'This I cannot accept without reservations,' and that was all. Her bitter disappointment at being left on the sidelines of the war deepened as her chances to be called to 'active duty' dwindled: 'I am more and more cruelly torn, day after day,' she wrote to her brother, 'with regrets and remorse for having been so weak as to follow your advice [to leave France] a year ago.' In the bitter remarks she made at that time, one can sense her revolt at being kept out of the war. The limit of her forbearance was reached when Simone Deitz refused to turn over to her the mission in France for which she had been accepted. She was so much disturbed that she lost whatever little inclination she still had for food. 'But you will kill yourself,' remonstrated her friend. She replied that she did not care. In the end, when Simone Deitz's departure was cancelled, she rejoiced. If she could not go, none should go. Nothing less could satisfy her.

Simone Weil left her lodgings about half-past nine and returned home in the afternoon. Yet there were occasions when she did not come back at all, and the office boy would find her in the morning asleep at her work-table, where she must have passed the night after forgetting the time till it was too late for the last Underground train.

Much against her will, as we have seen, she had been set to work on projects of an intellectual order for which indeed she was eminently qualified. Was there not the peace to foresee and for which to organize? 'At present nobody here is worrying about that kind of thing,' she had been told. 'You do it.' Though the articles previously mentioned in this chapter were the result of her dialogue with the committees on political matters in France, it is not difficult to see that a large share was written as a self-questioning dialogue with herself. Such also was the conception behind her 'Prelude to a Declaration of Duties Towards Mankind' which was afterwards published in France as *L'Enracinement* and in English as *The Need for Roots*. The thought of this work flows slowly, like a river; the expression is tentative, and the reader often has to make an effort to discipline his attention. But the reasoning is sound, and the logical structure is strong enough to support the conclusions based upon it.

*The Need for Roots* is a kind of spiritual testament: it reconsiders each theme, defines it, and stamps it with the seal of a personality intensified by the proximity of death.

Simone begins by synthesizing the two aspects of her thinking which had been violently antithesized in the past—the 'gros animal', the collective on the one hand; cultural values, the theme of *Venice Preserved*, on the other.[14] She upholds, in principle, the idea that we 'owe our respect to a collectivity, of whatever kind—country, family or any other—not for itself, but because it is food for a certain number of human souls.' Indeed, she says, every collectivity is unique; if we destroy it, we cannot replace what we have destroyed. And 'the sustenance that a collectivity provides for the souls of its members has no equivalent in the whole universe.' Every collectivity plunges roots deep into the past and extends itself into the future: all are therefore precious, and man is under an obligation to preserve them.

But this does not mean that collectivity is something above mankind. Certain collectivities, 'instead of serving as food, do just the opposite: they devour souls'. Others do not manage to provide souls with nourishment enough. Still others are dead; they do not devour souls, but 'they do not nourish them either'.

The first duty of governments, then, is to discover the personal needs of the soul. In the 'Draft for a Declaration of Obligations Towards Mankind',[15] Simone Weil's argument is presented more forcibly. The needs of the soul are, she says, order, liberty, obedience, honour, punishment, risk, property, etc . . . and —above all—truth: an incomplete list, to which must be added the need for roots.

Rootedness may be defined as follows: 'A human being has roots by virtue of his real, active and natural participation in the life of a community, which preserves in living shape certain treasures of the past and certain expectations for the future'.[16] Uprootedness, on the other hand, is the consequence of military conquest; or if not, it may also be a result of the 'power of money' or of 'economic domination'—or, simply, of the social relations within a country, which are capable of turning a human being into a foreigner in the heart of his own collectivity. Education as it is conceived today is also a factor in uprootedness.

Workers, for example, have been the victims of moral disintegration within the French collectivity. Their social condition is 'an absolute and perpetual dependence on money'. Simone Weil condemns that 'mixture of confused and more or less false ideas known under the name of Marxism, a mixture to which, since Marx's day, it is, generally speaking, only very ordinary middle-class intellectuals who have contributed', a pseudo-science which is foreign to the workers and indigestible by them, for it has been emptied of nearly all the truth contained in Marx's writings'. 'Under the same name of revolution', Simone Weil writes, 'lie concealed two conceptions entirely opposed to one another. One consists in transforming society in such a way that the working class may be given roots in it; while the other consists in spreading to the whole of society the disease of uprootedness which has been inflicted on the working class.'

What we ought to look for in the claims of the workers 'is the sign and token of their sufferings. Now all, or nearly all, of these demands express the suffering caused by uprootedness': here, then, is where the trouble lies.

Let a realistic list of the workers' sufferings be drawn up, and it will supply us with 'a list of the things that need changing': the shock suffered by the boy when he first enters the factory; the discipline of concentration during working hours; 'the type of stimulants which make for the overcoming of laziness or exhaustion'; the kind of obedience demanded; the inability to have a view of production as a whole—a very long list, no doubt, but one that could be made.

Once drawn up, this list should be submitted to the technicians. The prerequisite of carrying out any reform is 'the idea itself of posing in technical terms problems concerning the effect of machines upon the moral well-being of workmen. Once posed, the technicians have only to resolve them; just as they have resolved countless others.'

'If there is one conviction which stands out with irresistible force in the works of Marx, it is this one: that any change in the relationship between the classes is only illusory if it is not accompanied by a transformation in technical processes, expressing itself in entirely new types of machinery.' Beside that remark, other measures proposed by Simone Weil seem merely augmentative.

It is not truly feasible to speak of forming a workers' youth movement, she writes, unless its participation in a real intellectual culture is possible. What makes it difficult to communicate culture to the working class 'is not that culture is too high, but that it is too low. It is a singular remedy, indeed, to lower it still further', before dealing it out, bit by bit. The cure consists in translation—not popularization. 'The art of transposing truths is among the most essential and least known.' To practise it, it is necessary to be at the centre of a truth, 'and possess it in all its nakedness, divested of the particular form in which it happens to have found expression'. Incidentally, Simone adds, the search for methods for transmitting culture would be even more salutary for culture than for the people. Instead of being 'an instrument manipulated by professors for manufacturing more professors who, in turn, manufacture more professors', culture would come out of that ivory tower in which it inevitably deteriorates.

In summary, ' "a condition of any working-class" culture is the mingling of what are called "intellectuals"—an awful name, but at present they scarcely deserve a better one—with the workers'. Such mingling must be real, not fictitious, and 'undertaken with the idea of affecting a *rapprochement* between culture and people, thereby giving culture a new direction'.

But to return to the problem of uprootedness in general: like it or not, Simone Weil writes, 'for a long time now, only the nation has assumed the chief responsibility of the collectivity to the human individual: that of maintaining throughout the present the links with the past and the future'.[17] This leads her to an analysis of French patriotism, which she sums up concisely. Quoting Shakespeare's famous line, that England 'hath made a shameful conquest of itself', she notes that in France kings have 'assimilated' the conquered peoples—that is, deprived them of their roots. 'The Revolution melted all the populations subject to the French Crown into one single mass, by their enthusiasm for national sovereignty.' And 'the influence of the *Encyclopédistes*, all of them uprooted intellectuals, all obsessed with the idea of progress, killed any chance of inspiration being sought in a revolutionary tradition'. National sovereignty rapidly proved to be an illusion; patriotism then changed its meaning and became oriented towards the State. However, 'the State is a cold thing which cannot inspire love, but which kills and eradicates anything else that might be loved; so one is forced to love it, because there is nothing else. Such is the painful predicament which confronts contemporary man'. To take the State for an object of fidelity—that is idolatry pure and simple: 'The real sin of idolatry is always committed on behalf of something similar to the State. It was this sin that the devil wanted Christ to commit when he offered him the kingdoms of this world. Christ refused. Richelieu accepted.'

In truth, 'the development of the State despoils a country'. The State lives and fattens upon its substance, ending by exhausting it, until finally the State becomes an object of hatred. To complete the paradox, the State, 'the object of hatred, repugnance, derision, disdain, and fear . . . under the name of *patrie* demanded absolute loyalty, total self-abnegation, the supreme sacrifice'. And it has been given what it asked for, 'it has been accepted and served in accordance with its demand, worshipped with a frightful quantity of human sacrifices. A loveless idolatry—what could be more monstrous, more heart-rending?'

Simone Weil observes that such State idolatry shocked the workers—but, ironically, 'didn't shock the Christians'. As soon as the State looms behind the country, she writes, 'justice is far away': 'When there is a lot of talk about patriotism, little is heard about justice; and the sense of justice is so strong among the workers, even if they are materialists (because they are always under the impression they are being deprived of it), that any form of moral education in which justice hardly figures cannot possibly exercise any hold over them. When they die for France, they always need to feel that at the same time they are dying for something very much greater, taking part in the universal struggle against injustice. For them, to use a now famous expression, patriotism is not enough.

'The same rule applies wherever a flame, a spark, however indistinct, of truly spiritual life burns. To kindle this fire, patriotism is not enough. And for those in whom this fire is wanting, patriotism, with its supreme demands, is far too exalted; it can be a strong enough incentive only in the form of the blindest national fanaticism.'

In matters of national pride, writes Simone, not only is there unlimited licence but, under pressure, an obligation to rise to the highest possible degree of licence.

'It has happened, it does happen and it will happen to France to lie and to be unjust, for France is not God, by a long way. Christ alone could say: "I am the truth." That is not permissible to anyone else on earth, neither men nor collectivities—indeed still less to collectivities. . . . There is no holy nation.' 'Our patriotism comes straight from the Romans. That is why French children are encouraged to look for inspiration for it in Corneille.' The pagan virtue of patriotism passed from Rome to France without being baptized.

The soul of the country must be refashioned 'and the temptation to do this by resorting to lies or half-lies is so strong that it requires more than ordinary heroism to remain faithful to the truth'.

Simone Weil predicts in this context that the French Government which is to be established after the liberation 'will have to face the triple danger' of blood lust (the desire for revenge against Germans and collaborationists), the mendicity complex (common among deprived countries), and the inability to obey (the result of having had to obey the Germans for so long). Against this triple threat, there is, she says, only one remedy: 'To give the French people something to love; and, in the first place, to give them France to love—to conceive the reality that can correspond to the name of France in such a way that as she actually is, in her very truth, she can be loved wholeheartedly.'

In the very notion of patriotism there is a contradiction. The country is a limited and imperfect entity; yet it makes unlimited demands. But this contradiction is only apparent. The human condition is made up of analogous contradictions, 'which must be recognized, accepted and used as a foothold for climbing above the merely human. Never in this world can there be any dimensional equality between an obligation [such as patriotism] and its subject [the nation]. The obligation is something infinite, the subject of it is not.'

'We are all united in the name of our country. What are we, and what contempt shall we not deserve, if the least trace of a falsehood is to be found in the thought with which we think about our land? . . .

# False grandeur

'One can either love France for the glory which would seem to ensure for her a prolonged existence in time and space; or else one can love her as something which, being earthly, can be destroyed, and the value of which is all the more apparent.

'These are two distinct ways of loving . . .

'The latter alone is legitimate for a Christian, for it alone wears the Christian badge of humility and belongs to that kind of love which can be given the name of charity.'

We have, then, to find 'a method for breathing an inspiration into a people'—a new problem which must be boldly studied, disregarding the idea that 'the inspiring of a people is a mystery reserved for God alone and therefore beyond all method'. Thus, 'looking on day by day at the changing situation in France, it is necessary to bear in mind a conception of public action as a means of education for the country'. It is in consideration of this problem at once spiritual and sociological, that Simone Weil suggests solutions.

Solutions, however, interest her less than the question: Who would be capable of taking radical and far-reaching action?[18] To the French government in London, the words of St Paul might apply: 'Strength is made perfect in weakness.'

The true purpose of the French movement in London was to be a 'spiritual director' on a national scale. Its central goal, before the political and the military, was spiritual: to assist France to renew contact with her genius even in the depth of misfortune. The problem was, above all, to beware of pursuing aims that were not high enough, and also to avoid false ideas of 'greatness'. 'Our conception of greatness is the most serious defect of all, and the one which we are least aware of as a defect. . . . Our conception of greatness is the very one which has inspired Hitler's whole life.' The power of the idea of force is great: 'When the early Christians became solidly convinced that Christ, in spite of having been crucified, had subsequently risen from the dead and was to return before very long in his glory to recompense his own and punish all the rest, no tortures had any further terrors for them. Previously, when Christ was only an absolutely pure being, he was abandoned as soon as misfortune overtook him. Those who loved him most could not find in their hearts the courage to run risks

333

on his behalf. Torture gets the better of courage when, in order
to face it, there isn't the stimulus of revenge. The revenge need
not be a personal one. A martyred Jesuit in China is sustained by
the temporal grandeur of the Church, in spite of the fact that he
cannot expect it to assist him personally in any way. *There is no
other force on this earth except force,*' stresses Simone Weil.

We must therefore divest ourselves of all admiration for force,
at whatever cost, in our interpretation of the history of France.
Truly to love France, 'we must feel that she has a past; but
we must not love the historical wrapper of the past. We must
love the past that is inarticulate, anonymous, which has
vanished'. For 'by the very nature of things, it is false greatness
which is transmitted'.

There is another danger to be avoided, another responsibility
to be underlined: 'The modern conception of science is as
responsible as that of history and that of art for the monstrous
conditions under which we live, and will in its turn have to be
transformed, before we can hope to see the dawn of a better
civilization.' (In a schematic sense, this statement returns
Simone Weil to one of the essential themes of her work.)

The prestige of science is so vast that there are, so to speak,
no unbelievers in it. For several centuries past it has been assuring
us that force is what really governs all phenomena. It is affirmed
at the same time—and in the same breath—that human relations
should be founded upon justice.

'This is a flagrant absurdity. It is inconceivable that everything
in the universe should be entirely subjected to the rule of force
and that man alone should be exempted from it, since he is only
made of flesh and blood and his thought drifts about at the mercy
of sense-impressions.

'There is only one possible choice to be made. Either a
different principle must be perceived at work in the universe,
alongside force, or force must be recognized as being the unique
and sovereign ruler over human relations.'

The former possibility is in opposition to science as Galileo,
Descartes and Newton founded it; the latter, is irrevocably
opposed to humanism. To admit both at once, is to submit to a
lie.

# Force versus justice

The contradiction between science and humanism has not escaped anybody, 'although the intellectual courage to look it squarely in the face has always been lacking'. Attempts have been made to resolve the antinomy. Marxism tried to. It re-christened force 'history'. History 'takes the form of the class struggle: justice is relegated to some future time which has to be preceded by a sort of apocalyptic cataclysm'. These and other efforts, on the surface so diverse and at bottom so similar, present one and the same problem: that of falsehood.

'Force is not a machine for automatically creating justice. It is a blind mechanism which produces indiscriminately and impartially just or unjust results, but, by the laws of probability, nearly always unjust ones. . . .

'Where force is absolutely sovereign, justice is absolutely unreal. Yet justice cannot be unreal. This we know experimentally. Justice is real, deep in the hearts of men . . . .

'If justice cannot be erased from the heart of Man, it must have a reality in this world. It is science, then, which is mistaken.

'Not science, to be precise, but modern science.'

The Greeks possessed a science far superior to ours. Doubtless its superiority is not generally recognized. Few people have plunged 'into the atmosphere of Greek science as into something real and vital'; inasmuch as they have not, they cannot expect to recognize this to be true. Greek science was neither materialistic, nor profane: it 'was a subject of religious study'. This view of science, however, disappeared with the coming of the Romans, only to reappear briefly in the Middle Ages, under another guise, in gnostic thinking, and in circles of initiates. When science was revived in the sixteenth century to the applause of all . . . 'as in certain fairy tales, the science that was awakened after lying dormant for nearly two millenniums, no longer was the same. It had been changed. It was of another kind, absolutely incompatible with anything of a religious spirit', and indifferent to justice, whose ally it was made to be.

Whatever her longing to return to her homeland, Simone Weil's hopes were fading fast. Despite her pleas, Closon refused to take her with him in his next mission to France. He pointed

335

out that space available on the planes which were dropping agents behind the lines was precious, that only the most effective personnel could be sent. Furthermore, her proposal to be a contact in Occupied France keeping London informed of the state of opinion seemed of dubious value. And her arguments, too often repeated, were viewed as so many fallacies to cover her real thought, which she herself brought to light when pressed by despair. She wished, it was well known, to flee the 'idleness' and the security of her London job, to share in the life and the trials of the French people. But no one in authority would seriously consider an application for a mission of gratuitous heroism.

Thus thwarted in her plan, Simone was living through a drama of inaction. She foresaw the mass movements at the Liberation which must be prevented, the unleashing of passions which she compared to what she had witnessed in Spain. Her craving to be with her compatriots in their fight and in their suffering was transmuted, and expressed itself in other ways. The salary she received from the Free French for what she conceived as the unbearable privilege of a desk-bound intellectual burned her fingers and she would only keep part of it for herself. Out of solidarity, she hardly ate, would not finish the meals to which she was invited, refused apples for dessert 'because French children have nothing to eat', distributed to others the contents of the packages she received from her parents who had remained in America. What would have seemed to any other a gesture of futility became for her an obsession. This refusal to eat, this impossibility to nourish herself adequately, this almost clinical anorexia, had a physiological basis which was not apparent at this time, but which was revealed later. Totally unaware of the morbid origin of her revulsion to food, Simone believed herself to be motivated by reasons for not eating that were valid in her eyes: 'For an honest man, to defraud is never possible . . . Given the general and permanent situation of mankind in the world, it may well be that to eat all one wants is always to defraud'. She added: '(I have often defrauded)'.[19] To deprive herself of what was necessary had become a strict moral obligation. It seemed to her as though some divine law of compensation operated in favour of the unfortunate, and that the nourishment she refused

336

did profit in a mysterious way, that little child in France whose image haunted her.

She now detached herself from everything except from her detachment and from her own work, at which she laboured unremittingly. 'What she had to say' was her entire preoccupation—not that she attached any excessive value to it, but rather that it enabled her to forget the comparative safety of her privileged situation. She lived thus in a state of permanent creativity, her mind boiling over with ideas that came to her at every moment. She would hastily jot them down in her notebooks or on anything at hand, sometimes just to have done with them, sometimes to remind herself of them later, or to see 'what would come of them'. Their subsequent publication in the *Notebooks* or *La Connaissance surnaturelle* was far from her mind when she made these jottings. Her normal working practice was to write a piece as one continuous whole, at one sitting, almost without additions or erasures. It is therefore apparent that her notes are not related, as quotations might be, to articles or chapters that she subsequently came to write or would have written. She liked to experiment: in order to test ideas that came to her, she would sometimes give them expression without meaning thereby to pronounce a value judgment upon them; this exercise did not necessarily commit her. So it is not possible to assume that Simone Weil was entirely in agreement with all that appears in her *Notebooks* or *La Connaissance surnaturelle* or to try to reconstruct all her philosophy from such fragments alone.

A distinction should be made, however, between her personal statements, with their clearly expressed intent, feeling, *état d'âme*, and those doctrinal affirmations, those speculative or even assertive pronouncements about matters of fact, faith, morals, that may be considered sketchy attempts at systematization of thought. The former give to the aforementioned works the character of a diary, *un journal intérieur*, a spiritual document—at times even of a poem in prose. The latter, unlike the former, cannot always be taken at face value. By their very nature, they are out of context, or rather, without context. Their convergence, however, or (as Newman said) the 'assemblage', which they constitute when related to each other and to letters, texts written for publication, or utterances corroborated by knowledgeable witnesses, creates a consensus which can be interpreted.

While Simone Weil was suffering extreme anxiety over conditions in France, spring made its appearance in London, covering 'the fruit trees with white and pink blossoms'. The month of May came, with abnormally warm days interspersed with rain; the roses, which were also 'early and abundant', invaded 'the parks in profusion'. But all these wonders were hidden from her, although she wrote about them in her letters.[20] What she now saw of the sky, 'of a pale, profound and delicious blue', was a large patch enclosed between brick walls, for she had entered the Middlesex Hospital in mid-April.

Looking in at her friend's office one day, Simone Deitz had not found her there, and learnt that she had also been absent the day before. Disquieted by this, Simone Deitz called at 31 Portland Road, where she found Simone Weil prostrate on the floor of her room in a state of extreme weakness. After having revived her with a little brandy, she proposed to send for the doctor. 'Promise me not to tell anyone,' murmured Simone. 'That is impossible,' answered Simone Deitz. 'You would run the risk of not being able to work any more.' Simone Weil wept: 'All's over now! I'll be taken to the hospital.' After examining her, Dr Izad Bennett, a physician at the Middlesex Hospital, directed that she be hospitalized. She refused a private room, and was placed in one of the general wards.

The doctor in the Free French forces who had examined her in the United States had declared her in good health. Whether that medical examination, at a time when practically everyone of good will was being enrolled, was really carried out according to the rule is a question. Her parents, at least, believed she was well; her friends in London, though not greatly surprised to hear she was in the hospital, were also quite unaware of her real state of health.

Overruling her objections, Dr Bennett soon put her into a private room. Actually this suited her better, for she could not stand noise. But she would not agree to be moved until she was told that she was contagious. Two or three times a week Mme

Closon went to see her. Their talks about trifles and family matters were constantly interrupted by Simone expressing concern that she should not become a burden to anyone. She also saw Mrs Francis, and all the members of her intimate circle.

The condition of her lungs was not serious enough to exclude definite hopes of recovery; with thorough treatment there was little doubt that she would be cured. Yet, Simone Weil refused a pneumothorax; she wanted to escape all intervention. Also she rebelled against the 'obstinacy' of the English doctor who attended her and would not follow his prescriptions. Still worse, she did not eat or ate very little. The nurse in charge noticed that she was too weak to lift her spoon or fork and used to feed her like a small child, which Simone found hard to bear.

The thought that her mind had little or no command over her limbs was intolerable to her. Yet she had foreseen this special trial and had prayed for it less than a year before:

'Father, in the name of Christ, grant: That I may be like a total paralytic—wholly prevented from making any movement of the body, or even any attempted movement, that corresponds to any prompting of my will'.[21] But she had often mentioned in the past that suffering could not be supernaturally meaningful and fruitful if some perceptible consoling meaning could be ascribed to it at the moment of suffering.

In this way her state of illness brought into new light some of her favourite themes. Simone Deitz now recalled that she had heard her say: 'If one day I am entirely deprived of will, in a state of coma, then should I be baptized.' But she could not bring herself to broach the subject anew, any more than did the Closons, who felt that their privileged relationship with the patient forbade it.

It was Simone Weil who asked to see a priest. Through Simone Deitz, she received the visits of Father de Naurois, who came three or four times. He sensed that he was in the presence of a 'soul of rare nobility, a soul tormented to the depths by the mystery of God and the destiny of man, the mystery of Christ and Christianity.' At the same time, he experienced an odd irritation, ' . . . that is, in a manner of speaking, for my feelings as a priest, before this heroic and dying woman, left no room for more than a kind of human annoyance; the impression that the discussion she seemed to want was a waste of time.' He was 'annoyed' chiefly by the style of her arguments and of her thought as a whole: 'A style highly abstract and abstruse, of a rapid dialectic, and very "feminine", under which I could feel deep instincts and tacit decisions perhaps hardly reflected upon, and which appeared to me to be travestied, dressed up in "rationalizations" (as the modern psychologists say); in short, a thought that was elusive and at the same time prodigiously rich, which could not manage to grasp and formulate itself satisfactorily, and which would not accept fixed starting points from which to advance (or retreat).'

And, in spite of his admiration, he felt no affinity at all for her thought, which baffled him: 'I did not rate [it] very highly; it seemed to me too "feminine", too "khâgneuse"—too "Judaic", also.'

To go to see her, to speak to her, was all and the best he could do. On one occasion, he gave her his sacerdotal blessing before leaving, 'which she accepted with the fervour and humility of a great and experienced Christian'.

For she had arrived, he thought, at the end of her quest— 'at the intimate Encounter *de facto* with her long-sought God— in spite of the troubled surface waters of her soul, of the arguments, the minute differences, the constant evasions and slips' which rendered the discussion impossible. At the spiritual summit she had reached, there was the certitude that she had known God, while at the lower level of her being a 'wonderful and very humble simplicity' coexisted with an argumentative and disruptive intelligence.

She was preoccupied by the question of Limbo, which was a theme she had only recently taken up again with another priest, and Mme Closon and Schumann. She could not be content with a mere statement of the problem; she had to resolve it.

The first of these interviews has been reported by Simone Deitz: 'I told him: "I wish to be baptized, but I can do so only under certain conditions. I can't admit that infants who die without baptism are shut out of Paradise, and my attitude on this subject must not be in contradiction with Catholic dogma." The priest replied to me: "That will never do. You are too proud." '

This one position concerning Limbo could hardly have elicited

Passport photo of Simone Weil, New York, October-November 1942

31 Portland Road, Holland Park, London, where Simone Weil rented an apartment (upper left window) from January to April 1943

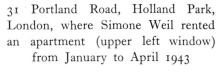

Mrs. Francis, Simone Weil's landlady at 31 Portland Road

such a categorical reply. Though uppermost in her mind, this problem was not the only one. The 'opinions' mentioned in her *Letter to a Priest* which were at the core of most of her conversations with churchmen arose in the course of their discussion. Father de Naurois alludes to them; it was these that shocked him. The barrage of objections directed against the articles of faith seemed to him to express a virtual refusal, an implicit negation of the formal content of revelation. The hypothetical character of Simone's 'opinions'—which she had underlined in her *Letter*— cannot have escaped him. But this 'perhaps' was not enough to annul the general impression of rationalistic contention, of an underlying modernism—in short, of opposition to the Church. And because of the vigour of her statements, he did not realize how close she was to death, since *in articulo mortis* the rules for the administration of the Sacraments are relaxed.

In her concern for the injustice done to innocents, Simone Weil remained adamant. God must accord what the Church did not; she was sure of it. By her refusal of baptism she found herself, as always, symbolically identified with the beings who inspired her with the deepest compassion. Their destiny was hers; and the doors of Paradise should be closed to her as they were to them. Yet, she was not without her own brand of private scepticism about the efficacy of this exclusion, and certainly, she did not lack the conviction that in the 'absence' of her being (that image which she must have conceived of being both there and not there), she would some day rejoin in fact (whether or not by right) those whose absence from such a place had been assumed on theological grounds. A paradox, to be sure—as such intuitive concepts frequently are.

Father de Naurois recalls that during his first visits, she questioned him eagerly about the alimentary and material privations of their French compatriots. Having left France at the end of 1942, he had some recent news to give her. 'But she hardly listened to my replies. She knew that the French were hungry and she was hungry with them. But one might almost have said "it had to be so".'

Yet, in spite of her physical weakness, she still had enough vital energy left to express the hope, not only of her return to health, but also her return to France. One day she said to Mme Closon: 'Do you think that when I have recovered, I shall be able to go back to France?'

At times, during her visits, Simone Deitz would try to calm her friend: 'I said she must not tire herself: "Keep quiet, and talk to me of God." She was silent then, and when the moment came for me to go, murmured: "Thank you for all you have said." The idea of God, it seemed, became more clear, more visible, when another's thought was joined to hers.

'Some time after that she said to me: "You are both she who is mediocre and mediocrity itself. You must accept this in yourself as I accept it in myself".*

'Only once did she mention the after-life: "If there is something in after-life, I shall come back. If I don't come back, it will mean that there is nothing".'

When did she give Simone Deitz that recently published document to be found at the end of the *Pensées sans ordre concernant l'amour de Dieu*? The handwriting is clear and firm, which practically precludes the possibility that it could have been written at Middlesex towards the end of her stay. Whatever its date of composition, it certainly bears some relationship to Simone's last illness, as if it had been written with knowledge or foreknowledge of what was awaiting her. And the conclusions it contains are similar to those that can be drawn from her talks with the Abbé de Naurois. Perhaps it was meant to be her final spiritual testament?

'I believe in God, in the Trinity, in the Incarnation, in the Redemption, in the teachings of the Gospel.' At the same time, she wrote: 'Up to now I have never made a formal request for baptism to any priest.

'I do not make it now.'[22]

As before, she did not want anything beyond the gift of love which she had received through her mystical experiences. The lover sustains himself with the awareness of his love; he does not know if he can or dare take the step that would clarify the intentions of his beloved. He hesitates because the step is so

*There is an untranslatable play on words in the original: *Tu es le et la médiocre. Il faut que tu acceptes les deux, comme moi je l'accepte.*

final: he would like to analyse and understand emotions that are so novel and so strong, forgetting that love is in itself its own justification. Thus in this matter of faith, Simone Weil felt that she was unable to believe in *all* dogma and so drew back, and chose to wait for complete enlightenment.

But faith held no further disclosures for her in the realm of reason, beyond the preliminary ones that she had already experienced. There was nowhere to go, she thought. To retreat would have meant another stretch of darkness. To walk forward would have been to step into a world of shadows. So she stood like a traveller in a tunnel who doubts if he will ever see the point of light that signals the end just around the next bend. She remained in the same spot, and constantly reaffirmed her personal creed that had not wavered from the moment she had left Marseilles.

Had they been dated from the hospital, Simone Weil's declarations would have abolished once and for all the controversy surrounding her final moments. These statements indicate that she would die a non-Christian and yet a believer. 'I hope, I strongly intend, to maintain the same attitude until I die.'

Faith, she wrote, was not belief, but love; it was not an intellectual acquiescence in those 'matters of faith' which are rigidly defined and formulated by dogmatic decree. It was an attachment of the heart 'to that truth which is perfect and intangible, locked deep inside' the mysteries.

Firm as was her resolution, she vacillated inwardly between the claims of her heart which experienced 'an intense and perpetually increasing desire for Holy Communion' and the demands of her reason. And her reason itself oscillated between attitudes of assent and dissent: 'I doubt in a sense even the things that appear to me the most manifestly certain.

'This doubt permeates all my ideas to an equal degree, those which agree as well as those which disagree with the teachings of the Church.'

To reach a decision was, for her, to break a link with truth— with what might be called an 'opposite truth'. To decide was to assume a position to which she was not called, to go against a vocation, to disobey God:

343

'I have the certainty that what I have said conceals no sin. Were I to think otherwise, I would commit a crime against my vocation, which demands absolute intellectual honesty.

'No human and informal influence that I can discern has brought about this attitude which can produce nothing but pain, moral discomfort, and isolation.

'Above all, pride cannot be the cause, because there is nothing to flatter pride in a situation in which a person appears to unbelievers to be a pathological case because he adheres to absurd dogmas without the excuse of social pressure, and in which he inspires in Catholics only the benevolent and slightly disdainful good-will of one who has arrived towards one who is on his way.'

Could Simone Weil be as certain of escaping the pitfalls of error as those of sin? Did she become a victim of the very 'philosophy' she had constructed? The unwary philosopher, once he has captured all of reality in the skein of his net, may also catch himself in the mesh of his own making.

But Simone Weil was well aware of the perils which await the soul on the threshold of the sacraments. In her 'Theory of the Sacraments' which she had sent to Maurice Schumann, she described one who is about to receive a sacrament:

'When the soul is in that state in which the approach to the sacrament is more difficult than the step towards death, it is very near that threshold beyond which martyrdom is easy.

'In a desperate effort to survive, to escape destruction by fire, the mediocre part of the soul, with feverish activity, invents arguments. It borrows from any possible arsenal, including theology and all the warnings concerning the dangers inherent to the unworthy reception of sacraments.'[23]

In the arsenal to which she had access, it seems that Simone Weil had seized upon a double-edged weapon. For she restricted pride to the social realm alone, and thus overlooked the most fundamental kind of presumption—a presumption which is of such a spiritual nature as to affect man in the deepest reaches of his soul, where he is one in kin with the angels, and where no group consciousness can penetrate:

'A part of the soul which might be at the time unperceived

344

by the mind longs for the sacrament; it is the part of truth within the soul, for "he that doeth truth cometh to the light".

'But the mediocre part of the soul recoils from the sacrament, hates it and fears it with a hate and fear stronger than that of the animal who retreats and flees from the threat of death. "For every one that doeth evil hateth the light". . . .

'The stronger the desire for God and therefore the more genuine the intended contact with Him through the sacrament, the more violent the upheaval within the mediocre part of the soul, an upheaval comparable to the reaction of living flesh confronted by fire. This upheaval, then, assumes mainly the characteristics of repulsion, of hate, of fear.'

To all those who knew her well, the personal humility of Simone Weil was beyond doubt. But humility is not the same as supernatural clairvoyance, nor does it involve the total and comprehensive understanding to which she aspired. And there was still 'the fear'—the fear with which the flesh recoils before what is from God, and holds back from taking the step towards him who calls without words. And so there is he who waits and ohe who is waiting for him—both wrapped in that sublime indifference of love; each having done all they could for the other. Nothing remains but the waiting.

From her bed in the hospital, she wrote letters to her family, with the return address of 31 Portland Road, as if she were still living there. Astonishingly enough, though her handwriting shows some unsteadiness, it hardly reveals the state of severe weakness fully documented in her medical records. Her attempts to delude her parents were entirely successful. She chatted with them about random things. In her next-to-last letter, written on the 4th of August, she mentions the maid who cleaned the room, 'a little girl of 19, fresh, pretty, very pleasant' but with hardly 'two ideas in her head, or even one'.[24] She speaks of British culinary customs, describing those fruit puddings known as 'fruit fools' (because they belie their true contents). With remarkable wit, she contrasts these misleading fools with the faultless fools of Shakespeare's plays, where they are the only characters who speak the truth. 'In this world, those beings alone who have fallen to the lowest degree of humiliation, far below mendicity, who not only receive no social consideration, but who are looked upon by all as deprived of the first dignity reserved to man, his own reason—these beings alone have the capacity to speak the truth. All others lie.'

Such are the fools portrayed by Velasquez, who reveal in their eyes that sorrow which comes from the possession of an incommunicable truth. Such is Simone Weil herself. Her reputation for intelligence is the 'practical equivalent of the label "fool" attached to these fools'. The praises heaped upon her since the École Normale 'are used to escape from having to ask: Does she speak the truth?' 'Such is the answer,' she writes, 'to the question of "what I have to give".' For 'the pure unalloyed truths, the luminous, deep and essential truths' are to be found in a world which is closed to all but to the fools or to those who resemble them.

Simone Weil's stay at the Middlesex could not be prolonged indefinitely. Her opposition to the treatments he had prescribed had irritated Dr Bennett. He called upon the Free French Forces' headquarters asking for some accommodation to be found for her elsewhere, since the hospital's facilities were needed for patients who would accept treatment. But Maurice Schumann, Mme Closon, and Simone Deitz were loath to agree with this request. He telephoned them several times, however, and insisted that he could not keep Simone Weil. They remembered that she had expressed the typical wish of the bedridden for a breath of pure air and a view of the countryside. Yet she would not leave London: it seemed to her that to move away from the Free French was to move further away from France. So her friends did not consult her; they authorized Dr Bennett to ask for her admission at the Grosvenor Sanatorium at Ashford in Kent. The answer he received, dated 7th August, contains the following observation, which seems singularly inappropriate: 'In reply to your letter of the 30th ult., I regret that I am unable to accept Mlle Simone Weil as a patient. We deal with industrial patients here and feel that she will not settle down with us.'

The administrator of Ashford Sanatorium would doubtless have not formed such an objection if he had been aware that the patient's sole wish, throughout her life, had been to mingle with such potential 'industrial patients'.

Simone Weil was nevertheless admitted on 17th August among those whom she had long wished to join. The day before her departure, she asked to have all her books packed up, as she wanted to have them with her: Plato, the *Bhagavad-Gita*, some Hindu authors and the works of some Christian mystics including St John of the Cross. She entrusted all her papers to Mme Closon, who went with her by car.

It was a two-hour ride. Mme Closon had provided herself with champagne to sustain the patient on her way, but Simone Weil was comforted only by the thought of rediscovering nature and of seeing trees.

She was given bed No. 104. It was located on the second floor, in the centre of the building, almost at the intersection of two wings; the rooms in this section were placed along an open corridor. Simone Weil had the good fortune to have a window that looked towards France. Below her room a gravel path which divided the lawn led to an open field, fringed with trees on the far side. The view extended past the ridge to a small valley and across to a distant hill, where the engines of the London-Dover trains would puff by at regular hours. Other gently rolling hills and fields, relieved by strands of trees, receded into the horizon.

Beyond the line where heaven and earth met, which closed her in, exiled into a strange land, Simone Weil could have imagined the French countryside extending beyond the landscape visible from her window: the meadows of St Jean de Lalande where she had pitched hay with the Le Telliers; the furrows of Carron de Gron where she had worked in the fields of beetroots, and the vines of St Julien-de-Peyrolas whose grapes she had picked while stretched out on the ground. And still further, perhaps, in a light that is not of this world, there was the city with the 'wooden scaffolds' and the 'river along which boats were being unladen' seen from the 'attic' to which the Host, for whom she was now waiting, had led her.

Simone Weil's card of admission to the sanatorium contained the following information:

## 24th August, 1943

*Occupation:* Rédacteur (C.F.N.L.)
*Religion:*
Too ill to be examined properly
*Highest known weight:* not known
*Weight on admission:* stretcher case.

She had a temperature of 102F., which dropped rapidly after a few days; her pulse also became regular. Asked whom to inform in case of emergency, she gave Mme Closon's name and address.

The painful struggle about her food began all over again. This time, she refused all nourishment. The English doctor tried to compel her to eat. Revolted and exhausted, she murmured, in a state of semi-consciousness, that she wanted to share the suffering of the French, that she could not eat. Finally the doctor gave in, and the order to feed her by force was rescinded. Her meals were brought to her as usual, but the food was untouched when the nurse came to remove the tray. . .

Now she appeared to be sleeping almost all the time and was hardly able to speak. On Sunday 22nd August Mme Closon went to see her. Simone asked her for some mashed potatoes: 'mashed potatoes, you know, like the ones my mother made, perhaps I could eat that' . . . Moved by her request, Mme Closon hastened to comply. But Simone Weil would not take any.

To Simone Deitz, who had come to her bedside, she said good-bye. 'You are like me, a misshapen piece cut out by God. But soon I will no longer be cut out; I will be added and united.'

She grew steadily weaker. On Tuesday the 24th August her life flickered out at half-past ten at night. The death certificate stated: 'Cardiac failure due to myocardial degeneration of the heart muscles due to starvation and pulmonary tuberculosis. The deceased did kill and slay herself by refusing to eat whilst the balance of her mind was disturbed.'

The allusion to apparent suicide involved the doctor in some administrative troubles: on 27th August there was a coroner's inquest which was reported in the local newspapers. 'French Professor starves herself to death' appeared on the front page of the *Tuesday Express*, Ashford, of 31st August:

View as seen by Simone Weil from Ashford Sanatorium, August 1943

New Cemetery, Ashford, Kent

## Tuesday Express

' "I cannot eat when I think of all my people starving in France", was the answer given by Professor Weil to a doctor when she reasoned with her for not eating.

'This came to light when an inquest was held on Professor Simone Adolphine Weil, a 34-year-old Professor of Philosophy, late of the University of Paris, by the deputy coroner, Mr A. K. Mowll at Ashford on Friday.

'Staff Nurse Wilks, of the Grosvenor Sanatorium, Kennington, said in evidence that Professor Weil entered the sanatorium on 17 August, from Middlesex Hospital, suffering from tuberculosis. She continued that the patient took very little food, and was very emaciated and she died on 24 August, at 10.30 p.m.

'Dr Henrietta Broderick, senior medical officer at the Grosvenor Sanatorium, in a statement said:

' "When Professor Weil came down she was fully convinced that we would cure her. We did not consider her in an advanced stage of tuberculosis, and that she had a chance if she took food. I had a letter from Dr Roberts [sic], of the Middlesex Hospital, in which he said Professor Weil was starving herself, and that she kept repeating that her food was to be sent to the French prisoners of war.

' "When she arrived," Dr Broderick continued, "she was tired, and registered no emotions. Later I gave her an examination, when a nurse had to turn her over as she was so weak. I did not consider the signs of tuberculosis in the chest coincided with the condition of the patient. Her limbs were stiff, and she wouldn't use them. She was slightly mentally unbalanced. On the morning of the 18th August, the day after she was admitted, I tried to get her to take some food. She said she would try. She didn't have any however except for some tea and water. The reason she gave for not eating was that she couldn't eat when she thought of the French starving in France. I consider the death due to cardiac failure due to degeneration through starvation, and not through pulmonary tuberculosis."

'The Coroner recorded a verdict of suicide while the balance of the mind was disturbed.'

A more striking headline was supplied by two Maidstone

349

newspapers, the *Kent Messenger* of Friday, 3rd September, and the *South Eastern Gazette* of Sunday, 12th September: 'Death from starvation, French Professor's Curious Sacrifice'. They added an odd bit of information of their own:

'Witness [Dr Broderick] produced a letter from Dr Bennett, the chest specialist at the Middlesex Hospital, who said she had starved herself in an attic in order to send food to French prisoners of war.

'Witness said Professor Weil had a curious religious outlook, and would say she had no religion at all.'

Two days after the telegram announcing her death, her parents received Simone Weil's last letter, dated 16th August, which contained the words: 'Very little time and inspiration available for letters now. They will be short, far apart, irregular.' Not one word, until then, had prepared the family for the announcement of her death; her illness had not even been mentioned.

Her burial took place on Monday, 30th August. It might have been a sad occasion, but to the seven mourners present it seemed that Simone had found her peace, that tears were inappropriate for the departure of one made for the life beyond. M. and Mme Closon drove to the station to meet a priest, who did not arrive, having missed the train from London. Mrs Francis brought a bunch of red roses tied with the French and English colours. As she was leaving 31 Portland Road one of the boys drew her attention to the way she had tied the ribbon: 'No, mummy, this is the French side, don't put it the English way up.' The hearse was waiting for them at the station, and they went straight to the cemetery. In the absence of a priest, one of the assistants read aloud the prayers of the Church. When the ceremony was over, the little group paid a call to the matron at the sanatorium. Then they returned to London.

> WEIL Adolphine Simone
> Grosvenor Sanatorium
> August 30, 1943
> Age: 34
> Conducted own service
> Catholic

1909-1943
French Refugee
Depth: 6 feet
Louis Closon
*Dir. du Cabinet du Commissaire*
*[Certificate of burial]*

In the third row from the hedge in front of a pine wood, No. 79 in the Ashford New Cemetery, the grave is marked by a square stone of white granite mottled with grey and bearing her name: at the foot of the grave a hawthorn bush struggles for life.

SIMONE WEIL

1909-1943

When the Liberation came, the workers of Saint-Étienne learned about their comrade's death and were not at all surprised. 'She used to eat too little,' they said.

As for her old master, Alain, he would not believe it. 'It's not true,' he repeated, 'surely she will come back!'

351

# NOTES
# BIBLIOGRAPHY
# INDEX

# Notes

THE READER is generally referred to the English translation of Simone Weil's works (published by Routledge and Kegan, London, except for the *Selected Essays*, published by Oxford University Press, and *Gravity and Grace*, published by G. P. Putnam's Sons, New York.) The author has translated the selections made directly from the French original. Quotations from published English translations are not always literal. For reasons of space, notes in this edition have been held down to a minimum. Abbreviations used in the Notes and in the Bibliography are as follows, by alphabetical order:

A *L'Attente de Dieu* (Paris, La Colombe, new edition of 1950)
CO *La Condition ouvrière* (Paris, NRF, Gallimard, 1951)
CS *La Connaissance surnaturelle* (Paris, NRF, Gallimard, 1950)
EH *Ecrits historiques et politiques* (Paris, NRF, Gallimard, 1960)
EL *Écrits de Londres et dernières Lettres* (Paris, NRF, Gallimard, 1957)
G *Gravity and Grace* (1952)
I *Intimations of Christianity* (1957)
IPC *Intuitions préchrétiennes* (Paris, La Colombe, 1951)
LP *Letter to a Priest* (1953)
N *Notebooks* (2 vols. 1956)
NR *The Need for Roots* (1952)
OEL *Oppression et Liberté* (Paris, NRF, Gallimard, 1955)
OL *Oppression and Liberty* (1958)
P *La Pesanteur et la Grâce* (Paris, Plon, 1948)
PSO *Pensées sans ordre concernant l'amour de Dieu* (Paris, NRF, Gallimard, 1962)
PT J.-M. Perrin and G. Thibon, *Simone Weil telle que nous l'avons connue*, (Paris, La Colombe, 1952)
SE *Selected Essays* (1962)
SG *La Source grecque* (Paris, NRF, Gallimard, 1953)
V *Venise sauvée* (Paris, NRF, Gallimard, 1955)
WG *Waiting on God* (1951)

The following refer to French magazines, except for *NA*:

CDS  *Les Cahiers du Sud* (Marseilles)
E    *L'Effort* (Lyons)
EE   *L'École Émancipée* (Saumur)
FLQ  *Feuilles Libres de la Quinzaine* (Lyons)
LCS  *La Critique Sociale* (Paris)
LP   *Libres Propos* (Nîmes)
NA   *Nuovi Argomenti* (Rome)
NC   *Nouveaux Cahiers* (Paris)
RP   *La Révolution prolétarienne* (Paris)
TE   *Le Travailleur de l'Enseignement* (Paris)
TR   *La Table Ronde* (Paris)

PART I: CHILDHOOD AND UNIVERSITY

CHAPTER I: CHILDHOOD AND ADOLESCENCE

1  [*Introduction*] Alain, 'Simone Weil', *TR*, April 1950, p. 47.
2  We are indebted for the biographical information that we have used to Simone Weil's family, teachers, former colleagues, and friends. Their names, as well as other sources used, can be found in our French book. See Jacques Cabaud, *L'Expérience vécue de Simone Weil*, Paris, Plon, 1957.
3  See Int. to *A*, (in the 1948 edition,) p. 17. This Int. was not included in the new edition of 1950 or following editions.
4  *WG*, p. 17.
5  *PT*, p. 140.
6  *SE*, pp. 175-6.
7  See B. Souvarine, 'A Note on S.W.', *Politics*, New York, February 1945, and U. Thévenon in *RP*, May 1952.
8  See *WG*, pp. 15-19, and *A*, Int. in the 1948 edition, pp. 32-35. See also *N*, p. 132.
9  *CS*, p. 87.
10 *PT*, p. 27.

CHAPTER II: UNIVERSITY

1  For this chapter and the following, much use has been made of S. W.'s file in the Ministère de l'Éducation Nationale.
2  On the influence of Alain and Lagneau on S. W., see M. M. Davy, *Introduction au message de S. W.*, (Paris, Plon, 1954,) pp. 36-69, for some valuable, but fragmentary remarks.

3  See *passim* J. Lagneau, *De l'existence de Dieu* and *Célèbres leçons et fragments*, particularly the latter, pp. 261, 262, 304.
4  *RP*, May 1952, p. 13.
5  *TR*, April 1950, p. 47.
6  G. Hourdin, 'Quand une agrégée se fait ouvrière', *Ecclesia*, December 1951.
7  S. W., 'Le sang coule en Tunisie', *FLQ*, 25 March 1937.
8  'Mémoires d'une jeune fille rangée' (Paris, Gallimard, 1958), p. 237.

PART II: TEACHER, ANARCHIST, REVOLUTIONARY

CHAPTER I: THE LYCÉE OF LE PUY

1  U. Thévenon, *RP*, May 1952, and A. Thévenon, Int. to *CO*.
2  J. Duperray, 'Quand S. W. passa chez nous', MS graciously lent to the author.
3  *Syndicat National des institutrices et instituers publics de la France et des Colonies, Bulletin de la Section de la Haute-Loire*, November 1931.
4  S. W., 'Après la visite d'une mine', *E*, 19 March 1932.
5  We are much indebted for these notes to the former pupils of S. W. See part I, ch. I, note 2.
6  On *affaire Weil*, see mainly *Le Mémorial de Saint-Étienne*, 20 December 1931; 13, 14 January 1932—*Le Nouvelliste de Lyon*, 14 January 1932—*La Tribune Républicaine de Saint-Étienne*, 14, 18 January 1932—*Journal de la Haute-Loire*, 19 December 1931; 2, 13 January; 4, 5, 6 February 1932—*Registre des Délibérations du Conseil Municipal du Puy*, 30 December 1931; 18 February; 15 March; 20 May; 25 July 1932—Reports in *Bulletin de la Section de la Haute-Loire*, January and February 1932, and S. W.'s file at the Ministry.
7  S. W., 'Une survivance du régime des castes', op. cit. above No. 3, January-February 1932, p. 148.

CHAPTER II: THE AUXERRE LYCÉE

1  This and other quotations in this chapter from letters to Thévenon, *RP*, May 1952, pp. 14-16.
2  *RP*, 25 August 1932, p. 14.
3  *RP*, 25 November 1932, p. 11.
4  See S. W.'s series of articles in *EE*, 18 December 1932; 8, 29 January; 5, 12, 19, 26 February; 5 March; 9 April; 7 May 1933.
5  See part I, ch. I, note 2.

6  See *CS*, p. 205. Marriage is defined as 'un viol consenti', but as a metaphor for the mystical union between the soul and God.

7  'Sur la situation en Allemagne', *EE*, 9 April 1933, pp. 453-454.

CHAPTER III: ROANNE and SAINT-ÉTIENNE

1  On the Rheims Congress, see *RP*, no. 126 (April) and no. 128 (25 May 1932); *TE*, February and July 1933; *L'Émancipation*, a supplement to *EE*, October 1933.

2  See A. Thévenon, *CO*, p. 8 and *E*, 29 July and 12 August 1933, for a report on two of S. W.'s lectures.

3  Duperray's MS is again the source for much of this material.

4  *CO*, p. 139.

5  For further details see *E*, 4 November 1933 and *TE*, December 1933.

6  The unfinished version in *OL*, pp. 37-124 is entitled 'Reflections concerning the Causes of Liberty and Social Oppression.'

CHAPTER IV: A YEAR'S FACTORY WORK

1  *CO*, p. 23. On Detœuf see S. W.'s letters in *NA*, no. 20, 1953, pp. 98-99. Unless otherwise noted selections are from S. W.'s 'Factory Journal', in *CO*, pp. 35-107.

2  *RP*, May 1952, pp. 17-161. See letters to A. Thévenon and to a former student in *CO*, pp. 15-27—material also used in this chapter.

3  *CO*, pp. 29-31.

4  In *CO*, pp. 125-59, also quoted later.

5  S. W., 'Réflexions sur la guerre', *LCS*, November 1933, p. 156.

6  See *WG*, pp. 19-20, also for following quotes.

CHAPTER V: THE LYCÉE OF BOURGES AND HOLIDAYS IN SPAIN

1  See part I, ch. I, note 2.

2  *CO*, p. 184. S. W.'s correspondence with A. Detœuf is also mentioned below. See *CO*, pp. 181-95.

3  See this correspondence in *CO*, pp. 125-59.

4  See *I*, pp. 18-23.

5  This article is reprinted in *CO*, pp. 161-74.

6  *Société des amis de Georges Bernanos, Bulletin Trimestriel*, June 1950, pp. 11-14, (*Cf. SE*, pp. 171-6), which we used together with information obtained from friends and comrades of S. W. See also the entries on Spain in *N*, pp. 32, 40, 154, 160-1, 346-7.

7  *FLQ*, 25 September 1936, p. 244.

PART III: METAPHYSICAL AND RELIGIOUS SPECULATION

CHAPTER I: FROM THE POLITICAL EVIL TO THE DIVINE
REVELATION

*The Political Evil*

1 *CO*, pp. 196-205.
2 See this study and the lecture on rationalization in CO, pp. 207-13
and 216-32, respectively.

*The Divine Revelation*

1 These letters of S. W. to her family are unpublished. The letters
to a friend concerning this trip are found in *NA*, no. 20, 1953,
pp. 80-103.
2 *IPC*, p. 52.
3 *WG.* p. 20.
4 S. W., 'La fresque romane de l'église Sant'Angelo à Asolo',
*Il Ponte*, June 1951, pp. 612-15.
5 See part I, ch. I, note 2.
6 *CDS*, no. 304, 1950, p. 435.
7 *WG*, pp. 20-1.
8 St. Paul, Ephesians III, 18.
9 *CDS*, ib. p. 432.
10 *CS*, pp. 9-10. *Cf. N*, 638-9, and also in E. W. F. Tomlin's *Simone
Weil* (New Haven, Yale Univ. Press, 1954), pp. 28-9.
11 *N*, p. 162.
12 *PSO*, pp. 11-12. Quotes from these poems, as those from
'Venise Sauvée' in next chapter, were translated with the help of
Mr. Nicholas Thacher.

*Pacifism*

1 See 'Sur les Nouveaux Cahiers', *NC*, 1 March 1938, p. 14.
2 *NC*, 1 December 1937, p. 10.
3 *NC*, 1 February 1939, p. 20.
4 *WG*, p. 22.
5 *N*, pp. 96-7. See also ib., pp. 25-6 and 32-4.
6 *Preuves*, February 1953, pp. 20-9. See *SE*, pp. 177-94.
7 Note S. W.'s interest in Machiavelli, *SE*, pp. 55-72.

CHAPTER II: PACIFISM IN COLLAPSE

1  See *N*, p. 156.
2  *NA*, no. 20 (1953), p. 101.
3  *NC*, 15 March 1938, pp. 11-13.
4  *WG*, p. 22.
5  *EL*, pp. 187-95.
6  See *Deucalion*, Oct. 1952, and *N*, p. 1.
7  *CS*, p. 317.
8  See *V* for all quotes concerning *Venise sauvée*.
9  See *Politics*, New York, vol. VI, no. 1 (Winter 1949), p. 40.


CHAPTER III: THE YEARS OF INTENSE SPECULATION

*Speculation*

1  *I*, pp. 24-55.
2  See *WG*, pp. 63-78, from which we select unless otherwise noted.
3  *N*, p. 3.
4  *N*, p. 28.
5  *N*, pp. 386-7.
6  *N*, p. 252.
7  See *N*, p. 258.
8  See *W*. pp. 81-142.
9  *CS*, p. 238.
10  *N*, p. 248. See also *CS*, p. 226.
11  *IPC*, p. 38.
12  *I*, pp. 103-5. We have here again an opportunity to understand to what extent S. W.'s thought and religious outlook were congenial to Spinoza's.
13  *N*, p. 350.
14  See *SE*, pp. 35-54.
15  *IPC*, p. 7.
16  See *I*, pp. 56-9 (Zeus and Prometheus), pp. 74-88 (God in Plato), and *SG*, pp. 67-126 (Dieu dans Platon), and pp. 127-8 (Sur le Théétète).
17  *IPC*, p. 14.
18  *I*, pp. 89-105.
19  *SG*, p. 96.
20  *I*, p. 3.
21  *P*, p. 166.
22  *CDS*, no. 310 (1951), pp. 426-30.

23  *CDS,* no. 263 (January 1944), pp. 40-5.
24  *Les Études philosophiques,* Jan.-March 1946, pp. 13-19.
25  See *N,* p. 39.
26  See *N,* p. 63.

*Mysticism*

1   *CDS,* no. 304 (1950), p. 436.
2   See *WG,* p. 24.
3   According to Rimbaud's expression: 'Et j'ai vu quelquefois ce que l'homme a cru voir.' *Le Bateau Ivre.*
4   *N,* p. 156.
5   Letter to Joë Bousquet, *CDS,* no. 304 (1950), pp. 431-7.
6   See *N,* p. 242.
7   *CS,* p. 249.
8   These themes are taken from *LP.* See also *CS,* pp. 67, 171-4, 233, 260, 269, 272, and also Thibon's selections in *P,* pp. 189-93.
9   *CS,* p. 132. See also *CS,* pp. 36 and 257.
10  *CS,* p. 270.
11  *CS,* p. 311.
12  *CS,* pp. 77.
13  See selections on this point in *CS,* pp. 248-50 and 291-4.
14  *WG,* p. 91.
15  *CS,* p. 310.
16  *CS,* p. 34.
17  See *LP,* pp. 49-57.
18  See also in *LP,* pp. 48-9 and 57-63.
19  *WG,* pp. 3-6.
20  *WG,* p. 11.
21  See *WG,* pp. 11-12.
22  See this exchange in *CDS,* no. 284 (1947) and no. 304 (1950).

*In the Folds of Friendship, in the Fields of Labour*

1   See *PT,* p. 43.
2   *CO,* pp. 261-73.
3   *CS,* p. 331.
4   *CS,* p. 74.
5   *PT,* p. 127.
6   See Thibon's account in *PT,* pp. 122-48, and *G,* pp. i-xii.
7   See *WG,* pp. 23-4.
8   Eugène Fleuré, *Simone Weil Ouvrière,* Paris, Fernand Lanore, 1955, pp. 93-6. Compare with *N,* pp. 79, 147-8, 169-71.

9 Jean Lambert, *Les vacances du cœur*, Paris, NRF, Gallimard, p. 235
10 *PT*, p. 32.
11 See *WG*, p. 96.
12 *PT*, pp. 43-6.
13 J.-M. Perrin, Int. to *l'Attente de Dieu*, ed. of 1948, p. 45. See also *WG*, p. 27.
14 *WG*, p. 25.
15 *WG*, p. 27.
16 Starting here, this section quotes from *PT*, pp. 41-5.
17 *WG*, pp. 32-3.
18 *P*, pp. vi-viii.
19 J.-M. Perrin, *l'Attente de Dieu*, ed. of 1948, Introd., p. 48.
20 For all selections to the end of the chapter see *WG*, pp. 37-47.

CHAPTER IV: NEW YORK

1 See *EL*, pp. 185-201.
2 Selections in the paragraph just ended: *CS*, p. 222; *CS*, p. 168; *N*, p. 193; *N*. p. 192; *CS*, p. 168. Like many Hindus Simone Weil seems to say that original sin was committed against God by God himself when He yielded as it were to his creature's desire to be.
3 *CS*, p. 232.
4 *N*, p. 191.
5 *CS*, p. 49. See also *N*, pp. 26-7.
6 *CS*, p. 91.
7 *CS*, p. 325.
8 *N*, p. 147.
9 *CS*, p. 111.
10 *N*, p. 175.
11 Respectively in *N*, p. 137 and *CS* p. 113.
12 *CS*, p. 86.
13 *CS*, p. 59.
14 See respectively *CS*, pp. 109, 285, 275 and 57.
15 See respectively *N*, pp. 41 and 130.
16 See respectively *N*, pp. 150 and 57.
17 See *N*, p. 150.
18 See *N*, p. 278.
19 See *N*, p. 179.
20 See *WG*, p. 4.
21 See *WG*, p. 5.
22 *N*, pp. 217-18.
23 See *LP*, p. 10.

24  See *LP*, p. 33.
25  See *Deucalion*, Oct. 1952.
26  See *CS*, pp. 204-7.

CHAPTER V: LONDON

 1  For this letter and the other letter quoted below, see *EL*, pp. 225
    and 229.
 2  *EL*, pp. 126-48.
 3  *EL*, pp. 58-73.
 4  *EL*, pp. 85-92.
 5  *OL*, pp. 169-95.
 6  See *SE*, pp. 9-34.
 7  See *SE*, pp. 211-18.
 8  *EL*, pp. 182 and 180.
 9  *EL*, pp. 109-25.
10  *EL*, pp. 45-57.
11  See *SE*, pp. 195-210, and *NR*, p. 221.
12  *EL*, pp. 201-15.
13  *EL*, pp. 218-57.
14  See *NR*, pp. 7-9.
15  *SE*, pp. 219-27.
16  On social uprootedness, *NR*, pp. 41-8, 51-5, 63-9.
17  On patriotism, *NR*, pp. 95, 100, 105-14, 122-9, 134, 140, 142,
    149-50, 162-4, 179-81.
18  On force and science, *NR*, pp. 206-11, 222, 227, 230-5.
19  *CS*, p. 177.
20  *EL*, pp. 233, 242 and 235.
21  *CS*, pp. 204-5.
22  *PSO*, pp. 149-53.
23  *PSO*, pp. 135-45.
24  *EL*, pp. 254-7.

# Bibliography

ABBREVIATIONS USED IN THE BIBLIOGRAPHY are the same as those used in the Notes.

The following order is observed: the earliest publication comes first; immediately underneath, the most readily available versions in French (preceded by a dash) and in English (in parentheses). Any other edition is given in a footnote. Extracts are only listed when they pre-date publication of the entire work in either language.

Poems are grouped under the heading 'Poèmes'. In the section devoted to correspondence, letters are listed alphabetically solely according to the recipient's name, whether there are one or several letters per recipient ('Lettre' or 'Lettres'). The English titles used in this biography which refer to texts which have not been translated are followed by the letters NT, 'Not translated', and the original French title. Those which refer to texts which have been translated under another title are followed by the letters WT, 'Working title', and the English title used in their translation.

On doubtful points, reliance has been placed on Michel Thiout's authoritative chronological listing in *Archives des lettres modernes*, Paris, (III), no. 26 (octobre 1959).

For further bibliographical information—unpublished correspondence, biographical sources, articles about Simone Weil—see Jacques Cabaud: *L'expérience vécue de Simone Weil*, Paris, Plon, 1957, pp. 388-401.


I. ALPHABETICAL LIST OF SIMONE WEIL'S WORKS
PUBLISHED IN FRENCH AND IN ENGLISH

'À propos de la question coloniale dans ses rapports avec le destin du peuple français' *TR*, no. 46 (octobre 1951), pp. 9-25;
   —*EH*, pp. 364-78;
   ('East and West: Thoughts on the Colonial Problem' *SE*, pp. 195-210).

# Bibliography

'A propos des Jocistres' *CDS*, tome XIX, no. 234 (avril 1941), pp. 245-6; under the pseudonym of Emile Novis.

'A propos du "Pater"' *A*, pp. 167-76; ('Concerning the "Our Father"' *WG*, pp. 143-53).

'A qui le pouvoir?' [Parmi nos lettres], *RP*, no. 179 (25 juillet 1934), p. 7.

'L'affaire Freinet' *LP*, 7e année, no. 6 (25 juin 1933), pp. 326-7.

'L'agonie d'une civilisation vue à travers un poème épique' *CDS*, tome XX, no. 249 (août-septembre-octobre 1942[1]), pp. 99-107; signed Emile Novis, anagram of Simone Weil;
–*EH*, pp. 66-74;
('A Medieval Epic Poem' *SE*, pp. 35-43).
('The Agony of a Civilization' (WT), *see above* 'A Medieval Epic Poem').

'L'Allemagne en attente (impressions d'Allemagne (août et septembre))' *RP*, no. 138 (25 octobre 1932), pp. 6-12;
–*EH*, pp. 126-42: article identical to following one.

'L'Allemagne en attente (impressions d'août et septembre)' *LP*, 6e année, nos. 10 et 11 (25 octobre et 25 novembre 1932), pp. 526-32, 583-90: article identical to preceding one.

'Allons-nous vers la Révolution Prolétarienne?' *RP*, no. 158 (25 août 1933), pp. 3-11;
–*OEL*, pp. 9-38;
('Prospects: Are We Heading For The Proletarian Revolution?' *OL*, pp. 1-24);

'L'Amour de Dieu et le malheur' [full text]: only in *PSO*, pp. 85-131; [first part of text] in: *Nova et Vetera*, Fribourg, Switzerland, no. 3 (juillet-septembre 1949), pp. 225-37;
–*A*, pp. 81-98;
('The Love of God and Affliction' *WG*, pp. 61-78).

'L'amour divin dans la création' *see* 'Descente de Dieu'.

'Antigone' *Entre nous*, Chronique de Rosières, Bourges-Rosières, (15 mai 1936);
–*SG*, pp. 57-62;
('Antigone' *I*, pp. 18-23).

'Un appel aux ouvriers de R.' *CO*, pp. 128-32.

'Un appel aux syndiqués de la C.G.T.U. Pour la démocracie syndicale! Contre les exclusions de tendance!' *RP*, no. 155 (10 juillet 1933),

---

[1]Reprinted in 1943 in 'numéro spécial' entitled 'Le Génie d'Oc et l'Homme Méditerranéen', same pp.

# Bibliography

pp. 15-16; signed by Charbit, Craipeau and S. Weill [sic], but obviously written by S. Weil.

'Après la mort de Briand' [Sur trois morts], *LP*, no. 3 (mars 1932), pp. 165-6.

'Après la mort du Comité des 22' *E*, no. 288 (2 janvier 1932), pp. 1-2; unsigned article attributed by Michel Thiout to Simone Weil.

'Après la visite d'une mine' *E*, no. 299 (19 mars 1932), p. 1;

'Are We Fighting for Justice?' (NT): 'Luttons-nous pour la justice?'

'Are We Heading For the Proletarian Revolution?' *see* 'Allons-nous vers la Révolution Prolétarienne?'

'*Attente de Dieu*' introd. J.-M. Perrin,[1] Paris, La Colombe, ed. du Vieux Colombier,[2] 1950; (*Waiting on God*, trans. Emma Craufurd,[3] London, Routledge and Kegan Paul, 1951; *Waiting for God*, id., introd. by Leslie A. Fiedler, New York,[4] G. P. Putnam's Sons, 1951).

'Autour de la mort de Fritsch' *E*, no. 303 (16 avril 1932), p. 2.

'Aux Astres' *see* Poèmes.

'L'avenir de la science' *CDS*, tome XIX, no. 245 (avril 1942), pp. 303-8: under the pseudonym of Emile Novis;

('Beyond Personalism') *see* 'La personnalité humaine, le juste et l'injuste' and note.


*Cahiers*[5] t.  I, Paris, Plon, L'Épi, 1951

t. II,   „   „   „   1953

t. III,   „   „   „   1956;

(*The Notebooks of Simone Weil*, trans. Arthur Wills, London, Routledge and Kegan Paul, 1956, 2 vols; *idem*, New York, G. P. Putnam's Sons).

'Le capital et l'ouvrier' *E*, no. 298 (12 mars 1932), p. 1.

'Cercle d'Études' *E*, no. 293 (6 février 1932), p. 2.

'Ces membres palpitants de la patrie' *Vigilance*, Paris, no. 63 (10 mars 1938), pp. 18-20;

–*EH*, pp. 344-50.

'Cette guerre est une guerre de religions'; this article first appeared under the title 'Retour aux guerres de religions' *TR*, no. 55

---

[1] Introduction suppressed in new 1950 edition and all subsequent editions.
[2] In paperback: *idem*, 1963: new preface by J. -M. Perrin.
[3] (In paperback: *idem*, William Collins & Sons, Fontana Books, Glasgow 1959)
[4] (In paperback: *idem*, Capricorn Books, 1959: incomplete).
[5] *See La Pesanteur et la Grâce* and note.

# Bibliography

(juillet 1952), pp. 39-48; then under the new title 'Cette guerre est une guerre de religions' *EL*, pp. 98-108;

('A War of Religions' *SE*,[1] pp. 211-18).

'Le Christianisme et la vie des champs' *La Vie intellectuelle*, Paris, Ed. du Cerf (juillet 1953), pp. 62-71;

−*PSO*, pp. 21-33.

'Christianity and Life in the Fields' (NT). *see above*.

('Cold War Policy in 1939') *see* 'Réflexions en vue d'un bilan'.

('The Coming World War' duplicate title for 'The Next World War').

'Comment a mûri le conflit interne du parti nazi' *RP*, no. 178 (10 juillet 1934), pp. 12-13; doubtful attribution.

('Concerning the "Our Father"') *see* 'À propos du "Pater".'

*La Condition ouvrière*, Paris, N.R.F., Gallimard[2] Collection 'Espoir', 1951;

'La condition ouvrière' *CO*, pp. 233-9.

'Condition première d'un travail non servile'[3] *CO*, pp. 261-73.

'Conditions d'une révolution allemande. Et maintenant?' par Léon Trotsky, *LP*, 6e année, no. 8 (août 1932), pp. 417-22;

−*EH*, pp. 117-23.

'La Conférence du Désarmement' *E*, no. 295 (20 février 1932), p. 1.

'Le Congrès de la C.G.T. (Lettre de l'Observateur), *LP*, no. 10 (octobre 1931), pp. 474-6.

'Le Congrès de la C.G.T.U.' *E*, no. 402 (28 octobre 1933), p. 2.

'Le Congrès de l'Union des Syndicats de la Région Parisienne' *RP*, no. 240 (10 février 1937), pp. 27-8.

'Le Congrès des Métaux' *Le Libertaire*, organe hebdomadaire de l'Union Anarchiste, Paris, no. 525 (4 décembre 1936), p. 6.

*La Connaissance surnaturelle*,[4] Paris, N.R.F., Gallimard, Collection 'Espoir', 1950.

'Contre la politique néfaste de la direction fédérale' [Lettre à un camarade syndicaliste], *TE*, 5e année, no. 5 (février 1933), pp. 8-9.

'Crise d'autorité?' *Syndicats*, Paris, no. 18 (11 février 1937), p. 5.

[1](Previous publications: 'A War of Religions' *The Paris Review*, Paris, no. 2 (summer 1953), pp. 80-8; 'A War of Religions' (Reprint), tr. R. Rees, *Twentieth Century*. no. 170 (Autumn 1961), pp. 102-10).
[2]*Idem*, in paperback, Collection 'Idées', 1964.
[3]Extracts in *Le Cheval de Troie*, Saint-Maximin (Var)—Paris, no. 4 (décembre 1947), pp. 525-34.
[4]'Prologue' of *CS* in E. W. F. Tomlin's *Simone Weil*, New Haven, Yale University Press, 1954, pp. 28-9; also in *N*, pp. 638-9.

# Bibliography

('Critical Examination of the Ideas of Revolution and Progress') *see* 'Examen critique des idées de révolution et de progrès.'

'Les dangers de guerre et les conquêtes ouvrières' *Syndicats*, Paris, no. 28 (22 avril 1937), p. 4.

'La déclaration de la C.G.T.' *Le Libertaire*, Paris, no. 519 (23 octobre 1936), p. 8.

'Dernier texte' *PSO*, pp. 150-8

'Dernières lettres' *EL*, pp. 185-257: Letters to Maurice Schumann, to her brother and parents.

'Désarroi de notre temps' *EH*, pp. 290-1.

'Descente de Dieu' *IPC*, pp. 9-171: collection of four texts:
'Quête de l'homme par Dieu,' pp. 9-15: ('God's Quest for Man' *I*, pp. 1-6);
'Reconnaissance de Dieu et de l'homme,' pp. 15-20: ('God's Quest for Man,' *I*, pp. 6-10);
'L'opération de la grâce' pp. 20-1;
'L'amour divin dans la création' pp. 22-171: ('Divine Love in Creation' *I*, pp. 22-41; 'The Symposium of Plato' *I*, pp. 41-71; 'The Republic' *I*, pp. 71-93; 'Prometheus' *I*, pp. 93-108; 'The Pythagorean Doctrine' *I*, pp. 108-71).

'Dieu dans Héraclite' *SG*, pp. 149-50.

'Dieu dans Platon' *SG*, pp. 67-126;
('God in Plato' extract, *I*, pp. 74-88).

('Divine Love in Creation') *see* 'Descente de Dieu.'

('Draft for a Declaration of Obligations towards Mankind' (WT): 'Draft for a Statement of Human Obligations').

('Draft for a Statement of Human Obligations') *see* 'Étude pour une déclaration des obligations envers l'être humain.'

'E. Gunther-Grundel: La mission de la jeune génération' [Revue des Livres], *LCS*, no. 9 (septembre 1933), p. 137.

'E. O. Volkmann: La révolution allemande' [Revue des Livres], *LCS*, no. 9 (septembre 1933), p. 129.

('East and West: Thoughts on the Colonial Problem') *see* 'À propos de la question coloniale dans ses rapports avec le destin du peuple français.'

'Ébauches de lettres' [1938? 1939?], *EH*, pp. 102-16;
('Three Letters on History' *SE*, pp. 73-88: I, II, & IV of original).

'Éclair' *see* Poêmes.

# Bibliography

*Écrits de Londres et dernières lettres* Paris, NRF, Gallimard, Coll. 'Espoir' 1957; (in part[1] in *SE*).

*Écrits historiques et politiques* Paris, NRF, Gallimard, Coll. 'Espoir' 1960; (in part[2] in *SE*).

'En marge du Comité d'Études' [La vie syndicale], *E*, no. 286 (19 décembre 1931), p. 2.

'En quoi consiste l'inspiration occitanienne'[3] *CDS*, tome xx, no. 249 (août-septembre-octobre 1942), pp. 150-8; under the pseudonym of Emile Novis;
—*EH*, pp. 75-84;
('The Romanesque Renaissance'[4] *SE*, pp. 44-54).

'Encore quelques mots sur le boycottage' *EH*, pp. 242-3.

*L'Enracinement*[5] Prélude à une déclaration des devoirs envers l'être humain, Paris, NRF, Gallimard, Coll. 'Espoir,' 1949; (*The Need for Roots*[6] trans. Arthur Wills, preface T. S. Eliot, London, Routledge and Kegan Paul, 1952; New York, G. P. Putnam's Sons, 1953[7]).

'Esquisse d'une apologie de la banqueroute'[8] *EH*, pp. 400-2.

'Esquisse d'une histoire de la science grecque' *IPC*, pp. 172-80; ('A Sketch of a History of Greek Science' *I*, pp. 202-8).

'Essai sur la notion de lecture' *Les Études philosophiques*, Paris, nouv. série no. 1 (janvier-mars 1946), pp. 13-19.

('Essay On the Meaning of Reading') (NT): *see* preceding item.

---

[1]Translation of the three following articles: 'Cette guerre est une guerre de religions', 'Étude pour une déclaration des obligations envers l'être humain', 'La Personne et le Sacré'.
[2]Translation of the thirteen following articles: 'À propos de la question coloniale dans ses rapports avec le peuple français', 'L'agonie d'une civilisation vue à travers un poème épique', 'Ébauches de lettres', 'En quoi consiste l'inspiration occitanienne?' 'Esquisse d'une apologie de la banqueroute', 'Lettre à Georges Bernanos', 'Méditations sur un cadavre', 'Ne recommençons pas la guerre de Troie', 'Quelques réflexions sur les origines de l'hitlérisme', 'Réflexions en vue d'un bilan', 'Réflexions sur la barbarie', 'Rome et l'Albanie', 'Un soulèvement prolétarien à Florence au XIVe siècle'.
[3]Reprinted in 1943 in 'numéro spécial' entitled 'Le Génie d'Oc et l'Homme Méditerranéen', same pp.
[4]('The Romanesque Renaissance' trans. Richard Rees, *The Twentieth Century*, London, vol. 168, no. 1003, (Summer 1960), pp. 209-18).
[5]In the new 1950 edition and in most subsequent editions, six pp. of additional text. In paperback, Paris, N. R. F., Gallimard, Collection 'Idées,' 1962.
[6](Extracts of *L'Enracinement* appeared under title 'Hitler and the idea of greatness' in *Commentary*, New York, vol. 10, no. 7 (July 1950), pp. 15-22).
[7]*Idem*, in paperback, Boston, The Beacon Press, 1955.
[8]Variant of article 'Quelques méditations concernant l'économie'.

# Bibliography

'Étude pour une déclaration des obligations envers l'être humain'
*EL*, pp. 74-84;
('Draft for a Statement for Human Obligations' *SE*, pp. 219-27).
'L'Europe en guerre pour la Tchécoslovaquie?' *FLQ*, 4e année, no. 58
(25 mai 1938), pp. 149-51;
–*EH*, pp. 273-8.
'Les évènements d'Allemagne. La grève des transports à Berlin.
Les élections' *RP*, 8e année, no. 140 (25 novembre 1932), pp. 11-12;
–*EH*, pp. 143-5. *see also* 'Note sur les récents évènements
d'Allemagne. Les enseignements de la grève des transports à
Berlin. Les élections allemandes.'
'Examen critique des idées de révolution et de progrès' *OEL*, pp.
178-85;
('Critical Examination of the Ideas of Revolution and Progress'
*OL*, pp. 134-40).
'Expérience de la vie d'usine' *CO*, pp. 241-59; *see* 'Réflexions sur la
vie d'usine' for previous partial publication.
'Extraits du *Phèdre* de Platon' *SG*, pp. 135-6.

('Factory Work') *see* 'Réflexions sur la vie d'usine.'
('The Fallacy of Personal Rights') *see* 'La personnalité humaine, le
juste et l'injuste,' and note.
'Faut-il graisser les godillots?' *Vigilance*, Paris, nos. 44 et 45 (27 octobre
1936), p. 15;
–*EH*, pp. 248-9.
'The Fire Sylphs' (NT): 'Les Lutins du feu.'
'Le flic roi. L'assassinat et l'enterrement de Fritsch' in collaboration
with P. Busseuil, *RP*, no. 126 (avril 1932), pp. 3-4.
'For the General Suppression of Political Parties' (NT): 'Note sur la
suppression générale des partis politiques.'
'For trade-union democracy (in the C.G.T.U).' (NT): 'Un appel aux
syndiqués de la C.G.T.U. Pour la démocratie syndicale! Contre
les exclusions de tendance.'
'Formes de l'amour implicite de Dieu' *A*, pp. 99-166;
('Forms of the Implicit Love of God' *WG*, pp. 79-142).
'Fragment (1936?)' *EH*, p. 217.
'Fragment (1939?)' *EH*, pp. 292-5.
'Fragment (1939?)' *EH*, pp. 313-14.
'Fragment (après juin 1940)' *EH*, p. 315.
'Fragment (1938-1939?)' *EH*, pp. 357-8.
'Fragment (1938-1939?)' *EH*, pp. 359-60.

# Bibliography

'Fragment sur la guerre revolutionnaire' *EH*, pp. 240-1.

'Fragments (1934-35-36)', *CO*, pp. 109-24.

'Fragments 1933-1938' [I-IV], *OEL*, pp. 163-77;
 ('Fragments 1933-1938' [I-IV], *OL*, pp. 125-34).

'Fragments d'Héraclite' [traduction], *SG*, 139-48.

'Fragments et notes' *EL*, pp. 149-82.

'Fragments, Londres 1943' [I-II], *OEL*, pp. 205-20;
 ('Fragments, London 1943' [I-II], *OL*, pp. 156-8).

'La fresque romane de l'église Sant'Angelo à Ascolo' *II Ponte*, Firenze, anno VII, no. 6 (giugno 1951), pp. 612-14.


('God in Plato') *see* 'Dieu dans Platon.'

('God's Quest for Man') *see* 'Descente de Dieu.'

(*Gravity and Grace*) *see La Pesanteur et la Grâce.*

('The Great Beast: Some Reflections on the Origins of Hitlerism') *see* 'Quelques réflexions sur les origines de l'hitlérisme.'

'La grève des plébéiens romains' *Syndicats*, Paris, no. 23 (18 mars 1937), p. 4.


'Héraclite' *SG*, pp. 139-50; general heading for 'Fragments d'Héraclite.' [Traduction des Fragments], and 'Dieu dans Héraclite.'

'Une histoire instructive' *La Tribune*, Saint-Étienne, éd. de la Haute-Loire (21 janvier 1932).

('Hitler and the idea of greatness') *see L'Enracinement,* and note.

('Human personality') *see* 'La personnalité humaine, le juste et l'injuste.'


'Idées essentielles pour une nouvelle Constitution,' *EL*, pp. 93-7.

('The *Iliad* or, The Poem of Force') *see* '*L'Iliade* ou le poème de la force', and note.

'*L'Iliade* ou le poème de la force'[1] *CDS*, tome XIX, no. 230 (décembre 1940), pp. 561-74, and tome XX, no. 231 (janvier 1941), pp. 21-34; under the pseudonym of Emile Novis;

–*SG*, pp. 11-42;
 ('The *Iliad*, Poem of Might' *I*, pp. 24-55).

[1]('The *Iliad* or, The Poem of Force', trans. Mary McCarthy, *Politics*, New York, vol. II, no. II (November 1945), pp. 321-31);
 'L'Iliade ou le poème de la force', *CDS*, tome XXVI, no. 284 (2e semestre 1947), pp. 538-64;
 ('The *Iliad* Or, The Poem of Force,' trans. Mary McCarthy, *The Wind and the Rain*, London, vol. VI, no. 4 (Spring 1950), pp. 228-47);
 ('The *Iliad* Or, The Poem of Force', trans. Mary McCarthy, *Pendle Hill Pamphlet*, Wallingford, Pennsylvania, no. 91 (December 1956)).

# Bibliography

(*Intimations of Christianity*) *see Intuitions pré-chrétiennes* and *La Source grecque.*

*Intuitions pré-chrétiennes*, Paris, La Colombe, Éd. du Vieux-Colombier, 1951[1]; (*Intimations of Christianity* edited and translated by Elisabeth Chase Geissbuhler, London, Routledge & Kegan Paul, 1957; this volume, which contains also selections from *SG*, offers the same texts as *IPC*[2] but arranged in a slightly different order).

'Israël et les Gentils' *PSO*, pp. 47-62.

('Is There a Marxist Doctrine?') *see* 'Y a-t-il une doctrine marxiste?'

'Journal d'Espagne' *EH*, pp. 209-16.

'Journal d'Usine' *CO*, pp. 35-107.

('The Laments of Electra and the Recognition of Orestes') *see* 'Plaintes d'Electre et reconnaissance d'Oreste.'

'The Legitimacy of the Provisional Government' (NT): *see below.*

'Légitimité du gouvernement provisoire' *EL*, pp. 58-73.

'Lénine: Matérialisme et Empiriocriticisme' [Revue des Livres], *L.C.S.* no. 10 (novembre 1933), pp. 182-5;

–'Sur le livre de Lénine: "Matérialisme et Empiriocriticisme," ' *OEL*, pp. 45-53;

('On Lenin's Book *Materialism and Empiriocriticism*' *SE*, pp. 29-36).

('Let Us Not have Another Trojan War' (WT): 'The Power of Words')

(*Letter to a Priest*) *see Lettre à un religieux.*

'Lettres à un ami' *see* 'Ébauches de lettres.'

'Lettre au Dr Bercher' extracts in *L'expérience vécue de Simone Weil*, pp. 309-10.

'Lettre à Georges Bernanos'[3] *Société des amis de Georges Bernanos, Bulletin trimestriel*, Paris, no. 4 (juin 1950), pp. 11-14;

–*EH*, pp. 220-4;

('Letter to Georges Bernanos' *SE*, pp. 171-6).

'Lettres à M. Bernard' *OEL*, pp. 125-59, under title 'Lettres à un ingénieur directeur d'usine.'

'Lettres à Joë Bousquet'[4] *CDS*, tome XXXII, no. 304 (1950), pp. 420-38;

–*PSO* [lettre du 12 mai 1942], pp. 73-84.

[1]This ed. of 1951 contains many slight mistakes.

[2]Except for pp. 20-1 from 'Descente de Dieu' in *IPC*.

[3]–*NA*, no. 2 (mai-juin 1953), pp. 104-9;

–*Témoins*, Zurich, no. 7 (automne 1954), pp. 2-6.

[2]Extracts of a letter (12 mai 1942) in *CDS*, tome XXVI, no. 284 (2e semestre 1947), pp. 565-6, in text often at variance with that of *CDS*, no. 304, and *PSO*.

# Bibliography

'Lettre aux Cahiers du Sud sur les responsabilités de la littérature' *CDS*, tome XXXIV, no. 310 (2e semestre 1951), pp. 426-30.

'Lettre à un camarade syndicaliste' *see* 'Contre la politique néfaste de la direction fédérale.'

'Lettre à Carcopino' *see* 'Lettre à M. le Ministre de l'Instruction Publique.'

'Lettre au Père Couturier' *see Lettre a un religieux*.

'Lettres à René et Véra Daumal' in *Simone Weil*, by M. M. Davy, Paris, Éditions Universitaires, Témoins du XXe siècle, 1956, pp. 32-3 and 38-9.

'Lettres à Auguste Detoeuf' *CO*, pp. 181-95; previous publication of one letter in *NC*, no. 16 (15 décembre 1937), pp. 4-5.

'Lettre à une élève' (1934), *CO*, pp. 23-7.

'Lettres à d'anciennes élèves du Puy' extracts in *L'expérience vécue de Simone Weil*, pp. 35 and 64.

'Lettres à un étudiant' *NA*, no. 2 (1953), pp. 80-103.

'Lettre à son frère' *see* 'Dernières Lettres.'

'Une lettre inédite à Jean Giraudoux' *Le Figaro Littéraire*, Paris (5 décembre 1959), p. 4.

'Lettre à Guillaume Guindey' [un ami], *OEL*, Introd. p. 7.

'Lettres à un ingénieur directeur d'usine' *see* 'Lettres à M. Bernard.'

'Lettre à Claude Jamet' *FLQ*, 2e année, no. 22 (25 septembre 1936), p. 244.

'Lettres à Gilbert Kahn' [un ami], extracts in *L'expérience vécue de Simone Weil*, pp. 227-8 and 229; also p. 221, quote 4 (inadvertently mentioned as addressed to Père Perrin).

'Lettre aux *Libres propos*' also under the title of 'Lettre d'Allemagne (20 août)' included in 'Conditions d'une révolution allemande. Et maintenant?' par Léon Trotsky.

'Lettre à M. le Ministre de l'Instruction Publique' *Études matérialistes*, Cannes (A.–M), no. xvii (décembre 1947), pp. 2-4;

('What is a Jew? A Letter to a Minister of Education.' *Politics*, New York, vol VI, no. 1 (Winter 1949), p. 40).

'Lettres à ses parents' *see* 'Dernières lettres.'

'Lettres au Père Perrin' *A*, pp. 13-69;

('Letters to Father Perrin' *WG*, pp. 1-49). Also extracts of other letters in *PT*, pp. 32, 41-2, 44-5, 46, 67, 76-7, and in 1963 paperback edition of *A*, pp. 248-5.

*Lettre à un religieux* Paris, NRF, Gallimard, Collection 'Espoir,' 1951;

(*Letter to a Priest* translated by A. F. Wills, London, Routledge & Kegan Paul, 1953; New York, G. P. Putnam's Sons, 1954).

# Bibliography

'Lettres à la Révolution Prolétarienne' [Parmi nos lettres]: *RP*, no. 126 (avril 1932), p. 11; *see also*: 'Premières impressions d'Allemagne', 'Le parti communiste allemand et les syndicats', 'A qui le pouvoir?'

'Lettre à Déodat Roché' *Cahiers d'Études Cathares*,[1] Arques (Aude), no. 19 (1954), pp. 175-6; –*PSO*, pp. 63-7.

'Lettres à Maurice Schumann' *see* 'Dernières lettres'. Extract of other letter in *Les Cahiers Protestants*,[2] Lausanne (Suisse), no. 6 (décembre 1956), p. 294; –*PSO*, p. 133.

'Lettre à Boris Souvarine' *CO*, pp. 29-31.

'Lettre ouverte à un syndiqué' *CO*, pp. 175-9.

'Lettres à Albertine Thévenon' *CO*, pp. 15-22.

'Lettres à U. Thévenon' [extraits], *RP*, no. 362, Nelle série, no. 61 (mai 1952), pp. 14-17.

'Lettres à Gustave Thibon' extracts in *PT*, pp. 55-6 (extract reprinted in 1963 paperback edition of *A*, pp. 251-3), 127, 128, 136-7, 140, 141, 144, 145, 146-7, 147, 151, 152, 152-3, 189; and in introduction of *P*, pp. v, vi, vii-ix, xxvi.

'Lettre à Xavier Vallat' extracts published by Eugène Fleuré in 'Culture et Spiritualité' *Air, Guerre, Marine*, Paris, no 71 (janvier 1953), pp. 1 and 4; also in *Simone Weil ouvrière*, Paris, Fernand Lanore, 1955, pp. 85-9.

'Lettre à M. X . . .' fragments, *CO*, pp. 33-4.

'Lettre à Jean Wahl' *Deucalion*, no. 4 (octobre 1952).

('The Love of God and Affliction') *see* 'L'Amour de Dieu et le Malheur.'

'Les Lutins du feu' [extraits], *Le Figaro Littéraire*, 1er décembre 1962, p. 6.

'Luttons-nous pour la justice?' *Preuves*, Paris, no. 28 (1953), pp. 3-9; –*EL*, pp. 45-57.


'La marche vers l'unité syndicale: une réunion intersyndicale au Puy' *E*, no. 282 (21 novembre 1931), p. 2.

'Le Maroc ou de la prescription en matière de vol' *Vigilance*, Paris, nos. 48 and 49 (10 février 1937), pp. 28-9; –*EH*, pp. 331-5.

('A Medieval Epic Poem') *see* 'L'agonie d'une civilisation vue à travers un poème épique.'

[1] In no. 2 (avril-juin 1949), pp. 4-6, partial publication.
[2] Also in *Réalités-fémina-illustration*, Paris, no. 148 (mai 1958), pp. 43 and 44.

# Bibliography

'Méditation sur l'obéissance et la liberté' *OEL*, pp. 186-93;
  ('Meditation on Obedience and Liberty' *OL*, pp. 140-6.)
'Méditation sur un cadavre' *EH*, pp. 403-7, variant of the following
  article.
'Méditations sur un cadavre' *EH*, pp. 324-27;
  ('A Note on Social Democracy' *SE*, pp. 150-3).
'Les modes d'exploitation' *E*, no. 292 (30 janvier 1932), p. 1.
'Morale et littérature' *CDS*, tome XX, no. 263 (janvier 1944), pp. 40-5;
  under the pseudonym of Emile Novis.
('Morality and Literature') (NT): *see above.*

'Ne recommençons pas la guerre de Troie'[1] *NC*, no. 2 and 3 (1er et 15
  avril 1937), pp. 8-10 and 15-19 respectively;
  –*EH*, pp. 256-72;
  ('The Power of Words' *SE*, pp. 154-71).
'Nécessité' *see* Poèmes.
(*The Need for Roots*) *see L'Enracinement.*
('New Factors in the Colonial Problem of the French Empire') (NT):
  'Les nouvelles données du problème colonial dans l'empire
  français.'
('The next World War') *see* 'Réflexions sur la guerre.'
'Non-intervention généralisée' *EH*, pp. 252-5.
('A Note on Social Democracy') *see* 'Méditations sur un cadavre.'
'Note sur la suppression générale des partis politiques' *TR*, no. 26
  (février 1950), pp. 9-28;
  –*EL*, pp. 126-48.
'Note sur les récents évènements d'Allemagne. Les enseignements
  de la grève des transports à Berlin. Les élections allemandes'
  *LP*, Nelle série, 6e année, no. 11 (25 novembre 1932), pp.
  590-1;
  –*EH*, pp. 383-5; variant of 'Les évènements d'Allemagne. La grève
  des transports à Berlin. Les élections.'
(*The Notebooks*) *see Cahiers.*
'Notes sur Cléanthe, Phérécide, Anaximandre et Philolaos' *SG*, pp.
  151-62.
'Notion du socialisme scientifique' *E*, no. 409 (16 décembre 1933),
  p. 2.
'Une nouvelle étape dans le mouvement des chômeurs' *La Tribune*,
  Saint-Étienne, éd. de la Haute-Loire (14 janvier 1932).

[1]('Words and War' *Politics*, New York, vol. III, trans. Bowden Broadwater, no. 3
(March 1946), pp. 69-73).

# Bibliography

'Les nouvelles données du problème colonial dans l'empire français' *Essais et Combats*, Paris, nos. 2-3 (décembre 1938), pp. 6-7; –*EH*, pp. 351-6; a variant of this article is in *EH*, p. 409.

('On Bankruptcy') *see* 'Esquisse d'une apologie de la banqueroute.'
('On Lenin's Book Materialism and Empiriocriticism') *see* 'Lénine: Matérialisme et Empiriocriticisme.'
('On the Colonial Question in Relation to the Destiny of the French People') (WT): ('East and West: Thoughts on the Colonial Problem').
('On the Contradictions of Marxism') *see* 'Sur les contradictions du marxisme.'
'On the Theaetetus' (NT): 'Sur le Théétète.'
'L'opération de la grâce' *see* 'Descente de Dieu.'
*Oppression et Liberté* Paris, N.R.F., Gallimard, Collection 'Espoir,' 1955;
   (*Oppression and Liberty* translated by Arthur Wills and John Petrie, London, Routledge & Kegan Paul, 1958); the English version is complete except for the Appendix, pp. 255-73 in the French version.
'Otto Rühle: Karl Marx' *LCS*, no. 11 (mars 1934), pp. 246-7.
'Où étaient-ils tous ces pacifistes?' *E*, no. 402 (28 octobre 1933), p. 2.

'Le parti communiste allemand et les syndicats' [Parmi nos lettres], *RP*, no. 141 (10 décembre 1932), pp. 14-15; unsigned, possibly by Simone Weil.
'La patrie internationale des travailleurs' *E*, no. 389 (22 juillet 1933), p. 4.
*Pensées sans ordre concernant l'amour de Dieu*, Paris, N.R.F., Gallimard, Coll. 'Espoir,' 1962.
'Pensées sans ordre concernant l'amour de Dieu' *PSO*, pp. 13-20.
'De la perception ou l'Aventure de Protée' *LP*, no. 5 (20 mai 1929), pp. 237-41.
'La personnalité humaine, le juste et l'injuste'[1] *TR*, no. 36 (décembre 1950), pp. 9-33;
   –under its real title: 'La Personne et le Sacré. Collectivité—Personne —Impersonnel—Droit—Justice' *EL*, pp. 11-44;

[1]('Beyond Personalism' trans. Russell S. Young, *Cross-Currents*, New York, vol. II no. 3 (Spring 1952) pp. 59-76; 'The Fallacy of Personal Rights' trans. Richard Rees, *The Twentieth Century*, London, vol CLXV, nos. 987 and 988 (May-June 1959), pp. 470-81 and 543-55).

# Bibliography

('Human Personality' *SE*, pp. 9-34).

'Perspectives: Allons-nous vers la Révolution Prolétarienne?' *see* 'Allons-nous vers la Révolution Prolétarienne?'

*La Pesanteur et la Grâce*,[1] introd. Gustave Thibon, Paris, Plon, Coll. 'L'Épi,' 1947[2];

(*Gravity and Grace*,[3] trans. Emma Craufurd, London, Routledge & Kegan Paul, 1952).

'Un petit point d'histoire (Lettre au Temps)' a variant of 'Rome et l'Albanie.'

'Un peu d'histoire à propos du Maroc' *Syndicats*, no. 17 (4 février 1937), p. 3.

'La Philosophie' *CDS*, tome XIX, no. 235 (mai 1941), pp. 288-94; under the pseudonym of Emile Novis.

'Plaintes d'Electre et reconnaissance d'Oreste' *SG*, pp. 47-55; ('The Laments of Electra and the Recognition of Orestes' *I*, pp. 11-17).

'Platon' *SG*, pp. 65-138: general title for 'Dieu dans Platon'; 'Sur le *Théétète*'; 'Sur le *Phèdre*'; 'Sur le *Phèdre* et le *Banquet*'; 'Extraits du *Phèdre*'; 'Sur la *République*.'

[Poèmes][4]: 'Aux Astres' brief extracts in *L'expérience vécue de Simone Weil*, p. 178.

'Eclair' *CDS*, tome XXVI, no. 284 (1947), p. 565.

'La Mer' brief extracts in *L'expérience vécue de Simone Weil*, p. 177.

'Nécessité' *CDS*, tome XXVI, no. 284 (1947), p. 566.

'La porte' *PSO*, pp. 11-12; also extracts in *L'expérience vécue de Simone Weil*, p. 178.

'Prométhée' *Études matérialistes*, Cannes (A.-M.), no. XVII (décembre 1947), p. 1.

[Vers lus au Goûter de la Saint-Charlemagne, Lycée Henri IV, 30 janvier 1926], Imprimerie des Presses Modernes, Paris, 4 pp. Hors commerce. Extracts in *L'expérience vécue de Simone Weil*, p. 29.

'La politique de neutralité et l'assistance mutuelle' *EH*, pp. 250-1.

'La porte' *see* Poèmes.

---

[1]From extracts edited by Gustave Thibon from notebooks, which, later published in full, became the *Cahiers* (vols. I, II, III).
[2]Other editions: Le Club Français du Livre, 1954; Plon. Coll. 'Racines' without introd., 1960; and in paperback, introd. Georges Hourdér, plon, le monde 10-18, 1962.
[3](Also: trans. Arthur Wills, New York, G. P. Putnam's Sons, 1952).
[4]For '*Venise sauvée*' poetic drama, *see* under own heading.

'Pour une négociation immédiate' *FLQ*, no. 54 (25 mars 1938), p. 90; possibly by Simone Weil.

('The Power of Words') *see* 'Ne recommençons pas la guerre de Troie.'

'Premières impressions d'Allemagne' [Parmi nos lettres], *RP*, no. 134 (25 août 1932), p. 14;
   –*EH*, pp. 124-5.

'Prestige national et honneur ouvrier' *Syndicats*, no. 26 (8 avril 1937), p. 2.

'Principes d'un projet pour un régime intérieur nouveau dans les entreprises industrielles' *CO*, pp. 207-13.

'Printemps de Méléagre' [traduction], *SG*, pp. 63-4.

'Le problème de l'U.R.S.S.' *E*, no. 406 (2 décembre 1933), p. 4.

'Progrès et production' (fragment), *EH*, pp. 398-9.

'Projet d'une formation d'infirmières de première ligne' *EH*, pp. 187-95.

('A Proletarian Uprising in Florence') *see* 'Un soulèvement prolétarien à Florence au XIVe siècle.'

'Prologue' *see La Connaissance surnaturelle* and note.

'Prométhée' *see* Poèmes.

('Prometheus') *see* 'Descente de Dieu.'

('Prospects: Are We Heading for the Proletarian Revolution?') *see* 'Allons-nous vers la Révolution Prolétarienne?'

('The Pythagorean Doctrine') *see* 'Descente de Dieu.'


'Quelques méditations concernant l'économie (Esquisse d'une apologie de la banqueroute)' *EH*, pp. 319-23. There is a variant on pp. 400-2: 'Esquisse d'une apologie de la banqueroute';
('On Bankruptcy' *SE*, pp. 145-9: translation of 'Quelques méditations . . .').

'Quelques réflexions concernant l'honneur et la dignité nationale' *EH*, pp. 394-5: variant of 'Réponse à une question d'Alain.'

'Quelques réflexions sur les origines de l'hitlérisme'[1] *EH*, pp. 11-60; ('The Great Beast: Reflections on the Origins of Hitlerism' *SE*, pp. 89-140).

'Quelques remarques sur la réponse de la M.O.R.' *EH*, pp. 390-1: a variant of item immediately below.

'Quelques remarques sur la réponse de la M.O.R. (Tribune de discussion)' *EE*, 23e année, no. 31 (7 mai 1933);
   –*EH*, pp. 197-202; *see* variant immediately above.

[1] See below: 'Réflexions sur l'origine de l'hitlérisme. 1. Hitler et la politique extérieure de la Rome antique,' central part of this three-part article, published in *NC*, 4e année, no. 53 (1er janvier 1940), pp. 14-21.

# Bibliography

'Questionnaire' *PSO*, pp. 68-72.
'Quête de l'homme par Dieu' *see* 'Descente de Dieu.'
'Qui est coupable de menées antifrançaises?' *EH*, pp. 339-43.

'La rationalisation' *CO*, pp. 215-32.
'Reconnaissance de Dieu et de l'homme' *see* 'Descente de Dieu.'
('Reflections concerning Technocracy, National-socialism, the U.S.S.R. and certain other matters') *see* 'Réflexions concernant la Technocratie, le National-socialisme, l'U.R.S.S. et quelques autres points.'
('Reflections concerning the Causes of Liberty and Social Oppression') *see* 'Réflexions sur les causes de la liberté et de l'oppression sociale.'
'Reflections in View of An Assessment' (NT): 'Réflexions en vue d'un bilan.'
('Reflections on Barbarism'.) *see* 'Réflexions sur la barbarie.'
'Reflections on the Economic Crisis' (NT): *see* 'Réflexions concernant la crise économique.'
('Reflections on the Origins of Hitlerism') (WT): 'The Great Beast: Some Reflections on the Origins of Hitlerism').
'Reflections on the Quantum Theory' (NT): 'Réflexions à propos de la théorie des quanta.'
('Reflections on the Right Use of School Studies with a View to the Love of God') *see* 'Réflexions sur le bon usage des études scolaires en vue de l'Amour de Dieu.'
('Reflections on War') *see* 'Réflexions sur la guerre.'
'Reflections upon Revolt' (NT): 'Réflexions sur la révolte.'
'Réflexions à propos de la théorie des quanta' *CDS*, tome XIX, no. 251 (décembre 1942), pp. 102-19: under the pseudonym of Emile Novis.
'Réflexions concernant la crise économique' *Syndicat National des Instituteurs publics de France et des Colonies, Bulletin de la Section de la Haute-Loire*, le Puy, 13e année, no. 68 (novembre 1931), pp. 69-72.
'Réflexions concernant la Technocratie, le National-socialisme, l'U.R.S.S. et quelques autres points' *OEL*, pp. 39-44;
('Reflections concerning Technocracy, National-socialism, the U.S.S.R. and certain other matters' *OL*, pp. 25-9).
'Réflexions en vue d'un bilan' *Preuves*, Paris, 3e année, no. 24 (février 1953), pp. 20-9;
–*EH*, pp. 296-312;

# Bibliography

('Cold War Policy in 1939' *SE*, pp. 177-94).

'Réflexions pour déplaire' *EH*, pp. 218-19, with a variant on pp. 392-3.

'Réflexions sans ordre sur l'amour de Dieu' *PSO*, pp. 35-45.

'Réflexions sur la barbarie' (fragments), *EH*, pp. 63-5; ('Reflections on Barbarism' *SE*, pp. 142-4).

'Réflexions sur la conférence de Bouché' *EH*, pp. 279-82.

'Réflexions sur la guerre'[1] *LCS*, no. 10 (novembre 1933), pp. 153-8; –*EH*, pp. 229-39;

('The Next World War' *International Review*, New York, vol. III, no. 1 (1938), pp. 7-11).

'Réflexions sur la révolte' *EH*, pp. 109-25.

'Réflexions sur la vie d'usine' extract from 'Expérience de la vie d'usine,' *Economie et Humanisme*, Marseille, no. 2 (juin-juillet 1942), pp. 187-204, signed Emile Novis, anagram of Simone Weil;

('Factory work' trans. Félix Giovanelli, *Politics*, New York, vol. III, no. 11 (December 1946), pp. 369-73).

'Réflexions sur le bon usage des études scolaires en vue de l'Amour de Dieu' *A* pp. 71-80;

('Reflections on the Right Use of School Studies with a View to the Love of God' *WG*, pp. 51-9).

'Réflexions sur les causes de la liberté et de l'oppression sociale' *OEL*, pp. 55-162;

('Reflections concerning the Causes of Liberty and Social Oppression' *OL*, pp. 37-124).

'Réflexions sur l'origine de l'hitlérisme. 1. Hitler et la politique extérieure de la Rome antique.' This is part II, and not part I as indicated in title, of 'Quelques réflexions sur les origines de l'hitlérisme.'

'Remarques sur le nouveau projet de Constitution' *EL*, pp. 85-92.

'Remarques sur les enseignements à tirer des conflits du Nord' (1936-1937?), *CO*, pp. 197-205.

'Réponse à une question d'Alain' (printemps 1936), *EH*, pp. 244-7; there are two variants of this article: 'Quelques réflexions concernant l'honneur et la dignité nationale' *EH*, pp. 394-5; 'Réponse au questionnaire d'Alain' *EH*, pp. 396-7.

('The Republic') *see* 'Descente de Dieu.'

[1]–*Le Travailleur*, Belfort, nos. 98 to 100, p. 3, and no. 101, p. 2 (du 2 au 24 février 1934);

–*LP*, no. 8 (31 août 1935), pp. 364-72;

('Reflections on War' revised text of 'The Next World War', *Politics*, New York, vol. II, no. 2 (February 1945), pp. 51-5).

'Responsibilities of literature' (NT): 'Lettre aux *Cahiers du Sud* sur les responsabilités de la littérature.'

'Retour aux guerres de religions' *see* 'Cette guerre est une guerre de religions' and the note.

'Réunion du 16 janvier' [Comité pour l'indépendance du syndicalisme de la Loire], *E*, no. 291 (23 janvier 1932), p. 2; in collaboration with U. Thévenon.

'Review of an article by Brion' (NT): 'La Philosophie.'

'Le rôle de l'U.R.S.S. dans la politique mondiale' *EE*, 23e année, no. 42 (23 juillet 1933), pp. 693-5;
–*EH*, pp. 203-8.

('Rome and Albania') *see* 'Rome et l'Albanie.'

'Rome et l'Albanie' *NC*, no. 48 (Ier juillet 1939), p. 24;
–*EH*, pp. 61-2; variant entitled 'Un petit point d'histoire (Lettre au *Temps*)', pp. 381-2;
('Rome and Albania' *SE*, pp. 140-2).

('The Romanesque Renaissance') *see* 'En quoi consiste l'inspiration occitanienne.'

'Rosa Luxemburg: Lettres de la prison' [Revue des Livres], *LCS*, no. 10 (novembre 1933), pp. 180-1.

'Le sang coule en Tunisie' *FLQ*, 3e année, no. 33 (25 mars 1937), pp. 75-6;
–*EH*, pp. 336-8: variant of the same text.

'[Schéma de la conférence de Simone Weil]' *E*, no. 416 (3 février 1934), p. 2.

(*Selected Essays* (1934-43), translated by Richard Rees, London, Oxford University Press, 1962. *See* above: *Écrits de Londres et dernières lettres* and *Écrits historiques et critiques*).

'La situation en Allemagne' *EE*, 23e année, no. 10 (4 décembre 1932), pp. 146-8;
suite, no. 12 (18 décembre 1932), pp. 178-80;
suite, no. 15 (8 janvier 1933), pp. 235-7;
suite, no. 16 (15 janvier 1933), pp. 249-51;
suite, no. 18 (29 janvier 1933), pp. 284-5;
suite, no. 19 (5 février 1933), pp. 300-1;
suite, no. 20 (12 février 1933), pp. 315-16;
suite, no. 21 (19 février 1933), pp. 329-32;
suite, no. 22 (26 février 1933), pp. 347-8;
suite, no. 23 (5 mars 1933), pp. 363-5;
–*EH*, pp. 146-94.

# Bibliography

'La situation en Allemagne' *LP*, nouvelle série, 7e année, no. 2 (25 février 1933), pp. 90-2;
—*EH*, pp. 386-9.

('A Sketch of a History of Greek Science') *see* 'Esquisse d'une histoire de la science grecque.'

'Un soulèvement prolétarien à Florence, au XIVe siècle' suivi d'un texte de Machiavel traduit par S. Weil: *LCS*, no. 11 (mars 1934), pp. 225-8 pour l'introduction de S. Weil, pp. 228-32 pour la traduction;
—*EH*, pp. 85-101; introduction et traduction;
('A Proletarian Uprising in Florence' *SE*, pp. 55-72, introduction and translation).

*La Source grecque*, Paris, N.R.F., Gallimard, Collection 'Espoir' 1953;
(*I* contains 5 items from *SG*:
'L'*Iliade*, ou le poème de la force' (The *Iliad*, Poem of Might), 'Zeus et Prométhée' (Zeus and Prometheus), 'Plaintes d'Electre et reconnaissance d'Oreste' (The Laments of Electra and the Recognition of Orestes), 'Antigone' (Antigone), 'Dieu dans Platon' (God in Plato [in part])).

'Sur la *République*' *SG*, pp. 137-8.

'Sur la situation en Allemagne' *EE*, 23e année, no. 28 (9 avril 1933), pp. 453-4;
—*EH*, pp. 195-6.

'Sur la situation en Allemagne. Quelques remarques sur la réponse de la M.O.R.' *EE*, 23e année, no. 31 (7 mai 1933), pp. 498-500;
—*EH*, pp. 197-202.

'Sur le livre de Lénine "Matérialisme et Empiriocriticisme"' *see* 'Lénine: Matérialisme et Empiriocriticisme.'

'Sur le *Phèdre*' *SG*, p. 129.

'Sur le *Phèdre* et le *Banquet*' *SG*, pp. 131-3.

[Sur le sentiment d'éloignement] *CDS*, tome xx, no. 249 (1943), p. 387, note 1: cité par Joë Bousquet dans son étude: 'Conscience et Tradition d'Oc' pp. 374-89.

'Sur les contradictions du marxisme' *OEL*, pp. 194-204;
('On the Contradictions of Marxism' *OL*, pp. 147-55).

'Sur le tas. Souvenirs d'une exploitée' *see* 'La vie et la grève des ouvrières métallos' and note.

'Sur le *Théétète*' *SG*, pp. 127-8.

'Sur trois Morts. Après la mort de Briand' *see* 'Après la mort de Briand.'

'Une survivance du régime des castes' *Syndicat National des Instituteurs*

# Bibliography

publics de France et des Colonies, Bulletin de la Section de la Haute-Loire, le Puy, 13e année, no. 70 (janvier-février 1932), p. 148.
('The Symposium of Plato') see 'Descente de Dieu.'

'Du temps' LP, no. 8 (20 août 1929), pp. 387-92.
'Théorie des Sacrements'[1] Les Cahiers Protestants, Lausanne, no. 6 (décembre 1956), pp. 295-305;
–PSO, pp. 134-47.
'These Palpitating Limbs of the Fatherland' (NT): 'Ces membres palpitants de la patrie.'
('Three Letters on History') see 'Ébauches de lettres.'
('The three Sons of Noah and the History of Mediterranean Civilization') see 'Les trois fils de Noé et l'histoire de la civilisation méditerranéenne.'
'Traduction des fragments'. see 'Héraclite.'
'Les trois fils de Noé et l'histoire de la civilisation méditerranéenne' A, pp. 177-89;
('The Three Sons of Noah and the History of Mediterranean Civilization' WG, pp. 155-69).

'U.R.S.S. et Amérique' E, no. 314 (2 juillet 1932), p. 1.

Venice Preserved (NT): Venise sauvée.
Venise sauvée tragédie en trois actes, Paris, N.R.F., Gallimard, 1955.
'La vie et la grève des ouvriers métallos'[2] RP, no. 224 (10 juin 1936), pp. 4-8, under the pseudonym of S. Galois;
–CO, pp. 161-74.

(Waiting for God) see Attente de Dieu.
(Waiting on God) see Attente de Dieu.
('A War of Religion') see 'Cette guerre est une guerre de religions.'
('A War of Religions') see 'Cette guerre est une guerre de religions.'
('What is a Jew? A Letter to a Minister of Education') see 'Lettre à M. le Ministre de l'Instruction Publique.'
('What Was the Occitanian Inspiration?' (WT): 'The Romanesque Renaissance.')
('Words and War') see 'Ne recommençons pas la guerre de Troie.'

[1]Réalités-fémina-illustration, no. 148 (mai 1958), pp. 42-9; The New Morality, Rome, anno terzo, 1963 (inverno), pp. 19-24.
[2]Also under title: 'Sur le tas. Souvenirs d'une exploitée,' Les Cahiers de Terre Libre, Nîmes, no. 7 (15 juillet 1936), pp. 3-15; under pseudonym of S. Galois.

# Bibliography

'Y a-t-il une doctrine marxiste?' *OEL*, pp. 221-54; ('Is There a Marxist Doctrine?' *OL*, pp. 169-95).

'Zeus et Prométhée' *SG*, pp. 43-6; ('Zeus and Prometheus' *I*, pp. 56-9).

## II. BOOKS ON SIMONE WEIL

BUGNION-SECRÉTAN (PAULE), *Simone Weil, itinéraire politique et spirituel*, Neuchâtel, H. Messeiller, 1954.

CABAUD (JACQUES), *L'expérience vécue de Simone Weil*, Paris, Plon, 1957.

DAVY (MARIE-MAGDELEINE), *Introduction au message de Simone Weil*, Paris, Plon, l'épi, 1954.

The Mysticism of Simone Weil, translated by Cynthia Rowland, London, Rockliff, 1951; Boston, Beacon Press, 1951.

*Simone Weil*, Paris, Éditions Universitaires, Témoins du xxe siècle, 1956.

DEBIDOUR (VICTOR-HENRY), *Simone Weil ou la transparence*, Paris, Plon, la recherche de l'absolu, 1963.

DRAGHI (GIANFRANCA), *Razioni di una forza in Simone Weil*, Roma, Caltanisetta, S. Sciascia, 1958.

EPTING (KARL), *Der geistliche Weg der Simone Weil*, Stuttgart, Friedrich Vorweck, 1955.

FLEURÉ (EUGÉNE), *Simone Weil ouvrière*, Paris, Fernand Lanore, 1955.

KEMPFNER (GASTON), *La philosophie mystique de Simone Weil*, Paris, La Colombe, éd. du Vieux Colombier, 1960.

MALAN (IVO), *L'Enracinement de Simone Weil*, Paris, Didier, 1961.

OTTENSMEYER (HILARY), *Le thème de l'amour dans l'oeuvre de Simone Weil*, Paris, Lettres Modernes, Collection 'thèmes et mythes,' 1958.

PERRIN (J.-M), DANIÉLOU (J.), DURAND (C.), KAELIN (J.), LOCHET (L.), HUSSAR (B.), EMMANUELLE (J.-M), *Réponses aux questions de Simone Weil*, Paris, Aubier, 1964.

PERRIN (J.-M) & THIBON (GUSTAVE), *Simone Weil telle que nous l'avons connue*, Paris, La Colombe, éd. du Vieux Colombier, 1952; *Simone Weil as We Knew Her*, trans. Emma Craufurd, London, Routledge & Kegan Paul.

PICCARD (E.), *Simone Weil*, Essai biographique et critique, suivi

384

# Bibliography

d'une anthologie raisonnée des oeuvres de Simone Weil, Presses Universitaires de France, 1960.

REES (RICHARD), *Brave Men: A Study of D. H. Lawrence and Simone Weil*, London, Victor Gollancz, 1958; Carbondale, Southern Illinois, University Press, 1959.

REYNAUD (ANNE), *Leçons de philosophie de Simone Weil* (Roanne 1933-1934), (présentées par . . .), Paris, Plon, 1959.

TOMLIN (E. W. F.), *Simone Weil*, New Haven, Yale University Press, 1954; Bowes and Bowes, Cambridge, 1954.

# Index

# Index

# Index

# Index

Morocco, 148-9
Mowll, A. K., 349
Munich agreement, 180, 181
Mystical experience, 169-74, 194-6, 237-42

Nature of Perception, 33-4
Nature of Time, 34-5
Need for Roots, The, 188, 327-35
Nouveaux Cahiers founded, 174

Otway, Thomas, 197

Pacifism, 40, 174-9, 181-6, 192, 196-7
Parties, political, 301-3
Pascaud, M. E., 43
Pater Noster in Greek, 258-9
Patri, Aimé, 196
Paulhan, Jean, 174, 250
Perrin, Father Jean-Marie, first meets Simone Weil, 252-3; his encouragement, 253-5; his hopes of her baptism, 267-71; her gratitude, 271-3; mentioned, 22, 163, 164, 204, 237, 238
Perrin, François, 174, 176
Pétain, Marshal, 196
Pètrement, Simone, 40
Philip, André, 298, 300
Pichon, 126
Planck, Max, 228
Plato, 224-8, 306-7
Poincaré, Raymond, 37
Political parties, 301-3
Primary Condition of non-Servile Labour, 254-5
Proust, Marcel, 233
Puech, Professor, 32

Racine, Jean, 233

Ranchet, Mme, 66
Redemption, 243
Reflections on War, 98-101
Reflections upon Revolt, 314-15
Renault works, 111-12
Révolution Prolétarienne, La, 47-8
Reynaud, Paul, 196
Rheims, Trade Union Congress (1933), 89-91
Rimbaud, Arthur, 233
Roanne Lycée, 91, 95, 98
Roché, Déodat, 218
Rolland, Romain, 40
Roman Empire, 188-92
Rome, 162
Roosevelt, President F. D., 281
Rosières foundries, 129-34
Roubaud, Lucien, 40, 249-50
Roustan, 44
Rühle, Otto, 101
Russia, 70, 84

Sacraments, 323-4
Saint-Julien-de-Peyrolas, 260
Saint Malo de Lalande, 40
Saint-Marcel d'Ardèche, 257-60
Saint-Quentin Lycée, 165-8
Saint-Réal, Abbé de, 197
Sartre, J.-P., 40
Schumann, Maurice, correspondence with Simone Weil in New York, 276-8; helps her in England, 295; correspondence with her in London, 319-24; visits her in hospital, 346; mentioned, 192, 265
Science, fallibility of, 228-30
Sea, The, 172-3
'Service, civil', 41
Solesmes Monastery, 168-9
Solomon, Professor, 28-9

# Index